ROBUST UNIONISM

BOOKS BY ARTHUR B. SHOSTAK

America's Forgotten Labor Organization
Blue-Collar World (with William Gomberg)
New Perspectives on Poverty (with William Gomberg)
Sociology in Action
Blue-Collar Life
Sociology and Student Life
Privilege in America: An End to Inequality? (with Jon Van Til and Sally Bould
Van Til)
Putting Sociology to Work
Modern Social Reforms
Our Sociological Eye
Blue-Collar Stress
Men and Abortion (with Gary McLouth and Lynn Seng)
The Air Controllers' Controversy (with David Skocik)

ROBUST UNIONISM
Innovations in the Labor Movement

ARTHUR B. SHOSTAK

ILR Press
Ithaca, New York

Library of Congress Cataloging-in-Publication Data

Shostak, Arthur B.
    Robust unionism : innovations in the labor movement / Arthur B. Shostak.
        p. cm.
    Includes bibliographical references and index.
    ISBN 0-87546-169-7 (alk. paper). — ISBN 0-87546-170-0 (pbk. : alk. paper)
    1. Trade-unions—United States—Case studies. I. Title.
HD6508.S5217   1990
331.88'0973—dc20   90-47094
                                                                        CIP

Copies may be ordered through bookstores or from
ILR Press
School of Industrial and Labor Relations
Cornell University
Ithaca, NY 14851–0952

Printed on acid-free paper in the United States of America
5   4   3   2   1

IN MEMORY OF

I. W. ABEL
President of the United Steelworkers of America

FRANK W. EMIG
Director of the AFL-CIO Department of Community Services

WILLIAM GOMBERG
Labor consultant and professor of industrial relations, University of Pennsylvania

LEO PERLIS
First director of the AFL-CIO Department of Community Services

BERNARD SAMOFF
Associate professor of management, University of Pennsylvania

Each of these men contributed to this volume shortly before his death, and each modeled a robust life that helped to show the way.

Royalties from the sale of this book have been assigned to the scholarship fund of the Antioch College degree program at the AFL-CIO George Meany Center in Silver Spring, Maryland.

I am not unaware of the shortcomings of the labor movement. . . . They do not seem to me as important or as deeply ingrained in the character of the labor movement [as] the process of social rebuilding which is going on. . . . a moving force recreating our social organization and achieving a distinctly new pattern.

Frank Tannenbaum, A Philosophy of Labor *(1951)*

CONTENTS

Contents   *xi*

PREFACE

Many unionists I have met in the nearly thirty years I have taught industrial sociology believe labor has more going for it than the mass media convey, but they lack current examples and details. This volume includes examples of labor innovations I uncovered while conducting four years of field research (1985–89) and a thorough review of the literature. I also draw heavily on thirteen years of teaching trade unionists at the AFL-CIO George Meany Center for Labor Studies. My case studies are based on personal knowledge, whereas elsewhere I rely on the writing of others. I received enthusiastic cooperation in gathering case material, suggesting that unionists are eager to read about one another's innovative efforts.

I would like to update the book from time to time and therefore welcome suggestions of innovations worth including and of changes in projects cited in this edition. Please write to me in care of my publisher.

Contrary to the impression of passivity conveyed by hostile commentators, the American labor movement contains many imaginative and risky ventures. If my account of such projects inspires new respect for labor's inventiveness, a major goal of this volume will have been achieved. If unionists are stirred to adopt the new approaches, so much the better.

JULY 1990
PHILADELPHIA

INTRODUCTION: THE TRIMTAB FACTOR

In every single democracy in the world you will find a vibrant, vital labor movement. The reason is that in a democratic society, where you have a system of checks and balances, a labor movement is absolutely indispensable. . . . There will always be unions as long as there are bosses.

Douglas A. Fraser, former UAW president,
meeting of the Northwest Labor Historical Society, March 1988

I am not talking about fault; I'm trying to look for answers.

Lane Kirkland, AFL-CIO president,
"The David Brinkley Show," Labor Day 1988

Large oceangoing ships moving at full steam require great force to turn their rudders, so small, adjustable flaps, called trimtabs, are placed on the keels of the ships to help steady or redirect them. When trimtabs are attached, deck officers need to exert only a small amount of pressure to put considerable force on the main rudder. The trimtab factor, in short, demonstrates "how the precise application of a small amount of leverage can produce a powerful effect."[1]

In a comparable way, a small but growing number of local unions, international unions, and departments of the AFL-CIO now serve as labor's trimtab factor. Their robust experimental efforts, some of which are discussed in this volume, demonstrate how a "small amount of leverage" can elicit major gains and help redirect the entire labor movement. Mistakes are made, of course, and disappointments are not uncommon. By the time this book reaches you, some of its cases may have suffered unexpected setbacks. Far more vital than any particular win or loss, however, is the willingness of labor's trimtab organizations to continue to take risks and explore fresh options.

Skeptics will ask, What significance, if any, can be attached to accounts of widely scattered and diverse projects? How are we to know whether they are representative of positive trends in the labor movement? And, even if they are representative, what can they teach us other than lessons to which any social movement will occasionally pay lip service?

The projects highlighted in this volume do not represent the vast majority of ongoing union endeavors. But, more significant, they do represent a major, and possibly decisive, current in labor affairs, one that may prove strong enough—with a steady assist from labor's trimtab factor—to redirect the entire movement. Whether or not this revitalization occurs hinges in large part on whether the lessons learned from high-risk innovations such as those described here are honored or neglected.

Countless unsung heroes and heroines have been at the helm in initiating and following through on the creative efforts discussed in this book. Not especially credentialed or privileged, these charismatic men and women share several characteristics:[2]

- Most maintain an old-fashioned faith in the labor movement. While keenly aware of its many foibles, they are boosters whose belief in what remains possible is contagious.
- Most are energized, even driven, by what they are doing, by their effort to enhance some vital aspect of the movement.
- Most rely on traditional virtues they believe are present in their union peers. They expect tolerance of criticism, persistence of effort, and confidence that a single person can effect larger events.
- Most have an exceptional ability to improvise on preconceived plans and reach for fresh possibilities.

Indeed, labor's change agents mix improvisation and vision so adroitly that detractors have little to use against them and supporters see a demonstration of conscience and intelligence working more effectively than ever before.

From start to finish the cases discussed in this volume refute the caricature of labor as a relic, as a dinosaurlike object unwilling or unable to adapt rapidly enough to "future shock." Rather, the cases illuminate the little-known and undervalued campaign by which influential labor organizations, labor's trimtab factor, seek to help the entire movement "revamp, adjust, transform, and adapt."[3] This campaign is firmly grounded in a tradition of self-renewal that has succeeded over and again across more than 250 years of American labor history. Accordingly, labor's energizing use of innovative projects—on behalf of an even more robust trade unionism—may yet make all the difference in the 1990s.

Part I

WORKPLACE ISSUES

Conversations among trade unionists at the AFL-CIO George
Meany Center range over every topic touched on in this volume.
But the heart of these discussions remains the nature of life in
the shop, in the office, on the loading dock, and at every other work site.
They focus on the challenge of improving the quality of life at work and
gaining power in the work force and society.

Robust efforts now receiving field trials include comprehensive campaigns, in-plant strategies ("working the plant backward"), adaptations
of the team concept, fresh attempts at technology control, and innovative
responses to threatened plant closings. Each of these efforts is considered
in chapter 1. An accompanying case study explains how Philadelphia-
area building trades unionists have linked up with progressive employers
in a "win-win" alliance of lasting significance.

Chapter 2 focuses on a very weak link in America's production process.
Inadequate concern for safety at work, a preoccupation of unions since
their U.S. start in the late 1700s, has inspired many robust responses,
such as attempts to regulate use of video display terminals, whistleblowing, and the disclosure of problems to shareholders. The case study
hones in on a remarkable alliance of workplace safety activists and local
unionists that is promoting both reforms that are overdue and those for
which the need is growing.

Finally, chapter 3 explores health reforms of which we can be proud,
such as union-managed employee assistance plans, union links to Alcoholics Anonymous, and union programs for handicapped workers. Sound
in their focus on cost-containment strategies, these reforms protect the
dignity and humanity of trade unionists and their families.

Taken together, the three chapters and two case studies show how
some locals, unions, and AFL-CIO components are working smarter,
rather than merely harder, to improve workers' lives. In so doing, they
are also helping to keep America's products and services competitive in
the turbulent 1990s.

Chapter 1
Seeking a Better Way of Work

America's biggest handicap is . . . its inability to generate an environment where the labor force takes a direct interest in raising productivity.
Lester Thurow, *The Zero Sum Solution* (1985)

The Transit Workers, Steelworkers, Machinists, and others . . . have begun to push back the boundaries of management's rights and to establish workers' rights to have a say in everything that affects their work and their livelihoods. . . . Management is too important to be left to the managers.
***Labor Research Review,* Spring 1987**

When I first began seeking material for this volume, I was struck by a provocative imbalance. My contacts in labor, management, government, and academia had their favorite examples of robustness in union organizing campaigns, safety and health projects, community service outreach, and "high-tech" programs. But when I asked about union-management relations on the shop floor, these same knowledgeable sources would grow pensive and finally shrug.

Their comments suggest that union-management relations at the shop level are inhospitable to labor innovation:[1]

Union business agent, New England: "You've got to understand we've had no leeway, no spare energy, and no real incentive to play around! We're under siege, and the attack is unrelenting. . . . Our goal is to make it through to the following morning and then to the next one."

Local union president, West Coast: "We can't rely on the National Labor Relations Board [NLRB]. We can't expect a fair shake from the media. We can't get anything useful from the 'pols,' and we can't figure out how to win over the kids in our ranks. With all of this heartache, you've got one hell of a nerve to expect 'innovation' from any of us!"

Rank-and-file activist, Midwest: "We are hanging on by our fingertips out here, and we feel real good when the same old stuff goes okay. Sure, we read and hear about lots of things that might help us. But there are shells of rusting plants, stories of suicide, and a lot of painful memories out here that discourage risk-taking."

I have come to consider defensive analysis of this sort serious and costly. Innovative unionists have attempted much more in the workplace than many labor activists realize.

Balance is vitally important in assessing the record. If unionists remain ignorant of shop-floor experiments, many will also remain inappropriately dour about labor's energy and unnecessarily bleak in their expectations of its ability to make a difference in the American way of work.

Accordingly, I want to provide brief accounts of union innovations at work that inspire a fresh evaluation of labor initiative and a brighter assessment of its potential in the 1990s. Labor has much to be proud of in workplace relations. Comprehensive campaigns, in-plant strategies, adaptations of the team concept, efforts at technology control, and responses to plant closings underline its adaptive capacity and resourcefulness.

Comprehensive Campaigns

Frustrated in the early 1980s by the National Labor Relations Board's failure to enforce laws protecting the right to unionize and by its reluctance to curb corporate union-busting techniques, organized labor responded with the "corporate campaign." Used effectively in the J. P. Stevens organizing drive, and later in a twelve-union coordinated effort against Litton Industries, the technique was also used successfully in a two-union effort in 1984 against Beverly Enterprises, the nation's largest nursing home operator. The approach coordinated adroit use of political pressure and shareholder involvement with embarrassing exposés of mismanagement to win strategic concessions. Beverly, for example, agreed to foster a "noncoercive" atmosphere in response to labor's organizing campaigns and to join a labor-management task force on improving patient care at unionized Beverly sites.

Because of steady improvements in the original design, a variation on the corporate campaign—the comprehensive campaign (CC)—has gained wide use, especially where word of Litton, Beverly, and other earlier successes has reached activists. The CC uses vulnerable characteristics of targeted companies against themselves to help labor in its struggle with management. This is done by putting an interlocking web of related interests, including banks, creditors, stockholders, and boards of directors, under severe pressure, through informational picketing, leafleting, and other strategies.

A successful CC entails an allocation of time and resources different from anything familiar to old-line unionists. As Robert F. Harbrant, president of the AFL-CIO Food and Allied Service Trades Department, explained to my classes at the George Meany Center, a comprehensive campaign requires a union to get smarter rather than merely tougher: "The kind of research we are talking about is exciting, exhilarating, and it can be effective if it is done properly.... You have to become like Sherlock Holmes and begin looking for clues [to the vulnerabilities of the targeted company] you may not have thought of in the past."[2]

Rather than requiring lawyers or consultants, a CC is created by and with grass-roots talent:

- First, the leaders study earlier CC projects to determine the most appropriate tactic for moving beyond a union-management impasse or winning contract gains.
- Second, the local's CC team begins sweeping research efforts: members trace every piece of potentially relevant information about the company. Particular attention is paid to the interlocking roles of company directors and to connections that might reveal critical vulnerabilities, such as whether a large loan is outstanding to a bank vulnerable to informational picketing.
- Third, the CC team prepares a corporate profile, which is a standardized analysis of the opposition: who are we up against, and how does it divide up power, expertise, responsibilities, and vulnerabilities both on the job and off?
- Fourth, and finally, the CC team prepares an offensive game plan it can summarize in about three vibrant paragraphs. A tentative timetable is set that is sensitive to the needs of the local and the company.

Harbrant urges local union leaders to prepare a corporate profile on every company under contract, whether the scene is amicable or antagonistic, and to keep it current for a time when it is needed.

Harbrant's experience has persuaded him that skeptics will be "surprised how interested members will be, and they will become your biggest supporters." When executed with care and imagination, comprehensive campaigns lift rank-and-file morale: "You...devise ways of breaking down the tasks that are at hand, begin meeting with some of your rank-and-filers, and get them involved."[3]

Harbrant insists that "if you don't engage in comprehensive power research, you are going to lose." He is not alone in his assessment, and other knowledgeable sources expect further gains. Economist Charles Craypo, for example, contends that "whether such ventures succeed or fail in the immediate objective, they always educate the membership and sharpen the leadership for future endeavors. To that extent they surely will be part of labor's future power."[4] The CC option can make excellent use of grass-roots talent and help unionists "transform themselves from students of history into historical actors."[5]

In-Plant Strategies

Believing that strikes are often best avoided, labor has come up with an alternative for use during contract negotiations. It "moves the struggle in the same direction that a good strike, under favorable conditions, might, but avoids the obvious traps."[6] This alternative, known as an in-plant strategy, entails six components of an overall effort "to run the plant backward":

- The local surveys the membership to learn whether it believes the company is in financial trouble, and is therefore a poor candidate for union resistance, or whether it sees the company as seeking to enhance already-sweet profits.
- Leaders make a special effort to learn whether the highest skilled, least replaceable members of the plant work force can be drawn into the campaign as the "point of the spear."
- Local union leaders and activists form a solidarity committee to serve as cheerleaders and provocateurs. As Jerry Tucker, of the United Automobile, Aerospace and Agricultural Implement Workers of America (UAW), has explained, "Members bring back the intelligence so critical to an effective strategy. And they produce the initiatives and the shop floor organization to carry out that strategy."[7]
- The solidarity committee closely coordinates its activities with shop stewards and with the local's bargaining committee. Off-site meetings are used to share and process information, especially in defining tactics.
- Extensive research is done to uncover as much as possible about vulnerabilities in the corporate entity.
- Finally, the local emphasizes long-term strategies, since a prolonged in-plant struggle often becomes a war of attrition. Staying the strongest over the longest period of time, as Tucker contends, "usually determines the outcome."[8]

Once it has taken the initial steps, the local is free to use other options, such as mass grievances, overtime refusal, "sickouts," or a "work-to-rule" process.

One well-known campaign, directed by the International Brotherhood of Boilermakers, Iron Shipbuilders, Blacksmiths, Forgers and Helpers, involved over eight thousand unionized cement workers. Dating back to May 1, 1984, and involving workers at some fifty cement plants nationwide, the campaign was the first such venture undertaken on a multiplant, multicompany basis.

Insiders recall that commitment to the new strategy was not easily built. First, manual workers had to be restrained from telling the company to "take the job and shove it." An in-plant approach precludes such emotional reactions and challenges the local instead to outthink the employer. Second, many manual workers, given decades of compliance and obedience, believed they lacked the power to force their aroused employer to make concessions. As Tom Balanoff, a leader of this campaign, explained, "Involvement . . . in protected concerted activity helped overcome feelings of powerlessness many initially had about the strategy."[9]

Building commitment to fight concessions was a lot easier, as was building commitment to the Brotherhood of Boilermakers itself. The strong relationship members felt with the labor movement was strengthened by anti-union blunders at several companies. "Staying-the-course" strategies were many and varied:

- Solidarity committees gathered funds—voluntary weekly contributions of five or ten dollars, often from 100 percent of a local—to assist members discharged for union activities.
- Local weekly newsletters dispelled anti-labor rumors, especially those initiated by the company to create dissension and confusion in the ranks.
- Workers met for morale rallies run by the solidarity committee and then entered the plant together. The shift ended in the same way, with workers singing "Solidarity Forever" as they left. Workers sang or whistled the song on the job as well.
- Some locals created solidarity T-shirts or buttons to wear on designated days or supplied stickers for use on hard hats.
- Rallies were organized outside the plant gate, frequently followed by informational picketing. Many spouses, children, and retirees participated while the workers were inside.
- Company parties, safety awards banquets, retirement dinners, and other social functions were canceled because workers routinely boycotted them or ran counterparties.
- Workers required to attend company meetings often wore earplugs or sat in stony silence.

Carefully orchestrated, each of these tactics lifted worker morale, generated useful news coverage, undermined executive morale, and brought victory closer.

Efforts to "depreciate productivity" commonly embitter labor-management relations. Never undertaken lightly, moves to defy management's prerogatives frequently result in penalties or even firings. Although victims are commonly aided by voluntary contributions from co-workers, and often return to their jobs as part of an eventual settlement of the dispute, their plight underlines the campaign's seriousness. In-plant strategies test labor's mettle by boldly adapting the concept of an orthodox strike to an employer's desperate need to meet tight deadlines with products that clearly pass muster. An example of labor's ability to play hardball when it must, in-plant strategies seem likely to spread and gain effectiveness where warranted.

Adaptations of the Team Concept

At the opposite end of the spectrum is in-plant cooperation, which management initiates in an attempt to share power. Executives of this persuasion cite as support for their view the 1982 best seller *In Search of Excellence*: "The excellent companies treat the rank and file as the root source of quality and productivity gain. They do not foster we/they labor attitudes or regard capital investment as the fundamental source of efficiency improvement." The nation's lagging productivity, which has "slowed to a crawl in the last two decades and shows little sign of revival,"[10] spurs corporate interest in such cooperative ventures as quality circles, self-management teams, problem-solving teams, and other experiments collectively known as "quality of working life projects."

Given the history of comparable offers that have turned out badly, labor has been skeptical. Its reaction had been influenced by two opposing sentiments. On the one hand, most workers want to make high-quality products and are pleased when they are recognized for ideas that substantially improve the work process. On the other hand, many workers remain suspicious of any offer by management to share power and are disillusioned when their ideas are rejected or ignored by distant corporate officials. As labor lawyer Staughton Lynd notes, "Workers deeply resent the trivial character of the decisions to which this opportunity is confined, and the manipulated nature of the process as a whole." On balance, most unionists would agree with the U.S. National Conference of Catholic Bishops that labor must "reject calls for less adversarial relations when they are a smoke screen for demands that labor make all the concessions."[11]

Although cooperative ventures remain problematic, some have provided novel pro-labor experiences. Journalist Michael Massing recalls, for example:

Today, UAW and auto executives travel to Japan together, go on retreats together, even publish newspapers together. Joint committees have been set up to deal with everything from productivity to absenteeism. These cooperative ventures have become so common that they have given rise to a new term: *jointness*. . . . Overall, the contract General Motors [GM] has with the U.A.W. calls for the company to spend $300 million a year on joint activities.[12]

Similarly, journalist John B. Judis writes:

> In the last decade, as the U.S. carmakers have been forced to mimic Japanese methods, they have worked with the UAW to create a strange but welcome hybrid of Japanese "teamism" and American industrial democracy. The shop-floor culture of American factories has been radically transformed, giving unionized autoworkers a far greater voice than ever before in determining their working conditions. At Chrysler, top management and union officials even meet to discuss the company's investment strategy.[13]

UAW locals enthusiastic about this development say they are getting more of the confidential cost and profit data they need from management to participate effectively in decision making.

Responses to "jointness" remain very uncertain in unionized workplaces. Labor has much reason to weigh the invitation to cooperate carefully, and the jury is still out on this critical matter.

Tackling Technological Change

Labor's challenge in tackling technological change is again to intervene as early and as effectively as possible, even while preparing for a struggle. Robert Schrank, an informed observer, warns, "In the last seventy-five years, more changes have taken place in the technologies that affect work than in all of previously recorded history. It is no wonder, then, that organizations like the AFL-CIO are reeling under the impact of a revolution that is overturning all traditional work roles and functions."[14]

Dennis Chamot, associate director of the AFL-CIO Department of Professional Employees, agrees that the situation is without precedent: "High-tech changes allow . . . the elimination of the worker by design . . . the physical relocation of work (as with the ability of publishing firms to have word-processing done in Barbados, and conveyed by satellite transmission back and forth to the States)." Chamot worries that the techniques developed by labor over the past hundred years "may not be sufficient to deal with current and future problems . . . that are qualitatively different than in the past. We are entering new waters. It is a time of regrouping and of exploration."[15]

The union struggle with technological change has always been vexing. Labor has generally welcomed productivity-boosting equipment while insisting on employment security, job retraining, and skills upgrading. As long ago as the 1890s, when the Linotype machine was displacing hand typesetters and undermining the Typographical Union, AFL president Samuel Gompers advised that union to "advocate a policy of not opposing labor-saving machinery, but plan so the workman could control the use of the machine through the union, instead of permitting the machine to control the printers." Today, labor historian Daniel Nelson characterizes this advice as "coming close to summarizing the relationship between technological change and the labor movement over the past century."[16]

Economist Sumner H. Slichter identified three common union responses to technological change: obstruction, competition, and control.[17] The first two are short-run palliatives that "would almost certainly lead to the decline or demise of the organization" if extended for long periods.[18] Only "control" represents a viable strategy.

Union leaders have focused on collective bargaining as a forum for either accommodating or forestalling technological change. The usual tradeoffs have been sweeping mechanization in return for new employee benefits. In the 1950s, for example, the United Mine Workers of America (UMWA) agreed to mechanization of the bituminous mines in return for seniority rights and union control of the industry's welfare fund, a tradeoff that eventually shrank the UMWA's ranks by 75 percent. Longshoring underwent a similar change in the 1960s, with a comparable shrinkage in jobs. The loss of jobs has been less dramatic in most other cases, and although few unions have fully implemented Gompers's 1896 advice, some have "enjoyed considerable success in developing techniques for managing technological change."[19]

Chamot contends that the microchip revolution is altering technology and work as never before. In response, the labor movement has sought new routes to worker control of technology. Some unions have pressed for a say in the earliest analysis of a work process, keenly aware that "most technical problems have several possible solutions."[20] Some have begun to win predesign consultations, so that management now solicits suggestions from employees before final decisions about shop redesign or machine purchases are made. This process helps reduce rumors about job loss and can boost workplace morale.[21]

Labor has also pressed for a conversion of "job security" to "employment security." Pioneered by the UAW, the Communications Workers of America, and the United Steelworkers, this arrangement helps keep members steadily employed, through lifelong retraining, by enabling them to adapt to radically transformed jobs. Where layoffs appear unavoidable, leading unions have pioneered in developing retraining projects unlike any that have come before. Previous efforts were confined to tuition payment for technical courses related to a current job. Today, employers fund courses that are relevant for jobs outside the worker's industry. In the past, the pursuit of a college diploma was disdained, but the new projects typically help workers get "life credits" toward a bachelor's degree, provide counseling, and, in especially large workplaces, include such innovative support as education counselors from the colleges. Most important, job retraining efforts that were once in the domain of personnel departments are now constructed jointly by labor and management, with labor holding its own in evaluating and improving the process.

Certain unions and locals are guided by the precept that "only partial solutions are available at the bargaining table. The rest . . . lie in legislative and political action."[22] Effective labor lobbying, which is discussed in detail in chapter 2, recently won passage, for example, of a right-to-know Occupational Safety and Health Administration (OSHA) regulation that increases pressure for health and safety considerations as new technology is introduced.[23]

Labor's ability to secure a federal law in 1988 restricting the use of "lie detectors" was scarcely noticed outside the labor press. Nonetheless, it was a significant triumph. Over 325,000 employees had been "branded as liars" annually, even though experts put the error rate for these tests as high as 30 percent and an innocent person had nearly a 50 percent chance of failing.[24]

Typical of the public information offered in support of the law's passage was a full-page ad by the United Food and Commercial Workers International Union (UFCW) that said:

> Polygraph testing, like the dunking stool, has no place in America. Workers do not abdicate their right to privacy when they go to work, as some employers would claim. . . . Beyond the coercive invasion of privacy, there is another problem with polygraph machines. They simply don't work. Study after study has proven that "lie detectors" detect stress, not lies. And what should be more stressful to a worker than being attached to a machine, and asked questions that could lead to being fired or denied work?[25]

Citing a 1983 report of the U.S. Office of Technology Assessment, which found the polygraph worthless as a screening device, labor charged that over 2 million tests conducted annually by private business were an inferior substitute for careful background checks and better auditing procedures.[26]

When proponents of polygraphs sought to exempt utilities on the grounds of "indispensable use," the International Brotherhood of Electrical Workers (IBEW) quickly did a survey of thirty-three large electrical utilities and told Congress only five were actually using the technology.[27] When proponents sought use in cases in which theft was suspected, a Senate amendment drafted in consultation with organized labor specified safeguards to assure workers fair treatment, such as a requirement that each test take at least ninety minutes and be conducted only by a licensed examiner.[28]

In sum, the bill labor championed appears to have reduced use of the polygraph by 80 percent and to have struck a heartening "blow for personal freedom in what should be the citadel of the mind."[29] Labor's ability to limit effectively the use of a technology it judged harmful cheered unionists eager for many other such victories.

Buffers to Plant Closings

Throughout the early 1980s, plant after plant fell beneath the greatest wave of closings in the postwar economy. A desperate effort to bargain for scarce retraining funds and for retraining legislation preoccupied discouraged unionists.

Fortunately, there were a few exceptions to union resignation. One was at the General Motors plant in Van Nuys, California.[30] Hints of an impending shutdown galvanized an extraordinary anti-shutdown campaign in 1981 that forced the auto company to reconsider. Contrary to prevailing attitudes, UAW Local 645 argued that a shutdown was *not* an unchallengeable management prerogative. Rather, it was a subject for thorough debate, since the implications for workers and the community were so severe. While acknowledging that plant closings were sometimes inevitable, the local set out to secure an unprecedented place for labor in the decision-making process.

Five years of mass demonstrations and emotional marches, thousands of protest letters to the chairman of GM, many press conferences, a face-to-face meeting with the president of GM, and the dogged determination of grass-roots activists eventually earned the local a rare victory. On November 6, 1986, the General Motors Corporation, which had not closed any workplaces since late 1982, announced that it would close eleven of its auto plants. The Van Nuys operation, however, was kept open. Its UAW local proudly declared that its anti-shutdown campaign had been the deciding factor.

Six distinctive qualities characterized the pioneering Van Nuys effort:

■ The campaign reflected thorough planning. Every aspect underwent continuous reassessment throughout the five-year effort. Its organizers studied earlier efforts to stop closings in order to learn from them.

■ The campaign was unabashedly bold. While other local unions sought to cut their losses by bargaining defensively over how many jobs would go and whether the company would help to soften the blow, this local rejected a path based on concession.

■ The local insisted that "prevailing wisdom" could be profoundly misleading. The leaders of the campaign "advanced a demand that both restricted the mobility of capital and advanced the power of labor at a time when, overall, capital's power was dramatically expanding and labor's declining."[31]

■ The campaign aggressively counterattacked, threatening a sustained consumer boycott of GM cars if the shutdown occurred. The warning mentioned "picket lines, press conferences, dealer complaints, demands for more meetings by church and political leaders, endless calls by the press, and lots of bad publicity—not over a week, or even a month, but at least a year—publicity that might spark other labor and community-based initiatives against GM in other parts of the country as well."[32]

■ The campaign was politically astute in making race a central issue without antagonizing white workers. Since the plant was 50 percent Latino, 15 percent black, and 35 percent white, gaining support from black ministers and Latino groups was absolutely essential. The campaign also included women as leaders from the outset: "We didn't make the coffee and pass out the donuts; we helped to lead the thing, and we were good at it."[33]

■ The campaign raised confidence in labor's ability to earn favorable media coverage. More than a hundred newspaper stories and magazine articles, rallies of more than one thousand UAW members, and celebrities such as Ed Asner, Jackson Brown, and the Reverend Jesse Jackson helped focus attention and boost morale.

These strategies enabled a small movement to change apathy into activism. Appropriately, a prize-winning documentary about the campaign (commissioned by the local in 1986) focused not on hapless victims but on robust workers as bold strategists and adroit organizers.

Since there is no foreseeable end to GM's mismanagement difficulties, the danger of auto plant closings remains and "future confrontations are not just probable, but inevitable."[34] Local 645 activists continue to threaten to stage a consumer boycott of GM cars, while hoping never to have to carry it out.

Even if the Van Nuys plant is eventually closed, much has already been gained by organized labor. As Eric Mann, a participant in the struggle, explains, "The perpetuation of the Van Nuys movement for five years, and its uncanny ability to land on its feet, have provided an important

symbol and a rich organizing experience for a labor movement desperate
for victories."[35] Local 645 activists have every intention of winning a
ten-year commitment from GM to the continued operation of their auto
plant. The UAW activists insist that decisions about the future of their
plant or of any other plant must involve the unionists and the community
at risk.

Questions Raised by Skeptics

Friendly critics press two major lines of inquiry worth consideration and
response. Some worry that expectations may exceed what labor can
deliver. Comprehensive campaigns, for example, have a mixed record of
success, and unless they hurt a company's pocketbook swiftly and substantially, they can go nowhere slowly.[36] Similarly, local union efforts to
co-opt in-plant cooperation projects often yield disappointing results.[37]

Proponents of the innovations insist the scales tip in their favor already,
and will do so increasingly with experience. Boosters of the comprehensive campaign, for example, point to major gains they have made in
educating and politicizing workers and their families. Furthermore, a CC
wins "large amounts of publicity, and is seen by the community as labor
taking the moral high ground, two components of victory which are often
lacking in traditional labor struggles."[38]

Similarly, supporters of turning cooperative ventures to advantage urge
patience and persistence. They blame current problems on supervisory
obstructionists who will soon pass from the scene.

Some critics voice a second concern that is the reverse of the first. They
charge labor experiments do not go far enough. They rail that workplace
changes are meek accommodations to prevailing realities. They argue
that labor lacks an alternative vision to the one now steadily transforming
work.[39] Leading critics Rob Kling and Suzanne Iacono, for example,
gloomily conclude that "in its most likely form, our 'computer revolution'
will be a conservative revolution that will reinforce the patterns of an
elite-dominated, stratified society."[40]

Many labor activists resent this indictment. They believe their work
lives, which they typically began as teenagers on the shop floor, equip
them to intuit an alternative vision, a remarkably humanistic blueprint.
They understand that "high-tech" equipment does not have to create
authoritarian workplaces and could "just as easily be deployed to make
jobs more creative, and increase shop floor decision-making. . . . The technology could be used to bring work under the more complete control of
the people who do it, rather than the other way around."[41]

To implement a vision counter to authoritarian initiatives, the AFL-
CIO continues to fund study tours for American unionists of Scandi-

navian experiments in technology reform. It also conducts joint labor-academic conferences on work and technology and provides "take-charge" information to concerned unionists through print, TV, videotape, and other media. Similarly, the International Association of Machinists and Aerospace Workers (IAM) broke new ground in 1981 when it urged labor to adopt new principles embedded in the union's "Technology Bill of Rights." No longer would the introduction of new technology be seen as an automatic or exclusive right of management. Instead, the process of change would be governed by socially beneficial goals and would be subject to development through bargaining. This vision of labor helping to govern new technology may yet secure "machines that fit the needs of people, rather than the other way around."[42]

A Further Look at the Record

The list of examples could be extended at considerable length:

- The CWA has adapted the notion of profit sharing (now called gain sharing), which has been around since the 1940s. The union insists that if productivity has improved, workers have a right to earn bonuses even when profits are flat.[43]
- The Bricklayers, Masons and Plasterers' International Union has joined with industry representatives to create a labor-management trust fund to promote expanded use of industry products and a related growth in jobs for union members.[44]
- The United Paperworkers International Union pioneered in aiding in community and workplace recovery in Weed, California, after a traumatic plant closing. The cooperation of town and union in creating an employee stock ownership plan for a reopened mill and in drafting a participatory agreement has earned well-deserved honors.[45]

Labor's record is comparably diverse and creative concerning technology:

- The UAW has participated in the nation's most extensive preoperation joint technology planning effort ever. Fifty-two auto workers and thirty-nine GM managers spent a year designing the Saturn Division, the first new GM division since 1911. The union played an integral part in planning every technical area, and UAW members helped choose Saturn's suppliers, ad agency, and dealers. Journalist Michael Massing noted, "As in the past, the UAW's reaction will serve as a precedent for American labor generally."[46]
- The American Federation of State, County, and Municipal Employees (AFSCME) has helped its locals set up technology committees

to provide model language for contracts and guide educational meetings.[47]

■ The Amalgamated Clothing and Textile Workers' Union (ACTWU) has joined with manufacturers to create a corporation for the purpose of designing new machinery and methods to help meet the threat of overseas competition.[48]

These examples demonstrate that certain unions remain as inventive in meeting workplace challenges as Samuel Gompers would have wished.

Summary

Given the diversity of corporate attitudes and behaviors, labor moves cautiously through changing realities in the workplace. Contrary to any impression of inactivity, however, its record includes several far-reaching experiments:

■ Comprehensive campaigns are highlighting corporate vulnerabilities and leveraging them for more gains than ever before.

■ In-plant strategies such as calculated interruptions and disturbances are being used creatively while enabling workers to remain on the job.

■ Rejoinders to the use of cooperative experiments are testing the integrity of the team concept and helping to ensure union gains.

■ Technology-control projects are winning advances for labor, using bargaining and legislative measures.

■ Efforts to prevent plant closings are redefining management prerogatives and enlarging labor's role in relevant corporate decisions.

Consistent with Gompers's advice to the Typographical Union in 1896, contemporary unionists are guiding the use of technology more than ever before, recognizing that "while the risks here are significant, labor is unlikely to hold onto its traditional gains unless they are taken."[49]

Affirming Co-responsibilities: Building Trades Locals in Alliance with Contractors and Users

The Built-Rite concept is simple—"motivating the guy with the tools." If you treat the rank-and-file workers as being important, then they will act important.
Construction Labor Report, October 28, 1987

No issue is more important for the future than the procedures through which the legal framework of collective bargaining evolves.
John T. Dunlop, *A Handbook of Great Labor Quotations* (1983)

We never were able to get together before. Our building trade demonstrations never did any good. We just made enemies.
Philadelphia building trades officer (1987)

William (Bud) Farally, a business agent with Local 19 of the Sheet Metal Workers International Association (Delaware County, Pennsylvania) and a particularly hard-working student at the Meany Center, urged me to attend the first presentation of the Built-Rite idea to a labor-management audience. Intrigued by his enthusiasm, I joined about 150 other registrants who filled every seat in the hall on April 15, 1988, to learn more about this experiment in cooperative labor-management relations.

Speaker after speaker, including a member of the U.S. Congress, the head of the General Building Contractors' Association, the head of the AFL-CIO Philadelphia Building Trades Council, and three direct participants (a business manager for a local of the International Association of Heat and Frost Insulators and Asbestos Workers and two corporate users of construction) praised the experiment and handled potentially explosive questions. I had previously conducted a long interview with Patrick Gillespie, the business manager of the trades council, and I had had the benefit of Bud Farally's contributions to my class at the Meany Center. I came away from the three-hour Built-Rite presentation with an even stronger appreciation of the serious risks and high level of skill involved.

The story dates back to the mid-1980s when Gillespie and several leaders of his craft locals concluded that something positive had to be done to change an increasingly dangerous situation: nonunion contractors had increased their share from $250 million in 1982 to $500 million in 1986, pulling more and more jobs away from union contractors.[1] To make matters worse, bickering among the craft locals had alienated those contractors who might have preferred union contracts. It had also encouraged the media to dwell on jurisdictional disputes, wildcat strikes, slowdowns, sickouts, and other obstacles to meeting tight construction deadlines.

In 1986, Gillespie cogently advised his trades council that "we have to clean up our act in order to survive."[2] He turned for help to a project created two years earlier by the Philadelphia Area Labor-Management Council (PALM), itself an exercise in collaborative relations. (PALM owes its existence to a joint effort of the Greater Philadelphia Chamber of Commerce and the Philadelphia Central Labor Council of the AFL-CIO).

PALM's Built-Rite acts as a forum for bringing together three traditional adversaries: contractors; the users of large-scale construction services, such as hotel chains, hospitals, and universities; and Gillespie's building trades locals. Before a job begins, a planning committee is formed composed of representatives of each of these three parties. To facilitate communication, PALM staffers, skilled in mediation, walk the parties through exercises that commonly lead to new collaborative agreements about how to put up, revamp, or take down a major building or construction project. No one is satisfied until substantial progress has been made in resolving what the parties call "negative attitudes." By the time the job begins, representatives of the new alliance have forged a fresh understanding of a safe and cost-saving building process. The agenda agreed to conveys a commitment to workers by the contractors and users that "we want this to be the best job you have ever worked on."[3]

All three parties jointly review blueprints, assess which locals should do what job, and try to anticipate and settle technical problems in advance. They also discuss budgets, clarify the quality of work that is expected, and review safety and health guidelines. These discussions are all firsts for many of the craft locals. Committed to a pragmatic, non-adversarial process, the three parties agree to a regular schedule of meetings throughout the duration of the building project.

Behind the scenes and relevant to any particular site are about 150 union and industry representatives who are divided into four Built-Rite task forces: productivity and cost effectiveness; communication and training; safety and health; and public policy, research, and public information. Each tripartite group meets monthly to resolve issues that in the days before Built-Rite might have resulted in jurisdictional disputes or work stoppages.

At the job site itself, Built-Rite employs what many admirers consider its most powerful component. Known as "toolbox" meetings, these twenty-minute weekly gatherings enable workers to learn what the locals, the contractors, and the user (owner) are up to and to convey messages to them. In sharp contrast to the posturing and defensiveness that used to characterize work-site discussions, the toolbox sessions, facilitated by PALM specialists, promote the freest flow of communication ever known in the building industry.

Finally, the process calls for a postjob review by the original members of the planning committee. This review provides closure by ensuring a frank and constructive critique of the "job agenda" set in the early planning stages. The safety record, the quality of work, feedback from toolbox sessions, the record on productivity, and the time schedule are closely scrutinized. Ideas are sought on how to do better next time, and recognition is given for exemplary contributions. Insofar as the review crowns the entire experience, it sets the stage for future Built-Rite construction jobs.

After members of the Built-Rite panel explained this process, they responded to a number of questions. They emphasized the simplicity of the process once it is instituted, the reductions in the number of delays, and the improvements in quality.[4] They explained that since Built-Rite began, over $950 million in construction had been delivered on time, on budget, and without a single work stoppage.[5]

Questions Raised by Skeptics

Critics, not surprisingly, wax nostalgic for the good old days when the building trades used "muscle" with abandon and "kicked ass" to win contract concessions. They also whisper that the only builders and contractors attracted to Built-Rite are those that are vulnerable to bad publicity, such as "Fortune 1000" firms that have building subsidiaries. They argue that since these firms represent only a small portion of the nation's builders, the impact of Built-Rite may be limited.

When I asked Bud Farally about these criticisms, he dismissed them as familiar and wrongheaded. There is no going back to the bad old days romanticized by nostalgic members, and the wide range of builders involved with Built-Rite belies the contention that only gigantic firms enroll.

Built-Rite's focus on mutual trust wins contracts "the old fashioned way—by earning them with competitive costs and quality."[6] Similar robust projects are now under way in Illinois, Kentucky, and Missouri, and the rewards are increasingly obvious. As Robert Hatch notes, "There has been a series of slow, deliberate, but progressively constructive steps toward cooperation. As allies we're working smarter, and that's definitely resulted in an improved climate."[7]

Chapter 2
The Priority of Safety

We know how to prevent many of the unnecessary deaths in the mines. What we seem to have lost is the will to do what good judgment and the law require. It makes me angry every time I hear about a miner killed because someone would not do his job.   **Senator Edward M. Kennedy, March 12, 1987**

They did not die in vain, and we will never forget them.
                              Frances Perkins speaking of the 146 victims
                              of the 1911 Triangle Shirtwaist fire

As workers have the most at stake—their very lives—they deserve the greatest say over workplace safety.   ***Steelabor* editorial, May-June 1988**

To understand labor's motivation to achieve a laudable record on safety, one should read the transcript of a typical congressional hearing on work-life hazards. In April 1988, for example, witnesses before the Senate Labor and Human Resources Committee told tales of horror of the kind that have become familiar:[1]

- An officer of a Massachusetts-based building and construction trades council told how he had asked an OSHA field office to inspect a GM site where workers were in danger. OSHA, however, required a formal complaint in writing. It was still being processed when a nineteen-year-old apprentice roofer, who had expressed concern about safety at this site, fell to his death—while his father, also a roofer, watched.
- A volunteer organizer for the United Farm Workers of America (UFW) explained that since OSHA had shut two offices in Texas, it took an inspector more than three hours to reach the farm sites in her area. Typically, the inspectors did not show up until "days to weeks" after the workers had left the location.
- A widow told how her husband, a maintenance worker, was crushed to death while repairing an elevator. She wanted to know why OSHA was still trying to come up with a standard to prevent such accidents when it had been researching the hazard since 1978.
- Two widows told how their husbands had been overcome by carbon

monoxide after entering a condensing tank in a zinc processing plant. They wanted to know why OSHA had still not established a safety standard for confined workplaces more than twelve years after beginning the task.

Other witnesses told of unnecessary deaths and maimings due to grain mill explosions, a hazard unions finally forced OSHA to address in 1988 by legal action. The new regulations, however, were severely weakened thereafter by the White House Office of Management and Budget (OMB), a process finally stopped by the Supreme Court in mid-1990.

Workers experience far more risk than the general public realizes, and far more than the White House seems inclined to let OSHA alleviate. It is a level of risk that contradicts both our national desire to boost competitiveness and our human concern for one another. As Ray Marshall, a former secretary of labor, has warned, certain members of the financial community "consider [labor's] interests to be negatives.... They approach occupational safety, health, and other job-related protections as 'necessary evils' or 'positive dangers.' "[2]

Lifting the Curtain

Unfortunately, as an editorial in a 1988 issue of Steelabor magazine noted, "Safety and health protection becomes visible only when it fails—when workers die on the job or a plant blows up."[3] Too few Americans wonder why construction workers, who constituted only 4 percent of the work force in 1969, suffered 15 percent of all workplace fatalities. Today, twenty years after the creation of OSHA, they account for only 5 percent of all workers and 26 percent of the fatalities.[4] And this has occurred despite a 45 percent increase in the number of OSHA inspections of construction sites between 1980 and 1987.[5]

Similarly, few people outside the transportation industry know that penalties against railroads guilty of safety infractions average only ten dollars a citation. And the Federal Railroad Administration (OSHA's counterpart) has a policy of not penalizing a railroad unless a safety violation found on an initial inspection is still uncorrected at an announced follow-up visit.[6]

Even when regulations appear strict, inflation and reductions in funding have seriously diluted OSHA's clout. The agency uses the same schedule of fines today that it established in 1970. The fine for companies that fail to provide a workplace free from serious health hazards has remained at $10,000, even though inflation has cut its value to only $3,400.[7] Budget cuts in 1988 restricted OSHA to only 1,125 inspectors, enough to inspect about 2 percent of the nation's nearly 5 million workplaces covered by federal law. Similarly, the 1988 budget for the National Institute for Occupational Safety and Health (NIOSH), the occupational research arm of the government, had less than half the dollar value it had in 1980.[8]

Congressman Tom Lantos (D-California), after hearings in 1987 on the record-setting number of accidents in the meatpacking industry, concluded: "When you don't use criminal penalties, when you settle fines at a fraction of the dollar, and when you have a policy that basically is an invitation to cheat, you certainly don't have vigorous enforcement of safety standards at the workplace."[9] To make matters worse, the restructuring of American industry between 1981 and 1983, preceded and followed by a maelstrom of bankruptcies and conglomerate takeovers, has further reduced union safeguards in critical industries.

The situation in meatpacking, the most hazardous industry in America, is typical. Organized labor now represents only 68 percent of the industry, down from 85 percent five years ago.[10] More than thirty out of every one hundred meat packers suffer work-related injuries and illnesses every year, a rate nearly four times that of all private businesses and three times that of manufacturing.[11] As the rate of unionization has gone down, there has been an upward climb in the number of days lost to injury and illness.

Once Over Lightly

Bookshelves bulge with volumes on unions and accident prevention, workplace hazards, and safety campaigns. Congressional hearings pour out still more volumes annually, rich in new facts, testimony, and suggested reforms. Single-focus magazines, such as *Occupational Health and Safety,* struggle to keep up with rapid developments.

Confronting this profusion of material, I have chosen three cases for their diversity and timeliness. The first highlights labor's ability to win groundbreaking safety legislation (VDT regulatory laws). The second demonstrates labor's ability to use safety "whistleblowing" and leverage stock ownership to advantage (anti-asbestos efforts). The third illustrates labor's ability to adapt major reforms to a work situation (the United Union of Roofers, Waterproofers and Allied Workers).

Curbing VDT Use

About 15 million video display terminals are in use today in American industry, and some 3 million new units are produced annually. As their use has increased, reports of arm pains, backaches, blurred vision, carpal tunnel syndrome, fatigue, headaches, muscular strain, night blindness, numb fingers, complications in pregnancy, skin rashes, and other ailments have proliferated. One study suggests that "as many as half of the estimated 13 million workers who spend at least four hours a day using VDT's are either in frequent pain or have missed work as a result of VDT-related problems."[12]

A major breakthrough came in 1987 when as many as ten thousand New York State employees gained the protection of regulations on the use of VDTs. The rules, designed by a labor-management committee required by the 1985–88 AFSCME contract, provided the following protections:

- Employees would have a greater say in any office changes.
- All VDT work stations would be upgraded to meet ergonomic standards.
- Managers would examine the impact of office automation on jobs and review how work was being changed by VDT use.
- VDT operators would be given a chance to vary their tasks and to exercise away from the machine.
- Noise would be reduced and temperature and humidity better controlled to reduce occupational stress.

Labor was disappointed that the recommendations did not address radiation exposure and did not require the government to pay for eye examinations and glasses for VDT operators. But the victorious AFSCME local applauded as "one of the biggest benefits" of the new policy the requirement that all state agencies upgrade working conditions.[13]

Despite bitter opposition from the business community, labor finally won passage in June 1988 of the first comprehensive VDT-regulating bill applicable to the private sector. Under the law, employers in Suffolk County, New York, who use more than twenty VDTs, would have been required by January 1, 1990, to

- pay 80 percent of the cost of annual eye exams for VDT-using employees and 100 percent for glasses and contact lenses, if needed;
- restrict continuous VDT work to three hours and provide a fifteen-minute "alternative task" break every three hours;
- provide adjustable nonglare VDT screens, five-legged chairs, detachable keyboards, copy holders, and adjustable light fixtures; and
- provide both written and oral training to employees in the use of the improved equipment and tips on how to avoid health hazards related to computer work.

The Suffolk County law also would have established a VDT review commission to recommend periodic improvements. Labor was keenly disappointed, however, in December 1989 when a state judge struck down the Suffolk law as superseded by existing state and federal statutes.[14]

Given that the federal government expects VDTs to be part of every white-collar job within ten years and that these machines "are likely to become the biggest cause of worker injuries in industrial history," IBM has recalibrated radiation levels much as labor has urged, and many businesses are now voluntarily adopting Suffolk-like VDT standards.[15]

Using Whistleblowing and Shareholders' Clout

Another promising tactic was used successfully in 1987 when ACTWU and the United Brotherhood of Carpenters and Joiners joined forces to expose use of dangerous asbestos materials in an auto parts company. Using their sixty thousand shares in the company and cooperating with some of the twenty thousand other shareholders, the two unions created a shareholder committee and won favorable attention from the media. In a statement sent to the shareholders, the unions "blew the whistle" on the company's practice of exposing workers to hazardous asbestos fibers at levels more than three times higher than the federal standard— a practice that unnecessarily endangered workers, was patently immoral, and heightened the risk of heavy fines and costly lawsuits.

In the ensuing proxy battle, the two unions earned support from public employee pension funds and large institutional investors, as well as from individual shareholders. As labor spokesman William Patterson explained, the union resolution on asbestos that emerged sought "to promote new thinking, and a reexamination of the corporate policy in this critical area." And as Carlos Puello, a worker in the company, rose to say, "We make the brakes that save your lives, and we hope you will take precautions to save our lives."[16]

When the tally from the vote was announced one month later, the two unions were pleased with a 25 percent total, far ahead of the predicted 1 to 2 percent. Pledged to sustain pressure for reform between annual meetings and to renew its resolutions on asbestos again and again, the unions expect management to see the light soon and agree to substantial safety-related changes.

Effecting Major Reforms

Roofers deal daily with the rigors of outdoor exposure, noxious fumes, extreme heat and humidity, and other occupational stressors. Their union, however, has stimulated significant accident and safety reform efforts at the workplace. A 1984 increase in union dues assures the union a steady and predictable funding base for safety efforts, immune from the vagaries of federal funding.[17]

The Roofers' program goes far beyond anything available from OSHA or NIOSH and fills a major gap in worker protection. According to Kinsey Robinson, secretary-treasurer of the union, the program includes the following:

- special hazard alerts on roofing products and research on their chemical ingredients;
- a monitoring program to determine the concentrations of hazardous exposures on the job, including air sampling surveys to measure coal tar pitch volatiles and solvent-based products;
- service on an industry committee to develop a safety and health standard for hot built-up roofing;
- regional conferences to explore with contractors the health and safety risks of materials (such as single-ply systems) and programs to assist the union's signatory contractors in complying with OSHA's hazard communications standard; and
- the use of bonuses sponsored by joint union-management committees for accident reduction.

To engage concerned local officers and grass-roots activists, the Roofers' program has an extensive outreach component. A brief injury and illness survey was distributed in 1985 to help the union begin its baseline research on the industry. A quarterly newsletter on safety and health is widely distributed, and slide/tape programs keyed to sections of the union's new safety and health manual help dramatize the need for responsive concern.

Initiated in 1978, the education and dissemination effort has steadily grown larger and more effective. What makes this program especially noteworthy is the ease with which the union could have ignored the challenge, given the macho culture of the work site, the short duration of most jobs, the migratory character of the young work force, and many other pressing demands. Instead, the Roofers union responded assertively and creatively and won a substantial spending base.

A Record of Innovation

Labor's struggle to achieve safe working conditions is so diverse that many other accomplishments warrant attention:

- The United Farm Workers launched a "Wrath of Grapes" boycott in 1985 to force California growers to stop spraying fields with five chemicals targeted as toxic by the union. Over 8 million pounds of these hazardous chemicals were being used annually in California alone. The Environmental Protection Agency has since judged all five "potentially dangerous" to farm workers.[18]

■ Thanks to a suit filed in 1986 by the Steelworkers, OSHA agreed to add 32.5 million workers to the coverage of its right-to-know regulation. Long overdue, the move inspired the *New York Times* to comment: "The wonder is that it should have taken 17 years and a Federal court order to bring this about."[19]

■ In 1988, the International Chemical Workers Union received nearly $5 million from the National Institute of Environmental Health Sciences to develop "hands-on" health and safety training for workers exposed to hazardous wastes and chemical fires.[20]

■ In 1988, the AFL-CIO Industrial Union Department took the lead in creating an international Center for Emergency Response to Chemical Disasters. Designed to lower the toll from disasters such as those in Bhopal, India, and Institute, West Virginia, the center will use teleconference systems to facilitate information exchange and cooperation between experts and officials of unions, companies, universities, and relevant levels of government.[21]

■ A $55,000 grant from a city agency enabled the New York Coalition on Occupational Safety and Health (NYCOSH), a labor and public-interest group, to conduct a one-month "job hazard hotline" in April 1988. Workers in the New York City area could call and learn from NYCOSH what the new state right-to-know law offered, where and when clinics on eliminating hazards would be held, and so on. Posters placed on subways, buses, and elsewhere urged use of this experimental service.[22]

■ Complaints from UFCW members working in a meatpacking plant in Dakota City, Nebraska, led OSHA to level a record fine of nearly $2.6 million in 1988 for violations of federal safety and health regulations. A week later, UFCW negotiators and the company agreed to a four-year contract that substantially increased the role of the union's safety committee, expanded employee participation in safety programs, and guaranteed workers access to their medical records. The company also agreed to hire a safety consultant to study operations and recommend changes.[23]

■ In 1989, the AFL-CIO initiated an annual Workers Memorial Day, a nationwide tribute to job safety and health and to victims of the workplace. At scores of rallies coast to coast, special attention was given to labor's recommendations for stronger OSHA legislation. A moment of silence was observed, followed by a solemn reading of the names of workers who have been killed in workplace accidents.

This record of continuous innovation provides strong evidence that a worker is far safer under labor's umbrella than in a nonunion workplace. When a union is the lone agent in an industry, as in the case of the UMWA in bituminous coal, the rank-and-file profits significantly:

> The annual number of inspections received by a union mine is far higher than its nonunion counterpart. The UMWA not only increases the number of inspections; it increases their *intensity* as measured by both the duration and scope of inspectors. Second, the UMWA substantially reduces the amount of time that elapses between the initial Mine Safety and Health Agency (MSHA) finding of a violation of health and safety standards and [the time] when mine owners actually correct that violation. Finally, the UMWA increases the penalty cost of violating an MSHA standard, providing greater incentive for operators to comply with the law.[24]

Union president Richard Trumka has reason to be proud of the UMWA's sophisticated health and safety programs and its record of success.[25]

Questions Raised by Skeptics

There is no shortage of ideas about why labor has not been more effective in the areas of safety and health, and unions take some responsibility. The Steelworkers Union, for example, although proud of its efforts and adamantly committed to increasing workplace safety, in 1988 conceded how hard it is to sustain such projects: "Guarding safety and health is not a glamour job. It never produces victories, like an organizing drive or a contract negotiation.... Safety and health protection is tedious and never-ending.... What's more, safety and health protection is complex. Every day there are new chemicals and new manufacturing processes that must be understood and evaluated."[26]

Skeptics doubt union locals can sustain their safety claims, given the small number of industrial hygienists in labor's employ. Their numbers are rapidly growing, however, and labor is securing a respectable share of available specialists.

Another concern of the skeptics is the costly delays in winning regulations. In 1979, for example, labor called for an OSHA regulation requiring employers to put warning tags or locks on machinery being cleaned or serviced. Since then, more than 1,000 related workplace deaths and over 540,000 injuries have occurred. Skeptics fault labor for its failure to get OSHA to act with appropriate speed.[27] Unionists insist, however, that their persistent lobbying was what finally forced OSHA to address the problem in 1988.

Finally, skeptics wonder about the efficacy of gains such as the city, state, and OSHA right-to-know legislation won since 1980 by coalitions of labor and environmental activists. Skeptics murmur darkly that these laws do not improve the understanding of average workers since exotic chemical names do not convey the toxic significance of materials. Unionists concede the point, but they see the educational task for a local's safety committee as an appropriate challenge. Familiarity with the impact of diseases and accidents remains a powerful spur to grass-roots activism in most union locals.

Summary

According to researcher David Weil, the evidence demonstrates that the safety advantages of a unionized work environment are widespread: "A new set of data demonstrate that unionized establishments are more likely to receive safety and health inspections, face greater scrutiny in the course of those inspections, and pay higher penalties for violating health and safety standards than do comparable nonunion establishments." Indeed, the Harvard researcher was so impressed by the evidence that he suggested "unions serve an important social function that has been overlooked up to now." Given labor's decline in the past decade, he thought labor's "critical role in the implementation of labor market [safety] policies argues for a reassessment of U.S. labor policy as a whole."[28] In that a worker is injured on the job every six seconds, or more than forty-nine hundred on an average workday, and more than eleven thousand individuals are killed on the job every year, or over thirty every day, reforms cannot come soon enough.[29]

Case Study
PHILAPOSH: "With a Little Help from My Friends"

American industry has always enjoyed a world-wide reputation for recklessness, and this is borne out by the accident figures which, even after years of "safety first" campaigns, still show both frequency and severity rates double those of Great Britain, France, and Germany.

Morris L. Cooke and Philip Murray,
Organized Labor and Production (1940)

The environmental and occupational safety and health issues are two sides of the same coin.
Howard D. Samuel, director, AFL-CIO Industrial Union Department (1981)

Now is not the time to make [environmental protection] ineffective because of some political objective to "get the government off of our backs." What we need is to get carcinogens out of our lungs, and put good jobs into our community. **John Sheehan, legislative director, Steelworkers (1981)**

In the late 1960s, labor was challenged anew by community activists intent on reducing accidents and hazards at work. For example, a coalition of VISTA organizers, public health physicians, retired miners, and leaders of coal union locals was formed to win benefits for victims of black lung disease. Although the UMWA was not involved at that time, it has since taken charge of this effort with distinction. Similarly, retired textile workers have received compensation benefits and strict controls on exposure to cotton dust through brown lung associations in mill towns in the South. ACTWU, the key union in this area, initially chose to remain on the sidelines, but much like the UMWA, it has long since redeemed itself by defending the associations and incorporating many of their demands into the union's own safety program.

By the early 1970s, labor was waking up to its responsibilities to take the initiative. Unions and progressive locals joined with community and environmental activists in various locations to form committees on occupational safety and health, otherwise known as COSH groups. Often operating outside the traditional union structure, the COSH groups have by now achieved major victories for workplace safety.

One such group is known as PHILAPOSH, and impressed by its media coverage and by forums I have occasionally attended since its founding in 1975, I interviewed its director, James Moran, to learn more about labor's part in its operation. We spoke at length on July 12, 1987, and on July 26, 1988. A high school dropout, fifty-one years old in 1990, Moran went to work in 1955 and soon joined Local 1612 (UAW). He served as a shop steward for years, rapidly earning distinction as a feisty activist. After being fired for leading a wildcat strike in 1970, Moran joined the COSH movement as an organizer. His travels on behalf of workers' safety have taken him up and down the East Coast and overseas to Finland, Ireland, Scotland, and Sweden. His experiences have earned him considerable respect from shop-floor unionists, who accept him as one of their own.

Started by about five union locals, PHILAPOSH is now sponsored by 167 locals in the Delaware Valley area (Philadelphia and southern New Jersey). They represent about 250,000 workers in public service locals, private sector manufacturing and trades locals, and private sector white-collar locals. Part of a network that includes similar COSH projects in California, Massachusetts, New York, North Carolina, Pennsylvania, Rhode Island, Wisconsin, and elsewhere, PHILAPOSH has an annual budget of over $150,000, three full-time staff members, and a remarkable record of accomplishment.

Labeled as "outsiders" back in the early 1970s, COSH stalwarts faced AFL-CIO hostility to environmentalists of every stripe, most of whom were perceived as threats to new construction and investment to generate jobs. Indeed, "the most heated conflicts between unions and environmental groups developed in the first few years after the shock of the 1974–75 recession . . . as companies intensified their efforts to force workers to choose between their jobs and their health."[1]

Turning to PHILAPOSH's accomplishments, Moran focused first on a 1980 campaign that experts believe was one of the most impressive of its kind.[2] In 1979, Moran and his volunteers from area locals organized the Delaware Valley Toxics Coalition (DVTC), made up of community, environmental, and labor groups. By 1981, DVTC had persuaded the Philadelphia City Council to pass the first city right-to-know legislation, a model for the nation then and now. Nine months of intense lobbying won the inclusion of unique clauses empowering both workers and community residents. Moran told reporters at the time that the key to victory was the broad base of DVTC membership. Its diversity ensured "the legislation couldn't be dismissed simply as a labor question, or an environmental one."[3]

PHILAPOSH continues to promote safety and health bills and testifies on their behalf. Moran, for example, has been tireless in his effort to secure the votes of state legislators for a "Crimes of Workplace Safety Act," a bill that would prod district attorneys to prosecute employers for culpable workplace deaths. Moran has a long list of cases of work-site fatalities he condemns as "needless, callous, and criminal" but which the district attorney declined to prosecute. The result, Moran charges, is "corporate murder, murder for profit. Employers make a calculated business decision to skimp on safety, and then pay the fine if they get caught." The bill PHILAPOSH wants passed would change this immediately, Moran insists, once employers realize their neglect could land them in prison.[4]

PHILAPOSH also makes a difference in community and worker education. Moran is a frequent speaker at evening and weekend forums to raise consciousness about work-site hazards, and he personally trains local union volunteers to serve as lay educators. For example, Ginny Jarvis, a staff member recruited from the United Electrical, Radio and Machine Workers of America (UE), has become an authority on VDT health threats to female workers. PHILAPOSH provides a variety of training sessions on reproductive hazards in the workplace, workers' compensation issues, contract language, and OSHA standards. Its new book, *Injured on the Job,* the first comprehensive guide to workers' compensation ever published in Pennsylvania and now in its second edition (1987), has won praise from Pennsylvania State University experts: "It succeeds impressively . . . should be in the library of every local union in the state."[5] Moran adds that PHILAPOSH has other equally fine publications to share with unionists.

PHILAPOSH also serves as a source of expert information. Staff members and volunteers can provide

- information from the PHILAPOSH toxicology library about a particular chemical and its health effects;
- an analysis of anything management offers as proof that something is safe, such as industrial hygiene surveys, air and noise sampling results, or asbestos removal procedures;
- help in designing questionnaires to learn the health concerns of members and to involve them in a local's efforts to improve safety and health;
- help in documenting and preparing requests for investigations by OSHA, NIOSH, or state and local agencies;
- industrial hygienists to survey specific areas for hazards or to accompany union representatives when government inspectors or management personnel walk through the workplace;
- evaluations of a company's medical program, complete with suggestions on how a local can protect members from improper screenings, invasion of privacy, and other abuses;

- information about public and private labs for testing samples of asbestos or chemicals; and
- referrals to sympathetic, objective doctors to serve as alternatives to management doctors, who are "typically not trained or are too pro-management to properly evaluate occupational disease."[6]

The scope of these resources continues to expand, Moran assures me, and many of the other twenty-five COSH groups around the country provide comparable services.

Another PHILAPOSH service available to local union affiliates and especially dear to Moran's heart is outreach to other organizations: "Often we can't win if we go it alone. PHILAPOSH is a bridge to the community. Our working relationships with groups like the Delaware Valley Toxics Coalition, the Pennsylvania Public Interest Campaign, and the New Jersey Citizen Action can help you win allies when public health and safety is at stake."[7] Outreach also extends beyond the region, since PHILAPOSH cooperates closely with other COSH groups and their overseas counterparts.

In 1989, PHILAPOSH received 771 technical requests, of which over 380 focused on workers' compensation questions, 28 on asbestos, 88 on chemical research, and 12 on drug testing. Staff filled 3,000 requests for their booklet on workers' compensation committees and 7,000 for PHILAPOSH fact sheets on AIDS in the workplace and distributed 5,400 copies of PHILAPOSH's newsletter, *Safer Times*. The speakers' bureau answered 12 requests from nonlabor groups and offered free health and safety forums to 11 local unions on a topic of their choice. Three work sites were surveyed at the request of locals, and many improvements were made on the basis of PHILAPOSH recommendations. PHILAPOSH received major funding from four sources: dues and donations from its 167 local affiliates, United Way, foundation grants, and funds raised through the sale of T-shirts, books, and buttons.[8]

Moran summarizes the focus of PHILAPOSH very clearly:

We would like the labor movement to focus on the rank-and-file, to focus closest to the shop floor. Nowadays it is preoccupied with contract negotiations and arbitration procedures. While they're important, they are far removed from the place of pain. They tempt labor into becoming technical, legalistic, and scientific, when it should instead remember its roots are *still* in the rank-and-file.

We also want labor to associate itself more sincerely with the larger community. The American people do not have labor consciousness, and very few have been educated about the labor movement. Coalitions like the COSH projects help people understand the good labor can accomplish—and they also help younger workers learn you never win a struggle forever; you have to fight the good fight over and again.

Moran also has ambitions that are more specific to the safety challenge:

PHILAPOSH would like to win a law that requires all employers to set up an effective work-site safety committee, one with guts and the power to match. Unions can bargain for this, but a law is the only way we can get it in nonunion shops, where they sure as hell need it.

We'd like to see an end to the squabbles between some people in labor and some environmentalists. It's time everyone recognized we're the *same* people, with the *same* interests, and this paranoia about "outsiders" only hurts us both. Thank God, the situation has been steadily improving, but we've still got a long way to go.

Above all, Moran concludes, PHILAPOSH would like its allies in labor to understand there is no quick fix for safety problems at the work site. The only path is grass-roots involvement, creative militancy, and a mix of perseverance, power, and caring.

Chapter 3
Health Promotion at Work

Hard experience teaches us that all but a few employers will cut every corner to avoid meeting their responsibilities, and that unsympathetic administration officials will use every foot-dragging technique known to delay enforcement. But experience also teaches us that we can make a difference, and that on health and safety questions, the labor movement is not just the first but the only line of defense for working people, whether they are union members or not.

**Lane Kirkland, president, AFL-CIO, at AFL-CIO
Conference on Safety and Health, November 1987**

Workers themselves must take charge of their own health and working conditions. Since workers and their unions usually face the powerful opposition forces of the owners and managers and their experts, this is not an easy prescription. **Ray H. Elling, *The Struggle for Workers' Health* (1987)**

The real question here...doesn't have anything to do with drugs. The philosophy underlying mandatory drug testing applies to everything else....Do you want to have a system at the workplace in which people are presumed innocent until proven guilty?...Or, do we want to turn all that around, and throw it away?

**Donald M. Fehr, executive director and general counsel,
Major League Baseball Players' Association,
in Douglas, *The Unionized Professoriate* (1986)**

America's labor movement has a vested interest in workplace health issues. While most workers get health-care coverage through their employers, far too many are also exposed to major health risks at their place of work. We are aware of some of these risks, such as flaking asbestos or sealed "indoor pollution," but are far less aware of others, such as toxic chemicals that have twenty-year latency periods before causing cancer. Moreover, far too few workers enjoy such health-enhancing options at work as a wellness program, a smoke ender's program, an athletic center, or exercise paths or receive bonuses for good attendance or weight loss.

Unions have a strong commitment to promoting workplace health, and that commitment is exemplified by the five robust projects described in this chapter:

- A relatively new union, unfettered by constraining traditions, has created a very successful labor-based alternative to employer-run employee assistance programs (EAPs).
- A dynamic older union has successfully adapted the fifty-year-old recovery model of Alcoholics Anonymous.
- A major union has created a sensitive and effective rehabilitation program for handicapped workers.
- Labor continues to challenge random mandatory drug testing.
- Labor is actively involved in shaping efforts by business to cut health costs.

While there are certainly other worthy examples, including the unique health-promotion projects of the United Farm Workers, the National Union of Hospital and Health Care Employees, and the United Mine Workers, these five cases clearly demonstrate labor's innovations in promoting health in the workplace.

Employee Assistance Programs

EAPs are defined as "job-based strategies for the identification, motivation, and treatment of alcoholic and other troubled employees." Introduced in the 1970s, EAPs initially helped plant supervisors learn a model for early intervention.[1] The model taught the supervisors to view repeated instances of impaired job performance as signals that a worker needed to be drawn into a "constructive confrontation." During this encounter, the troubled worker was given the choice if he or she wished to remain employed of either changing the self-destructive behavior or accepting referral to an alcoholism treatment and counseling center.

Although labor resented employers' unilateral imposition of the program, farsighted unionists appreciated certain aspects of the EAP model. First, it focused less on disease labels than on the existence of inappropriate behavior. Second, it empowered ordinary folk, like shop-floor supervisors, to play a constructive role as trained intermediaries. And third, it gave alcoholic employees a straightforward challenge to change their workplace behavior or accept the option of counseling, without commenting on how they behaved on their own time.[2]

Labor's own substance abuse specialists, however, found that employees who experienced both confrontation and counseling, rather than one or the other, made greater improvement.[3] Labor's goal thus became the development of an EAP model that did not give management sole responsibility for its initiation and control. Knowing that shop stewards, grievance committee members, and local officers could play a constructive role,[4] labor began to promote a jointly administered EAP. Unionists urged corporate America to believe that "the success of any such model depended upon the workers having full trust in it."[5]

It took the Association of Flight Attendants (AFA), a young union formed in 1974 and dominated by women (98 percent in 1974 and 87 percent at present), to show the way and challenge the labor movement to catch up. Elena M. Brown, a coordinator of the union's EAP, and Barbara Feuer, program director, both emphasized in conversations with me that the conventional EAP model, with its primary reliance on trained supervisors, would not do for flight attendants. These individuals change their work schedules monthly, work in multiple job sites (sixteen carriers), and perform their duties with a minimum of supervision. Indeed, supervisors often become involved only when major work-related problems occur or when new policies or procedures are to be implemented.

Accordingly, in 1980, the twenty-six thousand–member AFA came up with its own EAP design, one which provided a superior fit for the attendants. The union was keenly aware of the "family" allegiance among its members. Flight attendants regularly lodge, eat, and socialize with one another, putting them in a good position to know and care about colleagues who are abusing drugs or alcohol. AFA officers located 120 members, all of them full-time flight attendants, who agreed to take extensive training (ninety-six hours) to become peer referral counselors. EAP committee members, who are required to hone their skills regularly, now discreetly refer troubled co-workers who need treatment for alcohol or other drug use, crisis counseling, legal and financial advice, or guidance with marriage and family conflicts. In addition, there is a twenty-four-hour hotline for use by AFA members and their families.

One measure of the program's success is that in its first five years (1980–85), more than three thousand flight attendants and their family members sought help from AFA counselors in twenty-four cities. In 1989, 50 percent were self-referrals, 35 percent were peer referrals, another 17 percent came from supervisors or other management personnel, and 3 percent came from family and friends.

AFA thinks these figures attest to the confidentiality, sensitivity, and usefulness of a mutual reliance model, one that depends on there being goodwill and warmth among members. Certainly the program has succeeded in reaching a greater proportion of rank-and-file members than have conventional programs.[6] Much of the credit goes to the program's reliance on nonsupervisory agents and its pioneering focus on issues relevant to members. The AFA EAP was the first to create, for example, an EAP-linked program for battered women. AFA has demonstrated decisively that labor is able to recruit, train, and upgrade lay volunteers proudly identified as "health experts in the workplace... 'health ambassadors.' "[7]

Three other features of AFA's program are especially worthy of praise:

- EAP counselors are responsible for ferreting out and assessing treatment resources within their communities. Armed with screening information provided by AFA headquarters, the EAP makes sure that a troubled worker is put in touch with the best resources possible and that they will be receptive to the special work schedule and lifestyle of AFA members.

- EAP counselors substitute a very different message for disciplinary warnings from management. As AFA explains, "Our leverage is to say, 'We are your advocates; we are your union. But you can only continue this kind of behavior for so long before the company's going to get involved. And then you're going to be subject to some kind of discipline, and be in more trouble. Then it will be harder for us to help you.' "[8]

- AFA EAP counselors have earned the respect of supervisors throughout the industry, and management has become a booster. "The traditional adversarial relationship fell by the wayside.... Management says, 'We don't know how to identify this kind of problem. We don't have the expertise. Yes, we'll work with you on it.' "[9]

As Feuer notes, AFA's peer intervention model empowers rank-and-filers in a unique way by capitalizing on the humanistic strengths of its volunteers while building important new bridges to management.[10] The model beckons to locals everywhere in need of an effective alternative to employer-dominated EAPs.

Alcoholism Recovery Programs

Peter Sutherland, director of the Human Resources Group, a New York–based consulting firm, characterizes alcoholism as "the No. 1, 2, and 3 problem" in substance abuse.[11] Employers typically agree that with 18 million adults and 4 million teenagers afflicted, it far outdistances drug use in its toll at work. Alcoholics Anonymous (AA) is an unpretentious operation of sixty-three thousand self-help groups and 2 million members. Integral to the success of EAPs, AA has been amazingly successful, saving hundreds of thousands of lives since its founding in 1935.

Labor has been referring rank-and-filers to AA chapters since the mid-1940s when the CIO formally created a network of trained shop-floor referral "counselors." Recently, some locals have begun to shape a new and equally successful relationship with AA. Typical of such efforts is the EAP of the Tunnel and Construction Workers Union in New York City, which has devised an imaginative way of loosening the hold that heavy drinking and high rates of alcoholism have on the sandhog's way of life. In a 1985 case study, William J. Sonnenstuhl and Harrison M. Trice, two "giants" in this area, identified four salient features of the program:[12]

- The two full-time counselors in charge are both AA members with many years of practical experience in "twelve-step" programs. They were trained in the New York City Central Labor Council's peer counseling program, have completed a year-long hospital-based program, and have attended dozens of conferences and workshops on alcoholism.
- The counselors spend most of their time in the "hog house," or locker room, at work sites.
- When not at the work sites, the counselors take members to AA meetings, visit them in alcoholism treatment programs, or meet with them informally at home or a neighborhood coffee shop.
- The network of union members who serve as referral agents are all AA members.

Intensely loyal to their union, sandhogs have a tight gossip network about hard drinking and mental health problems. By bringing EAP counselors into their work culture, however, they are generally able to get troubled drinkers to admit their alcoholism, the difficult first step in any recovery process.

Thanks again to the closeness of the union, members of the EAP network are able to use a variety of tactics to keep members in the recovery group, including the distribution of jobs as a reward for not drinking. According to Sonnenstuhl and Trice, "Today, hiring...is as likely to occur in AA meetings as in the bars. In each of the hog houses, the AAs have their lockers together, and when someone returns to work from rehabilitation, they move his locker into their area, and make sure he has an AA buddy either on his gang or in his work area." Short AA meetings are held on the job, and AA members who pass one another at work express support with a wink or a nod. Alcoholic sandhogs stay in the recovery network "because the AA's and counselors teach them that they are, indeed, alcoholics. They cannot drink and sobriety will come only from remaining in the group."[13]

Sonnenstuhl and Trice emphasize the ability of this EAP to reverse the traditional attitude among sandhogs that symptoms of alcoholism are "ordinary matters."[14] To replace this suicidal misperception, the EAP emphasizes recovery and the use of the union as a "therapeutic community." Recovery, in turn, heightens loyalty to the union, since the EAP underscores labor's philosophy of having members support members, much as AA advocates having alcoholics help other alcoholics.

Assistance for Handicapped Workers

The IAM's Center for Administering Rehabilitation and Employment Services (IAM CARES) was created in 1981 to "pioneer in the development of innovative ways in which organized labor can participate in the important process of bringing disabled workers into the labor market, and enabling them to share as wage earners in the benefits of economic independence."[15] The program, which is administered by Charles E. Bradford, the executive director, and his deputy, Guy Stubblefield, has a number of innovative features:

- The employer is directly involved in the rehabilitation of every disabled individual who is placed.
- IAM district and local union officials provide help and backing through a buddy system for employers covered by an IAM contract.
- IAM's Placid Harbor Educational Center is used for staff training: "In this area we simply have no competition. No other grant recipients can offer the kind of in-service training through which we maintain and enhance the professional skills of our IAM CARES staff."[16]
- IAM CARES develops and tests new approaches to the provision of comprehensive specialized assistance to handicapped youth.
- Services are provided to the beneficiaries of Social Security disability payments: "IAM is breaking new ground; neither public agencies nor voluntary placement agencies have had much experience in dealing with this important social problem."[17]
- Employer misconceptions about the cost of modifying equipment for use by disabled workers are addressed and corrected; 60 percent of the modifications require an investment of less than one hundred dollars, and 90 percent require less than one thousand dollars.[18]
- Job sites that have never been available to disabled workers have been opened through the offer of a free prescreening service.
- The program has co-sponsored with the U.S. Department of Education a twenty-eight-minute videotape documentary entitled *We Can Do It* about six disabled workers who overcame their handicaps.
- A $1.8 million budget in government grants and $400,000 from the IAM has been successfully administered.[19]
- A comprehensive project funded by a 1986 demonstration grant of

$260,000 from the Department of Labor has been successfully implemented.

The number of handicapped workers placed by the twenty-five separate projects (two in Canada) of IAM CARES has risen from 59 in the opening year (1981–82) to 1,251 in 1989, for a record-setting total of more than 5,300 between 1981 and 1989. Although about one-third of those placed were IAM members and every effort was made to place clients in jobs covered by union contracts, the IAM CARES project does not require clients to have a union affiliation.

Established in fifteen major labor markets coast to coast and aided by more than twenty IAM district lodges, the project is particularly proud of its retention rate. Although 70 percent of its clients are classified as "severely disabled," IAM CARES reports that more than 80 percent remain in their posttreatment jobs, making the retention rate higher than that of the labor force as a whole. On the basis of this reccord, the IAM CARES project has been highly successful in competing for scarce federal grants: "The favorable response to our proposals indicates a growing appreciation within the government, and within the rehabilitation community, of the value of our union's sponsorship of these programs."[20] With the help of twenty-six staff, Bradford and Stubblefield plan to train and place 22 million partly or totally disabled working-age Americans,[21] at a time when less than 1 percent of the disabled workers who receive job training from other programs actually go back to work.[22]

Drug Testing

From 1984 to 1987, drug testing in industry jumped tenfold, and revenues of the drug-testing industry grew from $100 million to an estimated $1 billion.[23] More than half the Fortune 500 companies are now screening, compared to 3 percent in 1982, and more are joining all the time. A poll of workers in 1987 found that 81 percent agreed that some or all workers should be tested, and 88 percent said they would agree to be tested.[24]

Such surveys are lambasted by critics for their oversimplification. As sociologist William J. Sonnenstuhl and others say, "It is unlikely that respondents, when asked about supporting some vague concept called 'drug testing,' conjured up images of being required to provide a urine sample without just cause, being watched by someone while urinating in a cup, and being fired because of an unreliable finding."[25] Despite media pressure for random testing and a rush by corporate America to test, the AFL-CIO remains "adamantly opposed to blanket or random substance abuse screening and to testing without strictly defined reasonable cause."[26] Instead, the federation urges a joint labor-management response tailored to the specific work culture, along with passage of federal and state laws to ban tests that unnecessarily infringe on the privacy and dignity of workers. The AFL-CIO also urges strengthening the legal protections for those suffering from alcoholism or drug addiction.

The AFL-CIO argues further that technical limitations surrounding testing render the results highly unreliable, so that error rates, especially false positives, can run 25 percent or higher. Even accurate results leave critical questions unanswered. James Ellenberger, assistant director of the AFL-CIO Department of Occupational Safety, Health, and Social Security, asks: "What can tests really determine? Contrary to popular belief, drug testing is unable to establish whether an individual is addicted to a drug, under the influence of a drug, or unable to perform a job because of alleged drug use."[27] Labor remains firmly opposed to random testing because it implies that workers are guilty until proven innocent and because the experience is degrading.

Different unions emphasize different points in opposition. Kenneth T. Blaylock, former president of the American Federation of Government Employees (AFGE), has insisted that random testing is utterly wrong-headed: "It is ridiculous to believe [it] is a stronger solution to the drug abuse problem than stopping the flow of drugs into the country, keeping them off the streets by beefing up law enforcement efforts, teaching our children about drug abuse . . . and helping those who want to kick the habit through rehabilitation programs—all programs for which the Reagan Administration cut funding." Blaylock contends that the crucial issue is whether random drug testing of federal civilian employees is based on the detection of job impairment in the workplace. He says, "The resounding answer is no!"[28]

While ordering an immediate end to random testing of 120,000 AFGE members by the army, a U.S. district judge noted in March 1988 that testing of some 5,400 civilian army employees over a six-month period had found only thirty-seven positive cases, or less than 1 percent. He suggested that the army consider other alternatives, such as training supervisors to detect chronic drug use and conducting neurological tests to determine whether a worker's thinking and behavioral output are impaired.[29] Blaylock argued similarly that the old-fashioned approach to workplace monitoring, keeping an eye out for errors, would do the job just fine.[30]

The railroad unions have focused on fundamental constitutional issues. Their rejection of a May 1988 proposal by the secretary of transportation to institute random drug testing accused the government of trying to "strip rail employees of their individual rights, while ignoring the deeper problems surrounding substance abuse."[31] Attention, they argued, should be placed on rehabilitation rather than on FBI-like detection schemes. They advocated respect for the Fourth Amendment prohibition against unreasonable searches.[32]

Challenged to support their approach, the rail unions proudly point to Operation Red Block, a model drug-testing and rehabilitation project created in August 1987 as a result of negotiations between the Brotherhood of Locomotive Engineers and the CSX line, the country's largest carrier. This unprecedented contract allows for certain types of testing, "but does so with an eye toward prevention, education, and rehabilitation."[33] CSX's nineteen thousand employees are encouraged to acknowledge an alcohol or drug problem without fear of punishment or loss of employment. If they test positive, they are required to participate in a CSX EAP program.

Nearly a year after Operation Red Block was created, about 6 percent of all rail employees nationwide tested positive for drug use, whereas the figure was only 3 percent for the CSX employees. The union claims this improvement demonstrates the superiority of collectively bargained approaches over any narrow focus on mandatory random testing,[34] a claim since rebuffed by a high court in a ruling against the union.

Challenged to follow suit, the AFL-CIO calls attention to an agreement reached as far back as 1984 by Local 689 of the Amalgamated Transit Union and the Washington (D.C.) Area Metropolitan Transportation Authority. The agreement guaranteed that employees who tested positive would be allowed to remain on the job in a post that was not safety-sensitive while undergoing required treatment through an EAP. It guaranteed that successfully rehabilitated employees would be returned to their old jobs, although they would be subject to random testing during the subsequent six months. Finally, the agreement promised that testing procedures would be strictly controlled. Since the implementation of this program, the number of drug-related employee grievances has dropped from ninety to only two a year.[35]

Along with the focus on rehabilitation, the AFL-CIO urges its affiliates and management to agree to do the following:[36]

- Recognize alcohol and drug abuse as treatable illnesses, rather than instances of willful misconduct.
- Focus drug testing at the work site only on workers exhibiting job-related impairments that indicate drug abuse.
- Perform no tests until an employee has advised his or her union representative.

- Have the union and the employer select laboratory and testing procedures jointly.
- Permit employees to have their sample retested independently by a laboratory they have selected.
- Reimburse for all costs any employee who successfully challenges the accuracy of a positive result and compensate for related mental duress.
- Refer any employee who has a confirmed positive test to a previously agreed-upon rehabilitation or employee assistance program.
- When necessary, impose discipline that is progressive and proportional to the infraction and hazard presented.

In the furor over substance abuse, labor remains committed to protecting the privacy and dignity of every worker. Although labor has been on the losing side of recent key court decisions, its allies include civil rights advocates, civil libertarians, and rehabilitation-oriented health specialists.

Partnerships in Cost Cutting

Public and private expenditures for health care have increased an astonishing 700 percent in the last twenty years and are now running about $1 billion a day, representing over 12 percent of our entire gross national product.[37] Corporations are desperate to reduce the cost and protect productivity—two goals labor respects while insisting that the hard-earned rights of workers not be compromised. Labor faces the difficult challenge of helping to reduce health-care costs while protecting health-care benefits.

One result is labor's new interest in preferred provider organizations (PPOs). Before choosing a PPO, unions, directly or through consultants, assess health data such as the reputation of providers in the community, the number of sophisticated procedures performed, and outcome statistics. The unions then negotiate contracts at discounted rates for those services that are rated high in quality. In return, the PPO can expect a guaranteed pool of clients and efficient payment. Labor's distinct contribution to the choice of PPOs has been to discourage the use of "bottom-line" efficiency as the sole determinant. While teaching hospitals may not offer the cheapest services, for example, many workers believe they get much better and more sensitive care at such institutions.[38]

Labor is also making fresh use of the educational potential of its own press. Roy Dickinson, assistant director of research and education for the International Brotherhood of Electrical Workers, explains, for example, how his union is using its journal:

Two or three times each year we run articles featuring health care. First we focus on the fact that the cost of health care is a national problem. Then we move on to why it is important that our membership become involved. The idea of challenging what the physician says by saying that [patients] must have a second opinion or must be precertified before they go to the hospital comes as a shock to these people. They do not know why they have to do that now. We have to tell them why.[39]

"So far," Dickinson observes, "there have not been a lot of problems in members accepting the programs [the union has] instituted."[40]

Unions subject every cost-sharing or cost-shifting proposal from management to close scrutiny. They resist calls for high deductibles, restrictions on family coverage, substantial co-payments, and sharp cutbacks in the terms of service. They charge that the flexible benefit plans backed by some employers provide inadequate health-care coverage, especially for serious illnesses. In addition, such plans often exclude preventive health coverage for children, along with "well baby care" and employer contributions to dependent-care assistance.[41]

Painfully aware that family medical coverage took a forty-dollar bite from the average employee's monthly paycheck in 1988, an 18 percent rise from 1987 and the biggest rise in three years, labor advocates a better route to cost containment.[42] The AFL-CIO Committee on Health Care has, since 1985, urged management to join labor in efforts to economize by using tough administrative controls, hospital precertification programs, and PPO or health maintenance organization (HMO) plans; banning weekend admissions and preadmission testing; and providing incentives for securing second opinions and using outpatient care. Labor's suggestions remain part of a highly significant process of "discovering a self-interest in joint approaches to the broader questions of bringing the system under control."[43]

Other Breakthroughs

There are many, many examples of union breakthroughs in the area of health promotion. In addition to the examples above, the following are representative:

■ The Postal Workers Union Hearing Impaired Task Force described the problems of deaf workers directly to the U.S. postmaster general at union negotiations in 1987. The contract that resulted from these talks included, for the first time, language requiring telephone devices for the deaf, open-captioned training films, certified interpreters as needed, and other overdue provisions to accommodate the forty-four hundred hearing-impaired workers in the postal service.[44]

■ ACTWU is participating in a federal experimental program that extends HMO care services to the union's 130,000 retirees and dependents. The experiment should eliminate many of the inefficiencies inherent in the Medicare program and convert the waste into Medicare benefits.[45] Harvey Sigelbaum, president of Amalgamated Life Insurance, which is running the project for the union, boasted to the press, "We're a proven organization. We've been up and running not for two years, which is all the experience most HMOs have, but for forty years."[46] Convinced they can deliver benefits more economically than the government, other unions, such as the UAW and the UMWA, may soon follow ACTWU's example.[47]

■ The AFL-CIO annual conference on safety and health in November 1987 drew almost nine hundred union representatives to a two-day series of workshops on topics such as OSHA health standards, right-to-know legislation, the asbestos challenge, AIDS in the workplace, robots as a new health hazard, and health protection for health-care workers.[48] The AFL-CIO Committee on Health Care used the conference to detail innovative cost-control techniques that do not penalize patients. The committee also promoted model legislation for use in creating cost-containment laws at the state level and publicized its new videos for health education.[49]

■ Unions such as AFSCME, the Service Employees' International Union (SEIU), the National Union of Hospital and Health Care Employees, and others have created wide-ranging educational projects to train staff, stewards, and members. They are using the need for AIDS education to force management to join health and safety committees to monitor compliance with infection-control procedures. In 1988, in an effort to gain universal voluntary adherence to such procedures, San Francisco's Local 250, the largest health-care workers' local (thirty thousand members) in SEIU, arranged for several dozen stewards to attend university programs on how to educate co-workers about AIDS.[50]

■ Over 650,000 Americans, including unionized building services employees, carpenters, meat cutters, and teachers, were enrolled in 1988 in a new "preestimate" program. The doctors who run it under contract with a union-employer welfare fund achieve 25 to 35 percent savings by negotiating lower surgical fees before an operation.[51]

■ The Laborers' International Union of North America adopted a joint labor-management program in early 1988 to increase health education and counseling and to upgrade related research and data collection for its nearly 700,000 members. Angelo Fosco, the union's president, proudly explained, "To our knowledge, no other union has initiated such a broad program... [to help members and dependents] not only receive the proper treatment for health problems, but to learn to live healthier lives."[52]

■ Leaders from the UAW and GM met in April 1988 at the largest labor-management health and safety conference in the world (over 1,200 attendees). They assessed a teleconference they had sponsored that brought experts on AIDS to the attention of 330,000 UAW members in 150 GM plants, attended workshops, and heard an update on their UAW-GM Health and Training Center, which has "graduated" nearly 1,500 shop-floor personnel since it opened in 1985. Special attention was given to demonstrations of an interactive laser disk that can be used in health education projects.[53]

The list could be extended, but the point should already be clear: many of labor's efforts to promote health at the workplace are both inventive and successful.

Concerns of the Skeptics

Conflicting pressures on labor to expand health services, protect existing benefits, and yet help reduce costs has, inevitably, raised questions that warrant a thoughtful response. In particular, doubts about labor's clarity concerning certain health-protection matters arise in the stand self-interested unions take on smoking. Five unions in the Tobacco Industry Labor-Management Committee, a lobbying group sponsored by the industry since 1984, recently produced a booklet, for example, warning that anti-smoking rules imposed unilaterally by management may actually be a covert way of avoiding other health and safety improvements in the workplace.[54] Anti-smoking advocates in labor agree but urge, nevertheless, that the efforts to put an end to smoking be sustained. Although labor is encouraged by the fact that 65 to 75 percent of the work force no longer smokes and that smoke-free workplaces are increasingly common, it still objects to unilateral changes in working conditions, regardless of how sanctimoniously the company portrays its action. Anti-smoking unionists insist new policies should be established through collective bargaining rather than by corporate or legislative fiat. Research supports their contention, according to Bruce Miller, who notes that "companies that have made an active effort to include all unions in the initial planning are the companies with the smoothest transitions to a clean-air policy."[55]

Skeptics also wonder whether the entire effort to promote better health might not sometimes put the cart before the horse: "Asking a hospital employee to modify smoking habits at the same time that he or she is required to work on rotating shifts or to work on a severely understaffed floor may be ignoring [even more] significant health hazards. If the employee is worried about contracting hepatitis B because of poorly enforced isolation procedures for blood samples, will the worker be able to take seriously a company health promotion campaign?"[56]

There is similar concern about the new fascination among employers with "cafeteria" or flexible benefit schemes: "Low participation rates may reflect...that working families need more than salary reduction arrangements; they need employer contributions to make the benefit real. Designing flexible benefits that purport to address the needs of an evolving work force without adopting parallel personnel policies, such as adequate parental leave, further suggests a gap in employers' support for addressing workers' concerns."[57]

Health specialists in the labor movement are sensitive to this problem. They want and urge employers to postpone on-site wellness programs until workplace hazards have first been eliminated, such as indoor air pollution, heat and ionizing radiation, insensitive supervision, and sexual harassment.[58] Long experience has persuaded organized labor that the success of workplace health programs may hinge on first achieving "wellness" of the workplace itself.

Summary

According to the Bureau of Labor Statistics, there has been an upward trend in work-related illnesses and injuries. In 1973, for example, fifty-three workdays were lost for these reasons per one hundred workers, whereas seventy-six were lost in 1988.[59] Labor's campaign to upgrade employee health on and off the job has a long way to go before it will be considered successful, but it has tremendous incentive to get on with the job.

Part II

Part II

ORGANIZING AND REORGANIZING

D on't mourn for me. Organize!" was the last message Joe Hill, labor's legendary troubadour, sent out of a Utah prison before his execution in 1915 on a trumped-up murder charge. That message still resounds. Labor's first obligation is to help workers—unskilled, skilled, and professional—create locals that can balance the potentially overwhelming power of management.

Chapter 4 explores some of labor's problems in this process, while focusing on outstanding responses. These include updated versions of familiar organizing tools and some robust innovations: the use of volunteer and college-based organizers, approaches tailored to immigrant workers, the development of an associate member category and a privilege benefit program, and special drives to recruit professionals and health-care workers. The case study that follows describes a highly successful effort to form a new union among technicians whose employer had fired 85 percent of their predecessors in 1981 and promised the White House their union would never trouble the government again.

Chapters 5 and 6 examine successful efforts to create solidarity with professional employees and with working women. The case study summarizes a long, colorful, and ultimately victorious campaign to help clerical and technical workers at Harvard form a local resembling those at Columbia, Yale, and scores of other universities. Although Harvard has long sponsored a trade union leadership seminar, administrators adamantly opposed the new union. The successful organizing drive, aided by AFSCME, contains valuable lessons on strategic campaigns to draw in white-collar and service employees.

Chapter 7 explores inventive ways established unions maintain rank-and-file enthusiasm, such as the use of study circles, efforts to upgrade skills, affirmative action programs, and initiation ceremonies. The three case studies examine the use of telephone polling to take the pulse of the membership, an innovative approach to internal communications that uses sophisticated telecommunications, and a creative response to an adverse NLRB ruling, a response designed in part to "rally the troops." The four chapters and five case studies all emphasize the prodigious effort required first to attract and then to energize a membership that can help achieve labor's potential. Practically everything, labor understands, hinges on inventing and developing new ways to organize and reorganize ceaselessly and creatively.

Chapter 4
Encouraging Membership Growth

Obviously, most of the rejuvenation of the labor movement will begin in that movement itself. It will include both new strategies for organizing the unorganized, and for strategically wielding the economic power that labor has but does not use. The combination of these twin approaches will produce something very different from the business unionism that flourished for three decades after World War II. **Robert Kuttner, economist, *Dissent*, Winter 1986**

"We're preparing for an explosion of organizing," says James Velghe, president of Management Science Associates, Inc., an anti-union consulting firm. Such talk is the most cheering news unions have had in years.
Kevin Kelly and Hazel Bradford, *Business Week*, February 12, 1988

Although often lonely and enervating, organizing has always been "the sinews and lifeblood of the union." Epitomizing labor robustness at its best, the organizer is a "secret agent, salesman, public relations expert, writer, human relations expert, and, above all, charismatic leader."[1] The annals of organizing success crackle with examples of inventiveness and risk-taking, despite sometimes life-threatening opposition.

Organizing tallies, however, have disappointed labor since the 1955 merger of the AFL and CIO heightened expectations of new gains. Especially in the last decade, labor's response, therefore, has included more varied and impressive campaigns than previously undertaken, and although the cost in dollars and effort soars, the AFL-CIO and its many union affiliates expect to make impressive organizing gains in the 1990s.

Background

Labor's current innovations in organizing should be seen in their starkly sobering historical context:

- In October 1989, the AFL-CIO membership was listed at 14.2 million, about 1.6 million more than at the time of the merger in 1955, even though more than 57 million workers joined the labor force in the same period.[2]

■ At 17 million in 1989, union membership in AFL-CIO affiliated
unions and in all others outside the federation was down to about 16
percent of all full-time, nonsupervisory, nonagricultural workers, compared to 35 percent in the years following World War II.[3] Moreover,
80 percent of the decline had occurred since 1960.[4]
■ While the absolute number of union members has increased since
1955, union density declined by 12 percent by 1984, and that decline
was "unprecedented in American history."[5]

The good news takes the form of a reduction in the bad news: whereas declines in labor's ranks averaged 360,000 annually in the post-
recession years of 1983–85, the loss was only 21,000 in 1986 and
62,000 in 1987. In 1989, labor actually achieved a slight increase
and earned its highest victory level since 1981; a total of 87,000
workers were organized as a result of wins in more than 1,600
elections.[6]

Explanations for labor's organizing problems abound. One AFL-CIO
expert points to structural upheavals in the economy, intensified employer
resistance to unionization, the creeping paralysis of the legal apparatus
of collective bargaining, and the erosion of NLRB protections, as well
as the use of anti-union management consultants and sophisticated personnel practices. Labor, he acknowledges, has made mistakes: "Admit-
tedly, unions may not have been creative enough in tailoring their
organizing efforts."[7]

Economist Robert Kuttner contends that unions have been hiring too
few organizers. Many do not give appropriate priority to this function,
and some starve it for resources. Most will not cooperate in multiunion
joint organizing drives, and far too many resist hiring "hotshots" capable
of imaginative missionarylike work. Some actually fear that new members
may challenge incumbent leaders or reject prevailing union policies. The
labor movement, Kuttner warns, "is doing far too little organizing for
its own survival."[8]

Not surprisingly, therefore, organizing in the 1980s brought in no more
than 200,000 private sector workers each year, compared to 750,000 in
the 1950s.[9] Indeed, in the early 1980s, unions engaged in so few NLRB
elections, and won so few (45 percent, down from 75 percent in 1945),
that only 0.14 percent of the unorganized work force was organized as
a result of elections. Obviously, labor's share of the work force has been
eroded and achieving any comparable growth difficult.[10] In fact, unions
have to double their rate of organizing victories in the private sector just
to maintain current membership[11] or else organize without any use of
the NLRB representation election process.

A 1984 study of attrition in union membership attributes the declines to both a decrease in labor's organizing activity and a substantial increase in managerial opposition. Given that unionists in 1990 enjoyed a wage-benefits differential of about $180 a week more than nonunionists, corporate hostility is not surprising. That hostility, "broadly defined, is a major cause of the slow strangulation of private sector unionism."[12]

Although labor increasingly gains members in ways other than through NLRB elections, it has, nevertheless, suffered an annual decline of about 3 percent in its share of the work force. At current rates, its share could slip from its present rate of 16 percent to less than 10 percent by the year 2000, "a precipitous decline...of a magnitude comparable to the decline from the mid-1950s to the 1980s." Richard B. Freeman and James L. Medoff, the scholars who offer this grim warning, insist they are not predicting such a decline. On the contrary, they "would not be surprised to see a sudden burst in union organization,"[13] a prospect that may hinge on utilization of the robust ventures discussed in this volume.

Volunteer Organizers

While hardly a new concept, using volunteers as organizers fell out of sight in the 1950s and 1960s, when some unions became complacent about their numbers. George Meany spoke for many leaders at the time when he brusquely explained: "Why should we worry about organizing groups of people who do not want to be organized?... Frankly, I used to worry about the size of membership. But quite a few years ago, I just stopped worrying about it, because to me, it doesn't make any difference."[14] Since then, however, unions such as ACTWU, the CWA, and the UFCW have resurrected organizing programs based on the use of volunteers and have come to rely on them. In fact, a *Washington Post* reporter in 1987 solemnly contended that "the future of labor unions in America rests on the shoulders of [volunteers] who try to sell modern high-tech unionism door-to-door in the 1980s."[15]

A 1987 CWA campaign to unionize employees of MCI is representative. Rank-and-filers volunteered in response to conversations with CWA local officers and their reading of feature articles in the union paper. A training program held after work over a period of weeks provided the volunteers with information and conversational skills. They learned the criticisms, questions, and insults they were likely to encounter and appropriate responses. They learned how to use license plate numbers to locate the homes of potential members and how to parry doors being slammed on them. Above all, they learned how to "sell" CWA membership once they had gained entrance into a living room. They worked at night on their own time, and many recruited co-workers for the volunteer project.[16]

With 650,000 members, the CWA remains the world's largest telecommunications union, and it is eager to make inroads into the fast-growing nonunion sector of the industry.[17] The CWA believes that giving volunteers a strategic role in organizing campaigns helps "revitalize" the union since rank-and-filers intensify their commitment in the process of persuading others to join. The volunteers also provide valuable feedback from both new and "renewed" members.

Skeptics wonder how many rank-and-filers will actually volunteer for training and persevere at organizing. And how many will ultimately bring in enough new members to cover the costs of the volunteers' training, deployment, insurance, and supervision? Answers hinge on the commitment and resources of the sponsoring union. If its volunteer program is carefully organized and adequately supported, the rewards could satisfy even the most exacting skeptic.

College-Trained Organizers

One of the oldest questions in labor is whether organizers can be drawn from outside the ranks. As far back as 1879, Samuel Gompers advocated relying only on co-workers, since "wage-earners understood their problems and could deal with them better than could outsiders."[18] Throughout labor history, recruits from beyond the workplace have been suspected of harboring ulterior political motives that diverge from labor's best interests.

The question is raised again today by activists eager to tap the talents of young adults who have much to offer but have not come up through the ranks. One such proponent, Vincent Sirabella, organizing director of the Hotel and Restaurant Employees and Bartenders' International Union, initiated an ongoing experiment in 1970 that continues to emphasize six points:[19]

■ Organizing has to become labor's top priority.

■ Despite the image of young people as selfish and apolitical, ads placed in liberal publications such as the *Nation,* the *Progressive,* and *Dissent,* draw scores of responses from would-be organizers.

■ Selecting, training, placing, monitoring, and retaining or dismissing new organizers is an art that is neither esoteric nor hopelessly vague. It can be studied, systematized, practiced, assessed, and steadily improved.

■ Young college graduates can "go the course" provided they understand from the outset how much they have to learn from rank-and-filers with very little formal education.

- Young college graduates can learn to relate to all workers with ease, candor, and respect. If collaboration with organizers from the shop floor is mandatory, it can be effective and mutually rewarding.

Sirabella urges unions to give fair consideration to recruits with degrees from accredited colleges, rather than only those from the proverbial "college of hard knocks." He believes that success in organizing depends on using the widest possible pool of recruits.

Skeptics wonder whether college recruits will persevere, given the low salaries, long hours, and toil and stress involved. They worry that many may be covert ideologues who will pursue their own political agendas, regardless of labor's best interest. And they worry that prospective members will be turned off by organizers they dismiss as "bleeding-hearts" posing as the workers' best friend.

Sirabella's response is that his young recruits quickly earn the workers' full support. He finds them no more radical politically than labor can accept. While he has lost far too many, he is learning what is required to reduce their turnover. In his considered judgment, his twenty-year-old experiment demonstrates that college-trained organizers can be highly successful when employed in a sensitive and supportive way.

Immigrant Workers

Four million illegal immigrants and an even larger number of legal immigrants continue to wrestle with the intricacies of the 1980 Simpson-Rodine Immigration Act. To labor's credit, and especially to that of the SEIU and the International Ladies' Garment Workers' Union (ILGWU), for several years these potential members have been receiving union aid in dealing with this perplexing issue.

Even before passage of the Immigration Reform Act, the ILGWU was busy trying to protect workers who had tumbled into a "black hole" of shadowy employment. Sweatshops, reminiscent of those seen in the late 1800s, had begun reappearing in apartment basements in major cities, and recent arrivals from China, Korea, and the Dominican Republic were being systematically exploited. State inspectors found horrendous conditions, including fire hazards and blocked fire exits. Aware of the immigrants' desperate need for work, the ILGWU collaborated with New York state and city officials in creating a project to demonstrate a better alternative. An industrial condominium was developed in New York City where marginal garment companies could maintain decent standards at costs no higher than those they had been paying to maintain dangerously substandard facilities.[20]

By demonstrating "street smarts" in this way, the ILGWU has been able to use the complex problems raised by immigration regulations to win new members. Trained organizers act as counselors, helping immigrants who have arrest records, spouses who do not qualify for citizenship, and others with hindrances to naturalization. The union counselors have been particularly adept at helping workers reconstruct a "paper trail" to prove residence and employment before January 1, 1982, so that they can qualify for amnesty. A *New York Times* reporter judged the new members of the ILGWU extremely fortunate, since the availability of trained immigration counselors is "a rare advantage for illegal aliens."[21]

The ILGWU has also worked to resolve a quirk in the 1986 law that created a class of as many as 1 million workers ripe for abuse. Their present employers can keep them on their payrolls indefinitely if they began work before the law was enacted on November 6, 1986. But anyone who might hire them since then faces stiff fines if the workers do not have proper documentation. Because most do not qualify for documentation, they are unable to become legal aliens and are ineligible for employment with anyone except their current employers. Many have therefore endured wage cuts, overtime without pay, and much worse. As Mizaffar Chishti, an ILGWU lawyer, told the *Wall Street Journal,* "I don't think ever since slavery have we seen such an institution for bonded labor."[22] The union is seeking legal relief for the victims, while organizers emphasize the value in having union contract protection.

Unfortunately, sweatshops that exploit undocumented workers continue to undermine union organizing on both sides of the country.[23] In California, where the apparel industry is second only to New York's in sales and employees, the ILGWU is capitalizing on the shortage of immigrant workers to force employers to raise their standards. Union organizers have slowly won the confidence of many illegal immigrant workers and encouraged them to join the labor movement. An immigrant assistance project, for example, was created in 1987 by the AFL-CIO and its Los Angeles central body. Twelve unions donated $250,000 to open five counseling centers, and by November 1989, the project had been a source for leads in twenty-seven successful organizing campaigns.[24]

Elsewhere, "new coalitions are emerging. Telephone hotlines, union counselors, public service spots, educational brochures, and special assistance centers are being established in cities with large immigrant populations, such as Chicago, Boston, and New York."[25] Given that illegal aliens are expected to outnumber those granted amnesty by almost two to one, labor has its work cut out for it, with nearly 7 million employers and about 4 million unorganized workers at issue.[26]

Associate Membership and Privilege Benefit Programs

The range of new organizing efforts includes one silent, nonhuman "organizer" with very special appeal. The Union Privilege Benefit Program (UPBP) was begun in 1986 in response to the 1985 Executive Council report *The Changing Situation of Workers and Their Unions* and was guided by ideas advanced by the AFL-CIO Committee on the Evolution of Work (see chapter 14).

This strategy focuses on the importance of three types of workers whose numbers are growing:

- pro-union workers left behind when an organizing campaign fails to win a majority of potential members;
- former union members who have survived a plant shutdown and the ensuing disestablishment of their old local; and
- workers in anti-union settings, such as southern "right-to-work" states, who want some personal affiliation with organized labor.

To forge bonds with millions of such workers, the AFL-CIO in 1986 created the associate member category for workers who are not represented by collective bargaining. Although they pay only half the usual dues, they qualify for several valuable union-sponsored "perks" (the UPBP package). Naturally, the AFL-CIO hopes large numbers of associates will eventually become full members in its various union affiliates.

Already seventy-eight of the ninety AFL-CIO unions offer one or more of the UPBP perks, such as prescription drug plans, money market plans, inexpensive credit cards, inexpensive travel services, inexpensive legal services, and inexpensive health and life insurance. Other perks under consideration include an affordable auto club, a book club, a car-leasing service, a dental insurance package, a discount buying plan, an eye care program, funeral aid, and lending programs for school loans and mortgages. Cooperating unions are promoting the perks of associate membership to workers whose situations inhibit full membership.

In this novel way, the AFL-CIO hopes to retain some influence over the million or more members who leave labor's ranks each year in the aftermath of business failures, plant shutdowns, plant relocations, and retirement. Because these former members (28 percent of all nonunion employees, or about 27 million) tend to be sympathetic to unions, they are expected to serve as a strategic base for launching fresh organizing drives.[27]

Similarly, nonmembers "sold" on the considerable cost savings of the UPBP perks (an estimated 47 percent of the work force) are viewed as a potential organizing cadre. For example, Al Shanker, president of the

American Federation of Teachers (AFT), candidly explained to *Newsweek* that "once their names are on the mailing list, they're not just going to get the credit card. They're going to get our literature." Impressed by the overnight success of the first UPBP perk, a low-interest charge card, and by the rapid growth to nearly 400,000 associate members, *Newsweek* concluded that "in time, union solidarity may be measured as much by the size of one's credit line as by respect for the picket line."[28]

Skeptics worry that UPBP perks may trivialize the reasons for joining a union. They feel the motivation should not be reduced to gimmicks, bargains, and trinkets. Union membership, they grumble, should not be merchandised. Instead, it should be promoted as an act of self-empowerment and as a proud endorsement of full citizenship in the workplace, as one component in a vision of a loftier social order.

In rebuttal, economist Audrey Freeman expects the UPBP program to encourage people to "begin to think of labor as a social support movement or a citizens movement, and not just as a high-wages movement."[29] Similarly, Thomas Donahue, secretary-treasurer of the AFL, explains, "The associate membership program is the backbone of our effort to build our unions. . . . If the American way is to invent new methods to overcome old obstacles, we are clearly reaching that goal." In fact, Ray Denison, the first president of UPBP, expects his membership project to double the size of the federation (by 1990, eleven unions reported having over 400,000 associate members).[30]

Health-Care Workers

In sparkling contrast to the bleak statistics elsewhere, union membership among America's 7 million health-care workers shot up from 14 percent in 1980 to 20 percent in 1990.[31] Organizers agree with labor economist Harley Shaiken that the health-care industry is for unions today what the auto industry was in the 1930s.[32]

Accordingly, SEIU, a particularly successful union in this sector, with 350,000 health-care workers as members, tailors every campaign to the local community.[33] For example, as a result of an outreach effort in Los Angeles, one hundred Baptist church leaders announced union meetings from the pulpit, urged parishioners to attend, and helped in other ways to reach the target group, 90 percent of whom were church-going black women.[34] A related strategy focuses on associate member benefit programs, an option that shields the identity of a member from employer reprisals while linking workers in different workplaces, promoting "union consciousness," and keeping hope alive for a better organizing climate.[35] Not surprisingly, in 1989, unions won 59 percent of elections in the health-care industry, compared to only 47 percent in manufacturing.[36]

Upgrading the Recruiting System

Labor continues to revitalize more familiar organizing strategies, as indicated by the 1985 decision of the AFL-CIO to strengthen its fifty state AFL-CIO bodies. Valued for their political clout in state politics, these groups can also play a strategic role in coordinating the organizing campaigns of unions in their areas. Until 1985, however, barely half the workers represented by AFL-CIO unions paid any part of their dues to state federations, which stumbled along on inadequate yearly budgets averaging about $50,000.[37] Now a dues plan proposed by the Committee on the Evolution of Work (see chapter 14) and passed by the 1985 biennial AFL-CIO convention promises to double their income and upgrade their organizing role significantly.

Another strategy for reorganization is know as the "blitz." This technique builds quick and intense organizing momentum, thus requiring precise scheduling, reliable research, and careful coordination to succeed. During a 1988 project, for example, fifty teams, each made up of an organizer and a volunteer, targeted nine hundred employees of the Tappan plant in Springfield, Tennessee. All of the teams had attended a workshop on blitz tactics, sponsored by the USWA, where they had learned that thirty-eight other Tappan plants were unionized. They also learned that four of the company's directors at the headquarters in Sweden were officials of unions with whom the company dealt cordially. After role playing various situations they could expect to encounter in home calls, the fifty teams fanned out on schedule, proud to assign nearly half the union's force of 115 organizers to the first blitz ever mounted by the USWA.[38]

Unions are also making traditional strategies flashier and more convincing. Most unions, for instance, have moved beyond flyers and pamphlets to widespread use of high-quality, custom-made videotapes produced by union video centers that solicit ideas from field organizers. Some organizers now carry portable video display units so they can use these persuasive videos to sell prospective members on union enrollment. Many are now using portable computers, linked by modems with mainframe equipment at headquarters, to track card signing, to record factual and subjective data from house calls, to locate houses of potential members by using license plate numbers, and to replace random leafletting with personalized computer-generated mailings.

Summary

In 1985, Al Shanker was asked to comment on labor's adoption of new organizing tactics. He replied, "If we rely only on traditional techniques, then we are guaranteeing the labor movement's continued decline."[39]

Evidence of labor's commitment to nontraditional ventures is apparent in the percentage of NLRB election victories in 1989, 50 percent, the highest since 1976, and the opening in 1989 of an AFL-CIO organizing institute.[40] Evidence of the AFL-CIO's sensitivity to the diversity among the unorganized is found in the fact that 50 percent of the institute's first 105 trainees were female and 25 percent were black, Hispanic, or Asian.[41]

Since its postwar membership peaked in 1975, the AFL-CIO has added more than 80,000 members, and the federation now has the most members in its thirty-four-year history.[42] It is little wonder, then, that hope remains for organizing breakthroughs in the 1990s, especially among white-collar, service sector, public sector, and professional employees.

Reorganizing the Air Traffic Controllers: A Test of Union Indispensability

> If President Reagan's crushing of PATCO was seen as a symbol of labor's weakening, then surely today's election victory is a symbol of labor's resurgence.... We remain confident that workers—whether blue-collar or professional—will seek the collective strength of union organization when their job-site problems go unresolved.... PATCO was destroyed, but the problems remained, and, in fact, grew worse. Labor's anthem, "Solidarity Forever," includes the line: "We can bring to birth a new world from the ashes of the old." That's what happened today when the controllers voted to build a new union. **Kenneth Young, AFL-CIO spokesperson, June 11, 1987**

> There is still much to learn, but the odyssey of the air traffic controllers provides at least one clear message—we have entered a new era in the history of labor-management relations.
> **Paul M. Swiercz, *Atlanta Constitution*, July 22, 1987**

At a party to celebrate the emergence of the National Air Traffic Controllers Association (NATCA), prominent labor leaders, such as Captain Henry Duffy of the Air Line Pilots Association (ALPA) and Lane Kirkland, president of the AFL-CIO, joined concerned lawmakers, such as Senator Frank R. Lautenberg (D-New Jersey) and Congressman Leo Molinari (R-New York), in a glittering mix of three hundred jubilant people.[1] The party on June 11, 1987, hailed a major organizing victory thought impossible six years earlier when the Reagan administration had decertified NATCA's predecessor, the Professional Air Traffic Controllers Organization (PATCO) and fired 11,345 PATCO strikers. Ballots opened on the morning of June 11, however, indicated that the controllers who had crossed PATCO picket lines to replace the strikers had voted 7,494 to 3,275 to create NATCA, their own labor union.[2] And it would affiliate with the same parent union, the 35,000-member Marine Engineers' Beneficial Association (MEBA), an old and proud affiliate of the AFL-CIO, that in 1970 had helped create PATCO.

NATCA's victory crowned a long and costly organizing drive. It was an achievement the Reagan administration and other critics of labor had not expected and could not casually dismiss. The celebrants at the June 11 party saw it as a vindication of union indispensability and as a major sign that labor's prospects of organizing were strong.

I had worked with PATCO as a survey research consultant (1980–81) and had conducted five major surveys of its fourteen thousand members.

In addition to analyzing the results for union officers and activists, I attended prestrike meetings at headquarters and spoke at PATCO events in Boston and Chicago. After the strike was unexpectedly defeated in August 1981, I maintained ties with a successor group, the United States Air Traffic Controllers Organization (USATCO) and, two years later, with its replacement, PATCO Lives. In collaboration with David Skocik, who had served as a PATCO press representative, I wrote *The Air Controllers' Controversy: Lessons from the 1981 PATCO Strike*, the only full-length book available on the subject. I remain in touch with ex-PATCO activists, ocassionally attend reunions of strikers on the strike's anniversary, and write newspaper essays urging an "amnesty" that would permit the fired strikers to be rehired.[3] I am, in short, a longtime PATCO supporter, and I took special pleasure in joining the June 11 celebrants in welcoming the air controllers back into the ranks of organized labor.

Organizing Strikebreakers

Labor's critics had been confident no union in the foreseeable future would again confront the controllers' sole employer, the Federal Aviation Authority (FAA), and the ballot count is particularly important from that perspective. After the FAA succeeded in firing 75 percent of its controllers in 1981, their replacements came from three sources: About thirteen hundred were ex-strikers who broke ranks and scurried back to protect their jobs. Several thousand were new hires who seemed to have no compunctions about strikebreaking. And about one thousand were former military controllers. Initially treated royally by a grateful FAA, this instant work force enjoyed high morale and generous earnings. Overtime, for example, increased 240 percent from 1980 to 1985.[4] Controllers seemed unlikely to unionize again, and a self-confident FAA assured Congress that no labor organization would come between management and its new work force in the imminent future.

Further bolstering its situation, the FAA hired high-priced consultants to help sensitize field managers to the needs of their new nonunion controllers. Human relations committees were formed at every site, and substance abuse counselors were brought in to encourage offenders to join rehabilitation programs. No effort was spared to remove incentives to reunionization.

Not surprisingly, the first two efforts to unionize the new controllers proved weak and short-lived. Organizers from the AFGE were interested initially. But Kenneth T. Blaylock, president of the union, could not gain membership support for a dues increase earmarked in part for this organizing campaign. ALPA was next to announce its intention to create a separate unit for the controllers, but it too soon decided that the costs outweighed any possible benefits. To complicate matters still further, the AFGE and MEBA (which had originally supported PATCO) got into an embarrassing jurisdictional dispute that took months before the AFL-CIO resolved it in MEBA's favor. Opponents of unionization among the new controllers cited this dispute as proof of labor's immaturity.

When the NATCA organizing campaign financed by MEBA finally began to make headway in 1986, the anti-union controllers resurrected the ghost of the 1981 PATCO strike and the ensuing dismissal of over eleven thousand strikers. Reunionization, they warned, would lead to another such disaster, since the only thing unions knew how to do was strike, and lose, over and over again.

Even a cadre of working controllers who initially favored unionization had major misgivings. Some thought affiliation with a maritime union such as MEBA was awkward. They preferred a union made up exclusively of air traffic controllers, even if they had to create it themselves. Some resented the dues structure proposed by NATCA, which set per capita allocations aside for both MEBA and the AFL-CIO. And some favored a union other than MEBA, such as the AFGE, ALPA, or even the Teamsters. Given all these obstacles to unionization, the positive vote achieved by NATCA represented a remarkable triumph.[5]

How NATCA Did It

John Thornton, who directed NATCA's organizing campaign and had been a PATCO officer, believes there are five keys to the win, each of which offers valuable insights for other organizing drives:

■ NATCA organizers became known as good listeners and learned a lot from controllers' reports of the downward spiral in their working conditions.

■ The controllers' grievances became NATCA's priorities. Working controllers felt, for example, that staffing levels were increasingly inadequate since traffic was up by 17 percent while the number of fully qualified controllers had been reduced from 13,348 in 1981 to 9,107 in 1987.[6] Equipment had become dangerously outmoded, and childish dress codes were back in vogue, sending three controllers home, for example, for not wearing socks with their sandals.[7] Above all, resentment focused on the violation of civil rights in the FAA's zest for drug testing.

■ The organizers knew that MEBA was anathema to former PATCO dues payers who had crossed the picket line and was rejected by those who preferred a nonunion association of professionals to an AFL-CIO union of workers. In rebuttal, the organizers emphasized that NATCA would have to deal with the same employer, the U.S. Department of Transportation, with which MEBA had many decades of relevant experience. Moreover, MEBA had never meddled in PATCO's affairs but had provided advice and generous financial backing when asked.[8] Further, MEBA's link to the AFL-CIO was characterized as a strategic asset, since it linked controllers to labor's political influence on the Hill, where Congress decided the wages and working conditions of the controllers.

■ The organizers were flexible enough to finesse a rift that threatened to divide the controllers. FAA supervisors insisted a NATCA win would mean the triumphant return of PATCO strikers, thereby creating hostility between pre- and poststrike controllers. NATCA organizers, however, insisted this matter would be addressed only after the union had won its representation election. And, to the chagrin of PATCO stalwarts in and outside the ranks of controllers, these same organizers refused to take a position for or against rehiring the strikers.

■ The NATCA campaign was buttressed by a full-time staff of five and a volunteer force of over a hundred controllers, some of them former PATCO members who had been restored to FAA posts as a result of rehiring victories in court. A key insider, placed adroitly at each of the FAA's 414 work sites, assured potential members that NATCA took a nonadversarial and collegial approach to labor-management relations.

Above all, the organizers insisted NATCA locals would be far more helpful than the FAA's human relations committees ("They could only say where the Coke machine could go at their tower. Or should the coffee fund go to buy a microwave.")[9] NATCA, in contrast, would reform ill-advised managerial policies, such as those covering drug testing, and would end arbitrary infringements on the constitutional rights of employees.

Putting the Win in Perspective

At the AFL-CIO biennial convention in October 1987, Lane Kirkland cited the NATCA win as "not massive, but symbolic," as proof that "we're on the road again to a resurgent labor movement."[10]

Why was this particular organizing win so significant? Because anti-labor forces were still gloating in 1987 over the 1981 PATCO fiasco and were certain the FAA would never again bargain with a union of its controllers. The enormous loss of jobs and the unprecedented decertification of PATCO were seen as a harbinger of anti-union triumphs to come, until NATCA unionized a new FAA work force in 1987 and the gloating had to stop.

As a MEBA spokesperson explained, the win demonstrated labor's ability to organize nontraditional workers: "It shows what can be done to organize professions, as MEBA has proven already in organizing other groups, such as sheriffs, scientists, and engineers. And I am confident the NATCA experience will demonstrate to Americans in other professions the distinct advantages of joining together to achieve goals the professional person alone cannot hope to achieve."[11]

The post-1981 controllers were welcomed into "solidarity" with unionized teachers, nurses, technicians, librarians, journalists, union staffers, writers, and other white-collar professionals.

The question of rehiring is being resolved. As many as 3,000 of the 11,345 strikers wish to return on terms that a majority of NATCA members judge to be unacceptable. Many, for example, want their seniority restored, a move that could allow them to bump out of desirable posts those hired after the 1981 strike.[12] Some labor strategists insist that NATCA members, only 15 percent of whom were ever members of PATCO, owe the PATCO strikers an enormous debt since the 1981 strike exposed FAA inadequacies and led Congress to legislate useful reforms. NATCA delegates voted four to one at their 1990 convention in favor of PATCO rehiring the strikers. Hope persists that a compromise can be found that will protect NATCA privileges while allowing at least some of the ex-controllers to be rehired.[13]

Labor's victory resulted from a combination of persistence (a three-year campaign), payroll (MEBA put over $1 million into the effort), and persuasion (pro-NATCA controllers helped workmates realize their vulnerability to an increasingly haughty FAA). Listening skills and diplomatic compromises surmounted the lingering doubts of the work force after 1981 and enabled NATCA organizers to "write the book" on how to work successfully with initially hostile or resistant individuals.

Creation of the new air traffic controllers union, the most stunning second act in modern labor history, conveys an important message about positive prospects for labor and the indispensability of unions. With its many acts of mismanagement, the FAA helped to push anti-PATCO controllers into NATCA's ranks, reminding labor that many employers can be relied on to create recruits for union organizing campaigns.[14] As MEBA staff member Alex C. Cullison explained, "The annals of history will perhaps recognize that the renewal of the postindustrial labor movement started with the same vocation—air traffic control—that for six fleeting years represented a symbol of labor's ostensible decline."[15]

Chapter 5
Solidarity with Professional Employees

There wouldn't be a profession if it weren't for the unions. Before the unions, actors were equated with thieves and prostitutes. It was only through their unions that they gained some status, and had to be dealt with as a profession by employers and the public. It was only because of their unions that they couldn't be ignored.

Ralph Bellamy, former president of Actors' Equity, in Douglas, *The Unionized Professoriate* (1986), 48

We're building new types of professional organizations. I believe it's the way to address not only the problems of our professions, but the problems of society as a whole.

Jack Golodner, director, Department for Professional Employees, AFL-CIO, in Douglas, *The Unionized Professoriate* (1986), 53

To prosper in the 1990s, labor has to achieve unprecedented success in organizing professional employees, the fastest growing occupational group in the country. Conventional wisdom mistakenly holds that unions have little or no appeal to actors, doctors, engineers, journalists, librarians, musicians, nurses, performing artists, and athletes. But, in fact, as many as 29 percent of these professionals are already in trade unions, compared to 17 percent of all American workers. Twenty-nine different unions are now actively involved with the AFL-CIO Department for Professional Employees (DPE), the country's largest interdisciplinary group of professionals.

Membership in the Union of American Physicians and Dentists, for example, has jumped fourfold since 1982, to forty-three thousand members. As Barry Liebowitz, president of the Doctors Council, explains, "The need for union protection is blurring the distinctions between employees who wear a blue collar or a white collar, or those who wear green surgical scrubs or a white lab coat."[1] Moreover, when one subtracts professionals who are barred by law or hidebound by custom from unionizing, such as administrators and the self-employed, the proportion already in unions is as high as 40 percent.

Contrary to public opinion and media suggestion, labor has enjoyed disproportionate success with professional employees for many decades. As Jack Golodner, president of DPE, says "The labor movement, as far as professionals are concerned, arrived a long time ago. It's just the myth-makers, the academics, the press, our government leaders, and all those people who are suppose to shape public opinion, who have not recognized that."[2]

The story of how professionals are steadily coming into labor's ranks is helpful in explaining why thousands of others may do so soon. But first one must reconcile the alleged contradictions between professionalism and organized labor, for they challenge labor's prospects with this elite group.

Professionalism

The notion that many professionals are wary of organized labor is predicated on their individualism and autonomy, their control over passive clients, and their individual upward mobility. Deference to professionals as an occupational elite seems to reflect the division of the world along intellectual lines, a presumed correspondence between the public interest and that of the profession, and a tendency for professionals to be politically and socially conservative. While athletes, lawyers, and physicians vary in their adherence to this model, many find in it some safeguard against the propensity of society to whittle away at their favored treatment and special privilege.[3]

Unions are particularly challenged by certain traits that conflict with values historically held by labor:

■ Individualism promotes a "me-first" attitude at odds with labor's principle of solidarity and sacrifice for the collective good.
■ The value professionals place on individual upward mobility includes an implicit requirement to give up old social ties and obligations, an expectation at odds with labor's support of allegiance to one's social class of origin.
■ A professional way of life has frequently meant acceptance of avant garde values that conflict with labor's preference for more traditional lifestyles.

It is hardly surprising that tension exists between certain professionals and many trade unionists.

To compound the situation, the professions are in enormous flux. Occupations claiming to be professions, such as teaching and nursing, are not necessarily seen as such by the public. As a result, individuals may be denied the prestige they seek and sometimes find it difficult to establish their professional authority or to obtain political clout. Other professions, such as law and medicine, are under increasing pressure to strengthen their regulative codes of ethics or accept increasing government interference. Moreover, there are pressures from consumers to reduce mystification and increase accountability, as demonstrated by welfare recipients who have organized to assess their treatment by social workers, women who are criticizing the behavior of their gynecologists, and so on.

Challenges to the privileges of professionalism, in combination with a new militancy among professionals intent on securing a better work life, promise turmoil for years to come. In this context, robust unionism has had and can continue to have significant appeal to performers, medical interns, athletes, academics, nurses, and teachers.

Performing Arts Unions

Despite their legendary individualism, competitiveness, and pride in setting their own standards, performers have a long and proud history of unionization, beginning with musicians in 1896. The oldest of the three big performers' unions, the Actors' Equity Association, was formed in 1913, despite bitter opposition from producers. George M. Cohan, for example, committed $100,000 of his personal fortune to destroy the upstart union. After winning affiliation in 1917 with the AFL, Equity went out on strike, closing thirty-seven plays and preventing the opening of sixteen others. New members flocked to join, and astonished theater managers capitulated. A five-year contract was signed that included practically all of the union's demands. As Dick Moore, an Equity staffer, notes, "The prototype for organizing the performing arts had been established."[4]

In 1933, the Screen Actors Guild (SAG) was formed, and initially it too faced fierce employer opposition. But in 1937, when 98 percent of the union's film actors voted in favor of an organizing strike, the heads of the major studios backed down and the union was on its way.

The last of the "big talent" unions to organize, the American Federation of Television and Radio Artists (AFTRA), dates back to 1937 in radio and to 1950 in television. Like Equity and SAG, AFTRA has always differed from most unions in having unpaid volunteers serve as its president, officers, and executive board members, who supervise a paid staff.

All three of the performers' unions are also unusual in that their members negotiate far more than minimum salaries. Particular attention has been paid to propping up the livelihoods of those many members whom stardom eludes. For example, in 1954, AFTRA became the first union to establish a portable, multiemployer pension and health plan.

Unemployment caused by technological displacement, such as VCRs, tape recorders, compact discs, and cable television, is currently the greatest single threat to performers. According to Moore, the profession remains a "nightmare of pitfalls and insecurities," and "whatever protection or stability America's performers have achieved...has been largely through their unions."[5]

Doctors Council

Begun in 1959, the Doctors Council represents more than three thousand New York City physicians, dentists, optometrists, podiatrists, and veterinarians at public and private hospitals, city agencies, HMOs, and dental and health-care clinics, from the largest emergency room in the world to the city's prisons and coroner's office. Growing quickly, this unique organization is now the largest union of attending doctors in the country, and it clearly demonstrates elite professionals will unionize if they are recruited in a sufficiently sensitive and robust way.

Linked to fourteen similar unions of doctors elsewhere in the country, the Doctors Council relies on three guiding principles that are especially intriguing:

- *Make the well-being of patients a paramount concern.* The council has forged strong links with community groups that seek to monitor the scope and quality of services provided in health-care institutions. Council members are encouraged to report examples of mismanagement, such as lack of supplies or inoperative equipment, and the council contends that "our fate as health care professionals is inseparable from the fate of our patients."[6]
- *Make the forging of ties with nonmedical unions a paramount concern.* The council lobbies with locals of AFSCME, the International Brotherhood of Teamsters, the American Nurses' Association, and other groups in support of efforts to contain health-care expenditures, to ensure safe storage of toxic substances, to protect hospital workers from the risk of AIDS, and to discourage the subcontracting of health care because it reduces accountability.[7]
- *Make the renewal of the labor movement a paramount concern.* Although the council is proud of its role as a traditional union, it is also proud of its role as a path breaker. According to Barry Liebowitz, its president, "We look to other unions, older and more experienced, for we still have much to learn. But we also believe we are at the forefront of a new labor movement—one that is redefining its strategies

and is seeking innovative ways of addressing a rapidly changing work environment."[8]

Convinced that the "corporatization of American medicine is forcing doctors to see the need for collective action," the Doctors Council looks forward to continuing growth and increasing significance.[9]

Professional Athletes

The Major League Baseball Players Association (MLBPA) was created in 1968 by "one of the most . . . economically exploited groups of workers . . . in the country."[10] Since 1922, their sport has been the only one exempt from the nation's various anti-trust laws. This has given club owners more than sixty years of disproportionate power and, in effect, has indentured ball players to clubs for the duration of their playing lives. Based on a "reserve clause" dating back to 1868, when baseball became a business, the situation forces a player to deal only with the club that originally signed him. As a result, players have been grossly underpaid in relation to the industry's revenues, and the average player leaves after only four years in the major leagues.[11]

Seeking the right in an open economic market to sell their services to the highest bidder (a right known as free agency), unions of professional athletes in basketball, football, and hockey achieved significant legal triumphs in the 1970s. Courtroom victories in major anti-trust cases helped limit the right of club owners to collude in setting salaries of professional athletes.

Baseball remains the exception. Players have negotiated free agency clauses in their team contracts, but even with the clause, owners often violate the agreement with imperial indifference. The MLBPA has gone to the courts to defend its preference to negotiate only a minimum salary and the conditions of free agency, rather than to engage in far more traditional collective bargaining. But as Donald M. Fehr, executive director and general counsel of the MLBPA, has said, "Although you wouldn't bargain wage rates . . . in this particular circumstance you would have to bargain percentages of industry income to be divided to the players."[12]

Players' unions in major sports are beginning to win what they call "the great experiment," their legal battle for free agency. Victories come slowly and sometimes only after costly setbacks, such as the fruitless twenty-four-day strike of sixteen hundred football players in the fall of 1987. Progress continues to be made, however:

- On October 31, 1989, an arbitrator ruled that major league baseball clubs had engaged in "conspiratorial conduct" in 1986 aimed at killing free agency and were therefore liable for $10.5 million in damages owed to 139 players represented by the MLBPA.[13]

■ On November 9, 1989, the National Football League Players Association warned the NFL Management Council of its intention to seek decertification as a union unless a two-year-old impasse in free agency negotiations soon ended. Gene Upshaw, executive director of the union, explained that "players would rather protect their rights as independent contractors than subject themselves to the monopolistic whims of the NFL and its clubs. Decertification would result in twenty-eight unions bargaining with twenty-eight club owners, free the players to initiate their own free agency moves among the clubs, and strip the clubs of their exemption under anti-trust laws."[14]

■ On March 19, 1990, professional baseball players returned to work after a month-long lockout, the third in the past twenty years and the second longest in baseball history. A journalist who specializes in sports concluded, "It is clear the players got most of what they wanted. They defeated management's attempts to radically alter baseball's economic structure through revenue-sharing. They achieved large gains in such financial areas as pensions and minimum salaries. And they held tight through a 32-day lockout, further strengthening an already potent union.... The MLBPA's new contract is one that other unions can only dream of."[15]

Confident of their ability to make the best of either negotiations or courtroom decisions, and proud of their record in improving working conditions and safety provisions, as well as their support of players who are cut, unions of professional athletes expect many more wins in the coming decade.

Faculty Unionization

Largely as a result of the fiscal crisis of the 1970s, colleges and universities have been radically transformed as workplaces. As Mary G. Edwards explained in 1988 in the *Chronicle of Higher Education,* "Increasingly, curricula are modified by administrators in response to educational needs. In addition, the character of the faculties is changing as marginal employees, whose work is more like piecework in a factory than traditional college teaching, increase in number across the country."[16] As a result, advocates of faculty unionization expect substantial progress in the 1990s if three serious obstacles can be overcome.

The first is the chilling effect of the 1980 Yeshiva University decision, in which the Supreme Court ruled faculty in private colleges may be regarded as "managerial" employees and therefore have no right to bargain collectively under the National Labor Relations Act. The impact has been profound. More than twenty faculty unions have been decertified, and at least sixty-two institutions have cited the decision so as to avoid negotiations with faculty unions.[17] In January 1988, the U.S. Court of Appeals, citing the *Yeshiva* decision, ruled there was no basis for collective bargaining at Boston University since the teachers were "managerial employees." The NLRB reached the same decision in 1988 against faculty unions at Fairleigh Dickinson University, American International College, Livingstone College, and several others.[18]

A second obstacle concerns the inclination of faculty unions since *Yeshiva* to restrict the focus of their negotiations. Since 1980, most have concentrated on a narrow range of issues, such as wages, benefits, and provisions for review and tenure. Critics bemoan the inattention to other vital matters, claiming the unions "have been silent on one of the most important aspects of our work as faculty members: our right to shape the curriculum, control our own workplace, and influence the quality of our students' education."[19] They warn that unless their unions plunge into ongoing debates over the future of higher education they will be judged, fatally irrelevant.

A third obstacle to organizing concerns the increase in part-time faculty, who may already constitute as much as 40 percent of all college faculty.[20] Part-time faculty members and teaching assistants, whose grievances include poor salaries, inferior working conditions, and the lack of a career ladder, are creating the new bargaining units in higher education. But, ironically, full-time faculty, who might welcome and profit from the militancy of their part-time colleagues, are often alienated from them. Many faculty unions, for example, have acceded to demands from administrators for two-tier pay systems. Some remain silent on the subject, while others advance the interests of tenured professors only. Far too many condone the marginal status of part-time faculty by agreeing to their differential pay, ineligibility for tenure, and limitations on their course and text selections. Not surprisingly, outraged part-timers at some institutions have attempted to secede from faculty unions and form their own locals.

Fragmentation of the labor movement in higher education exasperates union supporters. The American Association of University Professors (AAUP) has historically represented faculty interests, but a majority of faculty today are represented by either the National Education Association (NEA) or the AFT (AFL-CIO). None of these groups is clearly more significant than the others, however, and their rivalry often diminishes effectiveness, alienates faculty, and, in locals weakened by divided loyalties, enhances the opportunity for administrators to impose contract terms.

Hope for progress in faculty unionism depends on four ongoing developments. An anti-*Yeshiva* bill is regularly reintroduced in the House of Representatives, and AFL-CIO lobbyists, along with those of the AFT and many individual faculty unions, are pressing for hearings and passage. A few states, notably California and Ohio, have already voted to allow unions on campuses even if there are decision-sharing systems that resemble those cited in the *Yeshiva* decision.[21]

Additionally, scathing dialogue about campus issues, which animates the pages of faculty union publications, has gradually influenced local union priorities. Long-standing traditions, such as peer review and faculty self-government, are under attack for contributing to the "excessive costs, waste, intellectual and moral hypocrisy, and the overriding failure of higher education to fulfill its social function." Faculty unions are being urged to oppose these "pervasive weaknesses."[22]

Efforts persist, meanwhile, at reconciling the conflicting interests of full- and part-time faculty, and agreement is growing that the salaries of part-timers must be increased so that it is no longer advantageous for administrators to exploit these faculty financially. Efforts continue to reduce rivalry and encourage cooperation among AAUP, NEA, and AFT affiliates, and the new militancy of the NEA, along with the new professionalism of the AFT, lead some observers to hope negotiations for a merger may be possible.

Research indicates that campus faculty nationwide "tend to be dispirited. . . . Perhaps the single best description of faculty morale is 'shaky.' " With 170,000 of about 400,000 full-time and 300,000 part-time faculty already unionized,[23] labor activists expect the size of the current membership, combined with union reforms and poor faculty morale, to precipitate major advances in faculty organizing in the 1990s.

Unionism among Nurses

Only 25 percent of the nation's 1.6 million registered nurses and 600,000 licensed practical nurses are now covered by collective bargaining agreements, making nurses a major organizing concern.[24] Nonunion nurses are being actively sought by the AFT, the CWA, the SEIU, the UFCW, the Retail, Wholesale and Department Store Union, the Steelworkers, the Teamsters, and the 36,000-member United Nurses of America, created by AFSME in 1990. In that registered nurses and licensed practical nurses earn half the average hourly wages of workers with comparable education, organizers expect many nurses to be joining unions in the 1990s.[25]

Regardless of affiliation, the issues raised by hospital-based locals are the same. Unionized nurses seek greater respect for their profession, more protection from job changes that dilute skills, better job security, a higher salary scale, help with child care, and more liberal provisions for retraining. Most recently, the list has been extended to include protection from speed-up orders and from wage compression.[26]

To the astonishment of the general public, more and more nurses have gone out on strike in recent years. Even more surprising has been the rate of victories. A 1988 report on a successful ten-day strike in 1987 by 225 nurses against Red Cross centers in Southern California is typical: "The Red Cross was caught totally off guard. They thought 'their' nurses would not strike, and Red Cross management had a hard time relating to what was happening. First of all, the nurses were union workers telling management what to do. Second, they were nurses telling doctors what to do. And thirdly, they were women telling men what to do."[27] Summarizing the experience, an officer of the SEIU local that won this strike concluded that "the most important lesson we all learned is not to be afraid to take our power. Only good can come of that."[28]

One area in which nurses' unions provide a model for others involves control of technological change. Throughout its history, nursing has required sensitive adjustment to innovations. Beginning in the mid-1970s, nurses' unions moved to "humanize" medical technology to reduce work-related stress. They also sought to influence the terms of retraining and to control the impact of technology on nurses' employability.

Monitoring in obstetrical, coronary, neonatal, and postoperative intensive care units provides a good example of how nurses' unions have influenced the impact of technological change. Health-care personnel initially resisted the tedious process of monitoring "high-tech" machines. As a result, alarms to alert nurses to problems were added. Speculation then developed that the next move would be total automation, including computer-generated suggestions for treatment and possibly automatically administered medication. Sensitive to the threat such possibilities posed to their employability and skills and to the quality of their patient care, nurses' unions effectively discouraged the introduction of such technology.[29] As sociologist Heidi Hartmann notes, a strong commitment on the part of nurses "to the importance of intensive personal nursing at the bedside, and to support for the patient's family, seems to underlie decisions about many monitoring systems that purposely have not been totally automated."[30]

As Hartmann explains, the achievement of nurses' unions in influencing technological development in their field breaks new ground:

> Today nurses are more often consulted when information technology
> is introduced into hospitals and other health care settings than they
> previously were. Nurses are also among the developers of special nurs-

ing applications of computer and information technology, including video and telecommunications systems. Manufacturers and vendors have employed nurses to improve existing systems. . . . In contrast to earlier computer-based systems with implicit models of the work of nurses, several of the most recent specific nursing applications are based on explicit philosophies of nursing.[31]

Unionized nurses now have a vote in decisions about technology. This vote benefits both their profession and the public interest and is one other unions would do well to study and win for themselves.

Teachers

Teaching is another of only a few professions that have been open to women for a long time, and it remains dominated by females. As in nursing, the rank-and-file is organized largely outside the AFL-CIO, with the NEA claiming 2 million members in 1990 and the AFT (AFL-CIO) about 720,000 members.[32] Much like the American Nurses' Association, the NEA initially prided itself on being above the fray as a professional association, and until the late 1960s it engaged in collective bargaining very reluctantly. More recently, however, it has dramatically altered its position, raising the possibility it will soon merge with the AFT.

Teachers have been on the defensive since the early 1980s when the teaching profession came under several prominent attacks. Since the major target was the quality of classroom teaching, the effect on professional self-esteem was considerable. To their credit, the AFT and the NEA have succeeded in redefining the issue and have earned new support from federal and state legislators. As a result, the starting salaries of teachers are becoming competitive with those of recruits to alternative careers and new contract terms encourage high-quality teaching and the retention of experienced teachers while bolstering the influence of teachers over curriculum and governance (site-based management).

Just as nurses have gained valuable influence in decisions about medical technology, AFT and NEA locals in the last few years have secured unprecedented leverage in educational management. The AFT boasts that its members "are challenging the outdated notion that teachers should be unquestioning cogs in an education machine." Instead, "they're leading a movement to revitalize our nation's public schools by breathing life into the pages of education reform reports and the rhetoric of the reformers."[33]

Especially intriguing are ongoing robust experiments that restructure relations among the teacher, principal, and school board so that power and responsibility are shared in fresh ways:

■ In Dade County, Florida, the AFT local negotiated a unique "Professionalization of Teaching" clause that greatly empowers the staff in forty-four schools. One school has redesigned the schoolday to relieve overcrowding; in another, teachers rather than administrators select textbooks, formulate budgets, and develop schedules. The Dade AFT contract also enables teachers to serve on the committees that hire school administrators and recruit new teachers.[34]

■ In more than two hundred cities, teachers participate in the AFT's Educational Research and Dissemination Program. A replacement for prescriptive in-service training, the program is compiled, tested, and taught by teachers, in response to the particular needs of local teachers. For example, a unit on classroom management has given District of Columbia junior high school teachers new strategies for reducing disruption and fighting.[35]

A spokesperson for the NEA, which encourages many similar projects, characterizes the emphasis on teacher initiative as "the most significant move on a single issue since both unions got into collective bargaining."[36]

Probably the best publicized experiment in expanding initiative is the 1988 AFT contract in Rochester, New York. Characterized by a reporter as a "revolution in the making," the contract signaled a readiness "to take unprecedented risks in a bold attempt to do something this country has failed to do: adequately educate large concentrated groups of poor, disadvantaged students."[37]

Rochester teachers negotiated a healthy new salary schedule ($45,000 for the average teacher by 1990) and secured a large say in matters ranging from curriculum to security. School-based planning committees of teachers and administrators help decide the goals of each of the city's fifty-one schools and determine how to achieve them. In return, the teachers' salaries are determined in part by how well their students do. Furthermore, teachers take responsibility for up to twenty students each by visiting their homes, keeping in touch with their parents, and helping them succeed. The teachers have also agreed to longer workdays and to a longer school year. Seniority no longer dictates assignments, and experienced teachers who fall short of standards set by peers are given outstanding peers as mentors. Those who do not improve are counseled to leave the profession.

Rochester's experiment is being watched closely by teachers' unions across the country. Adam Urbanski, head of the Rochester AFT local, is convinced the contract will benefit students precisely because teachers are empowered to make critical instructional decisions: "Of course there are no guarantees," he explains, "but there are no guarantees in life. There is certainly, however, greater promise now for more teacher productivity."[38]

Department for Professional Employees

Sensitive to the diversity of professionals, the AFL-CIO in 1977 created the Department for Professional Employees as a unifying provider. With twenty-nine of the federation's ninety affiliates as members, DPE is now the largest interdisciplinary organization of professionals in America.

From the outset, DPE ventured into areas that were new to organized labor. As Jack Golodner, director of the department, explains, "We lobbied for the creation of the National Endowments for the Arts and the National Endowments for the Humanities. Many members of Congress who were there in the 1960s when those two agencies were created would say that if it wasn't for the AFL-CIO (and if it wasn't for the unions of professionals within the AFL-CIO) this government would have no commitment to the cultural life of our country."[39]

Similarly, DPE is now actively seeking to unionize professionals such as the self-employed who have never before been targeted. Golodner explains:

Why are they talking to us? Because ... they feel powerless, not vis-à-vis an employer, but vis-à-vis the purchasers of their services. Independent freelance writers, for example, face a mammoth industry in selling their product. They have their organizations, but because of the laws, and because of the National Labor Relations Act, they have never been able to qualify as "an employee organization" protected by the law, and viewed by the law as capable of entering into collective bargaining. We say "nonsense" now to that! We're not going to be limited by the law in that respect. We will define who is going to be a part of tomorrow's movement, not the law.[40]

DPE's research, lobbying, and negotiating services help explain why many thousands of professionals, including the self-employed, may soon join any one of the department's twenty-nine robust affiliates.

Summary

Professional unionization still faces a tradition of arch-individualism, obstacles in case law, and stark opposition from some employers. Enthusiasts cite evidence, however, that growing numbers of professionals are unionizing even in "right-to-work" states such as Texas. They talk hopefully of reversing the *Yeshiva* mandate and of winning pro-labor decisions in free agency cases. They believe more and more employers are coming to see the merit of co-existing with progressive locals, as big-city school districts do across the nation.

Proud and creative individuals wedded to their vocational calling, America's professionals comprise a stronghold of more than 4 million trade unionists that, despite its handicaps, has the capacity to win new gains in technology control, co-management, and other critical matters. Ably guided by the Department for Professional Employees, professional unions could prove to be the "point of the spear" labor needs in the 1990s.

Chapter 6
Women and Unionism

The daily work lives and struggles by black women and white women... have contributed to our understanding of how to bring about change. They point to the importance of women's work culture for generating the ideas and values that are central to any movement's ability to challenge management's evaluations of workers' worth and rights.

Karen B. Sacks, *Caring by the Hour:*
Women, Work, and Organizing
at Duke Medical Center (1988), 216

Most people in the community really don't understand what a nurse is faced with, and what the understaffing problem means. There is educational and political pressure that unions can use effectively. There are innovative things unions can do in order to successfully organize, and represent the [female] employees who are turning to us for assistance. It is important to be creative and comprehensive in our approaches.

Vicki Saporta, director of organizing, Teamsters, in Gagala,
Union Power in the Future—A Union Activist's Agenda **(1987), 199**

Women have been labor militants since the start of the modern factory system in the 1800s. Indeed, labor historian Philip S. Foner insists that "it was the militancy and perseverance of women workers that laid the foundations of trade unionism—this, in the face of the double obstacle of employer–public hostility and the indifference of most male-dominated unions."[1]

Women constitued about 31 percent of the labor force in the 1950s. By 1988, that figure had grown to 47 percent, and it is expected to go over 50 percent before the turn of the century. While union organizers can point with pride to the gain of 470,000 women members since 1977 and to an increase of 17 percent (from 18 percent in 1960 to 35 percent) in the proportion of rank-and-filers who are women (now about 7 million), labor still represents only 13 percent of more than 50 million women workers. Labor educator Ruth Needleman notes that women are currently joining unions in greater numbers than men and account for at least 50 percent of labor's growth in the last twenty years. She contends that "the future of organized labor may depend on its ability to reach this new generation of female workers, and turn them into union members, activists, and leaders."[2]

Polls taken in 1983 and 1985 indicate that 67 percent of national labor leaders and 49 percent of the leaders of locals do not believe unions are putting sufficient resources into organizing women.[3] That 75 percent of union organizing budgets in the 1970s and early 1980s went into campaigns in the manufacturing sector, even though 90 percent of all new jobs were being created in the female-dominated service sector, provides some corroboration for this view.[4]

District 925, SEIU, has become "the preeminent example of the new style of female organizing."[5] Initiated in 1973 as a nonunion association of working women, 9 to 5 approached ten unions before the SEIU agreed in 1981 to give it a charter as a national affiliate.[6] Led by women, District 925 organized over sixty-five hundred office workers by 1986, won twenty-five of its twenty-six certification elections, and has been growing by about 20 percent a year.[7] Its sister organization, the National Association of Working Women (NAWW), forms preunion groups that focus on assertiveness training, self-help projects, and organizing around issues of local concern. District 925 and the NAWW provide support for each other and offer a promising model for tandem organizing.

In addition to its organizing efforts, labor is active in the fight for pay equity, in efforts to improve family welfare through mechanisms such as parental leave, and in the struggle to divide power more equitably between males and females in its own ranks. All three issues are explored below.

Pay Equity

Research suggests the wage gap between men and women began to narrow in the late 1970s or early 1980s as women began to fare better in the job market.[8] Nevertheless, they remain disproportionately in sex-segregated and poorly paid jobs and are paid less than seventy cents for every dollar earned by men. Labor economist and former secretary of labor Ray Marshall cites studies that have found "less than half of the gross earnings differentials can be accounted for by such human capital factors as education, training, experience, and skill requirements."[9]

Labor has been deeply involved in the struggle to reduce sexist pay differentials. A 1974 courtroom victory by AFSCME against the state of Washington first focused national attention on the case for pay equity. Under pressure from the union, the state agreed to commission a study that confirmed AFSCME's charge that there were substantial pay inequities among state employees. When the state refused to institute remedies, the union filed suits with both the Equal Employment Opportunity Commission and a federal district court. Although AFSCME initially won in court, the decision was overturned in 1985. By that time, however, Washington wanted no more of AFSCME's badgering and agreed to an out-of-court settlement that established a $42 million fund to correct pay differentials.

Similarly, AFSCME struck the city of San Jose, California, for nine days in 1977 before convincing the city to study its internal pay system. This research demonstrated that female employees in the city were being underpaid by about 18 percent. Negotiations resulted in the establishment of a $1.5 million fund so that adjustments of 5 to 15 percent could be made in the salaries of sixty female-dominated job classifications.

In the decade since the San Jose win, AFSCME has been joined in its fight for pay equity by many unions in the private sector, including the SEIU, the Newspaper Guild, and District 1199 of the National Union of Hospital and Health Care Employees. Increasingly, pay equity has become "a device for rallying support, launching campaigns, and energizing a labor movement looking for a focus."[10]

Labor has earned some very special rewards for its leadership role. Michael E. Gordon, in a study of union organizing, offers a revealing tale in this regard:

> I met an organizer from AFSCME who reported that organizing female workers was somewhat easier now because of the widespread publicity given the concept of comparable worth. . . . For a long time, the women he tried to organize felt an uneasiness about the size of their paychecks in comparison with men who, in many cases, performed less socially significant jobs. The term "comparable worth" became a label for these discriminatory experiences. Once labeled, it became easier for women to recognize a shared consensus about this socially constructed feature of their work environment. Hence, it became easier to build a labor organization around this shared meaning.[11]

Building a successful strike action around comparable worth has also become easier, as a 1984 organizing effort at Yale University demonstrated. Seeking to win its first contract, Local 34 of the Hotel and Restaurant Employees Union, a predominantly female, white-collar local, overcame determined opposition by using three effective strategies:

- focusing on unwarranted discrepancies in pay in comparable female- and male-dominated jobs;

- deciding to return to work temporarily in the midst of the strike to secure the sympathy of students and faculty; and
- departing from precedent by opening bargaining on the issue of pay equity to public view.

All of this, as Charles C. Heckscher concluded, "formed a strategy that was more complex, and in the end more effective, than a focus on collective bargaining alone."[12]

Convinced the 1990s will bring women to more and more prominence in the labor movement, labor analysts forecast a substantial increase in labor-initiated pay equity campaigns, making pay equity "the single most important women's issue to emerge onto the collective bargaining agenda in the last decade."[13]

Family Care

Thanks in large part to extensive lobbying by organized labor, the Senate Labor and Human Resources Committee in July 1988 approved the $2.5 billion "Act for Better Child Care Services" (ABC), aimed at the more than 14 million working parents who spend an average of $3,000 a year for child care. Seventy-five percent of ABC's funding is reserved for low- to low-moderate-income families, who would receive a voucher to defray the costs of child care and gain access to expanded facilities run by the state. Much of the remaining ABC funds would be devoted to improving the quality of child-care facilities. If and when the bill, or some close version, finally earns passage, it will set standards for such matters as staff qualifications, staff-child ratios, and safety regulations.[14]

In addition to lobbying on behalf of families, the labor movement has for a long time sponsored local and national initiatives to raise consciousness about family issues. Among its recent victories are the following:

- The 1987 UAW-GM contract included coverage for the costs of nonmedical custodial care for employees or retirees in ill health who want to live at home. This long-term-care benefit, believed to be the first employer-financed program of its kind, assists home-bound Alzheimer victims and others who are severely impaired.[15]
- ILGWU contracts in 1988 provided 135,000 members in East Coast states with up to six months' unpaid parental leave.[16]
- In 1988, the Steelworkers established joint union-management committees at three major steel mills to survey child-care needs and assess options.[17]
- A major rally was held in Washington, D.C., on May 14, 1988, to promote a comprehensive national family policy. The American Family

Celebration was organized primarily by the Coalition of Labor Union Women, aided by scores of unions and diverse groups such as the Black Women's Agenda, the Girls Clubs of America, the Italian-American Labor Committee, the Jewish Labor Committee, the National Council of Catholic Women, the Organization of Pan-Asian American Women, and the YMCA and YWCA.[18]

Keenly sensitive to the need for coalitions, labor has worked closely with nonunionists on behalf of shared family-life concerns.

More than 120 countries around the world provide parental or maternity leave compared to fewer than 40 percent of American businesses. Japan, for example, mandates that businesses provide twelve weeks of parental leave at 60 percent of normal pay, while West Germany requires fourteen to twenty-six weeks at full pay.[19] In this country, a presidential veto in 1990 stopped a parental and medical leave bill that would have provided twelve weeks of unpaid leave for the birth or adoption of a child or to care for a seriously ill member of the immediate family.[20] Research suggests that 20 to 30 percent of all full-time employees are caring for an elderly parent or other relative.[21]

An estimated 9 million children need high-quality day care, and that number is expected to increase by 3 million over the next three years.[22] Unions such as ACTWU, the UFCW, the ILGWU in Philadelphia, the SEIU in Hayward, California, and AFSCME at fifty sites nationwide have operated their own child-care centers for many years, but nationally the picture is bleak.[23] Indeed, in 1988, only about 750 of the nation's estimated 6 million employers provided any form of child care at all.[24]

In February 1988, Jerry Klepner, the legislative director of AFSCME, described child care as an issue "taking on a momentum that's making it virtually irresistible."[25] Since 75 percent of America's schoolchildren and 67 percent of all preschoolers are likely to have a working mother by the year 2000, labor lobbies for gains in this area with a special sense of urgency.[26] Joyce Miller, president of the Coalition of Labor Union Women, explains: "Incredibly enough, the United States is the only industrial nation—except for South Africa—that does not have a national family policy. This is an absolute disgrace, and it cannot be tolerated any longer."[27]

"Physician, Heal Thyself!"

Union-promoted gains in family policy and related issues such as the adequacy of women's pension plans and the quality of the workplace environment are inadequate unless the agent of change is changing itself.

At the heart of this challenge is the ability of male unionists to share power equitably with their "sisters" in the labor movement. Numbers provide a measure of slow but noteworthy progress:

- In 1989, the AFL-CIO Executive Council was made up of three females and thirty-five males; as recently as 1980, the council had been composed of only males.
- In 1988, five unions had elected female presidents, the largest number since the 1955 merger of the AFL and CIO.
- By 1987, the proportion of female officers in unions with a majority of female members reached an all-time high, with female leaders in the AFT, for example, rising from 25 to 32 percent from 1980 to 1985 and in AFSCME from 3 to 14 percent.
- By 1987, at least four AFL-CIO state federations had a female officer, and one, in Connecticut, had a female president. As recently as 1968, there had been no female officers and until 1985 no female presidents.
- By 1985, half the states had a woman as president of a central labor council, and a dozen had more than one female officer.
- By 1985, women constituted about 32 percent of the staff members of national-level unions, about twice the percentage in 1980.[28]

In some cases, the changes reflect a policy decision by the union, such as that reported by Albert R. Karr in July 1988: "A candidate slate has proposed a rule adding a woman and a minority person to the white, male executive board of the Oil, Chemical, and Atomic Workers Union."[29] Thus, gradually and in a variety of ways, organized labor struggles to improve internal gender equity.

Coalition of Labor Union Women

Whatever progress women have made in labor has resulted primarily from their own efforts. CLUW is an outstanding example. Founded by thirty-two hundred women in 1974, CLUW, with over eighteen thousand members, is now the largest national organization of trade union women and the first interunion organization founded since World War II that has an agenda written by and for such women. Since its inception, it has become "the major voice of trade union women, bringing women's issues to unions, and forming the links between women and organized labor."[30]

CLUW's achievements and accomplishments have been varied. For example:

- In 1986, the New York chapter produced the first union guide to contract language pertaining to child care.

■ CLUW's Center for Education and Research sponsors studies of issues affecting working women, disseminates the findings, and offers training to improve women's participation in union affairs.

■ The organization presents testimony before Congress, state legislatures, and regulatory bodies on such issues as pay equity, child care, and equal rights.

■ CLUW prepares "friend of the court" briefs in legal cases relevant to working women.

■ It cooperates in massive nationwide voter registration drives.

■ It sponsors educational conferences and programs on topics such as personal and job-related stress and health and safety reforms.

CLUW's founders were instrumental in persuading George Meany to change his mind in 1973 and support the ERA. The same women pressured the AFL-CIO Executive Council to endorse various women's issues and wrangled an AFL-CIO staff position for a coordinator of women's affairs. As scholar Diane Balser notes, CLUW is a "striking example of the success that can be achieved by a working women's group that has a solid union base and a good working relationship with the existing male leadership."[31]

Coal Employment Project

The considerable progress being made by women in traditionally male occupations can be traced to such single-industry campaigns as the Coal Employment Project (CEP). A nonprofit organization founded in 1977 by women miners, it has sought ever since to end sex discrimination in their industry. Endorsed in 1983 by the UMWA, CEP has brought several major class-action suits on behalf of women victimized in coal mining. The project has also documented problems of sexual harassment in the mines and sponsored training programs for prospective women miners. It has also raised money to send women miners to national conferences and testified at state and federal hearings on behalf of women miners.[32]

Cooperating closely with the UMWA, CEP campaigns for inclusion of parental leave provisions in new union contracts, builds floats for Labor Day parades, assists families in economic need, backs female delegates to the UMWA convention, and slates candidates for UMWA local posts. In the context of so many achievements, it is interesting to note those of greatest pride to CEP staff:

■ In 1986, for the first time in the UMWA's ninety-six-year history, a woman was elected to a full-time district office.

■ Attendance and commitment at the annual National Conference of Women Miners, sponsored by CEP, have improved every year since 1979. Workshops focus on sexual harassment, sex and race discrimination, assertiveness and confidence building, mine health and safety, and strengthening the union. Participants see films on women and mining, hear invited speakers (from groups such as CLUW), enjoy labor music, and offer one another advice and support in union, workplace, and personal matters.

■ In 1983, CEP inspired the UMWA convention to adopt unanimously a parental leave clause as a contract demand, an issue that "has won a permanent place in the minds and hearts of women miners."[33]

CEP is not resting on its laurels. Rather, it is busy expanding its activities to include women in other male-dominated industries, such as electronic services, trucking, and utilities.

Daughters of Mother Jones

Started as a traditional women's auxiliary of the UMWA, the Daughters of Mother Jones was created in 1990 for the purpose of bringing together female coal miners and the daughters, wives, mothers, and other female relatives of the seventeen hundred striking miners of the Pittston Coal Group, Inc., in Virginia, West Virginia, and Kentucky. It sought to duplicate successes in the coal mining region pioneered by the legendary Mother Jones in the 1900s: to help secure sympathetic national media attention for the strikers, to lift their morale, and to rally their family members. In an innovative way Mother Jones would have admired, they also strengthened the strikers' commitment to an effective strategy that substituted the principles of nonviolent protest for a more traditional reliance on guerrilla war.[34]

Visible at every major strike demonstration, the organization put the lie to the notion that the women of the coal region were too conservative to create a militant strike-support movement. Instead, the Daughters effectively conveyed to the nation the outrage and determination of the striking miners and their families, a factor of considerable significance in determining the successful outcome of the strike, one of the most important in current U.S. labor history.

Since the end of the strike in March 1990, the Daughters of Mother Jones have refocused their reform energies on the inadequacies of the public schools in coal mining counties. One of the founders explained to a reporter, "There's potential to develop chapters of the Daughters all over the country. And since Mother Jones herself crossed boundaries of different unions, there is a potential for women to help women in other unions."[35]

A Word from the Skeptics

Some critics question the value of certain reforms sought by women activists. For example, the proposed Parental and Medical Leave Act would have applied only to companies with fifty or more employees, thereby exempting about 95 percent of the nation's employers. Nevertheless, the U.S. Chamber of Commerce warns that "the real issue is the cumulative effect."[36] A spokesperson for women unionists agrees and insists that labor will exert unrelenting pressure to strengthen its terms.[37]

Other critics claim CLUW lacks substantive support from labor's current male leadership. They think it is therefore too weak to provide vital grass-roots activities and achieve significant feminist gains. Proponents explain that CLUW chose to build within an existing power structure and has had to use resources already in place. Depending on men known to be jealous of their prerogatives, CLUW, nevertheless, has managed to shape events and alter decisions while gradually increasing its influence.[38]

Women who are active in unions seem to retain the equanimity expressed in Addie Wyatt's closing words at CLUW's 1974 founding convention: "Remember, we are not each other's enemies.... Our unions are not the enemies because we are the unions.... We are telling our unions that we are ready, available, and capable to fight the fight.... The union is the most viable and available channel through which we can win our goals."[39] Knowing full well how much sexism permeates society, CLUW's activists remain committed to the process of liberation and the extension of equality in and outside of the labor movement.

Summary

To its credit, the labor movement has begun to shift resources in order to boost the loyalty of female members and strengthen labor's appeal to nonunion women workers. Spurred on by CLUW, CEP, and their many male allies, the labor movement shows encouraging signs of change.

Most polls indicate that nonunion female workers are more likely than their male counterparts to favor unionization.[40] Given that unionized clerical workers recently earned 39 percent more than those not in unions (the median weekly salary was $409 compared to $249) and that union women generally earn over 30 percent more than their nonunion counterparts, labor has much to offer millions of unorganized women workers.[41]

Encouraged by recent labor victories on behalf of pay equity, family care, day care, and the like, the nation's female unionists are likely to influence the labor movement in the 1990s as never before.

The Campaign at Harvard:
A Test of Union Availability

NLRB certification in 1988 of the Harvard Union of Clerical and Technical Workers (HUCTW) was characterized by AFSCME's president Gerald W. McEntee as "the premier test for our union," and many close observers of labor's prospects for organizing agree.[1] The NLRB representation vote upholding the AFSCME affiliate concluded a creative sixteen-year effort to unionize thirty-seven hundred university employees, most of whom were women. Although I was somewhat familiar with the campaign from media accounts, I did not realize how much could be learned from the effort until I interviewed insider Elisabeth Szanto in Boston on March 24, 1988. Few organizing drives have been as agile, intelligent, and creative as this one, and it deserves very close attention.

Background

Concurrent with the rise of feminism in the early 1970s, a small group of women employed as support staff at a Harvard University medical complex began to meet occasionally to share their personal and professional experiences. Many found they were not alone in feeling undervalued and overburdened on the job. And some wondered whether organized labor might provide some help. Contact was initiated with District 65, a freewheeling and progressive branch of the Retail, Wholesale, and Department Workers' Union. The women tentatively began to explore unionization through a new body they called the Medical Area District 65 ("MAD at Harvard").

While preliminary discussions were proceeding, District 65 affiliated with the UAW, and HUCTW found itself courted by one of the most macho unions in all of North America. Armed with a lengthy list of job grievances, the Harvard UAW secured a card count and forced the university into two NLRB elections, the first in 1977 and the second in 1981. Narrow losses—46 percent and 47 percent of seven hundred eligible workers in the medical complex voted support for the union—raised hopes of an imminent victory. These hopes were dashed in 1982, however, when lawyers for Harvard had the NLRB redefine the bargaining unit to include all of the university's clerical and technical staff, rather than only the staff of the medical complex. HUCTW had to redesign its entire effort from concentrating on seven hundred staff members in one complex to organizing nearly thirty-seven hundred office workers in over four hundred buildings across the campus. About 83 percent of the workers were women, and their annual turnover rate was close to 43 percent.

Support personnel at Yale University gained bargaining rights in 1983 after a heated strike against heavy-handed, bitter opposition. In contrast, staff at Harvard continued to confront seeming kindness and shrewd lawyering as the administration strove to address employee complaints, improve morale, and discourage employees from backing HUCTW's organizing effort.

Irreconcilable Differences

To complicate matters, the original cadre of workers and its allies from the UAW differed seriously in organizing style and strategy. According to journalist Robert Kuttner, the UAW officers felt the Harvard-based insiders were potentially uncontrollable and were not loyal enough to the UAW. The "insiders" resented some UAW staff members whom they considered autocratic and unsympathetic to white-collar organizing. Mistrust prevailed, and in 1985 the original organizers, having taken home critical campaign files, declared their independence from the UAW. The union, in turn, changed the locks on the office and hired a new team of organizers. Although most of them were women, none had ever worked for Harvard.[2]

To the university's delight, the newly formed independent HUCTW and its former supporter, the UAW, squared off for a bitter jurisdictional struggle. Harvard urged its office workers to see this as proof unions led only to costly complications, uncertainty, and strife.

Cut off from UAW financial support, seven HUCTW organizers worked for the next eighteen months without salaries, relying on fundraisers, flea markets, and crafts sales to pay their rent and phone bills. Throughout this crisis, HUCTW managed to draw more and more support from Harvard workers, while the rival UAW, with its staff of outsiders, made little progress.

Finally, in January 1987, the campaign took an unexpected turn for the better. An AFSCME officer who was attending classes at Harvard's Trade Union Program became fascinated by the events taking place. Impressed by the dedication and talent of the HUCTW officers, Robert McGarrah phoned his boss, AFSCME president McEntee, and urged him to come to Cambridge and explore the enormous potential of this operation. McEntee came and concluded that HUCTW was, quite simply, the strongest rank-and-file organizing effort he had ever encountered.[3] He offered his union's full and unfettered support, while promising

HUCTW it could remain autonomous and continue organizing as it saw fit. He backed up his words with an initial grant from AFSCME of $500,000, a photocopy machine, a computer, and other vital resources.

Ernie Rewolinsky, chief of staff for AFSCME, began a series of delicate negotiations with the UAW organizers. Their first reaction to the apparent raid on their project was to double their efforts on the Cambridge campus.[4] They insisted that HUCTW had nearly folded under financial pressure, and they bitterly resented any last-minute rescue attempts by a rival national union. Kristine Rondeau, head of HUCTW, confirmed the UAW's view: "If this didn't happen today with AFSCME, we would have had to close tomorrow."[5]

Rewolinsky finally succeeded in setting up a meeting during the AFL-CIO 1987 convention between UAW president Owen Bieber and AFSCME head McEntee to discuss the jurisdictional squabble. Everyone agreed that fractious interunion fights hurt organizing and only cheered Harvard administrators. "It's a tough drive because of the two groups," Ellen Sullivan, a UAW organizer, explained to the press, "because people are confused between them."[6] Bieber, however, took very seriously a poll indicating that his UAW unit had almost no support among Harvard clerks.

As a result, the UAW withdrew from Harvard in October 1987. UAW staff tactfully explained that overlapping organizing campaigns were causing "too much divisiveness for either union to succeed." If ending its Harvard campaign led to unionization of the university's technical and clerical employees, "it will have been the right thing to do."[7] Reserving the right to return if the AFSCME-HUCTW effort failed to win union representation by October 1988, the UAW urged support of its one-time ally and wished HUCTW good luck in its organizing effort.

Doing It Differently

Now that HUCTW finally had adequate financial support and leeway to go its own course, it rapidly expanded its organizing campaign. The staff grew from seven ex-Harvard employees to sixteen, and its organizing efforts became even more innovative. For example, it broke with traditional organizing tactics and engaged in an intensive, old-fashioned, "one-on-one" campaign. Instead of relying on impersonal mailings and leaflets, as the UAW had done, HUCTW recruited over four hundred volunteers, all of whom were Harvard office workers with union sympathies. After careful training, the volunteers fanned out to talk with co-workers in depth about how a union might alleviate job instability, improve fringe benefits, and upgrade their quality of work life.

But the organizers did not focus exclusively on these issues, as had the rival UAW group. Instead, HUCTW highlighted the new gains in personal autonomy and human dignity the union would provide for those at the bottom of the Harvard "pecking order." As Rondeau explained, "We do not organize around the issues. We change the way we look at ourselves, and our union. People should expect to have power and participation at work.... The issues then become problems to be solved."[8] HUCTW consistently emphasized empowerment of previously powerless underlings. Rondeau noted that young female employees were particularly energized "because, for them, the unionization experience is an extension of the political fight for women's recognition in general."[9]

Equally important, HUCTW emphasized the special needs of high-seniority, gray-haired workers. Its organizers did not take the easy course of focusing only on younger workers at the expense of older employees with years of experience. Instead, HUCTW pioneered in making the improvement of pensions and health insurance its highest priority, winning influential support from both older workers and gray-haired area activists, such as the Cambridge Committee of Elders.[10]

Another distinctive attribute of the campaign was that the organizers were careful not to denigrate Harvard. Consistent with the preference of many loyal white-collar employees, they did not characterize the organizing campaign as a holy war or assail the university administration. Rondeau told recruits unionization would actually help improve the Harvard they all cared about: "We've got a university to run and we're going to have to sit down and figure out the best ways of making that work. ...People who are part of a union care a lot about the university. They care about the overall mission of the university, both education and research."[11]

Joining the union was not portrayed as a vote in favor of "us" against "them." A popular button read "It's Not Anti-Harvard to Be Pro-Union." Rather, joining HUCTW was represented as a vote in favor of an even better Harvard, a finer workplace for employee and employer alike.

Also instructive was the organizers' decision to tackle Harvard's anti-union arguments directly. The most telling contention was that a union would seriously reduce the flexibility needed to run a complex academic operation. While HUCTW agreed that some managerial flexibility would be lost, organizers reasoned it was all for the best. The union assured prospective members HUCTW would stay as responsive as possible in its efforts to ensure personal dignity and employee rights: "When they want to fire somebody for no reason, they probably won't be able to. They're not going to be able to move somebody or retire somebody early or reorganize somebody out of a job at a whim."[12]

Union organizers seldom missed an opportunity to turn a seeming setback to advantage and keep the opposition off balance. Reaction to the publication of an anti-union briefing book for Harvard managers provides a typical example. Instead of ignoring or rebutting the book's harsh comments about unionization, HUCTW rushed to distribute nearly six hundred copies of the publication.[13] An accompanying note from the union boldly argued that Harvard had misrepresented critical facts, misunderstood the issues, and ignored the union's desire to cooperate in improving the university's operation.

HUCTW organizers gained support by using not only unexpected countermoves but also effective entertainment. Outstanding in this regard were the Pipets, a singing ensemble of Harvard University technicians who composed and performed pro-union lyrics set to familiar tunes. Harvard white-collar employees especially applauded a ditty entitled "You Can't Hurry Lunch," sung to the tune of the Supremes' "You Can't Hurry Love," and a bluesy feminist anthem, "Fifty-Nine Cents to Every Man's Dollar," which comtained the memorable line "You can keep your flowers, buddy; just give me a raise." The sale of low-cost tapes of favorites by the Pipets helped carry the union's message and made an engaging statement about the union's orientation.[14] Two candlelight vigils were held in front of the home of Harvard's president, and both included a serenade by the Pipets and nearly a hundred pro-union sympathizers.

As part of its effort to gain support beyond Cambridge, HUCTW solicited endorsements from such respected public figures as the Reverend Jesse Jackson, who spoke at a major rally on October 24, 1988. Letters of support were circulated from Coretta Scott King, Cesar Chavez, Congressman Barney Frank, the Boston chapter of the National Organization for Women (NOW), folk singer Pete Seeger, well-known Boston-area labor leaders, as well as the city councils of both Boston and Cambridge and Harvard's seven predominantly blue-collar (and male) unions.

Finally, the organizers earned favorable media attention with their persistent call for better on-site day care, an issue with special appeal to support staff who were starting their families. A kiddie picket line, featuring about seventy-five youngsters and over two hundred adults, drew media attention to the inadequacy of the child-care facilities at Harvard for low-income support staff. Harvard's seven child-care centers had very long waiting lists, cost over seven hundred dollars a month (in 1987), and served a total of only 388 children. Since clerical and technical workers earned only fourteen thousand to seventeen thousand dollars a year, parents had to spend half their salaries to pay for on-campus child care. Although ten scholarships were awarded in 1987, eighty families paid the full price. After doing an assessment of the situation, a monthly news magazine published by students urged Harvard, which boasted the largest endowment of any university in America, to show some heart and improve child-care options rapidly.[15]

Overall, the HUCTW organizing campaign effectively linked workplace and gender issues, as women unionists had at the turn of the century. A *New York Times* reporter noted three months before the election that "the HUCTW issue of affordable child care appears to be paying off."[16] Rondeau elaborated on the point: "The issue of child care must be seen as part of a package of women's issues which includes parental leave, pay equity, career advancement, job flexibility, and child care."[17]

Victory at Last

In May 1988, the NLRB certified HUCTW by a vote of 1,530 to 1,486, or a 44-vote margin, in a unit scattered across four hundred locations. At stake in the organizing campaign had been "the crown jewel of white-collar workers," including secretaries, museum personnel, library clerks, research and laboratory assistants, and dozens of other semiprofessionals."[18] Labor journalists believe this is "exactly the sort of work force the labor movement will have to learn to organize, if unions are to survive in the new service economy."[19] AFSCME hoped the HUCTW victory would "help dispel the notion unions are ailing institutions run by men for men."[20]

The stakes, in short, had been very high, and AFSCME and HUCTW relished the satisfaction of having won one of the most important organizing campaigns in recent history.[21]

Three months later a contract was signed that provided

- average wage increases of 32 percent over the next three years;
- a $50,000-a-year scholarship fund for child care and a model child-care center;
- eight weeks' leave at 70 percent of salary for mothers after giving birth and one week at full salary for fathers and adoptive parents;
- joint union-management planning and problem-solving councils in each area of the university;
- major improvements in pension benefits, including an uncoupling of the formula from Social Security;
- a provision for cost-of-living adjustments for retirees;
- an increase in the share of health insurance costs paid for by Harvard;
- strong language regarding affirmative action; and
- a joint union-management committee to address long-term needs.

HUCTW's chief negotiator, Kristine Rondeau, hailed the terms as proof labor could "win strong economic improvements and simultaneously develop a promising and forward-thinking relationship between the union and the university." AFSCME president McEntee predicted "many other workers in higher education across the country will take inspiration from these gains because their circumstances have much in common with those of Harvard workers.... The agreement lays a foundation for a whole new generation of working people, particularly working women and unions sensitive to their needs, to build upon."[22]

Chapter 7

"Reorganizing" Members

What gnaws at the psychological and moral roots of the contemporary worker is that most urban people, workers and owners, belong to nothing real, nothing greater than their own impersonal pecuniary interests. To escape from the profound tragedy of our industrial society is the great issue of our time.... For the worker the trade union has represented an unwitting attempt to escape from this dilemma. **Frank Tannenbaum, *A Philosophy of Labor* (1951), 106**

Unions need to rally their ranks, to bring their members into active participation in the lives of their unions.... Internal union democracy is no longer simply an ethical demand for more justice and better representation. It is a precondition for labor's survival. **"Organize!" *Labor Research Review*, Spring 1986, 2**

If labor journalist Abe Raskin can be trusted as a guide, then "reorganizing the organized must transcend all other union priorities if those inside, but divorced from any sense of genuine involvement, are to become bona fide trade unionists."[1] Without internal revival, Raskin warned in 1986, all of labor's other good intentions will falter and probably fail.

Controversy runs deep on this issue. Forty years ago, the strongest case for reorganizing was argued by Frank Tannenbaum in his seminal work, *A Philosophy of Labor*. Labor, Tannenbaum urged, should promote the close identification by members of the union as their "family" and of labor as their own mass movement. Unions had few objectives as vital as keeping their members engaged, informed, and enthusiastic so that rank-and-filers could regain dignity and "once again play the part of a moral person."[2]

Ever since Tannenbaum's day, certain labor realists have disparaged the positions of both Raskin and Tannenbaum. They argue that calls to reorganize are a waste of breath. Members, they say, get the quality of unionism they demand, and the matter is entirely in their own hands. Calls to improve morale or reduce apathy or to invigorate local union activities seem ill advised since members will get what they want anyway and such efforts distract attention from wiser priorities, such as lobbying, bargaining, and organizing.

Survey data, however, seem to favor the proponents of reorganizing. For example, in a poll of national union leaders taken in 1983, only 27 percent thought their members understood what a union does, while 62 percent thought they did not. Two years later, a national sample of local union officials was asked the same question and only 17 percent thought their members understood a union's activities, and 77 percent said members did not. Perhaps as a consequence, incumbents are often vigorously attacked at election time, the grievance process is often used capriciously, and contract demands are often complicated by "hype."[3]

Many local leaders regret that members do so much less than they might for their unions. As a consequence, locals suffer from membership apathy, poor attendance at meetings, and low voter turnout. Brian Heshizer reported in 1987 that 44 percent of union members polled designated "membership apathy" as the second leading internal cause of labor's problems, while 66 percent pinpointed "leadership apathy." Accordingly, 71 percent thought their unions should put "a lot of effort," and 24 percent, "some effort," into providing feedback to members. Only "job security" and "safety/health" on a list of ten issues outranked "providing feedback" as urgent objectives.[4]

Efforts to Reorganize

Not surprisingly, a number of robust strategies have been developed to improve communication and inspire new commitment:

- Telephone polls (case study, page 114) are helping leaders learn more about the rank-and-file, an effort made critical by dramatic changes in the composition of the membership.
- Telecommunications are helping to increase the exchange of information with members. Using this high-tech tool (case study, page 118) and others that are similar, the AFL-CIO and progressive unions are drawing their communities closer together.
- New organizing techniques (chapter 4) are building solidarity between members and potential members and enhancing sensitivity to needs such as child care.
- Aids such as a videotape of the contenders in the 1987 presidential primary are building labor's political effectiveness (chapter 11) and demonstrating the significance of rank-and-file preference in shaping labor endorsements.
- Labor education (chapter 9) is kindling new interest in union origins, labor history, and movement lore among novice members.

Virtually every project discussed in this book, of course, bears on the question of whether members are reorganized. Those I focus on below especially enhance the sense of the union as family and highlight the effort and resources this process may require. Together they underline the contention of Raskin and Tannenbaum that a social movement, labor included, is only as strong as its familylike bonds.

Drawing Members into a Dialogue

Turnout at local meetings tends to be low unless the agenda includes an announcement of an increase in dues, discussion of negotiating demands, or a hotly contested election. With its pioneering study circle program, the International Union of Bricklayers and Allied Craftsmen (BAC) offers a bold new option for perking up involvement.

In launching this experiment in 1986, BAC president John T. Joyce explained, "We are the first union in North America to attempt to adopt the study circle format. Democracy requires an ongoing dialogue between leaders and the people they serve. A modern trade union has to create mechanisms for a dialogue with its members. This is what the study circles are all about."[5] On the basis of conversations I have had with members, particularly Ed Cohen-Rosenthal, BAC's education director, and literature that documents the process, I am convinced unions across the country would profit from adaptations of BAC's project.

BAC has used study circles in an effort to give members new energy. At the time they were introduced, three major recessions had hit the construction industry and there was a growing move to use nonunion labor. By 1986, the 123-year-old union had lost more than a third of its members since 1970. Membership was down to only one hundred thousand, and the median age of the members was fifty-five.[6] Joyce warned that if BAC did not stem its decline, it might be forced to merge with a more viable union.

BAC turned to a format Swedish unions had used successfully for ninety years: voluntary, highly participatory, and democratic small-group study circles. BAC's study circles, for members and their families, have three explicit objectives:

- to promote understanding of BAC's long-range plans and obtain members' views on how these plans might affect locals, BAC, and the masonry industry;
- to raise the morale of members, their families, and BAC retirees through frank discussion and increased participation in the union; and
- to develop an effective communications mechanism for involving locals and their members more closely in the life of the union.

Beginning cautiously, BAC initially set up only twenty-six circles with 270 participants in 1986 and another thirty-two in 1987.

Led by trained field staff and business agents, the circles were an immediate success. As a BAC official explained, "Attendance for the five 2 ½ hour once-a-week sessions [in the first year] held, with little attrition, and members were participating with a vitality and enthusiasm surprising even to their study circle leaders.... The Study Circle Program had accomplished what we had set out to do."[7]

In addition, there have been unanticipated dividends. Circles serve as catalysts for settling intraunion disputes among locals. They draw out previously silent members. And they demonstrate the insights rank-and-file members can bring to an issue, both work- and nonwork-related.

Inevitably, the study circles have had their share of problems. Some tend to drift away from the BAC agenda, to run past scheduled adjournment times, or to become sessions for griping or placing blame. Remedial use of instructional videos and revamped training for circle leaders have substantially reduced these problems.

BAC was very pleased with responses to a 1986 study made by outside consultants to assess the program. Rank-and-filers who had completed the program had more positive attitudes toward BAC than a matched group of nonparticipants. Participants felt more confident about giving advice to others about union issues, and they had a more thorough understanding of the challenges facing BAC and the masonry industry, offering more support to BAC's long-range plans.

BAC is especially pleased that its study circles are not only opportunities to address substantive issues "but are also social occasions reminiscent of a time before World War II when union locals were places where members came together socially. Differences are aired, commonalities sought, members hear each other out, and the Union is stronger for it."[8]

One Step at a Time

Aware of my search for imaginative union achievements, Victor Munoz, president of the Central Labor Union Council in El Paso, Texas, introduced me to Mary Ann Snider, president of the area local of the American Federation of Teachers. Her proudest achievement has been "building our local, bringing it along, stage by stage." It is vital, she explained, to understand the process of a local's development in terms of stages of organizing and reorganizing the rank-and-file:

> In the first stage, you aim at making yourself visible. You want nonmembers and those in rival locals to sit up and take notice. You want people to realize you exist and to wonder what you are about.

In the second stage, at least in our situation, we moved to end a long and fruitless history of confrontation. We had not gotten very far butting heads with school administrators. And our chief rival, the El Paso NEA local, stung us with their charge we were being "non-professional." So we switched tactics and began to pursue consultation and learned how to win while compromising.

In the third stage, we widened the range of items eligible for negotiations and enlarged our sphere of influence. Members began to look to us for help on more and more varied matters, and we became more significant for our people and school administrators alike.

In the fourth stage, we moved our office out of a cramped cubbyhole into this comfortable suite and sent a message in this way that we had really "arrived" and were ready now to do the job we had earlier only wished we could.

Although the process took four years from the time Snider became president, the energy and activity of the local's office attest to its effectiveness.

A continuing effort is made to strengthen personal loyalties within the local, using a variety of strategies to promote the sense of family:

- A monthly calendar is sent to all seven hundred members listing a wide array of local activities and encouraging participation. An eight-by fourteen-inch wall poster, the attractive calendar includes a topical message designed to inspire action.
- One committee organizes an inventive range of social activities, including block attendance at baseball games, back-to-school socials, and workshops on topics such as makeup and color coordination.
- Another committee sponsors workshops on professional issues to aid career advancement, boost the status of the local, and promote a "family" feeling. Offerings in August 1988 included a week-long workshop on instruction and another on discipline and classroom management, an evening workshop on financial management, a one-day workshop on the consultation process, another entitled "Strategies for a More Successful School Year," and a final day-long workshop on the Texas Education Code of Discipline and Teacher Rights.
- Members are urged to attend AFT events that might further unite the El Paso local, such as the first Texas conference held to link paraprofessionals and teachers, a gathering designed "to help [them] get along better through understanding responsibilities and practicing mutual respect."
- Members are asked to comment on educational issues through monthly mail questionnaires. Results and commentary are shared with

members of the local, school administrators, the media, and AFT head-quarters. The survey for August 1988, for example, asked local members about school security and discipline issues, including their recommendations for changes in the student code of conduct booklet.

■ The local has two telephone-recorded hotlines. One offers labor news, and another provides child-rearing tips to El Paso parents.

In combination, these activities have lifted morale and promoted group spirit.

Snider says the effects have been profound, from finding new courage in confronting administrative mismanagement to receiving unprecedented support from key school board members, from the arrangement of regular consultation meetings with key school administrators to a provision for "comp time" for teachers participating in parent-teacher conferences. Snider adds:

> We know it adds up because we are gaining all the time on the other three unions competing with us for six thousand El Paso teachers, thirty-six hundred or more of whom remain nonunion. We won forty from our largest rival, the one thousand–member NEA local, last year, and we expect many times that number to sign up with us this coming school year. In a "right-to-work" state like this one, with its anti-labor character and hostile media, we've got to win our members all the time and in new ways, fresh ways, hold their interest.

The success of the El Paso AFT local demonstrates that energetic union leadership can simultaneously both strengthen union loyalty and provide essential educational services to the community.

Going about It in Earnest

Serious rifts among a local's members can develop over differences in sex roles, ethnicity, age, race, and so on. Boston's IBEW Local 103, for example, has had no choice except to try and improve race relations within the local. Donn Berry, a business agent in the local, is understandably proud of the changes achieved in attitudes toward racial difference:

> I was reared Irish-Catholic in an ethnic neighborhood where everyone was just like me, and I never spoke more than a few words to a colored person until the government forced our local into this quota stuff. . . .
> We had a lot of adjusting to do when we were forced to take outsiders, and black ones at that, into our union family. . . . There were some rough moments . . . and some things happened that we'd just as soon forget. But it was nowhere as bad as the media made it out to be, and we got

past the worst of it pretty soon. A lot of time has passed since then, and the [white] guys have made a remarkable discovery. Workin' along-side a black man for days on end, they've discovered he's got the same headaches, the same problems with the kids or old lady, that they have. [Now,] families picnic together, go to a ballgame, or just drop by.... It's personality and not race that really makes the difference.[9]

A reversal of racist attitudes is rarely spontaneous. In this case, it reflects the determined effort of the local and the courage and sensitivity of opinion shapers, white and black, in the rank-and-file.

This success story began inauspiciously in 1966 when the federal government imposed a "Boston plan" to integrate the building trades. By 1968, it had fallen of its own weight and a second plan was created. Craft locals were indifferent when the second plan also fell through three years later. Representatives of the unions had been minor players in writing the two documents, while community activists had preempted both center stage and federal funding.

By 1975, the squeeze was on. Boston's unionized contractors feared they would lose business because the IBEW local had too few black and female members to meet statistical reporting (quota) targets at a job site. By then an elected business manager, Berry suggested an audacious reform. He told his co-workers that waiting for blacks and women to seek out the local was a short-sighted exercise in disguised racism. Unless they adopted different tactics, the local would not survive; those contractors that were unable to satisfy quota requirements for minorities would soon shift to using nonunion workers.

Berry proposed that the local adopt a proactive stance. He suggested developing a new trainee program to supplement the local's apprentice program so as to boost the number of minority applicants for membership in the IBEW "family." Candidates would be able to waive both the age limit (twenty-four) and the aptitude test criteria of the apprentice program. Moreover, they would not be required to hold a high school diploma, as apprentices were, and there would be special options for appeal if they were dismissed from the program.

Berry was heartened by strong support from the local and sought similar approval from union contractors. A joint labor-management affirmative action committee was created to monitor the program, which was intended to be as race- and gender-conscious as the apprentice program was race- and gender-blind.

Since its inception in 1976, the program has had about sixty applicants each year. A six-member screening committee interviews the candidates, and every member independently scores each of them. At the same time, in an entirely separate process, one hundred new apprentices are accepted each year.

When an apprentice drops out or a contractor explicitly requests a black or female worker from the local, a trainee is contacted and sent out to the job site. He or she is then immediately enrolled in the local's apprentice schooling program and attends a four-hour evening course once a week for six weeks. On successful completion, the trainee is enrolled in the five-year apprentice program and is automatically taken into the IBEW. No one at a job site can distinguish an apprentice from a trainee.

This two-track plan has enjoyed remarkable success. Of the local's 3,800 members, over 250 are black men and over 100 are women (5 of them are black). Since 1976, about one-fourth of the local's apprentices have been minority members, and each year an additional eight or nine transfer in from the trainee program. (Women in Construction, a Boston group, provides help in recruiting women.) As Berry explains, "Our program [is] giving a fresh chance to some good people who might not otherwise get it. And we are bringing some talented people into our local we might not otherwise give the time of day to.... So, by taking a chance on the minorities, our 'family' is getting stronger,... and it is certainly a lot more interesting at the job site!" The success of the trainee program in finding and training minority workers has satisfied cooperating contractors and built new understanding among the local's increasingly diversified membership.[10]

Sealing a Pact

Jim Freese of Local 46 of the IBEW in Seattle shared with me a "union-as-family" ritual he designed to help seal a pact between new and old members. When he came on staff in 1986, he was eager to do "internal organizing." His candle ceremony has since proven highly effective in enhancing a sense of mutual commitment.

The ritual begins by having the students, stewards in a basic course in leadership development, sing "Solidarity Forever" on the final evening of the course. They are then joined by a delegation of staff members:

> I tell everyone, "We are going to do something that's a little unusual now. Trust us, it's harmless, and we're doing this for a point. I want you to close your eyes completely; just close them, and relax. I want you to take a deep breath in, and really relax. Exhale. Take another deep breath, and just feel a wave of relaxation."
>
> As I'm saying this, the lights dim down and go out, on the word *Exhale*. Then I begin a story... with their eyes closed and the room

dark: "A long time ago, there was no light, only total darkness. People were born, raised, worked, and died, within five miles of one geographic spot. There was no education, no hope for advancement, little health care, short life expectancy; very few, if any, comforts. It was dark.

"And then, at one moment, one person had an idea. They realized there was a spark of light, and the light was from within themselves. It was the person's idea." At this point I light my candle. I say, "Please open your eyes." Now, holding my candle in front of me, I continue talking: "The idea was the spark of enlightenment. By itself it was very weak. It reasonably followed that the only way to really protect this idea was to share it.

"Now, if you light someone else's candle, and someone else's, very quickly, the entire room is lit by candlelight. The power is not in the idea itself, and the idea itself is very weak. It's in the sharing of the idea." At this point I demonstrate this by blowing my candle out. "So, if for some reason my light goes out, I can reach over and relight it ...only because it's been shared. Okay, I'd like you all to blow your candles out." Everybody does this, and it's completely dark...except for one candle.

And I say something like: "Remember, the light starts nowhere else but within yourself. So our challenge is to find a light within ourself, and our duty, once we have found it, is to share it. For a light by itself, unshared, is worthless. Don't ever stop looking for the light within yourself, and don't ever let the light go out, because if you let the light go out, ... " and I put mine out, and there is nothing but darkness left.

From there I ask to have the lights put on, and we end the meeting in a very, very low key. I say, "Thank you for sharing your time with us tonight. Thank you for being here. I will ask you to do one thing: I'll ask you to not tell anyone about the candlelight ceremony, as that's a little surprise for the next group of people."

Freese freely admits that the ceremony has an "outrageous, fratlike, secret boys' club" quality. But the emotional impact is very real. Participants are genuinely moved and after the ceremony seem to bring a greater sense of "family" to their involvement with the local.

Other Undertakings

Skeptics sometimes scoff at labor's traditional props for "internal organizing": family picnics and excursions, baby pictures in the local's paper, scholarships for summer camp, dinners to honor recent retirees, and so on. But union activists contend that coverage of these efforts by the labor press actually aids solidarity. In addition to these events and those discussed in detail in this chapter, activists have devised a variety of other undertakings:

- The AFL-CIO campaign "Numbers That Count" is a coordinated field-proven strategy for "revitalizing our locals and renewing our members' commitment to the labor movement."[11]
- *History from Below* by Jeremy Brecher, published in 1986, tells rank-and-filers how and why they might want to uncover and tell the story of their locals.[12]
- AFSCME published a children's coloring book in 1987 entitled *Mommy, Why Do You Go to So Many Union Meetings?*

Clearly, labor's "solidarity" efforts are as strong and ingenious as ever.

A Word from the Skeptics

Those who doubt labor's intentions or capability continue to raise searching questions about "inside organizing." Some think efforts to achieve solidarity, such as those of the BAC and the El Paso AFT, preach only to the converted, while those indifferent to labor's ethos stay away.

In reply, proponents insist telephone, mail, and face-to-face surveys increasingly highlight the concerns of the rank-and-file. They point with pride to innovative tools such as VCR tapes that introduce the families of new members to organized labor. They note brisk sales of "Union, YES!" suspenders, buttons, and gym bags that help connect unionists from different organizations to one another. And they contend that the success of these projects vindicates labor's patient efforts to reach the unconverted.

Skeptics also contend that solidarity projects are vulnerable to two major obstacles: many members shy away from forming allegiances with a "family" that may include labor racketeers and may also inhibit free expression, intimidate a legitimate opposition, or otherwise undermine organizational democracy. The AFL-CIO, its ninety affiliates, and thousands of their locals, the skeptics warn, have no real appeal if their ranks include alleged racketeers and autocratic labor bosses.

In response, labor claims it has a cleaner record overall than any comparable social institution. Unions are required by the Landrum-Griffin Act and other legislation to conduct frequent, honest elections in which the rights of an opposition party are protected and from which convicted racketeers are barred. Further, efforts inside labor to reduce corruption are far more common than the mass media acknowledge. Archives of the newsletter of the Association for Union Democracy, for example, attest to vigorous and sustained efforts of nationwide grass-roots reformers. While internal political disputes are often ferocious, frequent victories for reformers restore faith and build unity in a local or international union.

Sociologist Harold Wilensky, one of the first scholars to research the behind-the-scenes workings of union headquarters, has chided those inclined to exaggerate labor's shortcomings: "If the non-union reader thinks organizational life in trade union headquarters is a bit seamy, let him look to his own organization with a critical eye, and the labor movement by and large will come out pretty well."[13] This cautionary note, written in 1955, remains appropriate, and those critics who point the finger at labor should first examine their own organizational culture unsparingly.

Finally, labor's admirers insist it remains a pioneer in tackling social problems such as racism:

■ Actors' Equity, for example, "has been in the forefront of the civil rights movement. In 1947, when the National Theatre in Washington, then the showcase of American theatre, barred blacks from admission, Equity decreed that its members could not play in that theatre. As a result, the theatre was closed for five years. When it reopened under different management with a policy of nondiscrimination, Equity returned."[14]

■ When Congress overrode President Reagan's veto of the Civil Rights Restoration Act in March 1988, the AFL-CIO proudly reminded readers of the *AFL-CIO News* that "from the start, the AFL-CIO and its affiliates were part of the broad civil rights coalition that pressed for legislation to clarify the intent of Congress, and prevent even indirect federal funding of discrimination."[15]

■ When the mayor of Washington, D.C., declared March 20–26, 1988, "Shell Boycott Week," over two hundred supporters cheered the AFL-CIO civil rights director and the presidents of the IBEW, the International Union of Electronic, Electrical, Technical, Salaried and Machine Workers (IUE), and the UMWA when they addressed an anti-apartheid demonstration at the oil company's Washington headquarters. UMWA president Richard Trumka said labor's message to Shell must be "we will not remain quiet while black South African workers are exploited."[16]

■ An hour-long TV production in January 1988 recounted the fifteen-year effort, vigorously backed by labor, to establish a national holiday honoring Dr. Martin Luther King, Jr. The program was produced with the assistance of the AFL-CIO and nine committed affiliates: AFSCME; the UAW; the IUE; the UFCW; the ILGWU; the Retail, Wholesale and Department Store Union; the SEIU; the United Steelworkers; and the Transportation-Communication Employees Union.[17]

Especially valuable are the efforts of the Coalition of Black Trade Unionists (CBTU), a "movement of rank-and-file folks, ordinary people who, over the years, have defied extraordinary odds in organizing themselves into a strong, independent force."[18] Since 1972, the CBTU has prodded, guided, and monitored activities to combat racism inside and outside labor. Representing 3 million black unionists and 23 percent of all trade unionists, the CBTU is the largest single organization of black Americans in the country.

Its efforts are supplemented by those of other anti-racism groups, such as the Labor Council for Latin American Advancement (LCLAA), which speaks for labor's 1.4 million Hispanic members, nearly 10 percent of the AFL-CIO's total membership.[19] Insofar as the percentage of Hispanic workers (9.4 million) who are joining unions is higher than that of any other ethnic group, the LCLAA warns that "no longer will Hispanics be silent or be content to be ignored by the labor movement."[20] In support of this position, a LCLAA representative took to the floor at the 1989 AFL-CIO convention to urge the federation to add a Hispanic vice-president to its executive council as soon as possible.[21]

Labor, in short, continues to struggle to meet the needs of its diverse members. To borrow a conclusion reached by researchers focused on women in construction, "If unions, as organizations, have tended to reflect some of the less attractive aspects of society at large, they certainly have both a proven record and vested interest in addressing these problems."[22]

Summary

In 1886, labor historian Richard T. Ely noted with approval the role social gatherings played in bringing "laborers and their families out of their isolation, and furnishing them with agreeable and congenial companionship." In the intervening years, labor's efforts have expanded substantially, although the fundamental goals have remained the same. As Ely explained, "The labor movement . . . is the strongest force outside the Christian Church making for the practical recognition of human brotherhood. . . . It is shown in sacrifices for one another in a thousand ways every day." In fact, he concluded, labor's cause was "so strong that for a man in a non-partisan position to oppose it is *prima facie* evidence of ignorance."[23]

Labor's effort to enhance the sense of "family" membership and heighten solidarity among the rank-and-file remains one of its noblest commitments. That effort, in all its forms, underlies labor's contention that it is not just another pressure bloc or merely a service-for-fee organization. Instead, as a social movement, labor struggles to unite "purpose with strength, and spirit with flesh," as befits a genuine family.[24]

Upgrading Telephone Polling

Telephone polling seems as simple as child's play, tempting the naive to think that anyone could use it effectively. This illusion has led some unions and locals to use the same services to conduct their telephone polls as they do to promote attendance at a rally or get out the vote. As a result, the call-termination rate is often high and open-ended responses are distorted or lost. Other unions have turned their polling over to professional firms, but their services are expensive and the professionals often lack insight into labor issues.

Phil Comstock, the executive assistant to the director of the Communications and Research Department of the UFCW, has begun to transform telephone polling with an ambitious project that could have enormous value to labor.

Background

Comstock worked his way through college as a telephone pollster and opened a small telephone polling company after he graduated. After meeting ILGWU stalwart Gus Tyler, Comstock accepted a position in union education in New England. He was soon invited to headquarters in New York City, as executive assistant to President Sol C. Chaikin. He put his polling experience to use in 1979, when the ILGWU commissioned its first phone survey of the rank-and-file. The results have informed key decisions of the union ever since and have inspired additional studies.

Comstock joined the staff of the UFCW in 1984 and has enjoyed similar support from that union and its president, William Wynn. But unlike the project for the ILGWU, which served that union alone, the UFCW projects are far wider in scope, reaching out to all AFL-CIO internationals.

Doing It Right

The Comstock dream is predicated on annual increases in union use of the UFCW's phone polling service. Already successful and widely endorsed by unions, the service has several distinct features:

- It is operated by labor for labor. Neither profit-hungry nor value-neutral, it is run by UFCW staff members who supervise trained phone interviewers. All go out of their way to earn return business from their major client—the ninety affiliates of the AFL-CIO.
- The service has an unusually talented staff. Interviewers hold master's degrees in social work or have equivalent training, and they are

expected to notice subtleties in responses to open-ended questions. Comstock is convinced that money spent on staff is an indispensable investment, and the comparatively high hourly wages of the interviewers ($9 to $13 in 1987) reflect this commitment.

■ The surveys focus on attitudes rather than on opinions. While many phone surveys capture only superficial responses to complex realities, Comstock's surveys try to measure the underlying attitudes that shape opinions.

■ The service is affordable. Because its overhead is low and its advertising investment limited, the UFCW service is able to charge 30 to 40 percent less for phone interviews than its commercial competition ($1.20 to $1.40 per minute, per interview, in 1987, compared to $2.80).

Perhaps the most important achievement of the UFCW project is the steady development of a data-based profile of contemporary Americans. The service has completed over eighty-seven thousand phone interviews, which are stored in a computer program, allowing data retrieval and analysis. A small battery of questions on topics such as aspirations and job satisfaction is the same in each interview so that the UFCW service is accumulating long-term data of major value to organized labor—provided, that is, unions make insightful and continuous use of it.

Why Bother?

Satisfaction with the shop steward or with an organizing campaign, willingness to support a consumer boycott or to serve as a volunteer organizer, and agreement with the union's stand on an issue are just a few of the topics the UFCW service has explored. Convinced that labor will continue to recognize the potential of phone surveys, Comstock is pleased with the growing variety of his commissioned projects:

■ Several unions have asked for needs-assessment studies to help clarify what nonunion workers want from unionization or what unionists want from their labor organization.

■ Other unions have asked for polls designed to clarify expectations of negotiations and the relative priority of issues to be negotiated.

■ Still other unions have sought assistance in tactical planning, such as surveys that explore alternative paths and priorities for the union.

Awareness of the potential value of thoroughly professional telephone surveys has clearly begun to spread, encouraging unions to employ the technique to meet their particular needs.

Get It through the Mail?

Even with minimal charges, a phone interview was billed at about $1.20 a minute in 1987. The use of open-ended questions can mean an average of twenty to twenty-five minutes per respondent. Skeptics are quick to scoff at the disparity between this cost and the cost of the stamp on the envelope used to return a questionnaire.

Comstock replies by comparing the number of contacts he has made through his phone surveys with the low response rate to surveys sent in the mail. Moreover, his interviewers, who speak a total of twelve languages, can restate and interpret questions in ways no mail survey can. Staff members also include a subjective reading of a respondent's mood, which is unavailable from a mailed-back questionnaire.

There are, nevertheless, two significant drawbacks to the UFCW phone polling service. The first problem is that it is dependent on a single individual, Phil Comstock. He is working very hard to help labor-based services similar to his succeed in Baltimore and in New York State. Both will cooperate with Comstock and then establish their independence as their staffs gain experience.

The second problem is that theoretically the UFCW could refuse service to a prospective client if the information sought could be used to organize workers in competition with the UFCW. Although the union's director of organizing approves all survey contracts, the prospect of such a conflict appears slim given the union's strong backing of the phone survey project.

Comstock hopes to develop eight to twelve satellite operations within five years, and he offers an annual workshop at the Meany Center to help promote this goal. He wants to prevent the original service from growing too big "because then you get obsessed with selling your service, rather than analyzing data.... I've helped to start this process in the labor movement, and I want others to get into it to help keep me honest.... The more people we draw in, the greater the chances of getting better and better approaches.... I'm hungry for more data, and that means more pollsters sharing more data." Far from worrying about the prospect of competition, Comstock welcomes the advent of colleagues and increased quantities of information.

Upgrading the Project

In December 1987, the UFCW moved its entire operation into new quarters designed to "put it one or two generations ahead of everyone." With $70,000 worth of customized software, the polling center has automated much of the phone survey process. Electronic input of a respondent's replies has replaced paper questionnaires. Open-ended questions predominate, and the computer "reads" and sorts open-ended responses more effectively than was previously possible. Narrative data, as well as statistical tables, can be accessed. As Comstock explains, "What we know will increase on a linear basis. But what we will be capable of doing will increase geometrically!" He expects the new facilities will convince many union skeptics to commission their first phone poll with his operation.

Summary

With over thirty unions among its clients, the UFCW phone polling service is now doing most of the survey work in the labor movement and is asking only $60,000 for a job commercial pollsters price at $135,000. The UFCW continues to explore attitudes rather than focus on ephemeral opinions, and it is using its expanding data bank to formulate one valuable hypothesis after another about unions and unionists.

Utilizing Telecommunications

How does a union maintain close, interactive communication when its members confront their first full-scale strike in thirty-two years? The challenge is even greater when the members are pilots because they are not typical union members: "Airline pilots are not likely candidates for the vanguard of the working class. They make, on the average, $80,000 a year, live in the fancier suburbs, and have a reputation for crossing other unions' picket lines."[1] Nevertheless, in 1985, the Air Line Pilots Association faced a situation at United Airlines that rapidly compelled the union to improve communications with its five thousand members.

Unions confronting the threat of a strike have traditionally relied on telephone networks and written communications to their rank-and-file. More recently, those with flair and funds have added phone conferences, but their use remains limited by high costs and complex coordination requirements. Furthermore, phone conferences rely on sound alone, which, in an age of shimmering electronic images, seriously limits their potential.

Teleconferences: A Better Way

The strike by United Airlines pilots in 1985 showed labor the potential value of teleconferences, a relatively new medium that combines audio and visual components in an interactive system. Participants thousands of miles apart duplicated the experience of a face-to-face meeting, using a medium that had, over the past fifteen years, demonstrated very substantial benefits:[2]

- Because they are easier to arrange than face-to-face gatherings, teleconferences enable more people to participate in making important decisions. Participants can share more resources and consider more perspectives than in face-to-face meetings.
- Leaders and specialists minimize travel time and costs and remain close to their resources, thereby increasing effectiveness.
- When the group task is well defined and there is little need for divergent points of view, teleconferences can reduce distraction by providing information that is targeted to a particular audience.
- Because participants have a shared concern, they are often able to establish trust quickly and to keep social protocols to a minimum.

Experts caution, however, that "the long-range impacts of teleconferencing will become apparent only as people with real communication problems and previous experience with the media begin to develop creative applications."[3]

Background

United's pilots were introduced to teleconferencing in 1981 during a brief period of unusual cordiality in union-management relations. A new contract had been negotiated that emphasized mutual respect, goodwill, and a cooperative rather than an antagonistic relationship.[4] To help convey this novel climate to a skeptical work force and to symbolize their new collaborative approach, both sides agreed to participate in the first-ever joint teleconference. The result was a closed-circuit TV program, starring officers of ALPA's local at United and representatives of the employer, that was broadcast nationwide to employees gathered at widely scattered locations. Questions were taken over the air and promptly answered by negotiators. The company picked up the bill, and later everyone involved agreed the show had been a great success.

Four years later, when contract negotiations began to sour, union leaders sought to replicate the 1981 teleconference. ALPA officers felt a special urgency because they believed that the costly and demoralizing failure of ALPA's strike at Continental was partially attributable to poor communications.

Gearing Up

While contract bargaining struggled along, a strike-preparedness committee (SPC) was created as a proactive response. The SPC's five pilots from United and one from Northwest were asked to address a fundamental question: how could ALPA pilots at United, who had not walked a picket line in thirty-two years, conduct an effective strike? Pilots from other airlines were invited to offer advice on strike preparation and management. Ideas received from the Northwest local carried special weight since it had won a major strike in 1981 and had subsequently held its own in tough labor-management relations. Pilots representing Northwest emphasized the strategic importance of two-way communication with the rank-and-file, and United ALPA officers took note.

With the stakes high and no time to spare, the United local hired a two-person team of communications specialists and charged them with mounting the first-class effort needed to prepare for a successful strike. The symbolic message to anxious members was that ALPA was not going to suffer a loss as it had at Continental. An additional nine pilots were added to the SPC, one for each domicile area in United's fifty-state territory, and the details of the strike preparations were immediately shared with an increasingly militant membership.

Fostering Family Spirit

As part of the strike plan, the SPC created an unprecedented family awareness network (FAN), a nationwide system of small mutual-aid committees of United pilots and dependents. The SPC resolved that families would be fully involved in any job action and charged FAN with accomplishing this goal. Attention would focus on reducing family stress and alleviating the pressure to resume the breadwinner's role that strikers often feel from spouse or children.

Groups of forty or fifty United pilots then went to Chicago for a special FAN training program in matters of mutual aid, such as ways families could economize by sharing meals, trading clothing their children had outgrown, or bartering home repairs. Nearly 650 pilots completed the course and returned home to establish FAN committees. The committees, composed of ten families each, held weekly meetings at the homes of trained leaders to develop the cooperation that would be needed during the strike that loomed ahead.

The strike-preparedness committee eventually produced sixteen videotapes that were offered at regular intervals to the new network. Week after week, pilots and their families across the country learned ways to reduce the stress of a strike, how to manage family finances while on strike, and how to retain coverage in benefit plans. Each videotape included a segment of answers to questions raised at the previous week's meetings of the family awareness network. Answers were phoned in to ALPA by volunteer leaders of FAN throughout the country.

Computer on Board

While FAN was being initiated, United pilots, who are thoroughly familiar with computers, quickly created a nationwide network that linked their personal computers with the ALPA mainframe. Using a computer bulletin board, the SPC was able to exchange information with remote ALPA offices and with individual United pilots who had use of a modem. Simultaneously, plans were made for the teleconference, the first ever used by a union in preparation for a strike. On May 5, 1985, twelve days before their strike began, the United pilots conducted the first of what proved to be five major teleconferences. Guided by media consultants, they followed several basic principles:

■ They featured well-known television personalities. Paul Anthony, a popular newscaster, moderated, and Daniel Schorr, the acclaimed news commentator, interviewed the leadership of the United local.

■ They varied the "menu." Each teleconference mixed news and opinion with entertainment, inspirational messages, and unrehearsed answers to questions phoned in by viewers.

■ Each show had an aura of professionalism. The program's complex operation, involving television and phone linkups with hotel rooms and arena space in nine cities, was technically well executed, and the quality of the production enhanced the self-esteem of commercial airline pilots nationwide.

As a means of sustaining morale and building resolve, the prestrike teleconference and its successors won enthusiastic support. Over eight thousand members participated and applauded the program that preceded the strike, and even more "tuned in" to those that followed.

Holding It Together

On May 17, the day the strike was called, members of the United local gathered at nine reception sites nationwide for the second teleconference. Last-minute contract negotiations were still going on in Boston, and local officers, at strike headquarters in Chicago, were preparing for any outcome. Meanwhile, a teleconference broadcast from Denver used live TV hookups to keep over eight thousand members up-to-date on developments. Rank-and-file members at TV sites across the country exchanged messages of encouragement and inspiration throughout the broadcast.

When negotiations collapsed at midnight, the United pilots officially went on strike, and at 12:45 A.M. the dramatic teleconference ended. The impact of the four-hour event was profound: 96 percent of the eligible pilots went out on strike, grounding 85 percent of the carrier's domestic flights.

Winning Over the Opposition

On May 18, the United pilots conducted another teleconference, this one addressed to a very different audience whose response could determine the outcome of the strike. Months earlier, in December 1984, the company had hired 570 pilots as standbys in case of a strike. ALPA immediately recognized the threat, and the SPC plotted a strategy to win the new recruits' allegiance to the union.

ALPA organizers went to Denver, United's main hub, where the standbys were concentrated. Day after day in meetings with the standbys, the organizers emphasized that United had already shown its low regard for them by declining to put them on the regular pilot's payroll and by paying them only thirty dollars a day for room and board. Moreover, if ALPA lost the strike and the company used the 570 pilots as replacements, their salaries would be at the bottom of the two-tier schedule the union was striking to resist. Regarding wages, ALPA's loss would be theirs as well.

When the organizers thought the moment was right, they rented buses and brought the 570 standbys from their hotels to a teleconference site. "We spirited them away from the company, right under their nose!" Captain Roger D. Hall, president of the local, proudly recalled. During the teleconference, the union extended an offer to pay the standbys' fare home if they would quit United. To the delight of the union and the consternation of the company, 566 of the 570 standby pilots later refused to cross ALPA's picket line at sixty sites across the country. As a result, United never flew more than 15 percent of its domestic flights during the strike.

Bringing It All Home

Buoyed by its victory with the standbys, ALPA held a third teleconference midway through what proved to be a twenty-nine-day work stoppage. This teleconference drew the largest audience yet, estimated at fifteen thousand viewers. Linking ten hotel ballrooms across the country, the show brought viewers up-to-date on strike events, dispelled rumors, and boosted morale.

Nationally renowned lawyer F. Lee Bailey offered a colorful message of support, as he had during the first teleconference. A licensed small-plane pilot well versed in the issues of the strike, Bailey used pilot jargon to advantage. The second featured speaker, Vietnam veteran Charles Plumb, brought the viewers to their feet with his motivational message. The five-hour show, the longest ALPA teleconference ever, appeared to be another resounding success.

Two weeks later, on June 15, when the unexpectedly long strike finally ended, ALPA broadcast one last teleconference. Held to three hours, it featured a deliberately slow and careful review of every clause in the United contract. Questions were called in from the ten audience sites and were answered on the air. The show then exploded into a ten-city victory party, telecast simultaneously from one uproarious site to another across the country.

Follow-up

Years after the event, United's strike leader Captain Hall continues to believe that nothing before or since has been as effective in uniting union members as was the series of five teleconferences. He remembers them as "the greatest display of solidarity the airline industry has ever seen!" Although their cost ($300,000) prohibits frequent use, Hall says, "We can mount one now in under a week, and won't hesitate to do so!"

ALPA used the format twice in 1987, once when Eastern Airlines pilots needed to participate in a nationwide exchange and once to brief United pilots on the $4.5 billion bid ALPA had just made for the stock of that airline. Most recently, two teleconferences were held in 1989 for the thirty-six hundred Eastern Airlines pilots who struck in sympathy with the line's machinists. The second of these was seen by twenty-two thousand viewers.

Transferable Lessons

Now confident about the form, ALPA expects to conduct more teleconferences in the future, guided by principles that other unions may also find useful:

- *Keep teleconferences short.* Two hours is about as long as viewer-participants can handle.
- *Engage magnetic TV personalities to attract viewers and set the tone.* Ed Asner and Martin Sheen, for example, put in brief appearances on the United shows.
- *Feature the wives and children of members.* Family involvement boosts morale.
- *Invite guests from cooperating unions, and make them feel genuinely welcome.* ALPA, for example, involved United Airlines representatives of the Association of Flight Attendants, which had honored ALPA's picket line for twenty-nine days.

A unique feature of teleconferences is that they enable two-way interactions to be both seen and heard. To use this feature fully, sponsors should allow as much time as possible for exchanges with audience members and should respond to their comments with respect and empathy. Used properly, teleconferences can maximize the trust, respect, and goodwill on which labor depends.

Catching the Spirit

ALPA made exemplary use of teleconferences in conjunction with its 1985 strike, but it was not the first union to recognize the value of this tool. The United Steelworkers used a teleconference in 1982 to share convention developments with rank-and-filers gathered at sites across the country. The response was so positive that the union held a fifty-five-site teleconference on June 21, 1986, to mark Save American Industry and Jobs Day. Co-sponsored by five major steel companies, the teleconference was promoted on more than four hundred billboards in thirty cities. TV time was shared with other concerned unions, including ACTWU and the CWA, and with celebrities such as singer Johnny Cash, actor Michael Keaton, and actress Cathy Lee Crosby.

Catching the spirit, the UAW broadcast its first teleconference to seventeen sites during its national convention in 1983. Shortly thereafter, AFSCME opened a $1.4 million network-quality radio and TV studio from which it has since conducted several teleconferences. It also leases access for such events to a number of other AFL-CIO unions.[5]

These unions, nevertheless, remain exceptions. The overwhelming majority of the AFL-CIO's ninety unions have still not organized their first teleconference, despite the advice of labor educators:[6] "ALPA's fortitude teaches that a well-prepared strike bolstered by a mix of new technology and 1930s-style small and family support networks can beat the union-busters."[7] New communications technology, combined with traditional personal networks, offer labor a powerful instrument for preparing for and withstanding the impact of a strike. ALPA has continuously refined this robust option, and it warrants adaptation by other unions.

Upgrading Responses to the NLRB

What is a robust response to a potentially devastating decision by the NLRB? IBEW activists in Local 46, Seattle, opted to retaliate with a strategy that is rich in useful lessons for the entire labor movement. At issue was a pro-union arrangement known as the prehire agreement. Authorized by Congress only for the construction industry, prehire agreements have been permitted since 1959 when section 8(f) of the 1947 Taft-Hartley Act was added to acknowledge "the need for contractors to fix their labor costs in advance of bidding, and the risk that unions would not refer their members to job sites without a contract established listing their wages, hours, and working conditions."[1] The agreements are signed before a contractor employs workers. A crew is then dispatched from the union hiring hall, and the job can begin.

For years, the nation's building trades unions have depended on the *conversion doctrine* to transform prehire agreements into standard labor contracts. Whenever a majority of the workers at a work site were union members, the agreement "converted" to a regular labor agreement, complete with full labor law protections, under section 9(a) of the Taft-Hartley Act.

Enter Deklewa

In 1986, John Deklewa and Sons, a contractor who had operated under union contracts for twenty-six years, had a bitter dispute with Local 3 of the International Association of Bridge, Structural and Ornamental Iron Workers. It led to an extraordinary NLRB decision on February 20, 1987. The company had signed a standard prehire agreement, but in the middle of the contract term, John Deklewa and Sons decided to hire nonunion workers and simply tore up its agreement. An astonished and outraged Local 3 filed charges with the NLRB and was initially delighted when the board ruled in the union's favor: Deklewa and Sons was ordered to honor the prehire agreement.[2]

But elation turned to surprise and then to dismay. To the astonishment of Local 3, the Reagan-appointed NLRB had also wiped out the time-honored conversion doctrine. Hank McGuire, a staff writer for *SPARKS*, the local's paper, explained: "The NLRB went on to say that when the contract expired, the contractor could just walk away. There would be no duty to bargain with the union! There would be no right for the union to picket! To put it bluntly, it would be as if there were no laws to protect the desire of craftsmen to have union representation." Moreover, the decision was retroactive: "Unless there had been an NLRB-certified recognition of a union as the collective bargaining representative for a group of workers, the contract would be considered to be of the pre-hire type."[3]

For all practical purposes, the *Deklewa* decision meant existing construction projects were suddenly considered to be operating with prehire agreements.[4] As a result, contractors eager to escape dealing with labor no longer had to bargain to an impasse, force a strike, and eventually win the decertification of the local. All they had to do was wait for a prehire agreement to expire, give notice of termination, and refuse to bargain. Thereafter, they were legally free to change wages, terminate benefit contributions, hire off the street, and institute exploitative job classifications, such as "pre-apprentice," "sub-journeyman," and "helper." In effect, they could arbitrarily change any term or condition of employment not dictated by law.

"Let's Turn It Around!"

Two months after the NLRB decision, the AFL-CIO's Building Trades Department sponsored a major conference at the Meany Center on organizing in the construction industry. Michael D. Lucas, director of the IBEW's Organizing Department, led a discussion of the ramifications of *Deklewa*. Responses and strategies were brainstormed, analyzed, and assessed by the forty attendees for a day and a half.

By the morning of the second day, Lucas and Jim Freese, a representative of Local 46 of the IBEW, Seattle, had arrived separately at the same insight: *Deklewa* did not have to be viewed as an unmitigated disaster. Instead, it could be seen as an opportunity to renew morale. They suggested a local might actually use *Deklewa* to "organize the organized." Freese left the conference determined to carry this message back to Seattle.

Impact in the Northwest

Seattle's IBEW Local 46 woke up the day after the *Deklewa* decision to find more than 160 agreements in the construction industry had been reduced to waste paper. They were no longer regular labor contracts converted from prehire agreements, since the local had never thought it necessary to earn NLRB certification or recognition based on majority status. And because they had never before been required, the local had never sought prehire agreements for groups of workers linked to separate contractors. Union members, Hank McGuire wrote, felt as if they had "just stepped into an open elevator pit!"[5]

The decision came at a time when the local was already under siege:

> We have less than 5 percent of the housing market, less than 10 percent of the multi-family housing market, and only 65 percent of the commercial-industrial market. The fact is that we have lost a tremendous part of the market, and it will be hard to get it back. . . . The situation we face has been created by ABC [American Builders and Contractors, chartered by the Business Roundtable]. They are anti-union, and have spent thousands of dollars to create a rabid hard core of non-union electrical contractors.[6]

Faced with the change, the local either had to accept its devastating implications or devise a way of protecting itself and its members.

Counterattack

Local 46 responded quickly to the NLRB decision. Led by McGuire, the local persuaded the Seattle Building Trades Council to plan a coordinated response through a special interunion committee representing the Laborers International Union, the United Association of Journeymen and Apprentices of the Plumbing and Pipe Fitting Industry, the Teamsters, the IBEW, and others.

Immediately, the interunion committee encouraged its legal staff to discuss the *Deklewa* decision in depth at its annual West Coast meeting. In early March 1987, the IBEW helped officers and representatives in all fifty states explore strategies to counter the NLRB decision, and at a subsequent San Francisco IBEW conference, procedures to deal with the legal ramifications were discussed in detail. The special interunion committee then convened the first statewide meeting of unions to review options. On June 8, 1987, over one hundred union business agents from all over the state of Washington gathered at the Local 46 hall to hear labor lawyers explore overt and covert aspects of the new NLRB ruling and to develop a sound plan of counterattack.

The "Deck Deklewa" Campaign

The heart of the plan was to convert a seeming setback into a robust campaign to renew union loyalty and commitment. Local 46 and other building trades locals sent out new "authorization for representation" cards to everyone who had worked in Seattle-area construction:

Old Wording	New Wording
I authorize a local union of the IBEW to represent me in collective bargaining with my employer.	I authorize Local Union No. _____ of the IBEW to represent me in collective bargaining with my present and future employers on all present and future jobsites within the jurisdiction of the Union. This Authorization is nonexpiring, binding, and valid until such a time as I submit a written revocation.

Once a majority of workers in a shop had signed cards, the local demanded voluntary recognition from the contractor in order to secure bargaining rights under section 9-a of the Taft-Hartley Act. If the contractor refused, the local tried to earn recognition through an NLRB representation election. And if the contractor questioned the validity of the list of card signers, the local arranged with the Seattle Church Council to verify names and arbitrate the matter.

With over 160 contracts to cover, the card-signing process proved very time-consuming, and, as McGuire noted, there was a real danger that contractors would attempt "to waste our time and money by forcing elections on us."[7] To reduce the danger, Local 46 urged its members to take new initiative. In June 1988, when the local's existing contracts expired, the local encouraged all workers to follow a four-step plan:

- Sign and mail back authorization-for-representation cards right away.
- Get others to do the same.
- Make sure the contractor knows you want Local 46 to represent you.
- Make sure the contractor knows you do not want to waste time and money participating in a drawn-out election.

Both McGuire and Freese were confident that if the workers followed the plan, all prehire agreements could be "converted" to standard labor contracts.

Carrying the Message

To help buttress its efforts, the union created effective promotional devices:

■ Thousands of two-inch "Deck Deklewa" stickers were displayed prominently on hard hats, T-shirts, lunch boxes, and lockers.

■ Thousands of flyers were produced to persuade workers that "Mama," a TV character created by actress Vicki Lawrence on "The Carole Burnett Show," wanted them to sign a bargaining card. The flyer quoted "Mama" warning, "When push comes to shove, lots of promises ain't worth diddly. A promise is a promise, but a contract is a guarantee. A union contract will make your bosses keep their promises."

The local emphasized to members that their union benefits were in jeopardy and the *Deklewa* decision could cost them their pensions, their union wages, their health benefits, and their grievance procedure unless they reaffirmed the union's bargaining rights by signing cards.

Every local represented on Seattle's interunion committee used the same leaflets and two-inch stickers, and McGuire was confident the message was heard. Over four hundred "Deck Deklewa" stickers were mailed to labor lawyers nationwide, alerting them to the fight. And in Seattle alone, hundreds of volunteers were recruited to call or visit unionists who had not yet signed authorization cards. As McGuire explained:

> *Deklewa* offers us all a chance to sell the IBEW. We grumble about the union and all sorts of stuff, but we have a tremendous benefit package, a great pension, good wages together with good jobs, the best training in the world, and we have much cleaner and safer jobs than non-union workers. We have lobbyists fighting for our rights at all levels of government, and we have a grievance procedure and attorneys to back us up.[8]

McGuire had enough confidence in his union to see the *Deklewa* decision as an opportunity.

A Word from the Skeptics

McGuire remains aware that some workers feel he exaggerated the danger in the *Deklewa* decision.[9] But he expects no reconsideration from the NLRB, and certainly no reversal of its decision. He remains convinced, as do scores of labor lawyers, that alarm is warranted.

Skeptics ask, What if the members of the various unions refuse to sign bargaining cards? What if the builders seize the opportunity to insist on conducting costly and time-consuming NLRB representation elections? Wouldn't it be better to leave the whole matter to the AFL-CIO Building Trades Department, its legal staff, and the lawyers retained by major building trades unions? They see little or no role for rank-and-filers and prefer to wait for the response of legal specialists and the emergence of a body of case law.

While Freese, Lucas, and McGuire value the contribution of labor lawyers, they are excited by the prospect of drawing dues payers out of their lethargy and converting them into activists. *Deklewa*, McGuire contends, "can be *the* catalyst to rouse our people like nothing we've had to go with in recent years. If we play our cards right, we can turn it to advantage, and come out stronger than ever!"[10]

Influence of the Campaign

For several years before *Deklewa*, the building trades had regularly lost thousands of signatory contractors who concluded that they no longer needed the union hiring hall. Under the conversion rule, however, walking away from the union was often a slow, cumbersome, and expensive process. This situation, of course, quietly boosted the fortunes of the building trades locals.

A major reversal of NLRB policy now allows these builders to repudiate their union relationships once current contracts expire, providing them with "the strongest bargaining position they have enjoyed in recent history."[11] But thanks to IBEW Local 46, the Seattle-area building trades have been the first in the nation to put together a coordinated response to the NLRB decision. The local's attorney has assured its activists, "You guys are on the cutting edge. . . . You are leading the entire country at this point."[12] Other building trades locals have been phoning, writing, and visiting Seattle to seek advice. Morale in Local 46 could not be higher.

Much remains to be seen. The IBEW is appealing the *Deklewa* decision to the courts and is considering a campaign for corrective legislation. Building sites throughout the Seattle area are festooned with sparkling two-inch stickers. McGuire and others in area locals have used the NLRB threat to lift morale and arouse new rank-and-file activism. Seattle unionists remain a model for locals nationwide of a way to capitalize on NLRB mischief. They have converted what first appeared to be a mortal threat into a manageable task, and, in that sense, they have already won.

Part III

UNIONS AND
THE COMMUNITY

L abor has always profited from the various organizations to which
members belong in addition to their locals. Thanks to its heter-
ogeneity, the movement has representation in social and community groups ranging in diversity from the African Violet Raisers to
the Zoological Society, from organizations in support of gun control to
the NRA itself.

Careful to chart a diplomatic path among the conflicting organizations
of dues payers, the labor movement also seeks pragmatic partners and
significant friends. Historically allied with civil rights, civil liberties, and
consumer groups, labor has recently begun to collaborate with ecological
and environmental organizations, global watch groups, peace movements, pro-democracy groups, and other agents of change. Unions were
conspicuous, for example, in the crowd, estimated at half a million, that
demonstrated for abortion choice and women's rights on April 9, 1989.

Chapter 8 explores the range of outreach services through which organized labor tries to meet its "good neighbor" responsibilities, including
efforts with the Red Cross, discussed in the case study that follows.
Another case study documents a successful effort to make better use of
a special community asset—those retired unionists who have much to
offer the labor movement and the larger community alike.

Chapter 9 hones in on a special aspect of the outreach challenge, the
high-quality educational services offered to members, staffers, and line
officers. An accompanying case study extends this principle to include
members of the Boy Scouts who are open to learning about the American
labor movement.

Together, the chapters and case studies urge overdue respect for the
community service outreach of organized labor. Having learned long ago
how to move adroitly in the minefields of community-based controversy,
especially when the rank-and-file is divided, labor strives to meet the
social needs of all Americans, whether or not they are dues-paying rank-
and-filers.

Chapter 8
Providing More Effective Service

Everything is useful which contributes to fix us in the principles and practice of virtue. When any signal act of charity or of gratitude, for instance, is presented either to our sight or our imagination, we are deeply impressed with its beauty and feel a strong desire in ourselves of doing charitable and grateful acts also.   **Thomas Jefferson, letter of advice (1771)**

In the labor movement we achieve splendid results in the transmutation of human material because we do (we must) approach our problem with the utmost faith and daring.... Trade unionism builds into the personalities of workers a sense of social concern, a willingness to make sacrifices, and a tendency toward team work and responsibility.
August Claessens, *Understanding the Worker* (1954), 21, 29

Community service remains organized labor's best-kept secret, both inside and outside the labor movement.[1] Otherwise competent labor histories, such as those by Foster Rhea Dulles (1955), Gus Tyler (1967), and, most recently, Seymour Martin Lipset (1986), do not mention the subject at all.[2] Similarly, as recently as 1985, the *AFL-CIO News*, the federation's main vehicle for communicating with its affiliates, ran an average of fewer than one article per issue on the topic. Even the highly acclaimed book *What Do Unions Do?* (1984) ignored labor's remarkable record of service to the community.[3]

There is evidence, however, that the subject is finally receiving well-warranted attention. From 1985 on, for example, the *AFL-CIO News* has steadily increased its coverage of community service activities. We now know, for example, that 260,000 requests for labor's assistance were handled in 1985, and that number is expected to reach 600,000 in 1990 (food and financial needs were first and second, with education a close third).[4] Critical agents in meeting that challenge in 1989 were 278 trained labor liaison representatives on the staff of United Way in 186 cities, 25 liaisons in Red Cross chapters across the country, and over 5,000 referral "counselors" trained to guide troubled co-workers (whether union or nonunion) to the services of appropriate community agencies.

Personal Preferences

Labor staff at United Way speak warmly about projects they helped accomplish in recent years. The following comments are drawn from interviews with unionists studying at the George Meany Center:

> We now provide six or more volunteers every Monday night to swim along with about twenty-four handicapped children.... When I saw how much good it did, and how few people were helping, I went around to the locals and asked for volunteers. Now I've got someone from AFSCME, someone from the building trades, and even a bus driver ... and we, the folks from labor, are keeping the project alive.

> Our area is the center of a six-state Rocky Mountain area that relies on us for critical medical services. We've got the biggest and best hospitals, so we have more than our share of kids in hospital beds. When we learned about the Ronald McDonald homes, we knew we needed one to house the relatives of these kids, but we did not know how to go about financing this. The building trades liked the whole idea, however, and I helped them set about raising funds and getting services volunteered (like the architect's drawings). They are building the home now, and we will have a big—I mean a *really* big—wingding when the opening occurs.

> We've got one of those "Please Touch" museums for children downtown, and it is *very* popular. They don't have much money, however, and so we found some volunteer electricians who keep the exhibits in repair and generally keep the place going.... The museum barely meets its bills, and without our union volunteers, the work just wouldn't get done at all.

Other staff members tell similar tales about successful blood drives, Boy Scout projects, first-aid education programs, and a variety of other activities.

Background

Shortly before his death in 1987, Leo Perlis, the first director of the AFL-CIO's Department of Community Services, explained in an interview that community service had always required a creative stance since no guidebook or codified tradition existed to show the way. He became head of the CIO's Community Service Committee in 1946 and brought both established and novel ideas with him to the same post with the AFL-CIO, a position he held for twenty-five years.

Perlis advocated a full partnership between labor and community agencies. He expanded the service role of unions and forged mutually rewarding alliances with the United Way, the Red Cross (see case study, page 144), the Boy Scouts (see case study, page 170), and other civic organizations. He firmly believed "we are, indeed, our brother's keeper. In our interdependent society, this, after all, is the bottom line."[5]

Of course, there were problems. Many employers failed to acknowledge the contributions workers made to United Way or plantwide blood drives. And even when an employer saw the wisdom of collaborating with organized labor, many newspaper reporters and radio and TV commentators minimized labor's involvement. The greatest challenge, however, was to improve the status of community volunteer activities within labor so service activities would receive an equitable share of labor's scarce resources, both human and financial.

Post-Perlis

Since Perlis's retirement in 1980, the department he created has expanded and upgraded its program significantly. Progress, guided by director Joe Velasquez, is demonstrable on nine major fronts:[6]

- *Direct assistance.* In the first nine months of 1988, labor liaisons answered more than 308,000 requests for food, 14,000 for financial aid, 8,000 for housing assistance, 7,000 for health care, 7,000 for job leads, and 4,000 for relief from alcohol or drug dependency.
- *Liaison network.* A grand total of 395 labor liaisons were employed in 1989, 50 more than in 1985. Many worked full time with chapters of United Way and the Red Cross, state AFL-CIO federations, and so on. Trained to provide access to services and advocacy for union members, these men and women are the backbone of labor's nationwide community services network.
- *Labor agencies.* Twenty-seven organizations existed in 1988 as nonprofit corporations under labor's control, each dedicated to serving the needs of the local labor movement. While their emphasis was on retraining projects, the labor agencies also helped the homeless, conducted preretirement classes, counseled Vietnam veterans, and trained union counselors to refer troubled rank-and-filers to appropriate community resources.
- *Union counseling.* Long considered central to community services, the counseling program includes a basic eight- to twelve-week introductory course, as well as advanced seminars and workshops. (In Bethlehem, Pennsylvania, for example, nearly sixty unionists received Red Cross training in disaster preparedness and response, covering topics

such as damage assessment, mass feeding, and the operation of a shelter.)

■ *Red Cross activities.* Two more union halls were added in 1990 to those participating in the Red Cross Disaster Coastline Project, bringing the total to 142 in eighty-five cities in thirty states. Each has phones, medical supplies, cots, and cooking equipment for use in emergencies such as hurricanes and floods. Similarly, in cooperation with city AFL-CIO labor organizations, sixty cities were targeted for special blood drives, and a 10 percent increase in blood units was achieved between 1988 and 1990. Hundreds of unionists received training in first aid, cardiopulmonary resuscitation, or safety training. And, at the request of the AFL-CIO Department of Civil Rights, blood pressure screening was done at meetings of the Coalition of Black Trade Unionists, the A. Philip Randolph Institute, and the NAACP.

■ *Conferences.* Twenty-two state-level gatherings were held in 1989 to highlight community service topics, such as responses to plant closings and ways to replace services eliminated by the Gramm-Rudman limits on federal spending. In addition, five hundred community service activists attended the 1990 AFL-CIO Department of Community Services three-day national conference.

■ *Pilot projects.* A meeting with the March of Dimes Foundation was held in 1987 to discuss ways in which that agency's Babies and You program could be applied to unions. Essentially an education and support program for future parents, it is aimed at helping women have healthy pregnancies and deliveries. Pilot programs were designed for four cities in 1987 and expanded to six in 1988.

■ *Workplace assistance.* A citywide conference launched an AIDS education project in Cleveland that focused on relieving fear and ignorance in the workplace. Soon afterward, nearly one thousand citizens were reached through small-group presentations. Similarly, almost ten thousand striking employees of the Kaiser Permanente Company received help on matters ranging from filling out applications for food stamps and for Aid for Families with Dependent Children to securing information on consumer credit, mortgages, and rent. Food was also donated for those on the twenty-four-hour picket lines and their families.

■ *Community assistance.* Union volunteers in Atlanta installed window locks in a crime-ravaged area; in Green Bay, Wisconsin, union volunteers built an outdoor play area for a nonprofit day-care center; and in North Little Rock, Arkansas, union volunteers created the world's largest sun dial as part of the state's sesquicentennial celebration.

Although this sampling is small, labor's community service activities are clearly diverse and valuable. In an era of diminished volunteerism, organized labor plays an increasingly significant role.

Labor and the United Way

The relationship between labor and the United Way is long-standing, complex, and constructive. In 1955, the newly merged AFL-CIO authorized an outreach by Leo Perlis, director of community services, to the United Community Funds and Councils of America (now the United Way). The organizations agreed to create the position of full-time AFL-CIO community services liaison and to train activists for placement in United Way offices across the country. Although United Way executives preferred that the liaisons be college educated, Perlis and his successors have insisted on hiring talented workers from the plant floor who view the role as a "calling."

In the intervening years, the relationship between labor and the United Way has grown immensely. An oft-cited study in 1967 found that when labor was involved in the annual fund-raising campaign the average contribution per employee was about 250 percent more than when solicitation was from management alone.[7]

Labor has also benefited from the relationship, particularly from the unexpected gains in "solidarity." According to Carol Kauss, a United Way labor liaison:

> To see teamsters working next to boilermakers, working next to a UAW member who was helping an AFSCME member, has meant much more to me as a trade unionist than the 225 pints of blood we collect. Then, two days later, to see these same people displaying their "I gave blood to the labor blood drive" T-shirt and again working side by side to feed the thousands of marchers from our Labor Day Parade.... To me, that's what trade unionism is all about.[8]

The personal dividend in "networking" and forging alliances across the gulf that can divide local unions is clearly profound.

Indiana as Prototype

The concrete accomplishments of the alliance between the United Way and the AFL-CIO have varied from place to place and from decade to decade, making generalizations difficult. The memories of one liaison, however, may be instructive. In an interview, B. G. (Pete) Culver, a protegée of Perlis and a key United Way liaison in the Midwest, recalled much success:

In 1948, we in the United Fund labor ranks were the first to get ordinary people convinced they should get the newfangled polio inoculations. In the early '50s, in my hometown, Terre Haute, we fought to shut down an outlying "poor farm," a disgraceful place where indigents were put to rot. The county medical society attacked us as commies, but we did not back down until the place got a reform-oriented direction. Today it is a decent rest home, thanks to our pressure and the director's skills.

In about 1953, when the returning Korean War vets were most adamantly opposed to having anything to do with the Red Cross, we helped straighten out that mess. And then our central labor body created the first "blood donor's insurance program," a plan by which you got credit for your donations and could expect to never fall short if your need was great.

Around 1958, we got a man to donate a building that we converted into a senior citizens' center. I got nineteen agencies to come in on providing services. Nineteen! Leo, my boss, a man I used to call "an angel with a union label," told me to make sure the whole community was involved.

In 1961, we raised over $500,000 for the United Way, far over our goal, and we concluded then it was time we had our own people—labor people—directly involved, rather than outside....

So today, we've got the kind of influence we deserve![9]

With a broad smile, Culver assured me that others among the hundreds of labor liaisons assigned to the United Way programs would have stories just as wonderful to tell, and he obviously took great satisfaction from this thought.

Widening the Focus: Nationwide Projects

Labor's achievements in community service are as robust today as they were twenty and thirty years ago:

■ Jerry Wright, a labor liaison with the United Way in Danville, Illinois, runs a successful pilot project (Medi-Share) that secures low-cost or free medical services for victims of plant closings. Wright has the cooperation of nearly seventy doctors, over twenty dentists, two hospitals, one major clinic, and ten drugstores. The project has assisted thirty thousand people who would otherwise have gone without adequate health services.

■ Arts Advocates in Cleveland familiarizes union volunteers with the city's many cultural resources and provides discount tickets to workers who might not otherwise take advantage of cultural opportunities.

■ A project in Orange County, California, conducts workshops led by professional clowns for union volunteers who want to learn clowning and arranges for graduates to entertain residents of area nursing homes.

■ The AFL-CIO Central Labor Council of San Bernardino and Riverside counties in California maintains a food bank that serves over three thousand families each month, without fanfare or fuss and without embarrassment to the recipients.

■ Bob Blessington has persuaded his United Way program in Wisconsin to join the state AFL-CIO in running a retraining project that includes a unique range of job-preparation skills.

Each of these programs is quite daring when seen in context. In some cases, the project was the first of its kind to be tackled by a particular cadre of labor volunteers. In all cases, the projects proved to be both novel and effective.

The "Jewel in the Crown"

Many labor activists consider their twenty-four-hour referral system for emotionally troubled workers labor's most important "social invention." Perlis believed labor could provide a vital link between workers with personal problems and mental health assistance available in the community. The link, however, was necessarily one only co-workers could provide for one another.

Originally called "union counseling," this lay referral system was initiated by the labor division of the National War Labor Board in 1942. In the years since, it has developed steadily and has grown in its appeal to shop-floor unionists with a talent for helping out. Over twenty-seven hundred rank-and-filers, for example, volunteered for training on their own time in 1988. In Chicago alone, three eight-week courses are filled annually. Shop stewards and local union officers learn about local social services, including their cost schedules, their accessibility, and even their informal reputations. They learn how to gather information about services and how to refer co-workers for help tactfully and respectfully. A required session explains the confidentiality standards that apply to all referral activities. This program, the only one of its kind, creates links that would otherwise not be forged between workers and the sources of help they need, much as Perlis envisioned and prescribed decades ago.

Other Overlooked Contributions

Any discussion of labor's robustness should include the often overlooked contributions labor makes to community services by

- assisting in both soliciting and distributing millions of dollars through United Way;
- assisting in disaster relief efforts of the Red Cross;
- bolstering community strike assistance and job loss or job response programs;
- locating and training networks of peer referral "counselors" directly in the workplace;
- attracting rank-and-filers to unpretentious seminars on AIDS in the workplace, alcohol and drug rehabilitation, abuse of the elderly, and other vital social issues; and
- rallying groups of volunteers to complete "hands-on" projects that would otherwise not be undertaken, such as revamping a senior center or upgrading a day-care site.

John McManus, assistant director of the AFL-CIO's Department of Community Services, is adamant about the importance of labor's role in community service: it is "the motherlode, this linking of alliances and compassion. . . . It is starting now to crescendo." Perlis foresaw the potential in 1975 when he advised organized labor that "community services is here to grow. It will stay and grow as long as people remain fallible and mortal. . . . [It] will occupy an ever-expanding place in the ever-new frontier of organized labor."[10]

A Word from the Skeptics

Criticisms of community service projects are of three sorts. First, some militants worry that talented local activists will be influenced by nonunion colleagues in community service and that this will undermine the cause of assertive trade unionism.

The second criticism reflects a preference for labor to create its own social service system. Many labor activists, particularly those who have traveled in Europe and Israel, raise troubling questions about labor's junior partnership in the human service system. They believe the movement would be better advised to establish its own (unionized) adoption, counseling, immigrant assistance, job retraining, and other services.

The third criticism focuses on gaps in the coverage provided by the labor liaisons. Despite efforts to monitor activities, the work of the several thousand union "counselors" is not regularly tracked at the local level, and, consequently, there are serious information gaps. Similarly, in a state like Maine, with fifty-eight thousand dues payers, there were enough resources in 1988 to support only one labor liaison, and twelve states had no labor liaisons at all.

Labor specialists doubt the risk of co-optation is great and believe labor participants are more likely to impress their community colleagues than to be overimpressed by them. They argue that emulating overseas unions, with their vast offering of social services, would prove divisive in a society where only 16 percent of the work force is unionized. In addition, the costs of emulating these unions are simply prohibitive. Finally, they note with satisfaction that groups like the New York State AFL-CIO are remedying coverage gaps: sensitive to a lack of services in some parts of that state, labor officials fund traveling liaisons known as "circuit riders" to help remedy this situation.

Summary

In *As Unions Mature,* an overlooked gem of analysis published in 1958, labor economist Richard A. Lester commented on the effort Perlis initiated to have labor branch out into new community activities. More than a hundred labor representatives were operating as full-time staff members of Community Chest and United Funds at the time, compared to 395 in 1989, and 60,000 representatives served with the Scouts, school boards, and welfare agencies, compared to over 300,000 today.[11]

Lester outlined the major reasons the AFL-CIO began to encourage such participation:

- Since rank-and-filers donated millions of dollars annually to various causes and volunteered millions of free work hours, unions were wise to systematize the contributions. Labor deserved to take some credit and use it as leverage to influence the policies of the recipients, as it did in pressuring the Red Cross to use the union "bug" on its publications and to have United Way offices and affiliates accept unionization by their employees.
- Cooperation with top management in a nonadversarial endeavor emphasized common interests and increased the social recognition and respectability of local unions and their labor leaders.
- Participation reduced the feeling that organized labor was a group apart from the community and increased reliance on unions in the community.
- Social involvement made good use of the missionary zeal of the membership by appealing to the idealism of youthful members and increasing acceptance of unions by women in the community.

After thirty-two years, Lester's analysis still remains sound. Many union activists agree substantially with his case for labor's robust involvement in community services.

Case Study
Cooperating with the Red Cross

Historians trace the relationship between organized labor and the Red Cross back to support the latter received during World War I from AFL president Samuel Gompers, who was the first labor leader to be nominated to the elite Red Cross Board of Incorporators (1923–25). Gompers's successor at the AFL, William Green, replaced him on the board in 1925, and relations at the national level have been cordial ever since.

Relations at the grass-roots level, however, were strained until the early 1940s. Major sources of controversy included "the refusal of the Red Cross to use the union label on its publications, perceptions of discrimination in distribution of relief to disaster victims, failure to adequately meet the needs of striking workers, and resentment of the appearance of an organization dominated by the socially elite."[1]

With the outbreak of World War II, the Red Cross rushed to set things right, and in 1942 it created a sensitive and constructive labor section at Red Cross national headquarters. Since then, there have been "ups and downs, twists and turns, and a few roadblocks. Despite these difficulties, the relationship has prevailed, and will continue as long as organized labor and the Red Cross share a sincere desire to work together in service to the entire community."[2]

Three ongoing projects are a source of special pride:

- *Carrier Watch:* Since the late 1970s, letter carriers, through the National Association of Letter Carriers, AFL-CIO, have monitored elderly people and invalids who are registered in the program. If there are signs they may need attention, such as uncollected mail, the letter carriers report their concern to the local Red Cross chapter.
- *Disaster Coastline Project:* Over 140 union halls in strategic locations from California to the Texas Gulf Coast to Florida have been remodeled with emergency generators and wiring to expand their communications capabilities. Union leaders have signed contracts with Red Cross chapters, which have agreed to use these buildings as administrative headquarters for disaster relief in extreme emergencies.
- *"Critical month" drives:* January and August have always been low-yield periods for Red Cross blood drives, and the problem is especially critical now because of misguided fears of contracting AIDS by donating. Labor has agreed to focus on this problem, and, while not disrupting present patterns of blood donation, it has offered to

work with unions in finding new ways to recruit and retain additional donors.

Other projects are in development, and, according to David Oliver, director of labor participation for the Red Cross, the twenty-five Red Cross liaisons recommended by the AFL-CIO and paid by the Red Cross never lack for innovative challenges.

One such challenge is an effort to broaden the base of active blood donors. The program is the brainchild of labor liaison Stan Gordon, who read that there is a shortage of less common types of blood, such as B. The health risks this shortage poses is greater for black Americans since they have a higher percentage of type B blood than do whites and it is a type that is generally in shorter supply.

Gordon outlined the ideas for a program to the national director of the Red Cross and with his approval launched the nation's first labor–Red Cross drive to encourage more blacks to donate blood. Thanks to the efforts of Red Cross–labor coordinators in forty-four cities, in August 1987, union members and their families provided 64,000 pints, or 13 percent of all the blood collected during that month. That fact gave Gordon confidence that labor could do as well, or even better, in 1988 if a strong, positive relationship could be established with labor's black brothers and sisters.

The specter of racism made the situation tense, however, and had to be confronted if the campaign was to succeed. Gordon explored all the angles with key members of the Red Cross and paid careful attention to their advice. He also reached out to the A. Philip Randolph Institute (APRI), a civil rights advocacy group long aligned with organized labor.

APRI president Norman Hill, an old friend and collaborator of Gordon's, pledged full support for the program and asked his Baltimore chapter head, Loretta Johnson, to convene the first meeting of black union leaders to assess the idea. About thirty people were invited, and when forty-five crowded into the meeting room, the sponsors were very pleased.

A full delegation of Red Cross officials, including several black staff members, explained the problem: persons such as sickle cell anemia patients and others who receive multiple transfusions need blood with certain markers, a requirement that makes matching difficult. Because proportionately fewer blacks than whites were donors, the Red Cross was looking to the black community for help in increasing the blood supply.

This analysis offended a few people in the audience, who rejected any thought that blacks had failed to meet their obligation. For a fleeting moment it looked as if the blood donor project might fall victim to offended pride before it ever really got going. Fortunately, at a critical moment, Lucious Webb, a labor liaison with the Red Cross who was well known and respected by the attendees, stepped forward and explained: "Brothers and Sisters, I've helped conduct hundreds of blood drives over the years in my job, and I will tell you, straight out, for every one hundred donors, only three or so have been black. You may not like hearing it, but that doesn't make it false.... We can do *better*. We must do better. And we will do better!"[3] When the applause died down, a small working group of volunteers was formed and the Baltimore campaign was officially opened.

Gordon and Hill expect AFL-CIO field staff, along with Gordon's Red Cross counterparts, to extend the project to Cleveland, Los Angeles, St. Louis, and Washington, D.C., all cities in which APRI has particularly strong chapters. On the basis of its success in these cities, the project will be expanded to the Red Cross's fifty-six blood-collection regions across the country. This novel effort at cooperation is critical in that the total volume of donated blood has fallen drastically since the beginning of the AIDS epidemic: blacks and whites alike will be beneficiaries of the program's success.

Cooperating with Retired Unionists

When he was more than ninety years old, Erik Erikson, one of America's most honored social psychologists, cautioned retirees against the traps of bingo, golf, and television. He urged a campaign to end policies that "doom a large segment of our population to inertia and inactivation.... The search for some way of including what [older Americans] can still contribute to the social order... is appropriate and in order."[1]

Three retired leaders of the Steelworkers would have agreed. Long-time friends who now lived in Sun City, Arizona, the trio included the late I. W. Abel, a former president of the Steelworkers; Walter Burke, the seventy-six-year-old former secretary-treasurer; and Larry Spitz, the seventy-six-year-old former subdirector of the New England region. Their success in founding a retirement organization called the Union Club highlights a resource labor is employing more and more effectively.

Labor's Uneven Record

Various unions have always sought to maintain ties with their retirees. Many, for example, send their national newspapers to emeritus members and include some news about them. Others, such as the ILGWU, IAM, IBEW, and the Sheetmetal Workers, sponsor clubs for retirees that may be underwritten by deductions from pension checks. A few especially robust unions, such as ACTWU, operate urban centers for their retired members that provide such amenities as pool tables, ceramics and knitting workshops, low-cost meals, and bus trips. In addition, the San Francisco Labor Council has pioneered in sponsoring a citywide retirees club; Connecticut's state federation has drawn about seven hundred retirees into a loosely knit organization; and about seventy retirees in the Washington, D.C., area meet monthly at the AFL-CIO George Meany Center for fellowship and mutual support.

Such experiments stand out, however, as all too rare endeavors. Many labor experts believe far too little money and staff time are allocated to retired union members, despite rapid growth in their numbers. If they conclude their locals have forgotten them, many former unionists may be lost to labor at a time when the movement cannot spare a single supporter.

Experienced Help Wanted

When the trio of former officers of the Steelworkers retired to Sun City in 1979, they were quick to agree a more energetic strategy was required if the state's several thousand union retirees were to "contribute to the social order."

So oppressive was the anti-union atmosphere in the "right-to-work" Sun Belt state of Arizona that most of the state's union retirees behaved as if they were undercover. Many kept their union membership a secret, almost as if it were a stigma, and many others were convinced that each union only took care of its own. If there was no Arizona phone number for a local of one's old international union, the retiree was just out of luck.

Larry Spitz was an exception. His phone had been busy from the time he arrived in Sun City as one after another retired union member called to ask his help in resolving problems with pension plans or mediating disputes with their unions or former employers. Word about Spitz spread through an invisible network of union retirees in Arizona who appealed to him for help. In consultation with Abel and Burke, Spitz decided to address the need for services for union retirees.

"Let's Give It a Shot!"

Spitz began by making guest appearances at Arizona locals. His fame as a morale booster spread rapidly, and he began to seek support for an organization for union retirees. At a meeting of a Phoenix local of the International Association of Bridge, Structural, and Ornamental Iron Workers, for example, members donated $725 on the spot.

With the help of his wife, Lilly, and the support of Abel and Burke, Spitz then called hundreds of labor retirees identified by the AFL-CIO and various unions. Many agreed a union retirement club sounded like a good idea and promised to attend an organizational meeting on March 23, 1979.

Eighty-five retirees made good on their promise and agreed to serve as incorporators for the club. Today, it has more than sixty-five hundred dues-paying members throughout Arizona (dues are three dollars a year for an individual; five dollars for a couple). Nearly seven hundred members in the Phoenix area regularly attend the monthly meetings of the "mother" chapter, the Sun City club, which boasts eighteen hundred members. Some thirteen other union clubs in Arizona are in various stages of development, all guided by the original Sun City operation.

Contrary to those who warned that workers from different unions would not join an amalgamated organization, the club now has members from eighty-seven different unions. Indeed, members represent virtually every industrial job and craft, as well as scores of professions.

Since its start in 1979, the Union Club has steadily expanded its services to encompass the concerns of the local and the national labor movement, of all retirees (whether from labor's ranks or otherwise), and of the sixty-five hundred dues payers in the club itself. Service to organized labor, for instance, includes a variety of activities:

■ a speakers' program that carries the message of the labor movement to the community, especially to high school students who will soon enter the labor force;
■ assistance in union organizing drives, including speakers at locals throughout Arizona who help raise morale and stimulate pro-labor attitudes;
■ advice to unions trying to negotiate improvements in benefits for retirees;
■ busloads of backers at Arizona AFL-CIO rallies, such as those held during the bitter and bloody Phelps-Dodge copper strike in 1987 and during crucial votes of the legislature;
■ letters to newspaper editors calling for repeal of Arizona's "right-to-work" law and advocacy of pro-labor policies; and
■ a free pamphlet that explains how to start an organization of retired trade unionists.

The Union Club also aids fellow activists, such as Cesar Chavez, by providing a speakers' platform, an audience of several hundred, extensive television and press coverage, and cash donations, which amounted to $1,200 for Chavez.

Burke and Spitz are especially proud of the club's concern for retirees in general. At their first meeting, the members resolved to fight for the repeal of a state sales tax on food. After forging an alliance with progressive churches and social welfare organizations, the club lobbied the Arizona legislature so effectively that in 1980 the lawmakers abolished the regressive food tax. The club continues to gain allies inside and outside the Arizona legislature in its continuing campaign to have the first $10,000 of pension income exempted from state taxation. In addition, the club reviews existing and proposed Arizona legislation for its possible impact on retirees and, when necessary, lobbies the state legislature for improvements.

This sort of pro bono work on behalf of everyone over the age of sixty-five has earned praise from anti-labor newspapers and influential figures throughout Arizona, which is widely known as an arch-conservative state. The club has also won many expressions of gratitude from older citizens throughout Arizona.

Above all, the club works to meet the special needs of its members:

■ A consumer repair committee provides retired repair people as unpaid consultants to members, especially those with high bills for home improvements or repairs or for auto maintenance.

■ A consumer's list provides names of professionals and repair people recommended by club members for performing good work at fair prices.

■ An environmental committee checks into water, ground, and air pollution hazards of concern to members.

■ A welfare committee assists members who are ill and helps arrange transportation, shopping services, and drop-in visits.

■ A sixty-five-member telephone committee calls hundreds of members each month to check how they are doing, providing a valuable barometer of needs and a list of the names of ill members for the welfare committee.

Spitz continues to provide personal interviews, make hundreds of phone inquiries, and handle correspondence on problems with pension plans, Social Security, and Medicare. The help and comfort Union Club members offer one another in times of grief and loss is especially moving. Spitz explains: "We have found, particularly in our early stages, that some women did not even know how to write a check or drive a car. Their husbands had taken care of those things all their lives, and suddenly the wife was left on her own. That person had been left absolutely adrift."[2] Spitz adds that the help and understanding of women on the welfare committee remains invaluable.

Gray Power

Initially shunned by political candidates in a notoriously anti-union region, the club is now courted assiduously by candidates from both major parties. The club also takes strong positions on volatile local matters. In 1988, for example, Arizona lawmakers were urged to pass

■ a rent-control law for tenants of mobile homes;
■ a resolution that would establish an Arizona Department of Aging; and
■ legislation modeled on an American Bar Association draft to encourage the establishment of board and care homes as a less expensive alternative to nursing homes.

Recommendations were also made to national lawmakers regarding issues such as those the AFL-CIO champions for all retirees, including passage of a comprehensive health plan.

Among its many roles, the club now serves as an educator, a consciousness raiser, a clarifier of issues, and a forum for personal views.

Union membership, once concealed in Arizona, has been elevated to a badge of honor. Equally important, the club helps many retirees reaffirm lifelong ties to the labor movement.

The Founders' Responses

I. W. Abel felt the club worked out far better than he ever expected. His original intention had been to meet occasionally to "schmooze" with some old-timers and once in a while to express their views in a hard-hitting "letter to the editor." None of the three founders expected their newfangled idea to "just run wild" and accomplish all it has.

Walter Burke was comparably enthusiastic: "The idea is a tremendous one! It is a phenomenal thing! Cats that normally stand and spit at one another actually cooperate, with no bickering, even over broad policy." Burke remains especially pleased with the club's impact on the Arizona legislature: "We rattle the cage of nincompoops making laws." He also takes pride in the promotion of women into key posts: "It's Larry's doing. Left to their own devices, the brothers would not promote women."

Burke would like to see the AFL-CIO "go out and find lots like Spitz and send such men out to Florida and California to create similar clubs, because the retirees there are just like here, an untapped treasure-trove! A real powerhouse! But unless they are soon organized they can forget their roots and whence they came!"

Larry Spitz agrees organized labor makes a major mistake when it expects little from its retirees and loses contact with them:

> The labor movement badly neglected its most important and potentially most loyal group of allies, its retirees. At best, it gave token recognition to this group, and it is paying a price for this neglect.... We have apparently had enough impact on the AFL-CIO Executive Council to prompt a number of discussions regarding recapturing the retired union members.... This shows a heightened recognition that what we are attempting in Arizona is most meaningful, as a resource, to the labor movement elsewhere.[3]

The Union Club experience suggests retirees across the country remain an important source of versatile and committed support for labor.

Spitz comments, "Apparently we're doing something right. Our members are intellectually alert, attentive, and a vocal audience. For the past five years we haven't had less than 650 people at any meeting!"

Beyond Arizona

Unfortunately, the Union Club has not been replicated in many other retirement communities. Challenged by this unwelcome isolation, Burke and Spitz continue to lobby on behalf of their idea with top AFL-CIO officials and with the leadership of the Steelworkers, the only union that makes regular monthly contributions to the club.

Until the Union Club model is recreated wherever union retirees congregate, its potential service to labor will remain unrealized. In a country growing older all the time, robust retirees deserve all the backing they need, especially from the labor movement many of them are still able and available to assist.[4]

Chapter 9
Labor Education

Sit down and read. Educate yourself for the coming conflicts.
Mother Jones, in Bollen,
A Handbook of Great Labor Quotations (1983), 33

What do I want from workers' education? I want it to teach me the truth about our economic system, our government, laws, customs, and traditions. I want workers' education to give me that which no other educational institution has given me since I first entered the public schools, and which I cannot obtain anywhere else.
Nettie Silverbrook (1928) in Kornbluh,
A New Deal for Workers' Education (1987), 3

Labor education is a dynamic enterprise, thanks to new technology, the professionalization of many practitioners, and the diversity of options available, including study on campus or off, as a participant or an observer, for one day or several years. This chapter focuses on three dimensions of labor education: programs that award degrees, including those at the Meany Center, in which I have participated for the past twelve years; AFL-CIO and other union education programs for members; and, finally, union-sponsored projects for nonunionists. Education is considered elsewhere in this book as well, in references to classroom exercises as an integral part of cooperative union-management efforts (chapter 1), accident-reduction efforts (chapter 2), health-promotion efforts (chapter 3), and so on. Clearly, this chapter provides only a partial treatment of a vast and many-sided topic.

Background

For nearly forty years, from its formation in 1886 through the early 1920s, the AFL withheld support for workers' education largely because of its distrust of middle-class intellectuals and left-wing activists. Several major unions, however, took the initiative. The ILGWU and the Amalgamated Clothing Workers of America (ACWA), for example, emphasized social change, industrial unionism, and the assimilation of foreign-born members. Courses in English and citizenship skills were particularly popular. More conservative trade unions sponsored classes that promoted a "craft culture" of sobriety, hard work, respectability, and solidarity.[1]

A spurt of union growth during World War I stimulated workers' education programs, and the ILGWU and ACWA pioneered in the creation of education departments. Between 1918 and 1921, several city labor federations linked forces with colleges and universities to initiate evening classes for adult workers. By 1921, as many as seventy-five worker "colleges" were offering classes in economics, law, speaking, writing, and other subjects.

The Workers' Education Bureau (WEB) was created in 1921, with approval and funding from the AFL, as a national clearinghouse for educational activities. Affiliates joined rapidly, and WEB served for decades as an agent of educational innovation. Its pamphlets on union administration, labor history, and the shop steward were praised in the mid–1930s as "the first serious and sustained attempt to give authentic recognition to the thinking worker."[2]

Also in 1921, the California Federation of Labor persuaded the University of California at Berkeley to establish the nation's first labor extension service. Within a very few years, similar programs had been started by Syracuse University, Harvard, MIT, Tufts, Amherst, the University of Cincinnati, and the University of Oklahoma. Although they were considered controversial, the programs were only mildly reformist and focused on the organizational needs of upright unions, excluding discussion of fundamental social change or industrial unionism.

This cautiousness was dramatically challenged between 1933 and 1942 by the first nationwide, federally supported adult education program in the United States. Known as the New Deal Emergency Education Program (EEP), it helped nearly a million workers attend workers' education classes in thirty-four states. Study focused on social issues, working conditions, and workplace reforms. Described by Mark Starr, a leading labor educator, as "the greatest impetus ever given to workers' education in the United States," the EEP had two major goals: the enhancement of critical thinking skills and the improvement of labor leadership.[3]

The EEP had a lasting impact because it made unions aware, many for the first time, of the need for ongoing, innovative educational programming. It introduced teaching techniques such as role playing, field trips, participant observation, self-governing committees, and panel discussions. The right of union representatives to participate in all educational plans concerning their members was emphasized, and the EEP established a tenet that educational institutions had a responsibility to serve employed as well as jobless workers. As Starr notes, overall, the EEP "played a crucial role in the transition from the multiple and frequently amorphous goals of earlier attempts to educate adult workers to a concept of labor education that serves the learning needs of workers in the context of their union institutions."[4]

Controversial throughout its existence, and mistrusted by some labor leaders because it was created by New Deal "outsiders," the EEP became a casualty of a profound shift in the American focus in the late 1930s. With war approaching, America's politics shifted to the right and the concept of workers' education was altered by ultrapatriotic motives. Focus was diverted from reform and social concerns to programs aimed at improving civilian morale and stimulating workers to support the war effort. Certain conservative AFL leaders who had always been hostile to EEP efforts to empower the rank-and-file breathed a sigh of relief. Many new CIO unions, however, hired former EEP teachers to head their new education divisions.

Labor education grew rapidly with the war industry boom. Many publicly funded state colleges, believing labor could influence the budget decisions of lawmakers, established labor extension programs of considerable scope and value. Between the late 1940s and the late 1960s, however, the fundamental purpose of labor education was questioned. Critics attacked the programs for training union officers only in the skills of their craft:

> Such training is clearly necessary, but it is not sufficient. The virtual absence of courses which seek to develop an understanding of how society functions, and the working class' role within it, reflects a view of the world by the leaders of organized labor which requires the fullest debate.... Labor education curricula must include these wider issues or be faced with the charge of irrelevance or, even worse, neglect of the values on which trade unions were founded.[5]

Curricula gradually appeared that understood labor itself to be a legitimate subject for study and sought to educate the whole person, rather than merely train the functionary.[6]

Not surprisingly, controversy persists. Some critics dismiss the "whole-person" approach as woolly-headed and favor a return to a more traditional labor union outlook.[7] Other critics condemn the "whole-person" approach for undermining class consciousness and dampening discontent.[8] Labor leadership continues to be divided, and this division contributes to the low and uncertain level of financial and resource support received by union and related education ventures.[9]

Universities and Workers' Education

One typical labor education experiment was the Economic Literacy Project conducted between 1983 and 1986 by a Boston College team in collaboration with the Massachusetts AFL-CIO. Locals of five major unions (AFT, ILGWU, SEIU, UAW, and the Marine and Shipbuilding Workers) were invited to participate.

The project rejected as antiquated the notion that management alone should conduct strategic economic planning, industrial development, and revitalization projects. That pattern, said project leader Charles Derber, relegated workers and their unions "to a largely passive role, buffeted by management decisions and confined to a position of reaction, rather than proactive participation and planning."[10] In contrast, the Economic Literacy Project sought to empower unionists by giving them access to knowledge previously reserved for management, such as information about global production and market trends, technological developments, and changes in educational requirements for desirable jobs.

Two assumptions guided the project and set it apart from traditional retraining programs:

■ universities and labor needed a new partnership that would provide labor with the analytical tools and information traditionally offered to managers; and
■ universities and labor needed a new social curriculum that would "stretch labor's sense of its capacities and rights to chart its own economic destiny."[11]

The ultimate goal was to help local unions design strategies for enhancing competitiveness in order to preserve and revitalize local industries.

According to Derber, events confirmed the soundness of the strategy and validated his assumptions:

I am totally convinced workers are ripe for this sort of approach. They have a huge storehouse of knowledge about their jobs and industry, but it goes unutilized. Our five-local project made plain how vital it is to provide ways to help this knowledge come out, to help workers crystallize their views and formulate strategies for renewing their industries.... They are capable of this, provided we in education lend a hand.[12]

Although one of the locals (the Marine and Shipbuilding Workers) fell victim to a total shutdown, another (the ILGWU) graduated from the three-year Boston College project able to help reconceptualize industry prospects in New England. It is now a pivotal player in a $200,000 state government industry-recovery program.

Looking back in 1988 with two years' experience, Derber could think of many ways in which the program could have been improved. Progress was slowed by the enormous amount of time required to win labor's trust, the suddenness with which local officers could be replaced, and the formalities required because of labor's penchant for doing things "the right way." Nevertheless, the accomplishments of the program were significant:

> Work with the Boston teachers' union has helped the union develop an educational program on the social and technical implications—for teachers, students, and the process of education itself—of the increasing use of computers in the schools. A project team is working with the Service Employees Union in Boston to implement a skills assessment, development, and training program for union members whose career mobility seems blocked in city hospital and other municipal settings. For two years, the project has also worked with a UAW local on the broad kinds of technical, economic, and organizational knowledge its members will require to keep their assembly plant competitive.[13]

"Our experience," Derber concludes, "suggests that unions, under auspicious circumstances, will recognize the need for ["economic literacy"] training, and will participate actively in innovative programs."[14]

Another example of an inventive relationship between a university and labor education is the Antioch University degree-granting program at the AFL-CIO's Meany Center for Labor Studies in Silver Spring, Maryland. Established in 1977 as a unique "college of the second chance," the Antioch–Meany Program "gives busy union officers and staff members an opportunity to earn a Bachelor of Arts degree in the area of their greatest interest—Labor Studies—while they continue with their trade union work." More than thirty adults begin annually, each recognizing that "the program is not suited to every individual. It requires self-discipline and perseverance over several years."[15]

In its relatively short history, the program has awarded degrees to 152 students after two or more years of study, and over 220 individuals from fifty-five unions in thirty-seven states and Canada are now enrolled. Each student visits the center every six months for a week of classes, including daily written assignments. Between these visits, students are expected to do 150 hours of research and writing for each five-credit course.

The program has four innovative features:[16]

■ Although they are tailored for a thirty-nine-year-old average learner, the courses are "generally executed with the sort of rigor and finesse that have come to be associated with corporate training centers for budding managers."[17]

■ College credit is given for competencies gained through work and union experience, completion of an apprenticeship, noncredit labor education programs of five or more courses, and passage of college-level examinations.

■ Time is reserved for informal small-group learning that takes place in a popular bar on campus, in dorm lounges, and in a prize-winning campus cafeteria.

■ New courses are added regularly on a trial basis, and student response influences whether the course is repeated, revised, or replaced.

Responses to a survey completed in 1987 by sixty-two alumni, whose average age was forty-six, offers revealing data: Two out of three did not think they would have earned a college degree without the program, and 86 percent felt more confident of their abilities as a result of completing it. No less than 93 percent felt the knowledge they had acquired helped them represent their membership more effectively. When asked the most important feature of the program, 60 percent praised the spirit of the center, the relationships formed, and the contacts established. And 92 percent said they would strongly recommend the program to others.[18]

Graduates' written comments were especially informative:

I was too old and "experienced" to consider returning to college with so many young people and new methods. But at the Labor Studies Center I was in the company of peers.

The reason I did not finish the first time was I was unsure as to a major. The ability to learn more about an area I live, eat, breathe, and love was never a chore.

This is the best—union people educating union people. My union membership has made it possible for me to earn living wages, get an education, and own a home. I have no problem serving it, or promoting this program.

A must! If we are going to make it in the 1990s and beyond, education is the only way!...Just think, if most business agents had the scope of knowledge presented at the center, we could get it all back!

It is hardly surprising that both the enrollment and the morale of staff and students are at record highs.

The Center for Worker Education (CWE) is an excellent example of a robust university-based labor education program. Created in 1980 by an alliance of the City University of New York (CUNY) and a unique citywide coalition of union locals, CWE offers both bachelor's and master's degrees and provides degree candidates with educational, career, and financial counseling.[19]

CWE also offers other services that address the diversity of New York City–area union members:

- literacy and high school degree programs;
- work-related two-year associate degree programs that provide preparation for entirely new jobs;
- a research facility focused on worker productivity and economics; and
- job training that is flexible enough to take advantage of employment opportunities and economic trends as they arise.

Once a semester, faculty and students of CWE assess all four components of the program and explore future developments.

CWE has pioneered in its strategies for addressing the grave problem of basic literacy:

- It encouraged labor to create the Consortium for Worker Literacy (CWL), a reform group with a single focus. Representing eight locals and over 300,000 members, CWL began research in 1985. Based on this research, it estimated that 50 percent of its constituency was illiterate in English and another 300,000 spouses and children over the age of sixteen needed help with reading skills.
- CWE staff members then taught CWL locals how to seek out members and dependents in need of help in becoming literate, rather than simply responding to the needs of those who came forward.
- Labor persuaded the New York State Department of Education to fund CWL's administrative expenses and the New York City Board of Education to pay teachers' salaries and provide staff for literacy project research and evaluation.

CWE continues to demonstrate to shop stewards and business agents that educational recruitment and retention are as important as grievance arbitration if union leaders wish to meet "their responsibility to their membership."

CWE is based on four premises, each of which departs from conventional wisdom about labor education programs:

- Programs should be preventive rather than reactive in focus. In contrast to government retraining programs that commonly exclude employed workers, the CWE program helps workers maintain their current jobs or retrain for new ones before job loss.

■ Programs should be tailored to union members by ensuring that teachers are sensitive to their students' struggles and their need for respect, by developing peer teaching and a buddy-support system, and by selecting congenial sites for classes, such as union halls, factories, housing projects, and churches.

■ Curricula should be organized around specific job skills, using job manuals to motivate improvements in reading comprehension, vocabulary, and other language arts skills.

■ CWE should work with the City University of New York to develop research on questions of direct concern to the program, such as whether shop stewards can be effective as paraprofessional teachers in introductory literacy classes.

As one striking measure of CWE's success, by 1987, its activities comprised one-third of all adult education classes provided by the New York City Board of Education.[20]

An assessment of a different type was offered in a newsletter published by UAW Local 259: "Students describe how they are beginning to speak up at union meetings, how they can now talk to their boss and the landlord and the doctor, how the classes give them a greater feeling of self-confidence, how proud their families are of their achievement." Later in the same article the local's officers note that "the program is a labor of love for our union, and we are committed to expand it."[21]

Nick Browne, a student of CWE and CWL, has offered a broad assessment and prognosis:

> Both programs are innovative and risky first steps in the assumption of entirely new responsibilities for unions. If taken to its logical conclusion, this will result in a new definition of the union role and a redefinition of its responsibilities to its membership.... Labor, in general, will have taken a gigantic stride toward resuming the large, day-to-day role in the lives of their membership that they once enjoyed ... [and] labor will regain a great deal of public good will, and refurbish a public image that has been, at times, less than glittering.[22]

Labor has demonstrated its ability to address the grave problem of basic education, which is essential in a society where "the grade level of literacy performance is going to have to go up about seven grades in the next twelve years." If CWE's example were to spread from coast to coast, labor would once again fulfill its traditional duty to members, "protecting their interests, not only in matters that exist, but in matters that will be."[23]

AFL-CIO and Union Projects

The ways in which labor is working on its own to address educational needs are equally impressive. The Meany Center is one example. In 1974, the AFL-CIO purchased a college campus in Silver Spring, Maryland, for $2.5 million and spent another $4 million to refurbish it. The center was intended to be a "cauldron for new ideas and an incubator for the movement's next generation of leaders." Yet its opening had been opposed for nearly twenty years after the 1955 merger of the AFL and CIO, according to the center's present executive director, Robert J. Pleasure, because labor education was perceived "as perhaps too ideological and not fitting the practical philosophy of a very practical labor movement." Pleasure himself has been characterized by the *New York Times* as a man who "talks passionately about the labor movement's need to educate future leaders."[24]

In the 1988–89 academic year, the center offered sixty-eight labor studies institutes and workshops (fourteen dealing with communications skills, thirteen with organizing, eleven with arbitration, and eight with negotiations). Included were twenty-two programs, characterized as "Union Building," that dealt with union leadership, labor law, issues facing labor today, and labor education. Over 51,000 unionists have taken such courses since 1974, and 5,340 attended in the 1988–89 year alone. (About 2,000 came for center offerings and another 3,000 for programs run at the center by their own unions.)

The center has been innovative in a number of ways:

- New courses are tested, improved, and then made available for transfer to union education departments. Two recent examples are courses in using microcomputers in negotiations and in survey research.
- Conferences on topical issues are rapidly convened, professionally executed, and quickly publicized through the labor press.
- Generic courses no single union could offer promote the cross-fertilization of ideas and the development of broader personal contacts. One perennial favorite is the new staff program, designed to improve the planning and personal skills of first-year union employees. Similarly, departments of the AFL-CIO offer advanced seminars at the center for workers from any union.

Through its combination of pragmatism and vision, the center encourages the belief that labor is "with it, on top of it, and helping to shape it," as one workshop member explained.

Among the center's facilities is a computer laboratory that is a "high-tech one-room schoolhouse." According to instructor Chuck Hodell, the lab is a joint venture of the AFL-CIO Human Resources Development Institute (HRDI), the Meany Center, and the AFL-CIO Department of Education. Equipped with union-made Zenith personal computers, it enables labor to test the Comprehensive Competencies Program (CCP), a "high-tech/high-touch" approach to basic skills mastery, leased from a major educational services firm.

Strategically placed where it is accessible to a variety of students, the lab at the Meany Center has four goals beyond testing CCP's utility for rank-and-filers:

■ to survey union-sponsored basic skills programs for purposes of comparison so that unions can learn from one another's experiences and profit from shared knowledge;

■ to collect outstanding instructional materials (particularly educational software) that strengthen the math and reading competencies of adult learners;

■ to develop customized educational software for use in labor education and to pilot ways of using personal computers to support the labor movement; and

■ to upgrade apprenticeship training and use to good advantage the experiences of labor's community of apprentices.

Lab instructors report an "incredible growing interest," especially when visitors learn the Meany Center lab shares insights with 285 similar CCP operations across the country.

The institute, which began by creating $30,000 computer-aided learning labs nationwide, then arranged for their transfer to eager state union operations. The "package"—a new learning setting, computer-aided instruction, and integrated CCP software—has seven innovative features:

■ CCP is individualized and self-paced; rank-and-filers can focus on their specific needs and take as much time as necessary to achieve mastery.

■ Progress is based on mastery of clearly stated learning objectives, rather than vague goals.

■ Learners advance and complete tasks as rapidly as they attain mastery; there are no artificial restraints on where one may seek personal challenge.

■ A variety of instructional options are offered, including print, audio-visual, and experience-based supplemental activities.

- Assigned materials contain mastery checks for each lesson to track progress, check retention, and pinpoint areas needing attention.
- CCP software provides test results instantaneously while storing data, such as the time spent on tasks, for quick and easy access.
- CCP learners take primary responsibility for learning activities. According to its developer, U.S. Basics, "This increases learners' sense of accomplishment and level of commitment, leaving teachers to concentrate on providing one-on-one help whenever it is needed."[25]

CCP provides instruction in areas ranging from basic literacy to apprentice training, from English as a second language (ESL) to labor history, for an average of only seven dollars per instructional hour (in 1987). It is remarkably popular with users: 90 percent would recommend it to others, and 75 percent like it better than they did their last regular school program.[26]

Rhode Island's Institute for Labor Studies and Research

State organizations such as Rhode Island's Institute for Labor Studies and Research (ILSR) provide distinctive educational services at a level between that of the AFL-CIO and specific unions. A private, nonprofit institution guided by a board of Rhode Island union leaders, the institute was founded in 1980 to redress a serious imbalance in public education. As one of its many pamphlets explains, "While there are many programs for management education, there are few for labor education. The Institute's programs and services provide leadership training, self-improvement skills, research, and technical assistance to all segments of organized labor and the community at large."[27]

The institute has provided training for the members of scores of Rhode Island locals, and participation has grown from about four hundred individuals in 1980–81 to nearly two thousand in 1989–90.[28]

In addition to offering such standard educational services as noncredit training for stewards, instruction in conducting effective meetings, and courses in the legal rights of stewards and dealing with the NLRB, ILSR provides some unusual offerings:

- Each year, the institute conducts literacy classes (English as a second language, high school equivalency, and adult basic education) at about seven unionized work sites. Of the more than two hundred unionists who participate, the majority are women and immigrants and nearly one-third are minority group members.
- In 1989–90, fifteen unions contracted with the institute to conduct customized training for their leadership and stewards in contract administration and related issues.

■ The institute's Labor in the Schools project has distributed over five thousand copies of a brochure for high school students, entitled *Your Rights on the Job*. It explains labor laws that pertain to teenagers, including their right to join or form a union. In addition, a curriculum guide, *Working in Rhode Island: Past and Present*, is being distributed to all social studies teachers in the state.

■ Through an arrangement with Rhode Island College, the institute offers college-level labor studies courses at its own offices. The institute also provides scholarships for union members who want to attend these or any of its programs.

■ The institute produces "RI LaborVision," which is seen on all cable TV channels in the state. The three-hour-a-week show features locally produced videos and labor news programming as well as award-winning films, such as *Union Maids, Harlan County,* and *Salt of the Earth*.

■ The institute co-sponsors the state's only annual conference on labor-management relations, at which a variety of views are aired and assessed.

Clearly, this small operation in our smallest state has a robust agenda.

Educational Efforts by Unions

For the past two years, I have joined several thousand public school teachers, paraprofessionals, and clerks for a two-day annual conference entitled "Programs for Teaching." Sponsored by the Health and Welfare Fund of Local 3, AFT, in Philadelphia, the conference in 1989, for example, included 225 workshops. Classroom teachers focused on creating a school environment in which learning takes place, reducing family violence, assessing the literature-based elementary classroom, relating to lesbian and gay youth, and using statistics to advantage. Other workshops addressed such occupational interests as office automation, special education services in mainstream classes, and time management strategies for school counselors. Labor studies was featured in a dramatization of the life of Mother Jones and in workshops on the U.S. labor movement and on problems of labor in Central America.

AFT members emphasize the boost the conference gives to their sense of professionalism. They are especially proud that labor is responsible for the event and that rank-and-filers lead most of the workshops. With its extraordinary diversity of offerings, the AFT conference demonstrates both the commitment of individual teachers to their union and the contributions of their union in organizing the event.

A very different educational service is provided by the UAW through its paid educational leave program (PEL) for auto workers. Jointly sponsored since its inception in 1983 by the UAW and General Motors' Human Resource Center, the program has developed curricula for local UAW officials throughout the country in economic literacy and the government process. Well-known academics, government leaders, and practitioners provide students with a better understanding of the global economy, the changing position of the U.S. auto industry, and new roles and options for organized labor here and abroad.

PEL participants Barry Bluestone, an economist at Boston University, and Charles Derber, a sociologist at Boston College, feel the program demonstrates that local officers can grasp esoteric matters when they are properly presented. According to Bluestone and Derber, more than four hundred grass-roots UAW leaders have begun to champion new reform ideas as a result of the program.[29]

Labor and Public Education Outreach

Labor has also offered educational services to people outside its ranks. In June 1988, for example, the American Postal Workers Union completed a historical preservation effort it began in 1968. At that time, the union purchased and donated an old postal service bus to the Smithsonian Institution's National Museum of American History. The bus had been used from 1941 to 1960 and had been "retired" when mail service by rail was curtailed. After being neglected in storage at the Smithsonian for twenty years, the bus was finally restored to its original glory in 1988, thanks to a grant from the union. After one last commemorative enactment of its route, the bus was retired in a colorful ceremony held at the Smithsonian. Former highway postal clerks provided tales of the bus's adventures during its nineteen years of service, and labor singer Joe Glazer sang about the life and times of highway postal workers.[30]

Job Corps

Since its founding in 1965, the Job Corps has provided down-to-earth job preparation for young people between the ages of sixteen and twenty-one. Seven major unions offer classes and find apprenticeships for youngsters trained at the 105 Job Corps centers across the country. In 1986, 106,000 trainees were enrolled, most of them high school dropouts, and 34,000 graduated. Of these, 70 percent were members of minority groups and 31 percent were female.

Unions have played a critical role in the development of innovative Job Corps programs:

- The International Union of Bricklayers and Allied Craftsmen has been involved in forty-four Job Corps programs nationwide through the joint labor-management International Masonry Institute, which teaches tile-setting, stone masonry, plastering, and bricklaying skills.
- The UAW program in Clearfield, Utah, attracts more than 240 students annually from across the country for advanced automotive training.
- The Transportation-Communication Employees Union offers eight programs, including instruction in accounting, clerical skills, data entry, and on-board steward service and commissary work, with the goal of placing students in jobs with the railroads.
- The Operative Plasterers' and Cement Masons' International Association participates in thirty-five programs involving over fifteen hundred Job Corps members who are trained in the skills of casting ornamental cement figures, stamping concrete, and producing styrofoam lettering.
- Trades taught by the International Union of Operating Engineers include the operation and repair of heavy equipment and surveying.
- Students in a program run by the International Brotherhood of Painters and Allied Trades receive instruction in drywall finishing, floor covering, glazing, painting, and sign-making.
- A year-long program of the United Brotherhood of Carpenters and Joiners features form-building, framing, drywall application, finish carpentry, and cabinet-making.

Strongly opposed to recent federal reductions in Job Corps allocations, the AFL-CIO continues to emphasize that the national economy gets $1.48 back on every dollar spent on the Job Corps.[31]

Labor Drama

"The Greatest Stories Never Told—Voices from the New American Workplace," a play co-produced in Los Angeles by the AFL-CIO's Labor Institute for Public Affairs and the Mark Taper Forum, premiered in 1987. One of many theater projects backed by labor in recent years, the production grew out of a ten-week workshop designed to give voice to the concerns of service sector workers. Thirteen members of nine AFL-CIO unions contributed time and experience to the project. Thomas Donahue, AFL-CIO secretary-treasurer, summarized its message to the opening-night audience: "The single most important issue of the service sector is ... dignity."[32]

A similar awareness motivates UAW Local 735 (Canton, Michigan) to use its Workers' Concept Theatre (WCT) to raise consciousness about social issues plaguing American workers. The aim of WCT is to create labor theater that speaks not only to workers but to entire communities. Some of the original scripts dramatize the human costs of layoffs and plant closings. Others portray significant events in labor history, such as the 1987 Hormel meatpackers strike, dramatized in "Sit Down '36" and "Jake's Brain," or the famous 1937 sitdown strike, recreated in "When You Strike Flint. . . ."

Touring union halls and high schools with its productions, WCT played to five thousand rank-and-filers and another five thousand teenagers in 1988 alone. Productions included the musical "Take Care," featuring about fifty unionists from District 1199, National Union of Hospital and Health Care Employees; "Lady Beth: The Steelworkers' Play"; and "Steel Town," a musical performed by the San Francisco Mime Troupe. WCT director Shaun Nethercott, who is familiar with workers' theater of the 1930s, believes labor theater can "spearhead a new dimension of unionism, encouraging all to examine their own lives as a source of art, and to recognize that theater is not an activity reserved for the few who now attend."[33]

A Word from the Skeptics

Those who question the effectiveness of labor's educational efforts note that little careful evaluation has been done, partly because the criteria for judging impact are ill defined and partly because neither time nor money has been allocated for such research. Defensiveness and disinterest in union ranks have also discouraged evaluation.

On the positive side, assessment workshops conducted at the annual meeting of the University and College Labor Education Association are increasingly well attended, and publications such as *Labor Studies Journal* contain a growing number of careful assessments of union educational efforts. For example:

■ An evaluation published in 1986 of the five-day Southern School for Union Women was based on a survey sent to nearly 150 women who attended in 1982 and 1983. It concluded the respondents "clearly felt the Southern School heightened their commitment to the labor movement, and gave them some tools to act on that commitment."[34]

■ A study published in 1988 of a 1983–85 CWA three-week training program in self-development for minorities used experimental assessment techniques to focus on the transfer of learning, along with external criteria to validate perceptions of trainees; overall, the program came out very well.[35]

■ An evaluation of the experiences of forty-one women enrolled in an Ohio apprenticeship program of the Brotherhood of Carpenters was published in 1988. Using statistical analysis, the study found the women were "strongly interested in, and supportive of the union, displaying more enthusiasm than their male peers in some areas."[36]

Many labor activists agree "resistance to evaluation of our training activities must be overcome.... This is essential in increasing the probability [that] the millions of dollars collected from union dues will be well spent."[37]

A second line of skeptical inquiry asks whether scarce resources are really being allocated for union education or whether support is basically limited to good intentions.[38] Evidence mounts, however, that unions are providing increasing financial backup:

■ At the 1988 IAM convention, the $2 million cap was removed on the amount of interest income from the strike fund ($91.5 million) that can be used for the IAM Education Center at Placid Harbor, in southern Maryland. The change means the union will pay travel expenses, as well as room and board, for members using the center.[39]

■ Reaffiliation of the Teamsters with the AFL-CIO in 1988 enabled that union to exhibit at the annual Union-Industries Show (New Orleans, May 4–8), where its booth, one of the show's largest, prominently saluted labor education.[40]

Although examples never constitute "proof," these support a cautious optimism regarding the increasing value many robust unions place on labor education.

Finally, skeptics wonder whether labor education will ever be the equal of corporate education. Certainly, there are encouraging examples that labor is coming into its own:

■ Since 1984, the Labor Education Service at the University of Minnesota, through its Union Leadership Academy, has taken 520 unionists from twenty-three unions in thirteen states through a situational leadership program that is fresh, demanding, and rewarding.[41]

■ Since 1961, the Department of Labor Education at Rutgers University's Institute of Management and Labor Relations has taken more than two hundred New Jersey unionists from over sixty unions through a six-week labor internship program; participants meet state Department of Labor personnel to exchange ideas, share concerns, and discuss controversial issues in a nonadversarial way.[42]

■ Since 1982, the UAW-GM Skills Development and Training Program has helped over 250,000 auto workers receive a total of more than 24 million hours of "joint training in job-related technical skills, basic education enhancement, and interpersonal and communication skills."[43]

■ The Sunday *New York Times* column "Where We Stand," by AFT president Albert Shanker, conveys to union and nonunion readers alike the insightful and creative approach of labor leadership.

■ The prestigious Harvard Trade Union Program, created in 1942, brings as many as thirty local union officers and staff members together every year for an intensive ten-week session entitled "Preparing Leadership for the Challenges of the Future."

Many other programs deserve mention, including those at the Steelworkers' educational campus in Linden Hall, Pennsylvania; the UAW's programs at their Blacklake, Michigan, educational center; and the IAM programs at the Placid Harbor Education Center in Hollywood, Maryland.

Summary

Unions are making an enormous investment in educational programs for their members and for the general public. Each year well over twenty-five thousand members attend residential institutes, and over sixty thousand shop stewards and local union officers attend seminars for a weekend or longer.[44] Labor is also focusing, particularly through the AFL-CIO Department of Education, on getting its message into primary and secondary schools.[45] Augmenting these contributions, the federation's Labor Institute on Public Affairs creates TV shows, video specials, and pioneering teleconferences. Controversial from the outset, labor education, buttressed now by a history of substantial achievement, appears ready to assume even greater significance in the 1990s.

Case Study
A New Boy Scouts Merit Badge

A union project does not need to be large scale or expensive to be robust. Sometimes a low-key, low-cost project directed at a particular population and guided by a handful of unassuming labor strategists can make significant gains. One example is a relatively new merit badge now available from the five million–member Boy Scouts of America (BSA).[1] Authorized in 1987 after several years of delicate and difficult negotiations, the badge is awarded on successful completion of a guided study of the American labor movement, aided and abetted by proud trade unionists.

Background

A cooperative relationship between labor and the Scouts dates back to 1913. Union members by the thousands have served, and continue to do so, as Scout leaders, members of troop committees, and supporters of scouting. Indeed, one in every four scoutmasters has come from labor's ranks.[2]

Leo Perlis, the first director of the AFL-CIO Department of Community Services, designated scouting as a major concern after the merger of the AFL and CIO in 1955. AFL-CIO affiliates volunteered their services to help build Boy Scout camps and facilities, sometimes joining management in co-sponsoring Scout units. They raised scholarship funds for low-income boys and earmarked United Fund contributions for scouting. Through the years, labor newspapers brought the appeal of scouting into millions of working-class homes. One measure of the involvement of union members is that by 1986, 1,440 members had received the AFL-CIO's George Meany Award for Scouting. Later, in 1989, 116 additional union members, representing nearly thirty federation affiliates, earned the award.[3]

Closing a Vital Gap

From its start in 1910 through 1967, the Boy Scouts steered clear of labor-management tension and seemed to enjoy the trust and support of both sides. Business provided financial donations and loaned executives for BSA functions; labor provided hands-on help with construction projects and invaluable troop leadership. The situation shifted dramatically in 1967, however, when BSA introduced a merit badge in American business. Although the pamphlet explaining the new badge contained a paragraph noting the existence of trade unions, the emphasis was put on the contributions of American business alone to our standard of living and global preeminence.

Union members involved in scouting felt challenged to respond. Once a badge had been created in business studies, they felt strongly one was needed in labor studies, too. Similar imbalances had occurred in the past. A badge in "energy" had been announced in 1978 but not in "environmental science" until 1983. A badge had been created for "American heritage" in 1976 but not for "citizenship in the world" until ten years later.

Making a Case

The first response from labor came when the National Labor Advisory Committee to the Boy Scouts, a volunteer committee composed of union members, drafted criteria for earning a labor badge. They included recommendations that a Scout talk with union members; visit a union local to determine what members do; diagram the structure of a union; define labor terminology; learn the rights and responsibilities of union members; explore the relationships between business, government, and labor; participate in a labor-sponsored community activity; and demonstrate an aspect of scouting at a union meeting. Activities were designed to encourage communication skills, which the advisory committee felt were pivotal to the development of constructive labor-management relations.

Block That Badge!

Opposition to the authorization of a merit badge focused on organized labor was immediate, emphatic, and effective. BSA relied heavily on financial donations from leading business people, some of whom sat on its executive board. Opponents warned that the badge would anger anti-labor activists, such as "right-to-work" advocates. Others felt it would place BSA on the wrong side of a continuing confrontation. A few opponents worried about paving the way for the introduction of other "pinko" badges in areas such as worker ownership or income redistribution.

By 1985, the controversy had become newsworthy, and the *Wall Street Journal* noted: "Anti-union people have objected. The National Right to Work Committee wants boys to learn about 'right to work' principles, not just about unions. The Scouts pledge balance."[4]

Personnel Journal also found the development noteworthy, although for different reasons: "Just when the media would have you believe organized labor is facing a crisis of anti-union sentiment and declining membership, labor has gotten a shot in the arm from a most unlikely source: the Boy Scouts of America."[5]

BSA made strenuous efforts to emphasize its objectivity. One prominent staff member, for example, assured the *Washington Times* that the purpose of the proposed badge was strictly educational: "It's a matter of enlightenment. We will not be encouraging or discouraging unionism. It's just another subject. We have a badge for beekeeping, but we're not necessarily encouraging scouts to become beekeepers." Another staff member observed that "some negative response was anticipated, but we felt the badge would be of benefit to our program. We have had a long association with the labor movement."[6]

The AFL-CIO, in response, reminded the public that about 25 percent of those involved in scouting were union members, far more than were beekeepers, and characterized its support of the proposed badge as a "perfectly sensible thing for us to do. It's a thing we have every right to do."[7]

Winning a Rewrite

A letter-writing campaign led by the National Right to Work Committee succeeded in defeating the first draft of the labor badge in 1985 and putting its supporters on the defensive. Stating its case against "compulsory" unionism, the committee demanded that the "right-to-work" movement be represented in the badge requirements and railed against the presence of a "paid AFL-CIO propagandist assigned to Boy Scout headquarters to develop the badge requirements."[8] By July 1985, the committee had won a delay in the entire process, and the badge was sent back for revision.

The AFL-CIO reacted with surprise and disappointment because, as spokesperson Alan Bosch said, "we had a whole string of committees that we went through."[9] Norman Osborne, another member of the National Labor Advisory Committee, told reporters that he remained optimistic of eventual passage since "we can't have the program torn apart by any one merit badge."[10] A triumphant leader of the "right-to-work" forces crowed, "It is clear we were right. I shudder to think what would have happened if we had not gotten onto this."[11]

Making Labor's Case

Forced by the vehemence of the opposition to move diplomatically, members of the National Labor Advisory Committee made three carefully phrased points:

■ Although the charitable donations of business were indispensable, the participation of thousands of unionists in troop leadership was comparably valuable.

- The language used in the pamphlet for the proposed merit badge would be sensitive and judicious.
- The existence of an explicitly pro-business badge and pamphlet since 1967 cried out for redress of the imbalance.

Patiently and with absolute conviction, the AFL-CIO delegates, led by Robert Harbrant, president of the AFL-CIO's Department of Food and Allied Service Trades, steadily built support for their position.

Finally, in late 1986, a nineteen-member committee of BSA, all of whom were corporate executives, met to resolve the matter. Years of persistent lobbying by labor had had an impact, but neither side in the "great badge war" was sufficiently confident to predict victory.

Showdown at BSA Corral

During a recess in the deliberations, a member of the BSA staff sought out an AFL-CIO representative. The labor badge would be approved, he explained, but at a price: the badge pamphlet would have to comment explicitly on alleged union crime and corruption. In response, the AFL-CIO delegates cited specific white-collar crimes and incidents of corruption in the companies of the very business people opposing the badge. Labor, the delegates said, was prepared to acknowledge allegations of corruption if and only if there was a comparable acknowledgment by business. Almost immediately, the labor badge was approved, and corruption was never mentioned again.

Preparing the Pamphlet

Writing the pamphlet for the badge turned out to be an arduous process, and the final forty-seven-page publication has several important weaknesses:

- Strikes are presented as utterly reprehensible, and references to major strikes in which organized labor takes pride are omitted completely.
- Labor history is often misrepresented, as in a reference to the Molly Maguires only as a group that "terrorized mine owners." The injustices that stimulated the creation of such an ultramilitant group are overlooked.
- Labor's community services, the AFL-CIO's international affairs activities, and other components of labor's outreach program are ignored completely.
- No mention is made of business's use of anti-union consultants, unfair labor practices, "runaway" shops, or other disreputable obstacles to union organizing campaigns and to labor-management cooperation.

■ Labor's culture, as amply explored in songs, poetry, novels, and folklore, escapes any attention whatsoever.

Also regrettable is the brevity of the pamphlet's bibliography. Bewildering in its omissions, it lists only eleven books, none published since 1984. These shortcomings may be corrected in revisions of the pamphlet and, in the interim, a Scout's personal adviser in securing the badge should be able to compensate for the deficiencies.

Summary

Informed observers foresaw that a labor merit badge would be controversial. As Harry Bernstein of the *Los Angeles Times* observed, "Organized labor has fought for years, with little success, to get public schools to teach students about the role that unions have played in American history. The squabble over the Scout badge is an indication of the trouble unions have had in trying to tell their story to youngsters."[12] It is encouraging, therefore, that in 1989 more than two hundred young men earned the labor merit badge each month. Furthermore, of fifty-seven badges awarded at the 1989 Scout Jamboree, the labor merit badge ranked twelfth in the number who earned it.[13] The significance of the Scouts' training and whether they will be committed to unionism remain to be seen. What is clear, however, is that the unionists who waged the eleven-year "great badge war" won. Responsibility now shifts to grassroots trade unionists who can draw more and more Scouts into learning about labor.

Part IV

Part IV

PUBLIC RELATIONS AND POLITICS

Many of the nation's union members feel labor is inadequately represented in the media and is the focus of inappropriate hostility. Chapter 10 explores several imaginative and well-financed efforts to improve this situation.

AFL-CIO economist John Zalusky reminded the media on Labor Day 1988 that organized labor has historically supported major legislative drives, such as all the civil rights acts and the successful bill to create Medicare. He forecast a significant intensification of legislative efforts in this decade: "If there's anything we've learned from the Reagan administration, it's that if we don't follow up what we get at the bargaining table with legislation, we'll lose it. You're going to see a lot more activity in this area."[1] Labor is eager to go beyond the gains that can be earned in negotiations with one company, and it relies on Congress, the state houses, and the courts for the initiative in solving broader economic problems.

D. Quinn Mills, a professor at the Harvard Business School, forecasts that the government "will be more and more the guarantor of the rights of the workplace."[2] If he is correct, unions will have to involve themselves more deeply in the political process, as unions do throughout Western Europe. Mills believes the process of new involvement is already under way and cites as evidence the gradual convergence of the labor movement's interests with those of the Democratic party. Twenty years ago, about a third of the members of the AFL-CIO Executive Council identified themselves as Republican. Today everyone on the council is a Democrat.[3]

Chapter 11 discusses a variety of robust political efforts and is followed by a case study that demonstrates labor's recent use of a videotape to poll members' preferences among candidates and establish labor's significance in a major contest.

Together, the chapters and case study document a new political enthusiasm that has enabled labor to register 87 percent of its 14 million members and 13 million voting-age family members. In contrast, of the population in general, only 72 percent are registered. Although barely half the electorate actually casts votes, labor sent at least 67 percent of its registered voters to the polls on Election Day in November 1988. Union members and their families provided Michael Dukakis with 2.5 million votes; 67 percent of the unionists voted Democratic, compared to 61 percent in 1985, when Senator Walter Mondale was the Democratic candidate. Many informed observers, after reflecting on this record, expect labor to become more politically active in the 1990s than ever before.

Chapter 10
Improving Public Relations

None of us in this hall enjoys great popularity in our nation because we are disturbers of the status quo, disturbers of the consciences of so many. But we don't seek popularity. We seek only understanding, and we can have that only if we explain ourselves better.

Thomas R. Donahue, secretary-treasurer,
AFL-CIO, *AFL-CIO News*, March 26, 1988, 5

If we wait for someone else to tell our story, it is never going to happen.
Lane Kirkland, president, AFL-CIO, *AFL-CIO News*, May 14, 1988, 3

Labor has long understood that the struggle to shape the image of a movement is a critical and often decisive one. Historically, it has used the media of the day to improve its image, share information, and boost morale. Archives at the Meany Center contain fragile labor newspapers published in the early 1880s; radio tapes made by labor personalities such as William Green, John R. Lewis, and Philip Murray; films used in pioneering labor education projects in the 1940s; and videotapes of labor's fledgling television ads in the early 1980s. The Chicago Federation of Labor owned and operated an AM radio station from 1929 to 1979, and the UAW owned and operated two FM stations in the 1950s.

Such efforts have been fragmentary, however, and unionists now acknowledge organized labor's painful public relations problems. These problems were vividly revealed in a 1985 Harris poll:[1]

- Fifty percent of the general population thought most union leaders no longer represented the wishes of their members.
- Nearly 67 percent of the nonunionists believed union leaders imposed their own views regarding strikes and other issues on their members.

Not surprisingly, a 1987 study concluded there has been "a long-term decline in the image of labor unions (as measured in national surveys) since the middle 1950s, a trend that seems to be somewhat more accentuated since the middle 1960s."[2]

As further evidence of the problem's seriousness, James L. Medoff published an exhaustive study in 1984 of the impact labor's negative image has had on its overall success. He noted a strong correlation between how workers vote in NLRB representation elections and their image of unions. He also documented ways politicians were responsive to public opinion about labor. And finally, he noted the absence of any public outcry against unfair labor practices when public opinion about unions fell very low.[3]

Balancing this gloomy picture, recent polls indicate the public also has some very positive attitudes toward certain aspects of labor unions:

- A 1988 Gallup poll found 61 percent of Americans "approve of unions," the highest percentage since 1957 and up dramatically from lows of 55 percent in 1979 and 1981.
- A compilation of fifteen years (1974–89) of Roper data reveals that more Americans side with the union (33 percent) than with the company (25 percent) when they first hear of a strike and before they have heard any of the details. This is a substantial change since 1978, when more people said they would side with the company (32 to 28 percent).
- The same study documents what Roper terms "a dramatic increase" in the number of Americans who have a high or fairly good opinion of labor unions—up from 36 percent in 1982 to 44 percent in 1986 and 50 percent in 1990.[4]

Equally significant, a 1989 survey found that workers aged eighteen to twenty-nine are more likely to have pro-labor attitudes than workers in any other age group.[5]

Labor Responds

Considerably challenged by its election losses in 1980, organized labor worried whether it had lost touch with its members and resolved to revamp its public relations.[6] A special $2 million assessment in 1981 was used to create the Labor Institute for Public Affairs (LIPA) to help labor take advantage of its sophisticated modern media. This effort was catalyzed in 1984 by the release of the AFL-CIO report *The Changing Situation of Workers and Their Unions* (see chapter 14), which urged substantial improvements in communication, including new training in media techniques.[7] Ideas that previously "would have been considered heretical or at least 'far out' " were now perceived as essential.[8] In 1985, for example, daily video highlights of the AFL-CIO convention were released via satellite to more than five hundred commercial television stations.

The three examples discussed in this chapter are representative of the diversity of approaches that have recently been developed to improve labor's public relations efforts. The first focuses on the "Union, YES!" campaign of the AFL-CIO, the best-financed and most extensive such effort ever undertaken by the American labor movement; the second, on the use of cable television; and the third, on labor's increasing use of videotapes. Taken together, they demonstrate labor's dedication to upgrading its image as never before.

"Union, YES!"

On May 11, 1988, the AFL-CIO launched a two-year multimedia project entitled "America Works Best When We Say 'Union, YES!' " Funded by $13 million from a record-setting 1987 allocation, it has been used in large part to sponsor television commercials on behalf of trade unionism. This approach, according to Lane Kirkland, president of the federation, had been vigorously supported by union members:

> Our affiliated unions reported there was substantial interest among their members in seeing unions portrayed in a positive way—for a change—on television. Quite a few members have taken the time to write to the AFL-CIO directly making the same point. They are frustrated with negative news stories and stereotyped portrayals of workers and unions on other programs. . . . We decided the members were right, and that a national communication campaign was worth the expense.[9]

Advertising on the three major television networks (ABC, CBS, and NBC) set a precedent many felt was long overdue. Labor's previous promotional efforts on television had been limited by low budgets, and national advertising had been subordinated to haphazard efforts by local stations. In contrast, the "Union, YES!" campaign was large enough in scale to ensure that in the initial month of May 1988 more than 91 percent of all viewers would see labor's new commercials at least four times, and some as many as ten times.[10]

Scheduled to appear in thirteen major television markets representing one-third of all domestic viewers, the "Union, YES!" commercials were shown during a variety of popular programs, news magazine shows, and sports specials. Each advertisement featured an anthem and the "Union, YES!" logo with an animated check mark to signify labor's active and positive role. Every commercial centered on a prototypical union member: a black female clerical assistant in a library, a white male telephone operator, a Hispanic female registered nurse, a white male electrician, and a white female secretary. Organized labor was thanked by the secretary for providing four months of job-protected maternity leave, by the electrician for barring favoritism in job-site rewards, by the nurse for enabling her to focus on patient care, and by the telephone operator for curbing office politics. A choral refrain of the campaign's anthem and a summary statement by a media star (Jack Lemmon, Tyne Daly, Howard Hesserman, and Edward James Olmos) wrapped up the commercial, which closed with a shot of the AFL-CIO seal and the American flag.

The successful television spots required the active cooperation of several unions. The boards of the Screen Actors Guild, the American Federation of Television and Radio Artists, and the American Federation of Musicians granted the AFL-CIO special status during the filming and recording of the commercials, which substantially reduced costs. SAG president Patty Duke Astin personally helped recruit talented members of her union for appearances, and both SAG and AFTRA recruited the top "voice" talent available for another series of announcements aired on the radio. A very appreciative AFL-CIO saluted this "extraordinary and unprecedented effort," of the sort that lends concrete meaning to the notion of labor solidarity.[11]

Radio Support

To bolster the campaign, LIPA created a series of radio commercials featuring NFL players voicing their support for labor unions. In addition, three customized versions of the "Union, YES!" anthem were prepared for specific audiences, one in country style, one in Spanish, and one with an urban contemporary focus. Each sixty-second spot contained twenty-eight seconds a union local could use to convey a message tailored to its situation. During contract negotiations, for example, a union local could explain its concerns in an effort to improve the bargaining climate. Sponsoring labor bodies were expected to write their own copy, hire an AFTRA announcer, and arrange for the radio station to integrate the message with the "Union, YES!" music.

First shipped to seven hundred labor leaders in April 1988, radio packets have been used in a variety of ways:[12]

- The Chicago AFL-CIO federation spent $75,000 for four hundred spots heard on eight radio stations, with a potential audience of over five hundred thousand workers. Each ad told listeners, "We believe Chicago works best when people have a say in what goes on at work."
- In Cleveland, several unions targeted workers between the ages of eighteen and twenty-five and broadcast the "Union, YES!" message on rock-and-roll stations during the 1988 Memorial Day weekend.

■ Over a two-week period, the National Association of Letter Carriers (NALC) ran sixty-second spots in the Washington, D.C., area that outlined "what the NALC has been all about for the past ninety-nine years."

■ In Pennsylvania, the "Union, YES!" message was used by the state AFL-CIO in its legislative campaign to increase the state's minimum wage. Listeners were asked to call their state senators and press for a vote on the bill, which was blocked in a senate committee.

Although they varied in focus and content, these relatively inexpensive radio ads consistently delivered a relevant message professionally and with style and created a very useful public relations model.

Other Media

Along with television and radio spots, "Union, YES!" print ads urging rank-and-file involvement have appeared in hundreds of union publications whose combined circulation is over 20 million readers. As each new phase of the campaign was launched during 1988–90, an updated print ad urged fresh grass-roots participation.

In addition to radio, television, and print, the "Union, YES!" campaign has had a number of other components:

■ Hundreds of locals, city labor councils, and major unions have incorporated the "Union, YES!" logo into their publications, banners, and other items. Camera-ready art was made available for use on T-shirts, hats, bumper stickers, and tote bags. The Phoenix Labor Council, for example, imprinted the logo on sun shields for cars, and the Pennsylvania State AFL-CIO used it on gym bags.

■ A fifteen-minute "Union, YES!" videocassette was available that inspired rank-and-file enthusiasm to help in the campaign and illustrated specific ways union member viewers could assist.

In its scope and bravado, the ongoing "Union, YES!" campaign has established a new standard for labor's public relations. Predicated on winning extensive membership involvement, this robust campaign could reward labor with improved morale for many years to come.

Labor and Cable TV

In Rhode Island, a public relations program called LaborVision demonstrates how labor can use cable television. According to Chuck

Schwartz, the project director, this effort has resulted in several new services:

> Rhode Island LaborVision is a weekly cable television program that is produced by the Institute for Labor Studies and Research [ILSR], a nonprofit, labor-affiliated education institution. LaborVision is broadcast on *every* cable television franchise in Rhode Island, and it can be viewed by nearly two-thirds of the state's 1 million residents. In 1986, over fifty different videos were aired. Most were produced by international unions or the AFL-CIO, and the topics covered included pay equity, sexual harassment, health-care cost containment, labor history, and plant closings. Among the films we showed were *Harlan County, U.S.A., Union Maids,* and several local productions, including *Life in Rhode Island Mills* and *Labor Salutes Providence 350.*
>
> Outreach for the television series has two components. Schedules of the programs are mailed quarterly to six thousand union members. In addition, advertisements (paid for by the featured unions) and news articles in local newspapers inform the general public of upcoming programs. The Institute has conducted several surveys to ascertain the size of LaborVision's audience. Forty-seven percent of Rhode Island union leadership surveyed indicated that they watched some of the programs. Nineteen percent, or a total of about one thousand people, on the ILSR mailing list reported watching at least one of the programs. Based on the ratio of ILSR participants to total viewer phone calls, the Institute estimates an overall accumulated viewership of around fifty thousand people.
>
> Two new projects have resulted from the cable television series. First, the Institute has established a lending library of videos about labor history, collective bargaining, and unions that is unrivaled in the area. These videos have been shown at union meetings and conferences, apprenticeship training and adult education programs, college seminars, and high school classes. In addition, the Institute, using community cable access equipment, has developed the capacity to film and edit its own videos. With the assistance of several volunteer unionists, the staff produces several programs each month that are first shown on cable television and then made available to the public in forums such as those described above.
>
> Rhode Island LaborVision has enabled the Institute to reach a much broader and larger audience than ever before. Many of the viewers who call are stewards, rank-and-file union members, or non-union workers who were not previously aware of the Institute and its programs. Television and video are the most powerful educa-

tional tools available today. Used in combination with traditional forums, such as steward training courses, workshops, and conferences, these media offer the promise of informing workers and the public about the goals, aspirations, and accomplishments of the labor movement.[13]

Little wonder that LaborVision is admired by labor educators and PR specialists coast to coast.

Although LaborVision has been a pioneer, it is no longer alone. In 1987, LIPA identified thirty-seven local and state cable television projects nationwide, and new projects are being added each month:[14]

- SEIU Local 790 in San Francisco reaches over 1 million northern California households with its news magazine show, "Talking Union." What began as a city project has since become available to public television stations throughout the West.
- The Chicago Committee for Labor Access has been airing a one-hour series, "Labor Beat," since 1986.
- Unions have a presence and a voice in Michigan through "Labor News Update" in Kalamazoo and "Images of Labor" in Grand Rapids.
- The New York City AFT produces "Inside Your Schools," a half-hour magazine-style series that explores issues in public education and features children and teachers from around the country.
- "Focus on Labor" is produced near Minneapolis by members of UAW Local 863 for viewing throughout the state.
- In Nashville, trade unionists from a variety of locals, the city and state central bodies, and the Nashville-based United Furniture Workers of America have joined forces to produce "Fraternally Yours," a creative interview show. Topics have included the state's right-to-know campaign and interviews with visiting South African unionists.

Pamphlets prepared by the AFL-CIO and other resources, including many on videotape, offer guidelines for replicating these successes. More than half of all television owners pay for cable access, and 20 to 60 percent have watched public access shows such as those created by labor. The medium is particularly appropriate for labor because "public access television humanizes rather than packages people, communicates ideas rather than sells them."[15]

Video and VCR Frontiers

Among the most exciting cable programs is one LaborVision calls "Labor Produces: Access to Solidarity," which features labor-produced videos from around the country. Unpretentious and varied in focus, the videos provide labor with the equivalent of an "electronic news magazine." Highlighting local union rallies or community service projects or the rewards of union membership, the videotapes are distributed by LIPA, which sends updated lists of hundreds of such tapes to unions and locals across the country.

Seldom before has labor made as rapid and effective use of a public relations tool as it has of camcorders, VCRs, and videotapes. The variety available attests to the breadth of labor's concerns:

- Using a style reminiscent of MTV to attract young viewers, Local 48 of the IBEW (Portland, Oregon) and the local chapter of the National Electrical Contractors Association joined forces to produce an eighteen-minute educational tape, *Teen Drug and Alcohol Prevention*. It features youngsters and parents discussing suicide and the detection and prevention of substance abuse.
- District 1199, National Union of Hospital and Health Care Employees, has produced a videotape series (*Bread and Roses*) about its extensive cultural activities.
- LIPA offers twelve half-hour dramatic specials covering such national issues as health-cost containment, education costs, the deregulation of natural gas, and health care for senior citizens. Done from the worker's perspective, the series, "America Works," goes on location to document the efforts of activists involved in solving these critical social problems. Audiences see the pros and cons of the issues argued by the people involved and are encouraged to take a stand of their own.
- The UAW has produced a videotape, *Would You Let Someone Do This to Your Sister?* which helps viewers understand sexual harassment at work.
- The Brotherhood of Painters has sponsored two videotapes, *Paint and Your Nervous System* and *The Latency Trap*, designed to alert viewers to chemical hazards.
- The Building Trades Department of the AFL-CIO offers locals everywhere use of such videotapes as *Unions in the Community* and *Building Our Future*.

Labor clearly has an extraordinary collection of video aids at its disposal. The challenges now are to develop attentive and responsive viewers and to keep the tapes timely and effective.

And Now . . . a Word from the Skeptics

Critics warn that sophistication in public relations cannot substitute for authentic change. According to Robert Schrank, an informed observer,

"To appeal to the new worker, the unions will have to develop a whole new agenda, including examining the usefulness of their unchanging 'fundamental principles.'... The labor movement will not get a new image by better use of the media unless it has something new to convey—and some new young leaders, particularly female, to say it."[16] This is a comment with which few unionists would disagree.

Other concerned parties think labor's public relations efforts are invalidated by a fundamental paradox: "The principal virtue of unions is that they serve the interests of their members. Their principal defect is that, by doing exactly that, unions seem to do little to benefit the public interest."[17] Labor's boosters see a response to this paradox in the vigor with which it has pursued "public-interest" politics (see chapter 11) and community service (see part III). What is good for labor, in the opinion of the Movement, is commonly good for everyone.

Finally, some skeptics would prefer to see resources now applied to public relations invested in more conventional labor efforts, such as community service, labor education, or workplace safety. Media visibility costs millions of dollars at a time when labor's dollars are badly stretched. In response, media proponents insist labor gets a much better return on its PR investment than is apparent. While proof of effectiveness is unavailable, the unions that have used media ads are firmly convinced of their value. They argue that public relations campaigns and more conventional labor efforts support each other. Labor's accomplishments provide indispensable material for PR, which, in turn, provides the recognition needed to ensure labor's continuation and improvement.

Innovative Uses of Traditional Strategies

Taking advantage of new media does not mean abandoning traditional forms of self-promotion. Donald F. Peters, a sixty-eight-year-old leader of the Chicago Teamsters Union, summarizes the value of time-honored strategies:

> You've got to keep your name out there, in front of people, where they will see it, know it, and remember it. We make a point, my Local 743, of always having a float of ours in the annual Labor Day parade and the St. Patrick's Day parade, and we also cooperate with newer parades, like those put together by Greek-Americans, black Americans, the Asians, or anybody else....I pay a company $200 per parade to see to it that our float is spruced up, made relevant, and included in the line of march. They call me when they learn of a parade we should 'show the flag in,' and I always say, 'Sure, go ahead, and make *certain* you make us look *good!*'[18]

Peters believes television and other high-tech approaches have a place in the labor leader's promotional tool kit, though primarily as a supplement to old-fashioned presence.

As the following examples illustrate, efforts to enhance the image of labor can include a wide range of traditional as well as modern strategies:

■ A prize-winning float was entered in the 1988 New Year's Day Rose Bowl Parade by the Bakery, Confectionery and Tobacco Workers' International Union, Local 37 of Los Angeles, and was seen on national television by millions. This event marked thirty-nine years of participation in the parade.[19]

■ The Sheet Metal Workers' International Association created a remarkable one hundredth anniversary exhibit at the National Building Museum in Washington, D.C. Members and apprentices of the union from across the country and Canada volunteered their time for a month to assemble the sixty-five-foot structure that housed the display. AFL-CIO president Lane Kirkland applauded the display for showing the union's "history of innovation, exploration, and readiness to respond to challenge."[20]

■ Both the IAM's logo and the AFL-CIO "Union, YES!" logo were brightly displayed on two professional race cars sponsored by the IAM that competed in the 1988 and 1989 Memorial Day classics.[21]

■ Lobbying behind the scenes prompted a Washington State delegate to the 1988 Democratic National Convention to tell a worldwide television audience, before announcing his state's vote, that the planes that brought every delegate to Atlanta had been "built in Washington by union labor."[22]

Examples abound of new successes in issue advocacy:

■ Informational ads placed by the UFCW in leading journals of opinion, such as *In These Times* and the *New Republic,* proudly explain the rewards of membership in the 1.3 million–member organization.

■ Television press conferences are facilitated by the million dollar AFSCME television studio, which is equipped to broadcast from remote locations through satellite transmission.

■ The Communications Workers of America provided a closed-circuit television system that broadcast to eight thousand Atlanta hotel rooms during the 1988 Democratic Party Convention. Substantial segments of union-related programming were included.[23]

- The Bricklayers Union and the Laborers Union constructed an "affordable" house in Atlanta during the 1988 Democratic Party Convention to call attention to the nation's housing crisis and to union labor's ability to help solve it.[24]

Summary

How much progress has really been made? Sara U. Douglas, author of *Labor's New Voice: Unions and the Mass Media,* poses this fundamental question: "[Can] labor use advertising to provide members with a sense of vigor, aggressiveness, and advocacy of change, while at the same time providing general public appeal by creating an understanding of labor as a responsible institution, fully integrated into the American system?" Douglas concludes the answer "appears to be yes" and emphasizes that "even the 'mildest' union advertising educates, informs, and encourages action."[25]

Among their other benefits, labor's new public relations efforts seek greater grass-roots involvement than ever before. The individual worker, for example, used to be depicted as an anonymous member of a large crowd, dutifully cheering, jeering, or marching. Now, typical rank-and-filers star on nationwide "Union, YES!" commercials. Others dream up, produce, and sometimes even star in cable TV or VCR programs on labor's behalf. Labor's morale, as well as its PR image, can only benefit from such activities.

Chapter 11

Enhancing Union Power

The plain truth is that labor is the chief representative force that keeps the real special interests from dominating American political life.

Lane Kirkland, *New York Times*, May 5, 1985, 31

Business is about twenty years behind labor in its political sophistication.... Give me a storefront with a handful of volunteers in sandals and jeans and they will make more important political strategic decisions in a day than Mobil can make in two years. The corporations can't move. They don't have the flexibility to make decisions. They're just too bureaucratic.

J. Brian Smith, in Broder, *Changing of the Guard: Power and Leadership in America* (1980), 215

In 1834, Eli Moore became the first trade union leader to win a seat in Congress. More than seventy years later, in 1908, organized labor made its first political endorsement. The decision to support Democrat William Jennings Bryan for president was a response to the use by business of its political war chest to elect Republican William McKinley in 1896. A process that began then has been evolving ever since. What has changed "is not just the scale of the effort—the millions spent in lobbying, political action, education, and propaganda—but its sophistication."[1]

Labor's first organizing manual for precinct politics was published by the CIO in 1938, and its first political action committee (PAC), the prototype for thousands of union and corporation fund-raising bodies, was created in 1943. Throughout the years, unions have made a concerted effort to use their political power effectively. According to William Olwell, head of the UFCW's $1.25 million PAC, "We're picking up the tools of the trade now. We're getting much more sophisticated in ... our fund raising, in our education, in our research. We're doing polling. We're looking at the media as a tool to be used positively for us, rather than just always castigating the media for giving us a black eye."[2]

Unions that have never had PACs see progress very quickly when they form them. In 1975, for example, the American Federation of Government Employees (AFGE) had no PAC. By 1978, however, a new AFGE PAC had raised nearly $150,000, which, as Kenneth T. Blaylock, president of the union, said, "is not a big amount, but it's a hell of a long way from nothing." Since then, the PAC has gained further recognition by providing access to computer networks that facilitate effective mail campaigns and focused response to politicians.[3]

Rank-and-File Perceptions

National labor leaders surveyed in 1983 and grass-roots leaders polled in 1985 strongly endorsed labor's efforts to influence political decisions, and fewer than 25 percent in each survey felt labor had too much political involvement. Rather, 69 and 72 percent, respectively, characterized labor as the strongest contemporary force behind the passage of social legislation. Similarly, 81 and 64 percent thought unions influenced laws passed by Congress, and 75 and 79 percent believed labor had a desirable impact on the results of elections.[4]

Yet only a minority (42 and 28 percent) believed unions adequately influence how our country is run, and a significant majority wanted labor to increase its political activity by making more consequential endorsements and taking a larger role in party decision making. Overall, both national and grass-roots labor officials seemed proud of labor's political influence and eager to see it increase.[5]

Sampling the Wares

Four political innovations are discussed in this chapter as a preface to the case study of labor's 1988 candidate-endorsement project. The first focuses on labor's ability to deliver the vote and command respect from those who shape policy and make laws. The second highlights labor's competence at coalition politics, while the third explores labor's use of the art of compromise. Finally, the fourth documents healthy controversy in labor's projects in foreign affairs. Together, all four provide a measure of how far labor has come in effecting political change since Moore's electoral victory in 1834 and how far it knows there is yet to go.

Delivering the Vote

Having effective access to voters, or even just the appearance of effective access, influences legislative decisions of critical importance to labor. When its political machinery is running well, its computerized lists are current, and its phone banks are efficient and persuasive, labor has few rivals as a political force. As David Bensman, a labor educator, insists, "the single biggest thing that has turned labor around" and renewed its spirit was its gains in 1986 congressional contests.[6]

Contrary to popular opinion, those gains had their basis in the ill-fated 1984 presidential election. In spite of Republican Ronald Reagan's overwhelming victory, polls showed that union households favored Democrat

Support for the Democratic Presidential Candidate among Families with a
Union Member, 1952–1984

Candidate	Year	Percentage
Truman	1952	56%
Stevenson	1956	53
Kennedy	1960	64
Johnson	1964	83
Humphrey	1968	56
McGovern	1972	43
Carter	1976	64
Carter	1980	47
Mondale	1984	57

Source: David Moberg, "Unions Are Having Difficulty Fathoming What Went Wrong,"
In These Times, November 21–December 4, 1984, 7.

Walter Mondale by 17 to 19 percentage points more than nonunion
households, a 50 percent differential. Victor Fingerhut, whose telephone
survey of AFL-CIO members found a margin of 49 to 41 in support of
Mondale, told the press that labor's tally was "a fantastic performance.
The unions ran on traditional themes, and the Mondale campaign essentially gave no backing to what the unions were doing. The unions
delivered their vote in the face of an incredibly stupid Mondale
campaign."[7]

One intriguing finding was the impact of white-collar union members.
According to an NBC poll, blue-collar workers favored Reagan 55 to
45. But when the sample included all households with a union member,
the numbers were virtually reversed. White-collar union members made
the difference, suggesting that the political influence of white-collar members on their unions is growing rapidly.[8]

Labor also played a crucial role in 1984 in maintaining the balance in
Congress. An AFL-CIO survey found that 72 percent of union members
voted for Democratic candidates for the Senate and 69 percent for Democratic candidates for the House. The political impact of organized labor
was a crucial reason a Reagan landslide produced only a minor fourteen-
seat gain for the Republicans.[9]

As the table illustrates, the record inspires guarded confidence in labor's
allegiance to Democratic presidential candidates.[10] To strengthen its impact, labor has consciously sought to improve its political communication. Increased delegate representation has been a consistent concern and
a measure of early success. Encouraged by the AFL-CIO Committee on
Political Education (COPE), unionists ran for and won a disproportion-

ately large number of delegate seats at the July 1988 Democratic Party National Convention. Although labor represented only 17 percent of the work force and a smaller percentage of eligible voters, union members made up 23 percent of the delegates, and union officials, 6 percent.[11] In assessing the increase of more than a hundred union delegates since 1984, the *New York Times* characterized labor as possessing "a strong voice in the places that matter."[12]

COPE worked relentlessly between the 1986 congressional races and the 1988 presidential campaign to update and refine its voter lists. According to COPE staff member David Gregory, computers have transformed the process of contacting voters:

> What do I see as the biggest gain in the last five years? No question about it—our new use of computers. We are getting better demographic data than anybody has ever had, and we are entering it into data banks nobody has ever been able to use before . . . [to] put together the best voter lists you have ever seen. Our computers can now provide separate lists of only women or only Hispanic women, or only black women forty-four to fifty-five, or any other cut you'd like.[13]

Nightly computer runs enable COPE to print personalized letters to union voters, addressing doubts uncovered in the previous day's telephone poll.

To strengthen its political base further, COPE created FRONTLASH, the AFL-CIO's first youth group. A nationwide organization based in state AFL-CIO and central labor body offices around the nation, it targets workers and students under the age of thirty, a group whose members often have little allegiance to labor or grasp of union history. FRONTLASH has five strong selling points:[14]

- Members join a unique coalition of students and young workers, two groups that rarely work together.
- Members draw strength from the FRONTLASH alliance with labor at city, state, and national levels.
- Members are invited to join labor clubs at high schools and colleges.
- Members help correct prejudices against unions by educating students and workers about union values.
- Members learn how to assume leadership roles while preparing for careers in the labor movement.

This nonpartisan youth program is intended to inspire political commitment in voters under thirty, who, as recent surveys show, comprise the group least supportive of labor's candidates. Since FRONTLASH began, its members have been operating phone banks, registering voters at their work sites, and turning out for labor rallies across the country.

Labor has learned more and more about marketing its political ideas and involving union members in the process. COPE, for example, continues to improve its One-on-One program, first used in 1984. Designed to enhance voter registration campaigns, the program trains shop stewards and rank-and-file members to seek out unregistered voters whom they can personally persuade to "vote labor." Continuously refined, the One-on-One program has successfully returned "both politics and organizing skills to the shop-floor level of labor leadership."[15]

Using the same process of active involvement, Carol O'Cleireacain, an economist for AFSCME, developed an idea championed by Jesse Jackson during his 1988 campaign which has "generally received high marks from economists." Jackson proposed raising capital for public housing, sewer systems, and other development projects by encouraging public pension funds to invest in federally guaranteed securities. O'Cleireacain, in turn, assured unionized public employees in Jackson's audiences that their pension savings would be protected.[16]

Broader in scope and duration, Jobs with Justice has activated union workers coast to coast. An educational and political program, Jobs with Justice draws civil rights, consumer, community, and religious groups together to work with labor unions such as AFSCME, the UAW, the Clothing and Textile Workers, the CWA, the Electrical Workers, the IAM, the Paperworkers, the Transport Workers, and the unaffiliated UMWA. Announced in June 1987 at a Washington press conference and at a four thousand–person rally in Miami, the coalition has been increasingly successful in involving the rank-and-file in political awareness efforts. Union members take an "I'll be there" pledge to participate at least five times in the next year in labor rallies, coalition events, or informational picket lines supporting workers' rights.[17]

Union leaders linked to the AFL-CIO's Industrial Union Department give Jobs with Justice its budget and clout. In return, they expect the program to conduct significant political rallies, offer testimony at congressional hearings, and forge strategic alliances with nonlabor groups. As UAW president Owen Bieber told the press, the new coalition is designed to "mobilize, agitate, and educate" the American public. CWA president Morton Bahr added: "For far too long, workers and their unions have been on the defensive. Well, today we draw the line, and say, 'Enough is enough!' "[18]

The result of all these efforts was summarized in a February 1987 article in *Business Week:* "Labor's political fortunes are finally looking up.... The country's shifting political mood is moving in labor's direction. Increased spending on social problems is no longer completely taboo. . . . Labor also is benefiting from a bipartisan consensus that America needs to be made more competitive worldwide. This has pushed issues such as minority unemployment and displaced workers to the fore." In the changing political climate, *Business Week* concluded, political players can no longer afford to ignore organized labor.[19]

Coalition Politics

Coalition politics is an art form complete with its own esoteric, covert, and dynamic norms. It is also an absolute prerequisite to political gain in our pluralist society. Efforts at joint labor-management lobbying date back to Samuel Gompers and his effort to boost productivity during World War I. Today, coalition politics takes a variety of colorful forms. One example is the coalition of companies and eleven unions formed in the late 1970s to lobby for control of the number of color televisions imported from Japan. Allan Cors, the business executive who initiated the coalition, observed years later: "It's been a joy to work with them. . . . They represent votes. If we come into a Congressman's office with the union representative, we can talk from the standpoint of political clout."[20]

Labor has always been open to collaboration with industry when interests overlap. As Thomas R. Donahue, secretary-treasurer of the AFL-CIO, explains, "We will take our allies in those fights wherever we can find them."[21] Several recent collaborative efforts deserve mention:

- The AFL-CIO was one of twenty-nine groups, including the National Association of Realtors and the National Association of Home Builders, that pushed for legislation in 1987 to hold down interest rates.
- The AFL-CIO was one of twenty-eight groups, including the Chemical Manufacturers Association and a variety of corporate and management organizations, to advocate successfully for passage of the High-Risk Notification Bill, which requires employers to notify workers if they are or have been exposed to work-site risks.
- The AFL-CIO, with General Electric, General Motors, TRW, Prudential Life, Johnson and Johnson, and other companies, was represented in the labor-management group that issued a blueprint in 1987 for controlling health-care costs. The study focused on six case histories of labor-management cooperation in cutting costs.

Probably the most widely publicized example of successful labor-management cooperation was the effort in 1979 to rescue Chrysler from the brink of bankruptcy. Longtime adversaries such as the UAW's Douglas Fraser and Chrysler's Lee Iacocca teamed up, as did corporate and

AFL-CIO lobbyists. Observers of the episode concluded that "the most important lobbying forces were Chrysler's dealers, the team of in-house and hired professionals, and the United Auto Workers."[22] Indeed, the UAW's chief Washington representative attributed the lack of friction among the parties to the shared recognition that the auto union was "the real source of political strength in the coalition."[23]

The Art of Compromise

The veto-proof passage by Congress in July 1988 of a bill requiring companies to notify employees sixty days before a plant closing was first urged in 1974 as part of a broad program to improve workers' rights.[24] The legislation was frustrated for fourteen years because of bitter ideological conflict. As the *New York Times* reported, "The bill is organized labor's most important legislative priority in this election year, and it has been strongly opposed by the business community as an unwarranted government intrusion into business affairs."[25]

Labor lobbyists never gave up, and after the 1981–83 recession, they intensified their efforts, reemphasizing the need for notification. Finally, in the spring of 1988, against the backdrop of the presidential campaign, an alliance with the mayors of large cities tipped the balance in labor's favor. A presidential veto in June 1988 led to a revision of the bill, hailed by the *New York Times* as "flexibly constructed . . . a responsibly modest approach to a valid national concern."[26] Passage of the bill by the House on July 13 by a vote of 286 to 136, or four more than the required two-thirds majority, was attributed to labor's willingness to compromise on its original demands and to assure Congress it would not put an undue burden on responsible businesses. Among the compromises labor reluctantly accepted was the exclusion from coverage of seasonal workers and workers on strike. The bill also exempts companies struck by natural catastrophes, including droughts. It no longer requires firms to consult with workers and community officials on alternatives to plant closings, and it forbids injunctions to prevent announced layoffs. Finally, it limits penalties for violation and exempts businesses whose efforts to raise capital in order to keep a plant open might be damaged by the notification of an impending closing. Nevertheless, organized labor's highest election-year priority was achieved and the revised sixty-day advance notice bill was hailed as a victory by the AFL-CIO.

A second major compromise, which received far less notice in the media, concerned the thousand-page trade bill that contained the original plant closing provision. The trade bill had taken three years to frame, and although a postveto bill still provided for a new $1 billion worker-retraining program and other labor goals, the AFL-CIO and key affiliates resented the watering-down of trade provisions. As Robert McGlottin, labor's chief lobbyist, observed, "We're past the issue of substance, and we're into politics."[27] Despite grumblings, labor did not oppose the trade bill and it was enacted.

Compromises are gained at a cost, sometimes a substantial one. A union official familiar with the internal debate about labor's legislative strategy complained that because of the compromises an inferior trade policy had been substituted for more promising trade action: "The immediacy is no longer in the bill, and it may not be worth saving, as far as many of our members are concerned." Quietly, however, a key union lobbyist acknowledged the political reality: "Our opposition won't keep it from being passed by Congress. We couldn't stop its passage."[28] Although the toll was frustrating, the compromise on trade terms became a mechanism for facilitating passage of a plant closing bill that had been stymied for fourteen years.

Foreign Affairs Policy

Although positions on foreign affairs have been singularly controversial within union ranks, labor has remained firmly "anti-Communist" and has steadfastly supported the administration's foreign policy and, in some matters, such as its early and significant support of Poland's SOLIDARITY, has done more than the U.S. government itself. Differences of opinion are likely to persist indefinitely.[29] But recent expansion of the dialogue inside the AFL-CIO suggests its foreign affairs projects have become more open to debate, a tribute to concerned parties on all sides of the argument.

Expansion of the scope of the foreign policy dialogue began on October 29, 1985, during the AFL-CIO fifteenth biannual convention. Kenneth Blaylock, then president of a major public sector union, initiated a spirited ninety-minute debate on Nicaragua. A policy concession, calling for a negotiated settlement, was reached after intense, private bargaining. The concession was not momentous, but the process was significant: participants had initiated the first open debate on foreign policy at an AFL-CIO convention in the federation's thirty-year history. And when it was over, as journalist Harold Meyerson noted, "The way American labor makes policy had changed measurably."[30]

As part of a broader relaxation in the tension within labor's inner circle and a new receptivity to self-criticism, the convention debate was a turning point. To pursue its own political goals regarding the trade deficit, runaway shops, the "guns-and-butter" ratio, the creation of genuinely free unions abroad, and the termination of South African apartheid, labor first had to reach a consensus on U.S. foreign policy. In 1985, to the credit of all parties concerned, labor took such a step.

Organized labor also conducts four dynamic and often controversial overseas training institutes directed by the AFL-CIO Department of International Affairs:

- the American Institute for Free Labor Development (AIFLD), active in Latin America and the Caribbean;
- the Asian-American Free Labor Institute (AAFLI), which works in Asia and the South Pacific;
- the African-American Labor Center (AALC), which provides assistance to unions in Africa; and
- the Free Trade Union Institute (FTUI), which monitors labor rights violations and provides assistance to unions throughout the world.

Financed by government grants amounting to more than $28 million in 1987 and by more than $4 million in AFL-CIO funds the same year, the institutes attempt to "promote trade union rights and independent democratic trade unions" in more than ninety countries.[31] Each year they teach tens of thousands of unionists, many of whom have no previous training in labor matters, how to formalize shop-floor matters, conduct a meeting of a local, negotiate a sound contract, speak up for community gains, and experiment with new union services.

AIFLD alone has trained more than five hundred thousand Latin American unionists since 1962. In El Salvador, for example, it has helped peasants buy land and organize community development projects. In an indirect and tragic tribute to the organization's effectiveness, the military junta kicked it out of the country in 1973, and a right-wing death squad murdered two AIFLD staff members in 1981.[32] Members of the institute staff, who are continuously criticized by some American labor leaders for their doctrinaire and hard-boiled "anti-Communist efforts," reject oversimplification of a very complex matter.[33] They apologize for nothing and regret only that repressive authoritarian regimes subvert their progress in promoting labor union gains and human rights advances around the world.

A Word from the Skeptics

Some critics question the wisdom of political policies that seem inspired primarily by desperation, such as labor's alleged interest in protectionist trade measures.[34] In response, political unionists insist that they deal with each case as it arises, adjusting their advocacy after an exacting review, and that they are very sensitive to the needs of consumers who fear the cost of labor's alleged protectionist policies.

Critics also contend many local union leaders and workers are largely indifferent to political efforts. Meyerson, a longtime political staffer for several unions, observes, for example, "Local leadership does not perceive politics as part of its job. There is even some resentment at having to do politics."[35] While this attitude may have been characteristic years ago, the jarring Mondale loss in 1984, combined with the toll exacted by eight years of the Reagan administration, seem to have politicized many leaders and rank-and-file activists.

Other skeptics question labor's allegiance to the Democratic party, which they feel takes labor for granted and downplays its agenda in favor of middle-class concerns. They argue for the creation of a third party for which labor would be the highest priority. Opponents insist that the clearest rebuttal lies in the abject failure of the third-party candidacy of Henry A. Wallace in 1948. Moreover, many who oppose a third party cite the "Liberal Quotient Box Score" of the Americans for Democratic Action which gives Republicans a 15 percent average in the House and 25 percent in the Senate, while Democrats average 77 percent in the House and 76 percent in the Senate.[36] On that basis, many union leaders remain content to see 95 percent of labor PAC funds go to Democratic candidates.[37]

Critics from the political Left, not surprisingly, condemn the AFL-CIO political agenda for its class collaboration. In its place, they urge "tapping anger at the big corporations, expressing an economic populism of the little guys against big business, and mixing in an economic nationalism that insists on reversing economic decline and growing inequality."[38] As evidence that such an effort might work, they cite Jesse Jackson's ballot-box success in drawing blue-collar votes.[39]

COPE representatives and mainstream union presidents disagree with leftist assumptions about the political attitudes of the rank-and-file and insist the vast majority of dues payers are actually somewhat conservative. They refer to 1988 survey data that show disproportionate rank-and-file support of candidates Pat Robinson and Representative Richard A. Gephardt, whose populist class politics and traditional values did not challenge "the system" as a whole.[40] They argue further that the undecided voters, 2 million of whom are unionists, tend to be nonideological moderates. And they trust the political strategists who contend the pool of potential voters who are thirty to forty-five years old is "the least ideological of all age groups."[41]

Especially sharp criticism is aimed at labor's inability to retain political clout. In the words of one union staff member, Joan M. Baggett, labor has been "playing defense."[43] Its failure to sustain proportionate union membership has enabled legislators to act with reduced fear of voter retaliation, has necessitated layoffs of union lobbying personnel, and has forced cutbacks in union budgets for lobbying, voter education, and political ads.

Labor's political activists, however, perceive a very different record and point with pride to several significant accomplishments:[43]

- the presence of the secretary of labor at an AFL-CIO convention in October 1985 for the first time since 1979;
- the defeat of several highly conservative candidates for strategic NLRB posts;
- the steady defeat of state "right-to-work" laws;
- the successful coalition effort to defeat the nomination of Robert H. Bork to the Supreme Court;
- passage of a federal law signed in July 1988 that substantially curbs the use of lie detectors;
- the inclusion of a $1 billion worker-retraining fund in the new trade bill;
- the steady increase in support of labor-backed bills that provide for parental leave, ban double-breasting, and require employers to track workers who may have been exposed to toxic materials;
- the dissemination of useful guidelines for political activists, such as the IAM's 1984 paperback *Let's Rebuild America;* and
- the increasing significance of COPE's Committee on Marginal Races, which includes twenty influential labor PAC directors and is described by one expert as "the most crucial [of the] kingmakers."[44]

Above all, labor politicos take credit for massive demonstrations of support through letter-writing campaigns and rallies for protection of the "safety net" from White House machinations. Numerous efforts to dilute human service programs have been successfully blocked by labor lobbyists and their congressional allies.

Perhaps the best indication of rank-and-file support is that each year rank-and-filers make large voluntary contributions to the PACs run by unions. Such donations are "pocketbook votes" of endorsement for labor activists who see themselves, in Jesse Jackson's phrase, as "odds-breakers and dream-makers." Many members seem to agree with researchers who have concluded, "In all fairness . . . unions would likely have fared much worse in the political arena if they had not increased their political activity since the 1970s."[45]

Prospects for the Future

Organized labor has come a long way since 1923 when economist Selig Perlman characterized politics as among the least appealing of labor's prospects: "The Federation leaders, as we know, regard their political work as a necessary evil, due to an unfortunate turn of affairs, which forces them from time to time to step out of their own trade union province in order that their natural enemy, the employing class, might get no aid and comfort from an outside ally."[46]

COPE and union political workers fully intend to increase voter registration and turnout, grass-roots lobbying, political education, and PAC fund-raising. COPE staff member David Gregory expresses an optimism many of his colleagues share: "Things have improved tenfold! We are getting a better response now than ever before.... We win when we're backing a candidate that's got the trust of people. Choice is made on trust, on issues, on personality, and if our candidate has that edge we can bring 15 percent more votes than the general public can."[47]

The labor movement was responsible for one-third of all the votes received by the 1988 Democratic presidential candidate, and 68 percent of families with a union member voted for the Democrat.[48] It is poised to assume even greater significance in American politics. A new climate inside the AFL-CIO increasingly favorable to the open discussion of controversial matters extends labor's potential influence still further, a prospect savored by union leaders, labor's political activists, and rank-and-filers alike.[49]

Case Study
Rank-and-File Participation: The Democracy at Work Project

Characterized by its sponsor, the AFL-CIO, as "the most extensive education effort ever launched by any organization to involve voters in presidential politics," the success of Democracy at Work (DAW) exceeded even the expectations of its designers.[1] Bold in concept and polished in design, the project provided grass-roots unionists with critical information about the leading 1988 presidential candidates and directly influenced labor's successful involvement in the contest.

Background

Anticipating a difficult presidential election in 1988, labor's political activists knew that simply endorsing a candidate would not suffice. Instead, voters needed to be directly involved in evaluating candidates and have a say in labor's decision making. As one anonymous analyst explained:

> Traditional vote-churning organizations, such as the labor union and the urban machine, no longer function as they once did, largely because the electorate itself has changed. The American public increasingly seems to be made up of individuals with few deep political or organizational commitments, who form what ties they do have on the basis of information from the media, and who don't like to vote for a candidate just on some big shot's say so.[2]

Accordingly, the AFL-CIO sought new techniques to illuminate the presidential hopefuls, poll the responses of concerned unionists, and guide labor's eventual endorsements.

Learning from Failure

Labor had learned a painful lesson in 1984 from its controversial pre-convention endorsement of Walter Mondale and his defeat. Some political commentators then and after had argued that the endorsement cost the Democratic candidate votes, and some astute unionists agreed:

■ Linda Rasmussen, president of a CWA local in Portland, Oregon: "Mondale had earned our support, and I think early endorsement is a good idea, but 1984 probably wasn't the best time to try it for the first time."

■ K. W. Flanagan, a delegate to the July 1987 CWA convention: "I don't think anybody was going to beat Reagan. We screwed up in 1984 by selecting so early. That turned a lot of my people off because it looked to them like the fix was in, and they were left out of it. I think a lot of them voted for Reagan as a result."[3]

Not surprisingly, the AFL-CIO officially rejects this analysis and reminds its critics that nearly 5 of 13 million AFL-CIO members were polled before Mondale was endorsed.[4]

No one disputed the need, however, to encourage still more participation by rank-and-filers in labor's endorsement process. Charges that "back-room deals" had been made to win labor's support, as leveled in 1984 by Senator Gary Hart and the Reagan election committee, could definitely not seem creditable this time around.

Making It Happen

To create an efficient and effective endorsement system, the AFL-CIO sent more than 3.5 million letters to unionists explaining why labor had backed or opposed candidates in key Senate and House races in 1986. To reach all of its members, specialists working for the AFL-CIO's Committee on Political Education relied on a sophisticated new computer system. Using that system, COPE joined forces with another federation unit, the Labor Institute on Public Affairs, and together they created Democracy at Work.

DAW decided to create a low-cost videotape featuring the candidates, possibly amplified by a booklet, that could easily be distributed to AFL-CIO affiliates. The sponsors were unclear about its scope and focus, however, partly because of their experience in 1983. At that time, COPE had invited Democratic senators Alan Cranston of California, John Glenn of Ohio, and Gary Hart of Colorado to answer labor-related questions before a video camera, and the session had unexpectedly turned into a grilling. Presidential candidates might be reluctant to subject themselves to such a session, which had been criticized by some even within labor's ranks.

According to Loretta A. Bowen, political director for the CWA, the 1983 videotape had concentrated on "purely parochial labor issues." As Rachelle Horowitz, political director of the AFT, observed, "Somebody went into a room with thirty-two people, and they all named their favorite bill. 'Are you for situs picketing? Are you for HR 22?' "[5]

In an effort to prevent a recurrence of this uncomfortable and narrow encounter, DAW members identified six goals for their project:

- to include as many announced candidates as possible;
- to give each a chance to put his best foot forward;
- to attract Republicans as well as Democrats;
- to demonstrate labor's responsible curiosity about the positions of all major political contenders;
- to avoid controversy and acrimony in favor of calm and reasoned presentations; and
- to restrict all speakers to the same limited amount of time.

In the spring of 1987, the leading presidential candidates were invited to come to AFL-CIO headquarters to make a four-and-a-half-minute presentation on the "unique leadership role of the presidency." They were told the videotape would provide "an opportunity to convince us you understand the aspirations of working-class people and will include our concerns in a leadership plan to serve all the people."[6] Each was also asked to provide in writing answers to questions on the trade deficit, the federal budget deficit, and the government's role in domestic social policy, as well as organized labor's role in the political process.

Cynics predicted few candidates would agree to cooperate, and certainly none of the Republicans. Because of lingering controversy over the 1984 preconvention endorsement of Mondale, some skeptics even thought certain Democratic candidates would decline due to "unavoidable schedule conflicts." Democracy at Work, they whispered, would prove to be just another example of labor's chronic inability to get its act together.

In fact, every announced presidential candidate accepted the invitation. A highly polished videotape made in the AFL-CIO building in April 1987 included Governor Bruce Babbitt, Senator Joseph R. Biden, Jr., Governor Michael S. Dukakis, Representative Richard Gephardt, Senator Albert Gore, Jr., the Reverend Jesse Jackson, and Senator Paul Simon from the Democratic party. Representing the Republicans were Vice-President George Bush, Senator Robert Dole, Governor Pete du Pont, General Alexander M. Haig, Jr., Representative Jack Kemp, and the Reverend Pat Richardson. At the same time, a special issue of the *American Federationist* offered twelve of the thirteen candidates' answers to four questions DAW had posed. (Pat Richardson chose not to respond in writing.)[7]

State federation bodies, city labor councils, and locals throughout the nation soon discovered that the videotape and its printed supplement had genuine appeal, and increasing numbers of unionists took advantage of the opportunity they provided. Impressed by the size and reaction of audiences viewing the tape, a reporter for the *Washington Post* commented that labor had put together "the hottest new video in politics—a sort of sneak preview of the 1987 campaign."[8]

According to members of the COPE staff, ten thousand copies of the video had to be created to meet nationwide demand. They found viewers felt the appeal was being made directly to them: their approval and votes were being solicited in a cogent, focused, and noncondescending manner. Rank-and-filers could not recall ever having been taken as seriously by the nation's leading politicians. They also appreciated the straightforwardness of the video, in contrast to the deceptive gimmicks of televised political ads. In addition, many union members were flattered by the candidates' greetings: "My friends of the AFL-CIO," "Women and men of labor," or, as Governor Dukakis, Representative Kemp, and Senator Simon said, "My fellow unionists." Such salutations were regarded as welcome recognition of labor's political clout and as a boost to the egos of rank-and-file viewers.

Guidelines for Utilization

To maximize the impact of the videotape and the special issue of the *American Federationist*, DAW established several guidelines for their use:

- Audience members were encouraged to share their reactions to the candidates and the issues.
- Audience members were urged to read the special issue of the *American Federationist* and to share their reactions with other rank-and-filers.
- No discussions of candidate preference or straw polls were to follow a screening of the tape. DAW was the educational phase of the AFL-CIO political process. Before the AFL-CIO General Board endorsed candidates in October 1987, members would be asked to express their preferences directly through their unions.[9]
- Only members of AFL-CIO unions and their families were permitted to attend, since federal election law forbade distribution of the written questions or the videotape to the general public.
- Scrupulous impartiality was to be shown to all speakers and to both parties: "The trust in the AFL-CIO displayed by the cooperation of the candidates must be reciprocated."[10]

Above all, unions were urged to assure their members that their preferences would "lead to a bottom-up, rather than a top-down decision about which candidate to endorse."[11]

Extending the Project

Rank-and-file response to DAW was so positive that two unions created a supplementary video of their own. The American Federation of Government Employees and the National Association of Letter Carriers joined forces to produce their own tape in which seven Democratic aspirants spoke about specific concerns of federal employees, such as "privatization" of federal programs and Hatch Act reform. All of the Republican hopefuls declined to participate.[12]

Inspired by these other unions, AFSCME printed a poll on candidate preference in its newspaper. Throughout the summer of 1987, the poll drew an average of two hundred mail ballots daily. A similar poll in the IAM's newspaper also earned a high response, with 84 percent showing a preference for the Democrats.[13] Other major unions then became involved in soliciting their members:

- The July 1987 issue of the *Carpenter* began a series of articles on political action that included each of the thirteen candidates' proposed solutions for dealing with the growing threat of foreign trade.
- At the July convention of the Brotherhood of Railway Carmen (BRC), seven hundred delegates representing two hundred thousand members filled out questionnaires on the candidates and issues, while the union's magazine solicited a straw vote from all BRC members.
- The July issue of *UFCW Action* focused on the candidates' views on the role of government in meeting human needs.

In addition, publications of state federations and city labor councils reprinted the candidates' written responses to labor's questions.[14]

Assessing the Impact

My impressions of the videotape paralleled those gained by COPE and LIPA observers at sessions similar to one I attended at the AFL-CIO George Meany Center:

- The tone was adult and informative. Audience members were given credit for possessing a general awareness of the key campaign issues.
- Each of the Republican candidates complimented President Kirkland and the AFL-CIO for offering the GOP a valuable opportunity to compare and contrast its front-runners with those of the Democratic party.
- Democratic candidates gave union members credit for open-mindedness in choosing among political styles.

- All of the speakers highlighted their efforts to help the labor movement over the years. Some took the opportunity to "set the record straight," such as Governor Bruce Babbitt who discussed his recent use of the National Guard to end a major copper mine strike in his state. The effect was to enhance the pride of union members in the significance of their movement.
- The presence of the Republican candidates finessed a "special-interest" charge that had long plagued labor. As CWA president Morton Bahr explained, "We've taken the curse off what happened to Mondale. No one will be able to accuse someone else of being a 'captive' of labor."[15]

Some viewers undoubtedly wondered whether unprepared answers might have better demonstrated each candidate's ability to think and speak spontaneously. And some viewers may have felt a second videotape, commenting on the policies and voting records of each candidate, would have been useful during the process of assessment and choice.

Lingering Doubts

Skeptics continue to ask whether DAW was merely a case of "preaching to the converted." Were those rank-and-filers who were willing to spend an evening watching the videotape the most politically alert and well informed beforehand while those who chose not to come the most politically indifferent? If so, DAW may ironically demonstrate how really difficult it is to get democracy to work.

Supporters of DAW reply that its greatest value was that it improved the self-definition of local union activists. It reminded people who staffed election phone banks, stuffed envelopes, and posted handbills of labor's steadily growing political clout. By galvanizing these vital activists, the tape helped invigorate democracy inside and outside the labor movement.

Summary

Labor educator Hig Roberts bases his judgment of the project on more than thirty years in union affairs: "It was a brilliant move, not because of what was or wasn't said, almost all of which will be forgotten, but because they actually pulled it off! They actually got the front-runners together and put the whole thing together.... People like to feel they matter, like to believe their opinions count for something, and this darn film helped them feel good about themselves!"[16] This assessment carries special weight because Roberts saw the tape over and over again with different audiences throughout the South.

Regardless of the Bush victory, the DAW project proved an important victory for labor in the 1988 presidential campaign. The consensus of the media, a proud *AFL-CIO News* boasted, was that the project "dwarfed any education campaign ever undertaken to involve voters."[17] It enhanced labor's political respectability and boosted political sophistication and morale in the ranks. Above all, it helped affirm a commitment to politics built from the ground up rather than from the top down, and it reinforced labor's far-reaching conviction that democracy *can* work.

Part V

UNIONS AND BUSINESS

In recent years, labor has brought an unprecedented vigor to its financial dealings with its employing companies. With corporate raiders and takeovers a constant threat to union-management relations, labor has learned the best defense is the capacity to take the offense. Union leaders have begun to study the intricacies of corporate finance so as to turn complex economic situations to labor's advantage. Chapter 12 explores the creative use of buyout bids by unions in the chaotic, deregulated airline industry. Two case studies follow that spotlight the advantages and perils of worker ownership, while a third explores the pros and cons of "pension power."

Chapter 13 analyzes labor's alliances with community-based reform groups. A case study follows that describes two locals that are building union-sponsored housing. A second case study highlights a promising alliance between building trades unionists and environmental groups. Characteristic of all these efforts is labor's new willingness to take risks and assume novel responsibilities.

Chapter 12

New Forms of Worker Involvement

The recent efforts of unions show that they can finance bids. And that could do as much to alter labor-management relations as any development in the past half-century. **Aaron Bernstein, *Business Week*, December 14, 1987, 125**

A lot of unions have been passive players in the financial markets. Now they are saying, "We don't have to be." They are actually getting up on the playing field and playing the game themselves.

Richard Belous, labor economist,
***Philadelphia Inquirer*, August 9, 1987, 12-C**

Margaret Brennan, a flight attendant for Pan American World Airways since 1969, earned media attention in 1987 for "acting more like a corporate raider ready to make a move."[1] Chairperson of a ten thous-and–member coalition composed of members of Pan Am's unions of flight attendants, pilots, ticket agents, and flight engineers, Brennan tried to force a thorough restructuring of the nation's seventh largest airline. The coalition's goals were to find another airline or investor to take over the troubled carrier, to replace top management, and, in return for reasonable labor concessions, to gain substantial ownership of Pan Am.

Along the way, as Brennan explained, she enjoyed the reactions of bewildered corporate managers: "It drives business people crazy to see unions acting like this. They can't accept what we're doing because we're stepping out of the union mold." As reporter Jennifer Lin noted, the idea of unions as financiers was emerging "as a significant trend in the labor movement and on Wall Street, according to labor economists, union leaders, and investment bankers."[2]

The New Activism

Historically, labor has been expected simply to react to the jockeying of companies on the finance battlefield. In a game that was byzantine and fast moving, labor was expected to do nothing but wait on the sidelines and hope for the best.

Now, however, in a sharp break with tradition, a small but growing number of unions are cautiously joining the fray. When financiers suspect a struggle over ownership is imminent, they have begun to explore the position unions may take, knowing they could prove to be a decisive factor. At the same time, a few unions are influencing, even controlling, the outcome of such events instead of meekly making the best of a raid attempt or takeover. They have advanced their own blueprints for restructuring and for buyouts. And, increasingly, they have actually become the pivotal players. They contend that the best way to confront corporate turbulence is by meeting raiders on their own terms, but with an agenda especially designed to protect union rank-and-filers.

Learning the Strategies

The boldest unions have turned to well-established investment bankers for guidance, while recognizing that such a relationship builds on an awkward history. At a meeting of steelworkers in Gadsden, Alabama, for example, an officer of the United Steelworkers characterized investment bankers as "tools of the boss class" and described a banker the union had retained to speak as "the best of a bad lot." Nonetheless, unions concede that they need investment bankers "as urgently as they once needed lawyers to fight injunctions."[3] In 1986, for the first time, an investment banker was invited to make a presentation to the AFL-CIO Executive Council. His talk focused on how takeover wars were affecting organized labor and what unions might do about it.

Not surprisingly, the high price of financial advice has restricted the number of unions using financial advice services, although the number has increased steadily. Leading attorney/financier Eugene J. Keilin of Lazard Freres charged $75,000 a month in 1986 plus 1 percent if he successfully negotiated a deal. He received $1.25 million for his services at that time on behalf of the TWA pilots.[4]

Background

In the mid-1970s, an agile union organizing campaign persuaded progressive churches to use their stock holdings on labor's behalf. During a stockholders' meeting at J. P. Stevens, for example, the clergy, as dissident stockholders, introduced and reintroduced resolutions condemning the company's bitter anti-labor policies. Their effort was widely credited with helping to force Stevens to bargain with ACTWU, which represented 20 percent of the mills' labor force.

A variety of "capital strategy" successes followed, including the 1982 bid by railroad unions to restructure Conrail and the brief 1983 collaboration of an IAM local with the (pre-Lorenzo) management of Eastern Airlines in an effort to cut costs and restructure.[5]

TWA and Its Unions

The first time labor decided the outcome of a major takeover battle was in 1985 at TWA. Financier Carl Icahn had made a bid for the airline in April, and the board tried to fend him off in the courts. Unable to do so, TWA's board chose Frank A. Lorenzo of Texas Air as its champion, even though TWA unions reviled him as a union buster.

TWA's local of the Air Line Pilots Association sought out Keilin and, after lengthy discussions, empowered him to offer Icahn significant concessions that it would not give to Lorenzo. When an IAM local offered similar wage and benefit concessions on behalf of the airline's machinists, the TWA board reconsidered and accepted Icahn's bid. In addition to freezing out Lorenzo, this "creative bargaining," a term strongly preferred to "concession bargaining," provided the ALPA local with about 7 percent of the company and the IAM with about 3.5 percent.[6]

Keilin earned labor's praise again in 1986 when he prompted the Steelworkers and USX to resume bargaining during a bitter dispute the union characterized as a lockout and the company described as a strike. After negotiations had been stalemated for eighty days, Carl Icahn started to buy USX shares and announced a takeover bid for the company. At that point, Keilin proposed that Lynn Williams, president of the Steelworkers, talk directly with Icahn in an effort to pressure USX to settle. He also explored the possibility of the Steelworkers making a separate deal with Icahn in which the union would offer concessions in return for equity if he was successful in obtaining USX. Not surprisingly, USX reconsidered its position. Fearing a deal between the union and Icahn might facilitate a takeover, as it had at TWA in 1985, USX rushed to reopen union-management negotiations, and Icahn soon dropped his takeover offer.

United Airlines and Its ALPA Local

One of the most dramatic examples of labor's use of innovative financial strategies involves ongoing negotiations between United Airlines, the nation's second largest carrier, and three locals representing its employees. Led by an ALPA local, the unionists continue a campaign to use its pension fund to buy the company, a move economist Robert Kuttner has described as "the almost unheard-of exception" to the conservative approach labor has historically taken to such funds.[7]

After a bitter twenty-nine-day strike against United in 1985 (see case study, page 118, on the local's innovative use of teleconferencing during this strike), the ALPA local spent eighteen months studying an idea highlighted during the last nationwide teleconference. Attorney F. Lee Bailey had suggested that one way to prevent future confrontations and influence the company directly was simply to buy it through some form of employee stock ownership plan (see case study, page 221, on unions and ESOPs).

Captain Roger Hall, now a first vice-president of ALPA, headed the local in 1985. He maintains that a $4.5 billion plan to buy United made by the Lazard Freres investment house was "solid, very solid."[8] According to Hall, within seven years, the ALPA local would have been able to become the sole owner of the sixty-one thousand–member company and to pay off any loans entailed. The time period could have been reduced to four years if the IAM and the Association of Flight Attendants had joined in the plan. Although technically the employees, and not the unions, would have bought United, union members could have participated only if one or more of the unions negotiated the deal. The buyout would have been accomplished using a new ESOP created by the unions for this purpose and controlled unofficially by them.

United's management, led by chairman Richard J. Ferris, was surprised and infuriated on April 5, 1987, when ALPA made its bid. "Our pilots are good people," he remarked. "I just wish they'd stick to flying."[9] The ALPA local, in turn, sharply condemned Ferris for jeopardizing a sound company through grievous mismanagement. It cited his decision to buy the Hertz Company and the Hilton International hotels as costly digressions from the airline business and as serious drains on its resources. It also claimed his decision to spin off profitable parts of the airline, such as United's lucrative reservation system, was reducing profits and thereby making employees more vulnerable to a raid.

Financed by a voluntary diversion of pension fund assets, a 25 percent wage "redirection" from pilots' paychecks into ESOP stock, and a 10 percent increase in productivity linked to changes in work rules, the local's $4.5 billion buyout plan stipulated that Ferris would have to go, the hotels and Hertz would follow soon thereafter, and the company would focus on the business it knew best. An ALPA spokesperson noted that "if we were running the airline, we'd probably have a newer, quieter, more fuel-efficient fleet of airplanes."[10] As concessions to the bankers who would have loaned the new ESOP the necessary $4.5 billion, the local also pledged that wages would be frozen and the pilots would not strike for the next seven years.

Underlying the local's plan was the belief that pilots are more vulnerable than other airline employees to corporate shakeups because their pay is based on seniority within a particular company. The buyout, the local believed, was well worth the concessions offered. As Jalmer Johnson, ALPA's manager of economic analysis, explained, "There's potential for substantial cuts in pay in the next round of bargaining in 1988. They have even threatened to liquidate the airline. We feel our future and the future of this airline are very cloudy. The pay cuts in the buyout are relatively small compared to the costs of interrupting our careers."[11]

At least one investment expert, Malon Wilkus, president of American Capital Strategies, agreed publicly that the local's overall strategy was sound, particularly its effort to forestall an expected crisis, rather than merely respond to one: "The pilots have put the company in play, and they can take it out of play if management agrees to treat them better. Even if they fail in the buyout, they may nevertheless succeed with a collective bargaining strategy."[12] That prediction proved correct in June 1987 when the board dramatically forced United to fire Ferris, sell Hertz and Hilton, and return the company to the business of running an airline.

United's pilots were elated, while other unions and labor specialists "were surprised the pilots got such big results."[13] Particular pleasure was taken in the removal of ALPA's nemesis, for as John Zalusky, an AFL-CIO economist, explained, "The only way to deal with Ferris was to get rid of the rascal. It became a case of who could do what to whom first and last." Captain Henry A. Duffy, president of ALPA, noted that although the company directors did not buy the plan, "they've bought our strategy. Now, our pilots have got to focus in on their bid for the airline." The *Wall Street Journal* tipped its hat to this "unprecedented attempt by a union to seek full control of a healthy company." And the labor specialist with *USA Today* felt ALPA's success "could embolden other airline unions, which haven't won many battles lately."[14]

In 1987, management warned that an ALPA buyout bid might produce "a very heavily indebted, financially weak airline with severely limited growth potential." Management said it would consider an employee buyout only if it were an all-cash offer, all the unions signed the pact, it provided a voice for the more than twenty thousand nonunion employees, and it contained a "satisfactory" management plan. In response, the ALPA local insisted the company's willingness to be even this specific showed the pilots their proposal "still had a chance."[15]

By mid-1987 more than four thousand of United's sixty-five hundred pilots had contributed more than $14 million beyond their regular dues to keep the buyout campaign moving forward.[16] But as Captain Rick Dubinsky, leader of the local, said, ALPA members foresaw a tough campaign: "We can afford to pay more for the airline than anybody else because we, and no one else, will have the concessions working for us. Management may have to be clubbed in the head by shareholders to see this." United pilots, the local contended, "are not prepared to settle for anything less than significant ownership of the company. Period. End of Statement."[17]

After more turmoil, in January 1990, the ALPA local succeeded in forming a coalition with the other two United locals (of the IAM and the Association of Flight Attendants) and with the line's largest investor, Coniston Partners, a New York investment firm. The coalition's ESOP bid, the first made jointly by all three unions, included about $2 billion in wage cuts over five years and contract terms insuring five years of labor peace. On April 6, 1990, the directors agreed to sell the company to the coalition.[18]

If and when shareholders and the three unions approve the deal, and the coalition's investment bankers succeed in raising the necessary financing, the new United Airlines will be the largest company in the world owned by its employees. Through the new ESOP, the 6,577 pilots will own 38 percent; the 25,623 machinists, 36 percent; the 13,237 flight attendants, 12 percent; and the 18,304 nonunion employees, 14 percent. Each union, as well as the salaried employees, will also have one seat on a new fifteen-member board.[19]

At a news conference on April 6, reporters reminded John Peterpaul, general vice-president of the IAM, that in the past he had been opposed in principle to employees becoming owners. His response explained his new, pro-ESOP position: "We have to put United into employee hands. We have to get involved so that we are taken out of the grip of outside interests." Similarly, Diane Robertson, president of the AFA, said, "We see it as an investment to get control of our destiny."[20]

Whether any bids will be successful remains uncertain. What is certain, however, is that as early as 1987 knowledgeable observers were already convinced the saga at United Airlines was likely to "prompt other unions to become more than bit players in corporate restructurings."[21]

Pan Am

One of the "most striking management upheavals in corporate history" occurred on January 22, 1988, when the outside directors of Pan Am, bending to the pressure of a union coalition, voted to oust the two top officers of the company. This "quiet drama," *New York Times* reporter Agis Salpukas noted, was a stunning display of the power unions have wielded in the airline industry in recent years: "In return for wage and benefit concessions, they have been able to call the shots in determining who gains control of an airline in a takeover struggle, and now, in the case of Pan Am, who must walk the plank when turnaround attempts have failed." Although the board had gradually been losing confidence in the airline's two top executives and probably would have ousted them soon, a director who insisted on anonymity confided to the press that "it was the pressure from the unions that brought about the shakeup."[22]

Months earlier a coalition of the Pan Am unions of transport workers, teamsters, pilots, flight attendants, and flight engineers had hired investment bankers to assess the company's financial situation. According to management, the company had expected to break even in 1987. But as early as July the union's hired experts warned that a loss of about $100 million seemed far more likely, and in January 1988, the chief executive officer acknowledged that the loss was $150 million. The union coalition then began to seek a competent, experienced buyer.

Overtures were made to Jay A. Pritzker, a midwestern financier and the chairman of Braniff Airways, and the coalition promised to seek $200 million in union concessions to assist his takeover. But the board was firmly opposed, and two of the coalition's members, the Teamsters and the Transport Workers Union, balked at the proposed givebacks. It quickly became clear that repeated attempts to seat Pritzker were going nowhere.

A lawyer for the coalition then suggested a new deal that would suspend efforts to find a buyer if top management was immediately fired, and the unions pledged about $180 million in concessions being sought by the board. While the same two unions remained cautious about the terms, the board accepted the deal and designated a new CEO acceptable to the union coalition. As Margaret Brennan, chairperson of the Pan Am union coalition, explained, "For the last year the joint labor coalition has cited change in management as a necessary element for Pan Am's survival. The board of directors has finally recognized this reality."[23]

Responses to the new corporate leader varied widely. The *New York Times* reported, "He was received warmly—a phenomenon not seen recently at Pan Am because of the work force's hostility toward much of the company's top management."[24] But not everyone was pleased. The head of the airline division of the TWU, the largest local at the airline, wrote to the board deploring its willingness to weaken the line's chances of survival by trading changes in management for union concessions. On the corporate side, an anonymous "participant in the ouster" told a reporter, "This is a historic event in the annals of corporate history. Here is a board of directors selling out their management in exchange for labor agreements, some of which have not been delivered. What will the new CEO do when he goes to the pilots for a new contract, and they say, 'We don't want to deal with you—send the board down here'?"[25] Another Pan Am executive complained that the move set a precedent for unions to seek the ouster of executives they did not like, and he concluded bitterly that "it's a travesty."[26]

The union coalition has continued to keep Pan Am's management off balance and sensitive to labor. In exchange for their concessions, the unions are to receive 21 million new shares of Pan Am common stock and an additional 15 million shares if specific profit goals are reached.[27] Such arrangements attest to the ways unions can take charge of their destinies in the high finance of airlines.

Summary

As Paul Rusen, a practitioner and former negotiator for the United Steelworkers, proudly explains, "We're starting to think like capitalists."[28] Such a sentiment may puzzle some labor old-timers, but many younger unionists welcome labor's high-finance efforts to protect its members directly and to help protect the nation's economy indirectly.

With more gains to date than losses, the unions at this frontier are likely to increase their expertise. Likewise, corporations are learning to deal respectfully with a new player that is increasingly their peer. Ruthless raiders, "greenmail" artists, and corporate plunderers threaten labor-management relations as never before. Either more unions will improve upon capital strategies pioneered by airline union locals or far more will be victimized in the financial "jungle." The appropriate choice would seem clear.

Turning an ESOP to Advantage: The Seymour Wire Case

An employee stock ownership plan enables workers to purchase stock in the company for which they work. According to Raymond Russell, ESOPs may be the most accessible mechanism for workers who are eager to own a stake in their employer's company: "It seems highly questionable whether the current efforts to make workers owners in the United States will lead to anything but illusory or transitory forms of workers' control in more than a small number of firms. The best chance of making them amount to something more than this lies with the ESOPs."[1] And that confidence in the potential of ESOPs is widely held.

ESOPs have gained in popularity since 1974 when a federal law encouraged companies to set up trusts in which employees could invest portions of their earnings as savings or deferred income. These investments are exempt from federal income tax, as are company contributions, which may be made in the form of stock, cash, or real estate. Trustees of the ESOP invest the employee and company contributions chiefly in the stock of the company itself. An ESOP thereby allows a company with a profit-sharing plan to borrow tax-sheltered money. It does not, however, require the company to give its workers participatory voting rights with which to help direct the firm, a fact that explains much of labor's skepticism about ESOPs.

About 75 percent of all ESOPs are investment rather than participatory in format, offering employees a stake in the ownership of their firm but no significant involvement in its management.[2] In contrast, a participatory ESOP requires that workers share in the decision-making power as well as the profits, making them attractive to a growing number of unions. To date, however, only a handful of ESOPs involve substantial sharing of power, as envisioned, for example, in the 1990 union bid to create an ESOP at United Airlines.[3]

Scope and Significance

By 1990, the number of firms with ESOPs was up to ten thousand, and they involved 9 percent of the work force.[4] Proponents expect involvement to reach at least 25 percent of all U.S. workers by the year 2000.[5]

Politicians favor ESOPs as a strategy to keep troubled firms afloat, protect jobs, and make credit available to rank-and-filers. As William Baldwin explained in *Forbes* magazine, "The theory goes like this: Rich folks can borrow money to make money; the rest of us can't. Give the worker access to credit, and he can bootstrap himself into ownership of productive assets."[6] The exciting projections offered by proponents of ESOPs can also create very high expectations among workers: "A 1985 study by the National Center for Employee Ownership, based on the performance of 147 ESOPs, projected that an employee earning the median wage of $18,000 in 1983 could expect to accumulate an ESOP share worth $31,000 in ten years, and $120,000 in twenty."[7]

To put this in perspective, the ten-year figure exceeds the net worth of half of all American families; the twenty-year figure exceeds the net worth of all but the top fifth. John Logue contends that "when all other considerations are equal, employee-owned enterprises outperform conventional companies in profitability, growth of productivity, volume of sales per employee, and number of new jobs created." Specifically, companies with ESOPs expand sales 5.4 percent faster and employment 5.1 percent faster than comparable companies without ESOPs.[8]

The potential effect on labor-management relations is profound, as Baldwin explains: "Beyond spreading the wealth, ESOPs promise an end to confrontation between labor and management, an end to featherbedding—and even an end to the welfare state. Who needs it when we all have a second income as capitalists?"[9] Another argument in favor of ESOPs, this one whispered rather than shouted, contends they are anti-union since they can effectively dilute working-class militancy. Companies with ESOPs suggest management really cares about employee well-being and a local union has become superfluous. In 1984, for example, an IAM local at the Ohio Brass factory in Mansfield, Ohio, initially opposed an ESOP buyout. When the union later sought representation under an ESOP successorship clause, it lost on a secret ballot by 114 votes to 2 and was decertified.[10]

ESOP Disappointments

Critics insist most ESOPs give workers very little power or influence. As economist Robert Kuttner notes, "The workers ordinarily end up with about as much influence in the management of the firm as Soviet workers have in managing the Kremlin."[11] What actually motivates creation of an ESOP, the critics conclude, is the desire for capital to be sheltered from taxes or for management to be sheltered from raids.

Another focus of criticism is that ESOPs are often substituted for funded pension plans. Because ESOP stocks are sold privately, an employee's retirement income depends not only on the success of the firm but on the judgment of management in setting the price on the shares of stock at the time an employee retires.

Two other weaknesses have emerged in the few cases in which employees have gained control through ESOP buyouts. These attempts at worker ownership, such as widely publicized efforts at Rath and at Hyatt-Clark in the early 1980s, often fail because the companies were already in serious trouble at the time of the attempt. And even when the companies succeed, workers may still have trouble obtaining adequate advice or sufficient credit to guide their efforts at self-management. Some commentators contend, in fact, it is worse to prop up firms temporarily with an ESOP buyout than to allow them to go under. Douglas Sease explains: "Industrial rescues are having the perverse effect of delaying the recovery of sick industries. An individual company or factory is saved, yet the underlying problem—excess capacity—remains somewhere down the road, and someone will have to give up. ESOP-backed rescues distort the process that weeds out the weakest members of the industry, leaving the stronger companies to compete."[12] Congress, these critics insist, should try to reduce the incentives to save aging and inefficient companies instead of liberalizing ESOP regulations to help keep them alive.

Labor responds that ESOP buyouts of troubled plants are feasible only when substantial federal, state, and municipal investment funds are available to provide critical support, such as plant modernization. Labor is adamant in emphasizing that an ESOP cannot effectively replace a local union. The false illusion that it can overlooks needs workers have

- to inform themselves about the wages and benefits of their industry or trade;
- to inform themselves about the true financial condition of their employer and to assess the meaning of that financial condition in terms of their own interests as workers;
- to negotiate with management; and
- to inform themselves about their own interests in the political and legislative processes of their community, state, and nation in order to act collectively on behalf of those interests.[13]

Having itemized their needs, informed workers scoff at the idea an ESOP could replace their union. As commentator James Smith says, "Owning a few shares of stock or having them beneficially owned by a set of trustees will not satisfy any of these needs."[14]

The most interesting perspective on ESOPs is that they can actually be turned to labor's advantage, as one was at Seymour Specialty Wire Company, a bustling New England factory organized by the UAW.

Seymour Specialty Wire Company: A Test Case

One of nearly 1,500 U.S. companies in which employees own a majority of stock, Seymour Specialty Wire Company in Seymour, Connecticut, is also one of 250 or so in which union and nonunion employees are represented on the board. It is one of very few U.S. companies, "perhaps the only one, in which employees have voting control [by five to four]. It is thus on the cutting edge of an array of issues arising at companies where unions have won board seats."[15]

The Seymour Wire ESOP works! Business has improved since 1985, when the employees bought their plant from an indifferent conglomerate parent using an ESOP the UAW helped structure. Since a strong UAW local initiated the buyout, Seymour Wire provides a model of healthy union expectations of the best possible result of ESOP experimentation.

Background

Seymour, Connecticut, is a small industrial town of fourteen thousand, located in what was once the center of the American brass industry. Because of its severe disinvestment and dozens of plant closings in recent years, it has been described as a "deindustrial valley."[16] In the early 1980s, Seymour had an unemployment rate higher than the state average, and workers were anxious about further job loss.

In 1983, the Connecticut State UAW joined a new coalition, the Naugatuck Valley Project (NVP), created by an alliance of statewide leaders of Catholic and Protestant denominations and the Connecticut Citizens Action Group. NVP sought to assert worker and community interests in response to rumors of pending plant closings, such as those in Seymour.

Early in 1984, some of the 250 workers at Bridgeport Brass, a century-old wire mill that was Seymour's second largest employer, heard rumors that its parent company, National Distillers, might sell the Seymour operation. The area's UAW staff representative urged the workers to consider buying the wire-making plant, which was profitable, although not profitable enough to please its corporate owners. The UAW representative referred the officers of the local in the mill to NVP. Guided by NVP and the Industrial Cooperative Association (ICA), UAW Local 1827 voted to pursue the matter in earnest. A subcommittee traveled to two other UAW buyout projects, Hyatt-Clark Industries in New Jersey and Atlas Chain in eastern Pennsylvania, where Bridgeport Brass workers were warned not to dilute worker ownership. On the basis of that advice, the local chose to create an ESOP and elected the new company's board of directors on a one-person, one-vote basis. They chose as chief executive officer the person who had been plant manager for eleven years.

By 1984, sales were up to $20 million and the company was the national leader in several product lines. Thus, when the local went to banks for a major buyout loan, six of the eight banks approached were willing to finance the deal. Employees were not required to put up any equity, but the union local agreed to accept a 10 percent wage cut to ease servicing of the debt. In April 1985, Bridgeport Brass was officially reborn as Seymour Specialty Wire, an employee-owned company.

So What?

Guided by the UAW, the Seymour Wire ESOP established a highly democratic structure of control and ownership:

- New employees are automatically included in the ESOP.
- Each department meets every two weeks to discuss all issues concerning the department and the company.
- Personnel policies and procedures are consistent for all employees, regardless of the color of their collars.
- The company holds quarterly shareholder meetings for its worker-owners, and 90 percent of its employees attend the annual meeting.

Overall, the switch from a branch plant to a participatory ESOP was "marked by a process of redefinition of roles that can be compared to that of a country which has suddenly been transformed from a monarchy to a constitutional republic, where rules and processes for decision-making must be reinvented almost from scratch."[17]

Role of the Union

Considerable awkwardness accompanied the new startup, as the president of the UAW local, Michael Kearney, recalls: "When we first established employee participation, management was a combination of patronizing to us and scared that we would start a revolution and their heads would roll. Workers didn't trust managers, either. But we learned that bucking heads doesn't work, and we started listening to each other and working together."[18]

Bolstered by its role as a catalyst, Local 1827 has grown stronger. With much deliberation, it has kept traditional labor-management issues within the bargaining process. By its choice, the time clock remains. Management still does the hiring. The standard grievance process has been maintained. And little change has occurred in production quotas. Nonetheless, the current climate of labor relations entails a healthy exchange as major decisions are made through a process of discussion and consent. As Kearney explains, "We sit around the table, rather than across the table."[19]

The Verdict

Even before the first year had passed, Seymour Specialty Wire was an economic success. After six months, ESOP members received a bonus, and wages were restored to prebuyout levels. Business has continued to prosper, thanks in large part to increased efficiency: "For eleven years as plant manager, Carl Drescher tried to get National Distillers to agree to buy a machine that now [1986] costs $1 million. And for eleven years he failed, despite the fact that the machine would have paid for itself in only nine months. The new board drawn from the plant took only fifteen minutes to authorize the purchase."[20] While the plant's previous absentee management may have known how to make money, the new worker-owners know how to make special-alloy wire and how to increase income for all parties.

Most important, the participatory ESOP has brought power and responsibility back home to the shop floor. As the president of UAW Local 1827 explains:

> Under National Distillers, . . . the only way we had any kind of control . . . was the grievance procedure. Now you don't have to worry about National coming in and saying, "Cut this out," and there goes twenty jobs. Anything that's happened in the company since we bought it, I've been called upstairs, asked my opinion. Once all the employees are involved in one step or another of that decision-making process, controlling their future—that should be the ultimate.[21]

Sharing power and responsibility remains "the ultimate" goal of this uncommon yet tentative and problematic work relationship.[22]

To be sure, it has not been easy. The local union president now likens the experience to "six tours in Vietnam."[23] The disruption of a legacy of more than one hundred years of assigned roles with traditional privileges has inevitably led to conflicts. Workers at Seymour have continued to use traditional weapons, such as slowdowns and sabotage, to force the removal of an unpopular supervisor. Although new roles remain undefined and accountability has not been established, both labor and management hasten to claim success in reaching their overarching goal, the preservation of their livelihoods in a setting that respects their adulthood.

Conclusions

Since their appearance in the mid-1970s, ESOPs have been used in seven major ways:

- for corporate financing;
- to defer compensation, as a substitute for more conventional pensions or in place of other benefits and wages;
- to raise employee motivation in order to boost productivity and profits;
- to create a market for the stock of a closely held company;
- to fight hostile corporate takeovers;

- as a trade-off for wage concessions; and
- as a strategy for transferring ownership of companies to workers.[24]

Edward Cohen-Rosenthal and Cynthia E. Burton conclude that as a vehicle for employee ownership, ESOPs are "not impossible, but only difficult. As an arena for union-management cooperation around financial participation, this is the most challenging one."[25] Joseph Blasi adds that ESOPs remain only one of several possible forms of employee ownership: "Perhaps the motives are correct, but the tool is wrong."[26] Certainly, well-publicized failures could still disillusion labor and evoke resistance to the ESOP option.

Naturally, labor prefers ESOPs in which ownership is coupled with authentic shop-floor decision-making power.[27] Seymour Specialty Wire Company and its few scattered counterparts remain significant test cases. Their continued success could model a strategy for large-scale adaptation throughout unionized workplaces.[28] As one union activist has commented, "Although worker ownership has had a disappointing history in the United States, and even though modern ESOPs have recently served as an anti-union tool, there is no practical or philosophical reason why unions and worker ownership . . . cannot co-exist."[29]

Three recent developments have heartened proponents of ESOPs. A full-page feature story in the March 19, 1990, issue of the *AFL-CIO News* heralded the ESOP-based purchase for $33 million of a prosperous Washington State wood mill by former employees who were members of a local of the United Brotherhood of Carpenters. Perhaps the hundredth such buyout since 1975, this one offers valuable lessons in how to leverage high-yield bonds, preferred stock, and the expertise of an ESOP-promoting state agency. Thanks to national coverage in the *AFL-CIO News*, the local has begun to attract deserved attention from counterparts across the country.[30]

Similar attention was given to the dramatic and unusual resolution of a four-year struggle by 1,050 striking members of UAW Local 376 and the Colt Industry's firearms division in Hartford, Connecticut. Purchase of the 154-year-old division was possible in large part because an unusual coalition was formed of labor, the state, and former plant managers. Strikers will return to work with $13 million in back pay, their seniority intact, a 13 percent wage hike, cost-of-living adjustments for future wages, pension credit for time lost on strike, and improvements in insurance and health benefits.[31]

In return for a $25 million investment from its pension funds, the state of Connecticut will have a 47 percent interest in the new company; the former plant managers, 12 percent; salaried workers, 12 percent; and members of the UAW local, 12 percent.[32] In addition, the local will have three representatives of its choice on a new eleven-person board. As Phil Wheeler, director of District 9A of the UAW, cheerfully told a regional labor newspaper, "It's a great settlement, but the ESOP is essentially icing on the cake."[33]

In 1990, the AFL-CIO's Industrial Union Department helped create a new Employee Partnership Fund to help members of locals finance friendly buyouts of companies where they work. This first-ever fund is expected to provide about 10 percent of the financing for a typical take-over, with the rest to come from loans arranged through an ESOP developed by the local involved. Unionists will thus have a ready supply of the capital they need but usually lack and that bankers regard as so critical to the ultimate success of an ESOP-financed buyout. Although there is no formal link between the AFL-CIO and the new fund, the expectation is that pension funds from many of the labor federation's ninety union affiliates will be used to invest in employee buyouts. Assuming it secures $100 to $200 million from private and public pension funds by 1991, the fund should be able to invest in buyouts worth ten times that amount.[34]

The officers of the fund are intent that it not be perceived as a "magic bullet" that will save any and all ailing plants. They have told AFL-CIO union leaders that all possible transactions will be evaluated on their financial merits. Only plants with a clear potential to survive will be considered. Worker-owners will be expected to accept wage cuts, agree to long-term contracts, and foster substantial gains in productivity. Naturally, with trade unionists serving as advisers to the fund, the traditions of collective bargaining in dispute settlement will be honored. Above all, pains will be taken to maintain the entire operation as a sound investment.[35]

Ron Bloom helped put together the $4.4 billion ESOP bid for United Airlines and is a partner in the Employee Partnership Fund as well as a New York investment banker. Asked by a reporter to explain the shift in labor's position from skepticism of ESOPs to cautious support, Bloom cogently summarized the situation: "One of the lessons some of the labor people have learned is that to not participate is to be a victim."[36]

Turning Worker Ownership to Advantage: The O & O Case

For six years, the O & O (Owned and Operated) Supermarket in the Philadelphia suburb of Roslyn served as a rare and fascinating example of a unionized employee-owned workplace.[1] Although employee stock ownership plans have gained wary acceptance (see case study, page 221), worker cooperatives have been largely neglected by the American labor movement. A business owned and operated by unionists working under a collective bargaining agreement they have negotiated with themselves thus raises three provocative questions:

- Why does labor remain so skeptical of worker cooperatives?
- What are the new arguments for changing this attitude?
- How could labor expand its role in developing worker cooperatives worth the effort?[2]

Although the lead O & O store was discontinued as a unionized worker-owned cooperative in the fall of 1989, its development and six years of success continue to provide useful and important information for unionists intrigued by this option to employee stock ownership plans.

Background

Contrary to popular opinion, labor's involvement in worker cooperatives goes back nearly two hundred years:

- As early as 1791, striking carpenters in Philadelphia formed a co-op to undercut the prices set by local employers.
- In the 1830s, Philadelphia cabinetmakers, tailors, hatters, and saddlers were operating within co-ops.
- The largest mass union in the 1880s, the robust Knights of Labor, sponsored more than two hundred small-scale worker-owned businesses that provided a broad range of products and services.

Wars and economic depressions caused the failure of nearly all the early ventures. Hamstrung by their small size and limited access to capital, few could handle rapid technological changes or economic downturns. After the demise of the Knights of Labor in the late 1880s, its successor, the AFL, committed itself exclusively to collective bargaining and actively scorned co-ops. Labor leaders, influenced by the AFL's new form of "business unionism," consequently rejected involvement with cooperatives. And for many decades worker ownership was abandoned as too controversial or too "radical."

Interest revived in the mid-1970s in response to the invention of employee stock ownership plans and the emergence of employee buyouts as a last-ditch strategy to avoid plant shutdowns. But labor was typically ambivalent about the financial liabilities entailed in buyouts, especially when the business for sale was in dubious health. Wary leaders of locals made little attempt to increase worker participation in the new ESOPs, and higher-level union leaders generally remained skeptical. In a 1977 survey, 77 percent of national union leaders described themselves as "basically negative" about employee ownership.[3]

Firms that emerged in the 1970s as a result of employee buyouts were typically dominated by management, thereby disappointing union activists. As William Foote Whyte notes, "When it became apparent there was to be little, if any, change in the previous pattern of worker-management relations, the atmosphere of euphoria that accompanied the success of the job-saving campaign gave way to alienation."[4]

By the early 1980s, however, labor had learned how to initiate its own employee buyout campaigns and how to secure substantial influence in the management of a new worker-owned firm, a hybrid organization that preserved jobs and provided hope for unions wracked by the woes of recession. A survey in 1980 of trade union leaders, in contrast to the one in 1977, found that only 29 percent had negative feelings about employee ownership. And, interestingly, no one who had direct experience expressed disapproval.[5] By 1985, experts such as economist Robert Kuttner suggested worker ownership held important promise for unions: "I hope labor unions will continue their cautious courtship of worker ownership, for it puts the labor movement squarely on the side of productivity, as well as security and democracy. . . . Unions have feared worker ownership as a Trojan Horse, but the horse can be theirs."[6] The question, however, of how labor might best take advantage of this option and claim the horse as their own remained open.

Local 1357: Heading Off Trouble

Wendell W. Young III is president of the fourteen thousand–member Local 1357 of the United Food and Commercial Workers Union based in Philadelphia. He began weighing the option of worker ownership early in 1980, the nineteenth year of his tenure, after his union had lost 40 percent of its members in supermarket and department store closings in the preceding years.[7] Kroger, a major chain across the state, was preparing to close forty-three supermarkets, at a cost of another thirty-two hundred jobs. The closings also jeopardized a sister UFCW local, which ultimately sank into trusteeship, $1.5 million in debt.[8]

Rumor had it A & P might soon close supermarkets in the Philadelphia area where members of Local 1357 worked, especially those where mismanagement had allowed labor costs to soar as high as 15 percent of sales income.[9] To make matters worse, the state's retail liquor store system was threatened by a scheme to privatize and disperse store ownership, a prospect that would cost Young's members thousands of state jobs as store clerks.[10]

Young turned to a group of outside advisers for assistance in meeting the A & P threat. Jay Guben, the leading adviser, was a successful entrepreneur and social activist with a flair for innovation. He rapidly became an expert in the intricacies of employee ownership and proposed a scheme for buying the state liquor stores. It later became the blueprint for the O & O purchase. As Young explained, "Jay's got a social conscience and he's a good businessman. A lot of these long-haired guys you see interested in worker ownership have great ideas, but they can't get in the front door of a bank."[11] Sherman Kreiner and Andy Lamas, two young lawyers who had founded the Philadelphia Association for Cooperative Enterprise (PACE), wrote the by-laws for the O & O co-op, wrote the O & O trust fund agreement, and, with Guben, produced an extraordinarily detailed training program.

Young also sought advice from the Industrial Cooperative Association in Somerville, Massachusetts; the School of Industrial and Labor Relations at Cornell University; and the National Center for Employee Ownership in Washington, D.C. In addition, union leaders with relevant experience offered excellent insights.

In December 1981, A & P closed the first of eighty-three stores in the Philadelphia area, at a loss of nearly two thousand UFCW jobs. Within three months, Young announced a plan "that left most of his members gasping and had other labor leaders questioning his sanity." He proposed to take over twenty-one of the A & P markets. As an O & O publication said, "It was the boldest move for employee ownership anybody had ever heard of, or even conceived. . . . The reaction from observers and retailing executives ranged from, 'This is Dunkirk without the boats,' to 'Wendell Young went to sleep in the walk-in freezer and turned his brain into frosty whip.' " Even staffers working for Young expressed doubts and were suspicious of outsiders like Guben and PACE. They worried about the new responsibilities and wondered if the visionary buyout plan was anything more "than a hastily-conceived morale builder for a membership in crisis."[12]

In mid-March, Young announced that six hundred of his nearly two thousand former A & P workers had pledged $5,000 each for a total of $3 million toward the $15 million price A & P had set for the twenty-one boarded-up stores. Moreover, members of the staff of Local 1357 were exploring loan possibilities with the Philadelphia Industrial Development Agency, the city's chief economic planning and promotion organization, and with the Philadelphia Citywide Development Corporation, a government-sponsored agency.

Framing a Deal

Astonished by the local's initiative, A & P executives reexamined their decision to shut down. After two months of intensive negotiations, the company agreed to an entirely new plan, hailed in May 1982 as "a glimmer of innovation in a year of bad news for labor."[13]

Under the novel terms of the plan, A & P agreed to create a new corporate entity, known as Super Fresh, which would gradually reopen A & P stores and give first preference in hiring to the union members who had been laid off. In return, Local 1357 agreed to a 20 percent cut in wages and fringe benefits, with the understanding that the amounts cut would be restored if and when business flourished—a target long since reached. A & P was especially pleased by the local's endorsement of work rule changes and an incentive plan aimed at holding labor costs down to 10 percent of gross sales. The local was gratified by a pledge to give employees unprecedented participation in management, including a voice in decisions about what items to stock, what hours to stay open, and what checkout system to use.

In deference to the concept of worker ownership, A & P agreed to give Super Fresh employees the first option to buy any reopened store that failed a second time. A & P also agreed to rebate 1 percent of gross sales annually, with 30 percent paid to employees and 70 percent donated to a new worker co-op trust fund. (Unfortunately, what would have been the nation's first worker-controlled venture capital fund to finance enterprises owned and operated by union workers never materialized.)

Under the terms of this unique agreement, Young's union members had two crucial choices. Nearly 99 percent chose to return to A & P, now renamed Super Fresh, with a new "quality of work life" plan that was still to be worked out. The others, a tiny group that retained the visionary notion of buying reopened stores themselves, risked taking out a $5,000 equity loan from the local's credit union to take a "leap into the unknown." Pooling their $5,000 loans, forty-five rank-and-filers strongly committed to worker participation and to gaining new power over their lives opted for "O & O" worker-ownership.[14]

Using Guben and PACE as intermediaries to avoid compromising its role as a collective bargaining agent, Local 1357 initiated the purchase of two stores at $150,000 each. The local's credit union helped provide seed money required of each would-be worker-owner, and the local pressured its bank to lend nearly $450,000 beyond the $300,000 purchase price to cover debts. The local used its regional, state, and federal influence to secure additional loans and loan guarantees. And the local instructed the law firm it retained to work out obstacles with the Internal Revenue Service. It also lent the worker-owners space in its building and donated office supplies. With an investment of over $300,000 of its own funds, the local made possible the emergence in October 1982 of the nation's first job-creation experiment in the form of a unionized supermarket worker co-operative, a sparkling new store in Roslyn and a much smaller store in Parkwood Manor, Pennsylvania.

O & O: A Dream Made Real

The final structure of the twenty-four-person Roslyn O & O Supermarket, however taxing it was to devise, was appealing to its forty-five rank-and-file backers. It contrasted significantly with a more conventional structure, as shown in the table on page 234. Other O & O features included the rejection of outside supervision of any kind and the refusal to classify jobs narrowly. In short, the voice of authority was "the voice of the worker speaking in a language that would make a regular personnel manager keel over."[15]

Learning to Promote Collegiality

Operating the O & O markets made perplexing personal demands, and those demands played an important part in the termination of the Roslyn, Pennsylvania, experiment in 1989. As PACE consultant Andy Lamas said, "To bring about a truly democratic workplace, you need two things: You need a structure that allows for it, and a capacity inside the individual to work within the structure."[16] Worker-owners had to learn how to get along and how to compromise, both of which were significant challenges for people with no history of responsibility for promoting collegiality. Getting along together had become a necessity, as Lamas explained to former A & P workers who were about to become co-owners:

It's an operational necessity that inside these supermarkets democracy must mean more than merely voting on an occasional basis. Worker-owners must find a way to do things quickly and efficiently so they don't lose out to stores with traditional structures, while still being democratic and participatory. We get them to learn their general re-

Comparison of O & O Structure and Conventional Structure

O & O Structure	Conventional Structure
Each owner was allowed only one share and each worker had one vote, so that someone who owned a $5,000 share had voting rights equal to those of every other owner.	Whoever bought additional shares gained more power, so that the more shares someone bought, the more votes he or she commanded.
Every full-time worker owned a job and could expect to hold and improve it for years. Reform efforts would precede dismissal for poor performance.	No worker had a special right to his or her job; all served at the pleasure of the employer, constrained only by a union contract and relevant legislation.
Every worker-owner agreed to serve on store committees so as to distribute managerial responsibilities, such as decisions about business planning, capital investment, personnel practices, product choice, and pricing.	Various levels of middle management handled all managerial tasks with little or no worker input.
Profits were shared in proportion to the number of hours worked.	Profit sharing, if any, favored supervisors and specific classes of employees.
Worker-owners elected a governing board of directors from their own ranks.	Stockholders elected a board of successful individuals from outside the firm.
The board hired a store manager, who served at the pleasure of those he or she supervised.	Management hired all supervisors, who were accountable to them.

sponsibilities to other members, to listen and consider differing opinions. The most important skill is learning to disagree without being disagreeable.[17]

PACE used exercises more closely resembling group therapy than job training to prepare O & O workers for the challenge. After training for six to nine months for fifteen hours a week, workers replaced learning simulations with actual experience in their own supermarket.

O & O's Demise

After six years of operating successfully, the Roslyn supermarket was sold to its major wholesale food supplier in the fall of 1989 and reverted to being a conventional unionized operation. Sherman Kreiner, a member of the original "brain trust," has identified three reasons for the sale:[18]

- The economic climate shifted adversely, and the opening of new nearby competitive stores severely reduced profitability.
- The Roslyn store decided to buy out six worker-owners, using a $150,000 bank loan, at a time when the cost of borrowing money proved burdensome and sales were being reduced by competition.
- The manager of the store was away "on loan," in an effort to buy another store for expansion purposes. Unable to find an adequate replacement, the Roslyn store floundered for several months.

According to Kreiner, Wendell Young, the president of UFCW 1357, remains convinced that the problems that forced the O & O to convert to a conventional unionized operation need not have occurred and do not impugn the excellence of the operation.

Impact of a Worker Cooperative

Worker cooperatives promote the extension of democracy to the work community through the principle of "one person, one vote." The average O & O member had more say in running his or her work life than do other American workers. Worker cooperatives also promote the hiring of management by labor. They alter the role of authority. Local 1357 members could actually fire their management for cause. And the O & O worker had more say than other wage earners in appraising management's performance.

Most important, worker cooperatives provide a chance to confirm one's adulthood, an opportunity subtly denied in conventional management relationships. O & O veterans of A & P employment remember irrational changes in store procedures and excessive secretiveness about a store's performance. They recall decades of indifference to employee suggestions. In contrast, many believe participating in O & O significantly improved their lives: "There's nothing like working for yourself. It gives you a feeling that you're mature enough to make your own decisions and take the responsibility for them. It makes you a better person."[19] That sentiment was frequently articulated and fervently felt.

Response of the Skeptics

Anything as novel as Local 1357's O & O project is bound to have critics. Conservative detractors grumble about the sharing of power with shop-floor workers. As Young explains, "An executive once told me it sounded like socialism to him. But I said we just wanted to organize stores the way he and his friends did their country club—everybody pays into a kitty; you elect some directors; you hire a manager. What's socialistic about that?"[20] Outright ownership, Young adds, "is a protection, not an ultimate goal. We believe in the private enterprise system. Our goal is not to own stores, but to save jobs. Owning them is just a last resort."[21]

Radical skeptics, in turn, condemned the O & O as a step toward class collaboration and a betrayal of militancy. Local 1357 was criticized for allowing concessions to O & O that might have undermined the local's bargaining position with other supermarkets: "Instead of organizing a militant rank-and-file response, which might have benefited all the workers, the union opted for a strategy which will positively affect only a small percentage of its members."[22]

O & O was also criticized for its dependence on loans from banks and the government and for its reliance on a single wholesaler (IGA). This concerned skeptics for several reasons:

- These parties would help O & O only as long as they believed its structures and goals did not threaten their interests.[23]
- The orientation of workers would shift from one of militant confrontation with employers to one of survival in the marketplace. Since worker ownership diverted workers' activity from class struggle, it weakened the labor movement.[24]
- Workers who gained ownership of a company tended, over a period of time, to identify less with workers-employees in other companies than with the company they now owned.[25]
- Worker ownership perpetuated the false illusion that workers' problems could all be solved in the workplace and at the company level, without resort to mass political action and union solidarity.[26]

To make matters worse, the concessions traded for ownership are alleged to give other employers an excuse to force contract rollbacks at their companies. As a result, critics say, workers end up competing with one another to offer employers the lowest possible labor costs, a race that working people always lose. Militants scoff at the notion that O & O could serve as a model for labor innovation, and they condemn its potential to distract labor from appropriate militancy.

O & O supporters, however, insist Local 1357's concessions in 1982 had long since been adjusted up to area norms and the quality of work life had become exemplary. As for their dependence on bank and government loans, they boast that they found sources of venture capital that were ideologically aligned with worker co-ops. The O & O stores also had adequate pro-labor sources of capital on which to rely.

These same supporters argue that customary relationships have to be distinguished from those that are potentially more useful:

■ Negotiated labor-management cooperation makes far more sense than militant action for resolving problems in worker cooperatives, and no local or union need apologize for recognizing this.

■ The risk that members of worker cooperatives might become "ideological capitalists" can be substantially reduced through focused prolabor educational efforts and leadership guidance.

■ Worker cooperatives "must inevitably be locally responsive. It is built into their democratic constitution. The O & O Supermarkets were significant because they were local. They represented the essential strength of grass-roots endorsement and face-to-face democratic choices.' "[27]

■ Worker ownership can prepare participants for larger projects, such as a citywide, state, or regional chain of worker-owned supermarkets.

Above all, worker cooperatives could set standards for worker rights, wages, and benefits that would serve as models for the local, its parent union, and the labor movement as a whole. As scholar Warner P. Woodworth suggested, "Organized labor needs to shift from a stance of disdain, or even suspicion, to a position of viewing worker ownership as a legitimate alternative to corporate bureaucracy. Employee ownership, instead of destroying the need for a union, may be the very mechanism for a revitalization of organized labor in the United States."[28]

Built-in Challenges

Some difficult underlying issues remain:

■ how to protect those who are not owners, such as part-time workers, from exploitation as second-class citizens;

■ how least to constrain the mobility of worker-owners by the prohibition against selling or transferring shares; and

■ how to encourage worker-owners to accept new applications rather than keep their numbers small so that they may increase the market value of their own shares.

In response, Local 1357 bargained hard with the Roslyn O & O to protect part-time workers against inequalities, and it persuaded the store to buy back shares when members chose to move on. The local also asked the O & O to boost its ratio of owners to part-timers from 51 to 70 percent.

The Union's Role

It may not be obvious why workers who are also owners need a union. Yet, as *Future Bread,* an O & O publication, notes, "People need protection, almost against another part of themselves. They need protection

to preclude personal issues becoming largely subservient to business issues.... Union membership forces the issue of worker interests to be
confronted, discussed, and resolved.... The location of business ownership does not change their importance and necessity."[29] O & O worker-
owners, PACE consultants, and Local 1357 officers believed union membership was an indispensable form of self-defense.

The union made several specific contributions to the worker cooperative. It served as an independent resource for the monetary evaluation
of particular jobs and benefits across work classifications. It facilitated
grievance resolution when personal issues, interests, or actions were in
conflict with those of the co-op. And it served as a lobbyist, educator,
and publicist, thereby increasing public information and support or seeking legislative intervention. While the union retained its traditional role
in representing members who were worker-owners, it acquired additional
responsibilities as an intermediary, counselor, advocate, and instructor
on behalf of the worker-owner option.

In spite of some built-in confusion about its role, and the substantial
cost (over $300,000) of the local's 1981–82 predicament, officers of Local
1357 remain proud of their robust part in the Roslyn O & O project.
Wendell Young, the president, explains:

> The primary objective of the union has always been to do everything
> possible to protect jobs. In this particular example, we went beyond
> protection and into job creation—a new field and a new role.... Be-
> cause it was perhaps unique for the union to be the organization
> initiating change, a potential exists for an expansion of the role of
> the union.... The models of worker ownership and shared decision-
> making may have a much wider applicability beyond the retail food
> industry.[30]

Although none of the officers of 1357 expresses regrets, and some note
the resilience of the small Parkwood Manor store, Charles Gentile, the
local's business agent for the Roslyn store, remains convinced they can
do the job even better the next time around.

Long-Term Value of Worker Ownership

As *Labor Research Review* has emphasized, the O & O Local 1357 story
remains part of what is still a new adventure: "Not too long ago worker
ownership was a pretty exotic subject within the American labor movement—interesting for labor intellectuals to discuss maybe, but not of
much practical significance."[31] Since the plant shutdowns and Rust Belt
community depressions that occurred between 1981 and 1983, unions
have begun assessing worker-ownership options. In May 1987, for ex-

ample, Local 1071-C of ACTWU helped create the first completely worker-owned and unionized apparel plant in Texas, one of only a handful in the nation.[32]

Why should labor unions care about worker ownership if successful projects are so rare? Economist Robert Kuttner argues that a commitment to worker ownership is essential to robust unionism:

> Worker ownership should be taken very seriously. It is immensely appealing as a philosophical proposition, for it solves a number of the knottiest problems of political economy. For those who value the efficiency and variety of free markets, worker ownership promises a capitalism where everyone is a capitalist. For those attracted to the fraternity and community of socialism, worker ownership promises an entrepreneurial socialism without bureaucracy. For believers in participatory democracy, worker ownership extends the ethic of political democracy to the workplace, the most stubbornly hierarchical institution in a democratic society. Besides, if labor unions are worth having, as a democratic counterweight to the immense political influence of business in a market economy, then worker ownership is a very good strategy for reinventing a labor movement.[33]

Wendell Young feels a similar sense of urgency:

> Labor leaders must change or they will be left behind. They need a new mandate and a new vision of work life that goes beyond the subclauses of some lawyer-built contract. The labor leaders themselves desperately need the power endorsement and driving force the worker ownership movement can provide.[34]

The activists in Local 1357, along with the staff members of advocacy organizations such as PACE, the ICA, and the National Center for Employee Ownership, are qualified to guide new projects and are eager to do so. They look forward to serving a new kind of unionist, America's proud worker-owners.

Turning Pension Power to Advantage: The Walton Case

The power implicit in labor's pension funds has been characterized as "largely an unfulfilled dream," but labor strategists have increasingly understood that their pension funds might shift the balance of power in the workplace. Unions have long been urged to use their assets to gain respect from management, negotiators, and adversaries.[1]

Since the late 1970s, more and more unions have invested their pension funds in building low-cost homes with union labor (see case study, page 262, for example). Several hundred locals and scores of unions have chosen AFL-CIO investment options. Some, such as ACTWU and the United Brotherhood of Carpenters and Joiners, have used their pension funds to leverage gains in organizing drives and corporate campaigns. In at least one case, the subject of this study, a union has forged new socially responsible investment possibilities by challenging tradition and law alike and daring to reinterpret its fiduciary obligations.

AFL-CIO involvement in pension fund investments dates back to 1964 when the Housing Investment Trust (HIT) was created. Since then, HIT, with 188 participating unions as investors, has financed more than $650 million in union construction of single-family and multifamily houses, retirement centers, and nursing homes. The average rate of return over the 1983–88 period was a commendable 11.4 percent, and administrative fees have been as low as 0.7 percent.[2]

What was needed to supplement HIT was a robust new venture that would develop a broad range of commercial and industrial projects. In June 1988, the AFL-CIO's Building Investments Trust (BIT) opened to fill that gap. As the AFL-CIO's pioneer in the field of major commercial and industrial real estate investment, BIT "seeks out prudent investments in union-friendly projects that will generate jobs and affect a positive impact on the host community."[3]

With an investment goal of $100 million for its first year of operation, the trust in its opening month attracted $15 million from the Bakery and Confectionery Workers' Pension Fund and a sizable commitment from the Bricklayers National Pension Fund. BIT has been characterized by President Lane Kirkland of the AFL-CIO as "an important initiative in representing the interests of working people." Floyd Hyde, a BIT officer, explained: "Let others invest in runaway manufacturing plants. We want to be people who work with communities to make them viable and prosperous."[4]

Randy Barber, a consultant to unions on pensions and related matters, insists labor "can meet social objectives and get a good rate of return," but he concedes progress to date is "only the tip of the iceberg of what is possible."[5] Balancing the risks of socially useful projects with fiduciary responsibility remains a challenge that can be surmounted only slowly and steadily.

Walton's Way

Until recently, the billions of dollars in pension funds co-managed by unions and employers were invested very conservatively. Little attention was paid to the possibility of building support for labor by requiring, for example, that union workers be hired to build any commercial development financed by the union pension dollars.

Since the 1985 decision in *Donovan v. Walton*, however, new opportunities have opened up, along with new controversies about the responsibilities of both labor and management trustees for pension funds.[6] Traditionalists especially value preservation of these funds, only 5 percent of which have historically gone into investments in real estate.[7] Anti-traditionalists have a leading spokesman in Dennis J. Walton, the business manager of Local 675, International Union of Operating Engineers (IUOE), in Pompano Beach, Florida, and a trustee of his local's co-managed pension fund.

Local 675's fund is guided by a joint labor-management committee of six nonsalaried trustees, three of whom represent labor and three of whom represent unionized contractors. Established through collective bargaining and subject to exacting legal requirements, the fund provides retirement benefits drawn from deferred wages, employer contributions of about $1 million a year, and interest earned on fund investments. By law, the fund is audited annually by an independent certified public accountant, and until Walton took charge it was unexceptional in every way.

Walton's crusade began in 1973 when he was appointed a business agent for his local. At his first trustees' meeting, the former crane operator found himself dumbly approving increases in fees for attorneys, administrators, and consultants and then agreeing to hold the following year's meeting in Hawaii. Until he won the post of business manager in 1976, Walton and the other trustees continued to accept the enigmatic advice of the expensive advisers they had on retainer. Walton now regrets having abdicated his authority in favor of the experts who routinely administered union pension plans.

The situation changed, however, one week after Walton assumed the top office in his local. He found himself on a multiunion picket line at a nonunion development being financed by both Metropolitan Life Insurance Company and Equitable Life. An electrician on the line pointed to a sign that said the insurance companies backed the construction companies. "Ain't that a bitch," he said, "we just handed these same companies ten million dollars of our money!"[8] That realization both surprised and infuriated Walton, who discovered in it a cause he would make his own.

Starting a Revolution

At the 1977 annual meeting of his local's pension fund, Walton raised searching questions but posed no direct challenge. He then began to investigate the entire issue as part of the evening program in labor studies at Florida International University, where he was working toward a bachelor's degree. By the 1978 annual meeting of the pension fund, he was ready to challenge the agents of insurance companies and banks who managed billions in union funds: "Who are these princes of privilege in three-piece suits? Have they ever walked a picket line? Have they ever seen the sorrow of unemployment when a family loses its car, its home? Have they felt the grief? How many times a day do they experience having to tell a man, a good union man, there just is not any work?"[9] If these agents had the best interests of plan participants in mind, Walton charged, they would not provide financial backing for open-shop, anti-union construction projects, as they had when Local 675's funds were used to purchase bonds from a utility company that relied on one of the largest nonunion construction firms in the country.

Walton drew the connection between fund investments and the soaring unemployment rate in Florida, at that time one of twenty "right-to-work" states. While commercial construction companies had once been nearly 90 percent union, union contractors were now rare, and many of those that had survived had parallel companies that employed nonunion labor.[10] Walton also documented the dismal rate of return on investments by the local's pension fund. At 1.8 percent, the return was far below the unimpressive 3.2 percent earned by all pension funds, union and otherwise, in the preceding ten years.[11] Walton argued that his local's situation was untenable: "When my Fund lost over $1.8 million in three years because of the poor performance of our bond portfolio, it was my fault, as much as it was our money manager's. When I looked around and saw more and more construction going non-union...I was forced into the realization that working people such as myself could not rely on professionals, but must seize their own destiny."[12] The time had come, Walton declared, to implement what he called the "pension fund revolution."

Taking to the Field

Walton devised a plan that would tackle three problems simultaneously: the use of co-managed union pension funds to finance non-union projects, the soaring rate of joblessness among union members, and the poor return on fund investments. Under his guidance, the six trustees fired the insurance companies on whom they had long relied, divested themselves of low-yielding bonds, and began to make carefully researched investments in Florida real estate. Walton was intrigued by the potential of his local's $28 million pension fund: "The day I learned I was a fiduciary, and a trustee, and I had the authority, and I had the responsibility, and I had the power, things started to change."[13] Guided by a small team of outside professionals, including an economist and a lawyer hired by the fund, Walton initiated a complex real estate development plan.

In August 1979, the fund made labor history when it paid $2.37 million for an unimproved ninety-five-acre tract ($25,000 per acre) of marshy land west of Pompano Beach. A buoyant Walton announced plans to build an office park exclusively with union contractors and union labor. In short order, the fund spent $4 million on improvements such as roads, water, and sewers and nearly $2 million more on a modern office building to house both the local and its pension fund. The local agreed to pay rent to the fund equal to an average 10 percent return.[14]

During its first full year of operation, the pension plan's real estate investments experienced a 78.6 percent return, while the yield on stocks and bonds was a dismal 1.07 percent; the average on all the plan's investments was 14.25 percent.[15] In accordance with a sale agreement made in 1985, the fund eventually sold eighty of its ninety-five acres to a commercial developer for nearly $14 million ($174,000 per acre).[16] The developer, in turn, was legally bound to hire only union labor for eighty-four thousand hours of building work on the site.[17]

On to Washington

In 1979, Walton was invited to testify before the President's Commission on Pension Policy, where he decried the situation in pension funds. He urged the commission to formulate guidelines to encourage the use of social criteria in the placement of pension fund assets, arguing that "investments in the stock of companies whose interests are adverse to union participants is destructive of the union movement itself."[18]

Walton assured the commission the regulations issued by the Department of Labor on July 23, 1979, were compatible with the consideration of social factors in investment decisions. In conclusion, he resolved, "We will be exploited no longer with our own funds, nor will we stay baffled and apathetic due to nebulous interpretations of ambiguous regulations."[19]

The Response

Provoked by Walton's challenge, the Department of Labor filed suit in May 1981 alleging the fund's trustees had violated the "prudent" obligation set forth in the Employee Retirement Income Security Act (ERISA). The department argued the trustees had breached their fiduciary responsibility by paying too much in construction costs, requiring too little from the union in rent, and otherwise entering into a transaction that was not in the best interest of the plan's participants and beneficiaries.[20] Outraged, Walton, who was named in the suit, responded immediately: "I find, after waking up to my real fiduciary duties, that the Department of Labor is suing me for breaching them. Could it be that they are the aggressive defenders of the status quo? Could it be they have the best interests of multi-nationals and the financial communities uppermost in their list of priorities?"[21]

Once he was named a defendant in this publicized government suit, Walton was ostracized by many of his colleagues in labor:

A lot of people just nod their heads and say, "Well, he's gone." "He's done." A lot of people pretend you are not even in the room at a cocktail party.... What mattered was that I had dared challenge the system! What mattered was that I had, and therefore, I had to be wrong. I had to be guilty of something. They didn't know just what. ... In the eyes of the mental midgets of big business and big government, we had to be wrong. Because when a union is sued by the government, in most people's eyes, the union is wrong even before it gets its day in court.[22]

Until the court finally spoke in 1985, Walton seized on speaking invitations that came his way. He indicted audiences of union trustees for offenses many had trouble conceding: "We, as labor trustees, have committed misfeasance, malfeasance, and nonfeasance.... We have been bogged down in ignorance and indifference.... We have been doing a great disservice to our people."[23]

The solution, Walton argued, was pension power, the "single most effective strategy for organized labor in the 1980s."[24] Walton based his conclusion on four specific charges:

■ The traditional investment managers had proven to be incompetent: "My question is, do we have to pay these people to lose money for us?"[25]

■ The banks and insurance companies to whom the unions entrusted their pension funds had not earned that trust: "What are we doing letting companies like Prudential finance our enemies, like the National Right to Work Committee [which used a Prudential loan to build its new headquarters] with our monies?"[26]

■ Union pension fund investors often selected inappropriate bonds. The promoters of most school bond issues, for example, "not only want to build ... non-union, but they want to pay the people that work in that building as cheaply as possible."[27]

■ The stocks favored by union pension fund investors are often in socially reactionary companies: "The cold hard fact is that if your pension fund is involved in the bond or equity market ... you are directly funding non-union, anti-labor companies. The Carpenters own shares in J. P. Stevens. The IBEW owns shares of Kodak and Haliburton. The CWA's plan owns shares in Kodak and Coors.... The list could go on and on for every union pension fund in this country."[28]

Pounding the podium for emphasis, Walton would explain, "What is ironic about the modern anti-union movement is that the investment managers ... are utilizing union pension funds to finance their own open-shop objectives!"[29]

Labor had "new instruments of battle," Walton insisted, and should not hesitate to use them to obtain real estate and construction loans (secured with property as collateral).[30] The goals of the union pension fund had to be both high returns *and* the creation of new union jobs. His own fund was an exemplary case in point:

One piece of property we bought for two million over nine months ago, we sold last week [September 1980] for four million dollars. Another piece of property we paid $25,000 an acre for has doubled in less than a year and a half. That is not the end. Whenever we buy property and sell it for development, a mandate in the sale is that any subsequent building on the site is done 100 percent union. We have increased our members' opportunity for work and doubled our money.[31]

Since the fund had taken this aggressive posture, Walton concluded, it was doing "very, very well."[32]

Built-in Sources of Stress

Walton suggests pension power projects need to meet a variety of challenges to succeed:

- The local must earn the full voting cooperation of the employers who contributed deferred wages to the fund since Taft-Hartley regulations give them 50 percent of the authority in its governance.
- The local should encourage amicable relationships at work sites underwritten by pension fund dollars to reassure trustees the investment is sound.
- The local must improve the productivity of its members to demonstrate the wisdom of using a union contractor.
- The local must reassure union builders that serving as a trustee will not preclude their working on jobs supported by the fund.
- The local must counteract a conservative preference to rely on stocks and bonds over real estate investments.

History, fear, and misunderstanding underlie a resistance to change in traditional patterns of pension fund investments. Unless and until a local can meet Walton's challenges, the likelihood of change in its pension fund investments remains small.

Judgment of the Court

Following an eight-day trial in May 1985, a federal judge ruled entirely in Walton's favor. The decision noted that although the Department of Labor's charges were "indeed serious, its bark is worse than its bite."[33] The judge not only endorsed union pension fund investments in real estate; he also implied that the fund, as a developer of a real estate project, could pay higher wages for union workers than for nonunion labor, even if doing so increased overall costs. This decision was immediately perceived as sending "a strong signal to trustees of jointly managed pension funds across the country."[34]

Walton's victory was "the only reported case under federal pension law in which the trustees of a pension fund beat the Department of Labor."[35] The judge noted with appreciation that the fund had taken three specific steps to honor the intent of ERISA:

- It had obtained an independent review of the project's economic viability, an expert feasibility study, and an evaluation of these studies.
- It had retained an independent real estate investment manager to negotiate the union's lease.
- It had adjusted the project to stay within budget.

In short, the Court found the trustees had exercised care, diligence, prudence, and skill, just as Walton had long contended.

A month after the decision, he discussed his response at an educational conference of union lawyers:

> I am sure that many of the attorneys in this room will tell you this case may well be...the most important victory for the trade union movement in the history of ERISA.... For myself, I am glad it is over. It feels like a huge rock has been lifted off my shoulders. I had seven years of war with the Federal government! It was seven years of the most intense investigation a union official has undergone. With no help ...from any other union in the country. And certainly no help from the International Foundation of Employee Benefits.[36]

In spite of all the complications, Walton saw the victory as fundamentally simple: "We were right. They were wrong. It was principle!"[37]

Spreading the Word

Working with his local's full-time attorney and its economist, Walton now regularly offers a one-and-a-half-day "Pension Fund Revolution" seminar. Union trustees learn how their pension funds can be used to acquire land for future development, how to ensure that only union contractors will bid, and how their pension funds can build and own office buildings, shopping centers, and commercial parks. Walton explains how to comply with ERISA regulations and create more employment for union contractors through direct equity investments. Participants are introduced to real estate experts who are registered investment advisers and can assume fiduciary responsibility. Not surprisingly, response to the seminar has been enthusiastic.[38]

In addition to teaching what can be done today, Walton continues to develop new possibilities for the future. In 1987, he joined with three real estate investment specialists to form the nation's first equity trust dedicated exclusively to augmenting labor's pension power. JHW Realty Advisors uses a direct investment approach to structure equity investments. Investments are thus recycled more quickly and typically yield higher returns than long-term mortgages, which tie up pension fund dollars for many years. With the National Bank of Washington as its master trustee and fiduciary, the new equity trust invites the involvement of international unions and locals.[39]

Promoting the Revolution

Walton's crusade has been well documented and well promoted. Copies of a dozen or more speeches given since 1980 are available from his office, as are pamphlets on ways to renew labor through pension power and a fifteen-minute videotape, *In Our Hands*. The marketing efforts reflect Walton's sense of urgency about change: "We can no longer function as we have in the past and be successful. . . . We're one small union, and we've created more than $300 million in local union work. Think of what would happen if that was multiplied by other unions."[40]

A Word from the Opposition

A spokesperson for the National Right to Work Committee is representative of those who are still angry about the 1985 victory for Local 675: "It's blatantly illegal. Under ERISA, pension investments are to be made for the maximum return at the minimum risk. You're not supposed to take into account any so-called social goals such as union-only employment. It's an increasing threat."[41]

Others see Walton's achievement as irrelevant rather than infuriating. In 1978, nearly 100 percent of the construction in Broward County, Florida, was union. Today, union construction accounts for only about 20 percent, in spite of Walton's projects. This reduction has led a spokesperson for a nonunion association of builders and contractors in South Florida to dismiss "Walton's folly" as inconsequential: "It's not going to help a whole lot . . . unless the Dennis Waltons can convince other union leaders. . . . I don't see that kind of unity in the national unions."[42]

Walton is well aware of his opponents' views. He insists that meeting social goals is the second greatest responsibility of a trustee, right after exercising reasonable prudence, and he contends the responsibilities are mutually compatible. Walton believes adamantly in the possibility of cooperation between unions and urges union presidents to create a joint multibillion pension investment pool. Insofar as the nation's unions have over $400 billion in joint labor-management pension trusts, the groundwork exists for significant joint action.

A more penetrating question is how far pension power can go in creating pressure to use union labor, services, and products. Walton's strategies to ensure developers employ union labor on jobs bankrolled by his local's pension fund have not yet been tested in court. Although he is confident he will win any legal challenge, he does not believe it is practical or feasible to influence the developers' commitment to unions after construction has been completed.

Walton himself is the target of some critics. His combination of idealism and pragmatism upsets many people, and his ability to attract media attention arouses jealousy. Detractors are quick to note his ideas have inspired little enthusiasm from his own union or the AFL-CIO Department of Building Trades. One national labor leader commented, "Dennis is a kind of loose cannon on the deck."[43]

Walton disavows aspirations for higher union office or a more lucrative career, explaining that "the easy course in life is not my style."[44] He rails against "the apathy and ignorance and arrogance that exist today in the labor movement,"[45] and yet he believes there is reason for hope. His close friend Andrew Banks, a labor educator, contends that "Dennis likes to run against the herd, but he's definitely not a champion of lost causes." It is that combination of optimism and outrage, high expectations and high jinx, that make Walton a "true pioneer and a visionary, the type of labor leader in short supply in recent times."[46]

Continuing Progress

As recently as the early 1980s, many trustees of union pension funds regarded the robust ideas of Dennis J. Walton as "wild and dangerous, liable to land them in jail and lose the money in their funds."[47] Today, he is bolstered by the fact his pension fund, 70 percent of which is invested in real estate, grew from $16 million to $44 million in eight years (1979–86). Since employer contributions account for about $1 million a year, real estate and development have earned more than $20 million of the $28 million gain, while generating more than $300 million worth of wages for union workers in the building trades.[48]

Walton does not regard his innovation as just another option among several. He argues that it is the most powerful of a diminishing number of strategies available to organized labor: "A picket line is not effective anymore! We can't beat them today in the National Labor Relations Board. And we can't beat them in the current political climate. But we in the building trades movement have about $90 billion in pension fund assets, and that is our money.... With that kind of power, we can beat them!"[49]

Gradually, examples of successful projects based on Walton's model are beginning to appear:[50]

- A $250 million development of hotels, office buildings, and high-technology manufacturing operations is being planned in Boca Raton, Florida, in which a substantial investment will come from the IBEW Local 323 pension fund.
- Plans are under way to build a $6 million facility for senior citizens in Boca Raton financed by union pension funds.
- A similar $9 million facility is scheduled to be built in Delray Beach.
- An agreement to build a $23 million, 288-unit rental property for seniors was funded through the AFL-CIO Housing Investment Trust pension fund.

■ According to the business manager of an Ohio electricians local, "Dennis Walton came here with his sermon, and he provided the motivation and direction to invest our Building Trades pension fund in Toledo, Ohio, in projects that generated over $80 million worth of work."[51]

Walton is infuriated by labor's sparse and timid efforts to utilize pension funds. He emphasizes that if one of every thousand dollars in pension fund assets were redirected into union-built projects, nearly twelve million man-hours or six thousand man-years of employment would be created.[52]

In spite of his disappointment in other funds, Walton takes enormous pride in his own: "What this local has accomplished is significant. There is no doubt about that. What we have achieved, no union in the country has achieved, or, for that matter, no union has even dared to try. We have changed things."[53] As members of a building trades union, Walton and his staff take particular pride in defying the stereotype of change-resisting hard hats.

Options for the Building Trades

Wide use of pension power is particularly important in the nation's twenty open-shop ("right-to-work") states. For locals of bricklayers, carpenters, electricians, hod carriers, sheet metal workers, and roofers, the alternative may be rapid erosion.

Neither Walton nor members of his staff harbor any illusions about members' loyalty to a union unless it is successful. As he explains:

You have to understand, the typical guy in construction down here is a white man in his mid-twenties, with a working wife and several kids, and a lot of debts. He has to work, and he isn't particularly choosy who signs the check. . . . Men in my local work union one week, non-union the next, and back and forth, without giving it a thought. Open-shop contractors are smart enough to pay very close to union scale. . . . I cannot count on anything like loyalty to the union, especially not from young guys with no background or experience, guys who want nothing to do with strikes and everything to do with staying on a payroll, any payroll.[54]

Unless Local 675 creates jobs for which unionized builders can hire young workers, Walton believes that even with wise investments, the union will lose more and more members.

Robert McMenemy of Local 675 has twenty years of experience in the political affairs of unions. He characterizes the situation quite starkly:

Let's not kid one another. Without the loyalty of the men... or the support of the builders, all they've got anymore is money, and that they've got a lot of. So they've got to begin using it to see to it their contractors get the work, so their men get the jobs, so their unions have some reason for being.... Either they wake up, and get into business, or they'll soon be completely out of business.[55]

To Walton, interunion cooperation is essential if his experience is to serve as a model for significant change:

If all of the union presidents got in the same room, and decided on a strategy for our pension funds, we could wipe out unemployment in the building trades.... And we would see a swelling in the ranks of our union membership... that big business and big government could not ignore. They would know the labor movement is here to stay.[56]

Walton concedes that the willingness to invest pension funds in real estate and get into the banking or insurance business needs to be nurtured. For now, such innovations continue to infuriate many conservative unionists.

Applications of Walton's Concept

Although it may seem radical to some, Dennis Walton's concept of pension power can benefit unions in significant ways:

- It reduces reliance on outside investment experts and helps provide union activists with authentic control over their co-managed pension funds.
- It provides union contractors with an attractive financial return for their commitment to hiring union labor.
- It raises consciousness about the indispensability of social criteria in labor's investment decisions.

Above all, the concept of pension power boosts some people's confidence in labor's future and demonstrates the possibility of using its economic power in bolder ways. With billions of dollars accrued in the Taft-Hartley pension funds they co-direct, unions have many opportunities to use what Walton describes as "the most effective tool we have in our arsenal today"[57]

Thanks to a major change in the Taft-Hartley Act won by labor lobbyists in April 1990, the nation's unions can now negotiate to create joint labor-management funds to relieve the housing crisis. The first of these funds, and the one that precipitated the change in the act, was won in December 1988 by Local 26 of the Hotel Employees and Restaurant Employees Union in Boston. In its negotiations with Boston's hotels, the five thousand–member local secured a five-cents-an-hour contribution per worker to help reduce down payments and closing costs for house purchases, interest payments on mortgages, and the cost of renting an apartment.[58]

More than $1 million accrued in the new fund in the first year while labor lobbied for the Taft-Hartley reform, and union and management trustees have since indicated a willingness to invest some of the funds in urgently needed efforts to build union-made affordable housing for rank-and-filers. So popular is this undertaking that Domenic Bozzotto, leader of Local 26 and the chief architect of the project, forecasts employer-assisted housing will prove to be "*the* next major fringe benefit that will be offered to employees."[59]

Walton's concept, albeit in a robust new format, goes forward—as does his opposition. In 1990, the Department of Labor initiated a second legal effort to end the social investment activities of Local 675. Regardless of the final disposition of the case, Walton's initiative assures labor's permanent interest in bold social investment strategies.

Chapter 13
Achieving More Effective Alliances

We must share in the problems of our city even if we have moved our families out to the suburbs. We owe something to the city, where we make our bread. We must put something back.

> Severino Bragiom, president, Boston Packing House local, in
> *A Handbook of Great Labor Quotations* (1983), 100

Unions have been most successful when they supported legislation important to wider constituencies than their own.... Political liberals who often join their opponents in dispraise of unions would do well to ask where else is to be found mass support for progressive legislation.

> Robert Lekachman, *Visions and Nightmares:*
> *America after Reagan (1987), 135*

Don't despair. Be as wise as my grandma. Pull the patches and the pieces together, bound by a common thread. When we form a great quilt of unity and common ground, we'll have the power to bring about health care and housing and jobs and education and hope.... We, the people, can win.

> Reverend Jesse Jackson, 1988 Democratic Party Convention

Labor's alliances with those who share its vision are almost as old as the movement itself, and the commitment to these friends is one most unionists endorse. When asked in the mid-1980s if the movement should seek closer ties with nonlabor reform groups, 45 percent of national union officers said yes, as did 47 percent of local union officers. Only 27 and 26 percent respectively were opposed.[1]

Unfortunately, the bonds between trade unionism and the larger community have often weakened. In the early 1950s, for example, "the general public...lost interest in the functioning of the largest democratic institution in this society other than the government itself."[2] Happily, thanks to remarkable activists on both sides of the divide, the general public is relearning the critical value of labor through public-interest coalitions. The late Michael Harrington, for example, urged readers of his 1988 autobiography never to forget that "in very practical terms, labor has more money, more printing presses, and more organizers than any other component of a potential progressive coalition."[3]

The case studies that follow this chapter each illustrate the complexity of collaborative efforts: one explores the cooperative efforts of formerly antagonistic groups of environmentalists and building trades people; the other describes a project in Boston in which bricklayers and laborers have joined with community activists to provide low-income housing. Taken together, the case studies suggest ways outreach can invigorate local unions, expand labor's horizons, extend its political clout, enhance its image, and "feed its soul."

This chapter documents three other examples of labor-community alliances: the Amalgamated Bank of New York, a remarkable survivor from the 1920s and a model for new labor banks; a coalition in California formed to protect its OSHA program; and the Pittsburgh-based Tri-State Conference on Steel. The underlying question is, How well are labor and nonunion groups promoting the idea of community, and how well are they succeeding in building solidarity, commitment, and continuity?

Labor's Bank

The Amalgamated Bank of New York, whose assets exceed $1.5 billion, is well known in banking circles for its innovations and its "inclination to tweak its big corporate rivals." Founded in 1923 by the Amalgamated Clothing Workers Union (now ACTWU) with barely $300,000, the bank is still owned by the 284,000 members of the union.[4] All members of its board are ACTWU officials, and the union receives the bank's profits, which totaled $9.8 million in 1988.

Labor's values have helped shape this "rogue bank, loudly touting a consumer ethic, and often de-emphasizing profits in favor of services."[5] Specifically, the bank pioneered in providing unsecured installment loans in the 1920s and in lending money to borrowers with no collateral but steady jobs (union or nonunion). It also led the way in providing free checking accounts to workers, money-market rates for small savers, and loans to workers on strike. Recently, the bank has distinguished itself in still other pro-worker ways:

■ It helped three New York locals of the Bridge, Structural, and Ornamental Iron Workers Union use pension money to finance below-market, no-points home mortgages for their members.
■ It teamed up with Metropolitan Life Insurance Company in a proposal to offer a comprehensive money-management program to the AFL-CIO's 14 million members.

■ It offered a variety of special services to the workers on strike during 1989 against Eastern Airlines.

Bank staff operate with a mandate to find new ways to demonstrate the bank's goal, which is emblazoned on a plaque in the lobby: "New York's First Labor Bank, dedicated to the service and advancement of the labor movement."

The implications of this commitment are outlined in a brochure the bank uses to introduce itself to potential union customers: "We speak the language of the trade union movement. We were founded by a union. We are run by union people. So we know what concerns union leadership. We understand the problems. We talk down-to-earth language. And we don't hedge. We deliver. Amalgamated has proven that banking and labor can blend in complete harmony. We manage the funds of labor unions, and we do a good job of it."[6]

Labor would seem to agree, as unions account for up to 67 percent of the bank's $1.1 billion in deposits (as of 1987), and its trust department holds an additional $3.2 billion in union pension and health and welfare funds. As one indication of the bank's solidarity, in 1981, when the National Football League Players Association went broke during a strike, it was given a $200,000 instant loan, even though it did not have an account with the bank. It has naturally done business with the Amalgamated ever since.[7]

Although the Amalgamated ranks among the top 1.5 percent of the nation's fourteen thousand commercial banks, it does not generally offer credit cards or home mortgages, and it has avoided interstate expansion and fierce competition for corporate loans. Instead, it focuses on providing friendly and careful service, knowing that "today, customers in open shirts and work boots outnumber those in business suits." As of 1986, its services were the second least expensive available to area consumers, and it has been named "the top bank in New York for average consumers" in three recent surveys.[8]

Labor banks were heralded as the wave of the future in the 1920s, but their history has not been easy. Thirty-six such banks were founded at that time, but only two (the Amalgamated and the Brotherhood Bank and Trust in Kansas City) survive as labor-owned institutions. The Amalgamated, however, has reported forty-four consecutive years of profit, and its return on equity and on capital exceed the average for banks of its size.[9]

The importance of the Amalgamated is not that it is a heroic anachronism but that it serves as an exemplary model for other banks. And, as a *Wall Street Journal* reporter alerted readers, labor banks may rise again: "Like the clothing workers who started Amalgamated, other unions see a chance to own a bank friendly to their members' needs and find new investment outlets for their growing assets."[10] In the past several years, six new labor banks have opened, led by robust union locals in the construction trades. Massachusetts members of the United Brotherhood of Carpenters and Joiners opened a bank in Boston in 1987, for example, and California carpenters opened an institution the following year.

Cal-OSHA: Toward a Safer Community

When George Deukmejian, California's Republican governor, cut $8 million from the 1987 state budget, he initiated a controversy that united the state's labor leaders and forged new community coalitions. At issue was the fate of California's occupational safety and health program, highly acclaimed for its commitment to protecting about 10 million workers in private industry. Deukmejian's decision to slash state funds from the program, funded jointly by the state and federal governments, cost the state $14 million in federal grants.[11]

Although money seemed to be at the heart of the controversy, opponents insisted the governor had other motives: "He equates Cal-OSHA with organized labor," said Democratic state assemblyman Richard Floyd. "He has a very narrow perception of things." The threat to Cal-OSHA provided organized labor with a statewide issue around which to build broad support for a safer workplace. This effort was remarkable in a state where less than 20 percent of the work force is unionized and labor's political power statewide is "unpredictable, at best."[12]

California's program in safety and health in the workplace had been a national leader since the early 1900s. Reaction to the governor's attempt to replace it with the more conservative and less adequately funded federal OSHA program was immediate and hostile: "Union response to Deukmejian's action has been 'every negative word you can think of.' "[13] A coalition was formed representing management, insurers, and labor, and it tried to find the critical $8 million the governor wanted to cut.

In short order, a union local in the construction industry, a state assemblyman, and 337 state employees joined in a suit to block the governor's actions. Cal-OSHA, they pointed out, was a nationwide model that had established exposure limits for 170 toxic substances unregulated by the federal agency and set more stringent standards for nearly 100 other chemical hazards. In addition, the program was exemplary in its regulation of asbestos removal, construction sites, and farm tool utilization.

To renew funding for Cal-OSHA against the governor's wishes, advocates needed to collect signatures from four hundred thousand California voters who agreed the issue belonged on the election ballot in November 1988. For help with this awesome task, labor turned to the thirty-six environmental, health, and public-interest groups that comprised the Coalition for a Safe Workplace.

Working across the state with local union volunteers, the California AFL-CIO secured more than seven hundred thousand signatures—nearly twice the number required to put the issue on the ballot—before its state labor legislative conference in June 1988.[14] Conference delegates pledged an all-out effort to win a "second life" for Cal-OSHA.

Early polls were encouraging, with one showing that 65 percent of the public favored restoration, even though 61 percent had not previously been aware that the agency was at risk.[15] When the vote was finally tallied, 4.5 million voters favored continued state support of Cal-OSHA, and 3.9 million opposed it, providing a 53 percent victory for the labor coalition.[16] Labor's real triumph was its ability to convince the public-interest community that Cal-OSHA should remain a model state-directed program. Support provided by the Sierra Club, the state's largest environmental organization, the state chapter of the American Cancer Society, and other groups was essential to the victory.

Tri-State Conference on Steel

Founded by ministers, community activists, policy experts, and militant steel unionists in 1979 as a nonprofit, community-based, public-interest organization, the Tri-State Conference on Steel has sought to prevent mill and plant closings in Pittsburgh, Pennsylvania, and Youngstown, Ohio. Tri-State consistently emphasizes self-reliance while many workers still place blind faith in the management of the steel companies. Its outreach to the steel mill communities of Pennsylvania, Ohio, and West Virginia has helped residents make new job-generating plans based on area diversification into the energy industry and the rebuilding of area railroads, ports, and bridges. These plans include a wide range of ideas and projects:

- Tri-State has developed a blueprint for a locally accountable and democratically controlled regional planning authority to manage investments earmarked for reindustrialization projects and run reopened mills.
- Tri-State has persuaded ten municipalities to form an industrial organization called the Steel Valley Authority (SVA). It has power of eminent domain (the right to take over private property for public

purposes) and the authority to buy, sell, or run companies. The SVA coordinates previously scattered efforts to retain jobs and relieves individual communities of some of the pressure when a plant shuts down or lays off workers. Its immediate goal is to prevent plant closings by threatening to take over the plants, while pursuing a long-range program of "regional reindustrialization."

■ Tri-State and labor lobbyists have drafted and are working to pass a state bill that would establish a Pennsylvania industrial development finance corporation. It would provide a source of equity capital for use in aiding manufacturing projects in distressed regions of the state.

■ Tri-State has convinced the Public Utility Commission and the Duquesne Light Company to work with the Pittsburgh Foundation and various community leaders to establish a $1.6 million revolving equity fund to help save viable manufacturing facilities and develop new ones.

■ Tri-State, the SVA, the Steelworkers, the Southside Community Council, Pittsburgh City Council representatives, and former LTV workers and neighbors of LTV have developed a plan to restart the company's Southside electric furnaces, using modern steelmaking technology. Plans for reopening include ownership by private investors, worker-stockholders, and public shareholders.

■ Tri-State has helped area unionists understand that certain redevelopment schemes, such as the conversion of factory sites into upscale residential projects, pose a veiled threat to blue-collar communities because they soon drive out less affluent manual workers.

■ Tri-State has helped area unionists think through the pros and cons of the reindustrialization drive in the Mon Valley at a time when certain parties advocate the development of commercial enterprises, industrial museums, new housing, and parks instead of the creation of new job sites.

Technology analyst Harley Shaiken characterizes the special interest this project inspires: "The Tri-State approach is exciting not because it's a blueprint—it's not—but because it's a rallying point for people seeking to gain some control over their lives."[17]

Other Worthy Examples

Additional examples deserve mention as evidence of the success labor has achieved in recent alliances with community organizations and social movements:

■ In December 1989, a coalition of labor, environmental, and other grass-roots community groups successfully ended the longest lockout in U.S. labor history, by the Louisiana branch of the BASF Corporation.

Leaders of the Oil, Chemical, and Atomic Workers Union believe BASF capitulated because the coalition's five-year-long exposure of the company's threat to the environment compelled more responsible corporate behavior. So great were the odds against this union win that an official of the Louisiana AFL-CIO contends "the BASF lockout will go down as a landmark in labor history."[18]

■ Gay activists and members of the building trades joined together in January 1990 to urge a Boston health center to deal only with union labor. Insofar as lesbian and gay workers were the center's main clients and supporters, the coalition won new construction work for the unionists. In turn, the building trades gave support to a benefit the gay activists held on behalf of the United Farm Workers, which has traditionally supported gay rights.[19]

■ The UMWA's ability to orchestrate an extraordinary nationwide solidarity effort, union and nonunion, helped bring to a successful end in February 1990 an eleven-month strike against Pittston Coal Company.[20]

■ In March 1990, a coalition of fifty labor unions, churches, and community groups announced a boycott of McDonald's in Philadelphia to protest the lower wage scale in effect in the inner city than in the suburbs. The company's initial response was to hire a union buster, but the Campaign for Fair Wages insists unionizing is not its immediate goal. Created by the Philadelphia Unemployment Project, the new coalition hopes its campaign will "focus more attention on organizing in the service sector," and it expects to take action soon against several other fast-food chains.[21]

■ A network in Eugene and Springfield, Oregon, now includes unionists, feminists, anti-racism activists, and other concerned citizens. It has rallied support for a teachers' union headed for a possible strike, planned boycotts of businesses using raw materials from union-busting suppliers, and published a monthly newsletter. On the eleventh morning of every month, it sets up a picket line at a plant struck since July 1988. Dennis Gilbert, a co-founder of the network, is convinced such community organizing "is to today's AFL-CIO what industrial organizing was to the labor movement in the 1930s."[22]

■ An unusual coalition of big business and organized labor succeeded in April 1990 in gaining passage of the nation's toughest state antitakeover law. A focus of nationwide debate, the bill, passed in Pennsylvania, was intended to thwart "that small band of about a dozen corporate raiders who have made a living over the past decade by putting companies in play."[23] Proponents expect similar bills to be introduced soon in other state legislatures. Labor is especially intent on including provisions that will maintain existing contracts for five years after a takeover, require severance payments, and establish disclosure requirements as a condition of pension fund raids.

■ In April 1990, a coalition of the AFL-CIO, the Natural Resources Defense Council, and the state of California was credited with forcing the Environmental Protection Agency to ban long-used chemical pesticides whose cancer-causing residues have been found in processed foods.[24]

■ A coalition in Connecticut now links the Naugatuck Valley Project (see case study, page 221) and the UAW with longtime advocates of economic conversion. Insofar as more than 700 state firms and 500,000 or so military-related jobs are at stake, the UAW, which nationally has pushed conversion policies since the 1940s, is using the coalition to pressure companies and public officials to find new markets for and create new retraining programs in military-dependent businesses. As the Reverend Kevin Bean, a coalition leader, explains, this issue "is now meat and potatoes on everyone's plate."[25]

All of these projects reflect a stirring in labor's ranks that questions the desirability of an economy narrowly guided by the profit motive. In place of that chilly perspective, they explore with keen interest the real meaning of community.

Hearing from the Skeptics

Alliances between labor and area activists are not immune from criticism. Skeptics mutter that scarce resources, especially unionists' time and energy, should be confined to work-site issues. They cite a long list of alliances in which labor ended up with little to show for its investment of funds, ideas, and physical labor. In fact, some skeptics warn that community groups primarily want to use labor to their narrow self-advantage.

Proponents of collaborative projects, however, devalue the danger. As one union activist said about a prominent research and advocacy group that courts alliances with local unions, "They've got a contribution to make, and a part to play, but it is much smaller than they think. They have their own political agenda, and we know it, and they know we know it, and we have to be on our guard. They want to use us, and we want to use them, but not anywhere as much as they'd like. So we keep our distance, though we stay in touch."[26] A fear of being co-opted by community or special-interest activists runs deep, grounded for some in the memory of historical manipulations of trade unions by ideologues of the Left and Right.

Many unionists believe broad-based alliances are a necessity. Labor cannot win public support during strikes and lockouts unless it has a track record of aiding community causes. Outreach gives local union participants new energy, they argue, rather than only taxing their strength. While some projects are bound to fail, the potential gain from community coalitions more than justifies the risks. Two close students of the subject, David Bensman and Roberta Lynch, explain: "The nature of the new [coalition-led] battles to save the steel industry is forcing the union to reevaluate its previous strategy of cooperation with the companies, its reliance on high-level lobbying, and its removal from local union struggles. This current crisis is bringing the union back in touch with its grass roots."[27]

Prospects for the Future

In the coming decade, labor may well expand its network of projects conducted with such strategic groups as the League of Women Voters, the National Association of Community Action Agencies, the National Association of Private Industry Councils, the National Council of Churches, the National Council of La Raza, the National Puerto Rican Forum, the NAACP, the National Urban League, the U.S. Catholic Conference, and the U.S. Student Association. Labor's outreach will probably continue to include labor-managed services (such as those offered through the Amalgamated Bank), sponsorship of focused campaigns (such as Cal-OSHA), and its commitment to democratic alliances (such as Tri-State). Long convinced of the need for innovative partnerships, labor offers funds, skills, technical resources, and access to the national media. "Perhaps more importantly," labor also brings "its heritage of solidarity, of decades of shared struggle."[28]

Linking Job Creation and Housing Needs

Tom McIntyre, a Boston-based vice-president of the International Union of Bricklayers and Allied Craftsmen (BAC), concluded in 1982 that labor was in a unique position to help protect local neighborhoods. Gentrification was driving property values and taxes so high that members of his union were being forced out of their homes and price inflation was preventing their adult children from locating in the area. Boston's working class was being steadily driven out of "urban villages" that were their historic enclaves. McIntyre resolved to do something about the rapidly increasing shortage of affordable urban housing.

Seldom at a loss for lilting phrases and colorful language, McIntyre now repeats the same cogent answer every time he is asked why BAC pioneered in building low-cost, not-for-profit houses: "Unions have been painted as a self-interest group. Our aim is to work on the grass-roots neighborhood level so that people begin to understand unionism is a force for good in their community."[1]

Labor has a long history of involvement in meeting housing needs, dating back to 1950, when the ILGWU and the Amalgamated Clothing Workers of America, along with representatives of smaller unions, formed the United Housing Foundation. Since that time more than fifty thousand cooperative housing units have been built with labor's help. The Teamsters Union has a National Housing Office, and the AFL-CIO Housing Investment Trust has more than $654 million in funding. In just the last decade, for example, the New York City Policemen's Pension Fund has invested $90 million in mid-priced housing, and the California Building Trades' Pension Fund, representing seventeen unions, has committed $268 million to union-built construction projects.[2]

In cooperation with another Boston-area labor organization, a local of the Laborers Union, McIntyre formed a partnership called the Bricklayers and Laborers Non-profit Housing Company, Inc., referred to ever since as B. and L. The rationale for creating the company was simply that it was "well-nigh time labor did something to upgrade its very poor image, and a very good thing would be to build affordable housing!"[3]

In the mid-1980s, B. and L. leveraged its political influence to acquire a tract of abandoned land from the city of Boston for a dollar, and it began construction of housing that unionists could afford. Such a venture was unprecedented in the Boston area, where the average price for a house at that time was the second highest in the United States. As McIntyre recalls, there were three critical hurdles:[4]

- The two BAC district councils that were involved had to learn how to see eye to eye and how to smooth over old disagreements.
- The two district councils had to learn how to coordinate plans with their new ally, the area laborers local.
- The members of a home owners' organization had to learn how to overcome their misgivings about organized labor and to trust the leadership of B. and L.

And, as McIntyre is quick to add, "an awful lot of luck" had to come the project's way.[5]

Having established new patterns of cooperation and trust, McIntyre obtained union pension funds, which were invested in certificates of deposit at a local bank where they earned 6 ½ to 7 percent interest. The bank then provided loans for construction below the market rate, at about 8 percent.[6] Since the land cost only a dollar and the developer's profit was set at zero, B. and L. could pass discounts along to home buyers.

The next step was to establish cordial relations with the neighborhoods in which the abandoned tract was located. As McIntyre explained, "You have to make it clear to community groups you are working *with* them, and not *for* them. . . . It takes a lot of patience to sit with community people. . . . Fortunately, we in BAC were spawned in these old neighborhoods, and we can 'swing and sway' with the groups. We understand the scene."[7]

Locating an architect was the next major challenge, as one after another declined the B. and L. job. McIntyre recalls that "we told them there were two conditions—the design had to be price competitive with factory-built housing, and they would get paid only when everything had gone smoothly, only when we actually got the land and were well on our way. So, many turned us down." In due course, however, eighteen two-bedroom brick row houses took shape, built and financed by union members. Priced exceptionally low ($69,000 in 1986) and assessed at $140,000 for a permanent mortgage, four of the homes were made available through a citywide lottery in which five hundred people participated. As McIntyre explained triumphantly, "We wanted to reach the '$3 bettor' and we wanted the lottery to prove there was no 'winking' or 'blinking' about the sale. We wanted to help the first-time buyer, and we pulled off the entire shebang!"[8]

Encouraged by its initial success, B. and L. undertook a much larger project involving the construction of 215 mixed-income rowhouse condominiums in two Boston locations. Only low- to moderate-income families were declared eligible to buy the one- to three-bedroom units, which were priced from $69,500 to $107,500, or about 40 percent below market value. Preference was given to neighborhood residents. Working through the Massachusetts Home Ownership Opportunities Program, a family of four with an income up to $43,000 was eligible for a mortgage at interest rates of 5.5 to 7.9 percent.[9] These terms proved so appealing that twelve hundred applicants bid in a lottery for 50 of the 215 units at the second B. and L. site; 16 units were purchased by the Boston Housing Authority for low-income renters.

Having seen the assets of B. and L. grow from $1.5 million to over $26 million, Boston neighborhood groups are now eager to have B. and L. projects in their areas. News of B. and L.'s achievements has spread, and McIntyre, who dropped out of school in tenth grade to lay bricks, is now invited all over the country to speak to labor and community groups about ways they can follow the example he has helped set:

> The key is getting a good bank to leverage pension fund monies, to enable you to borrow at a lower rate than other developers have to pay.... Then you want to get your building trades locals to put you in touch with the best contractors they know of.... Make sure everyone gets a decent rate of return, and don't ask anyone to take a vow of poverty but, as a zero-overhead developer, don't allow any "home runs," either.... Promise fifty but build fifty-five, and sell the extra five at market [value], thereby giving you some money with which to subsidize more low-income housing. Keep reminding yourself of all the good reasons you got into this to begin with, and never go soft or get timid.[10]

McIntyre is particularly pleased with invitations he gets to speak to locals of the Bricklayers, the Laborers, the Plumbers, and other unions. When he speaks, he emphasizes five points:

- *Do not try to change the world.* Just do the best possible job you can to build affordable housing, and downplay anything that has to do with controversial social "issues"!
- *Do not get drawn into assuring set-asides—for your own members, for the members of the unions who back you with their pension funds, or for anyone else.* If you do, the hostility of the neighborhood you are building in or the media will kill you: "We can't waltz with everyone, and we've got to disappoint some people, even our own people, some of the time."
- *Get the land for nothing or next to it, and get all the necessary city government approvals up front:* "We had the mayor and the governor

in our corner from the outset and never would have gotten to first base without them."

■ *Hire the best real estate attorney you can, and make sure the contract for the sale of land protects resales.* Use deed restrictions, imposed by the city, to limit resale prices to the consumer price index or to a maximum increase of 5 percent a year: "Keep speculators out!"

■ *Tell everybody from the outset what the deal is and be firm about it.* Offer 70 percent of the new homes to neighborhood people and keep the remaining 30 percent for other people in the city: "When people lean on us to change the numbers, we turn a deaf ear."[11]

Carefully adapted to meet an area's needs, McIntyre's guidelines should help union locals nationwide achieve their own successes in home building.

A Word from the Skeptics

Critics grumble that the small scale of B. and L. barely begins to meet Boston's considerable need for affordable housing. Some believe members of BAC and of other unions should have first claim on the homes built by their efforts. And many insist success in such a venture is impossible unless the leader is as tough and decisive, and also as rare, as Tom McIntyre. To all of this, he tersely responds, "Any progress is better than none! And labor has more than its fair share of talented blokes."[12]

A reporter for the *Boston Globe* put the $22 million project in perspective when he noted, "This is pretty radical stuff. . . . No federal funds. No limited partnerships. No sales commissions. No syndicated tax shelters, publicity campaign, extended planning procedures, environmentalist tedium, hearings, seminars, workshops, committees, reviews. Just do it."[13]

The B. and L. story, in sum, provides a robust model of how labor and neighborhood groups can meet shared needs in a "win-win" fashion. It suggests an approach to getting the job done swiftly and economically, whether or not one has what McIntyre delights in calling "the luck of the Irish."

Linking Job Creation and Environmental Issues

Relations between environmental activists and building trades unionists have been wary at best and frankly bitter at worst. The former
charge labor with indifference to Earth Day issues, and the latter suspect environmentalists put insufficient value on measures to protect
jobs. Communication between the groups has been minimal, and mistrust has been profound. The Job and Community Protection Program (JCPP), however, has created a new and significant opportunity
for overdue reconciliation.[1]

Seeing the Light

Thomas Hunter, a fifty-year-old business manager of Local 467 of the
United Association of the Plumbing and Pipe Fitting Industry in northern
California, designed JCPP in the early 1980s. He felt he had to do something about the loss of work his members were experiencing as more and
more construction jobs went to nonunion builders and union ranks dwin-
dled. Some new form of leverage against anti-union builders was des-
perately needed.

Hunter's creative response linked the Northern California Pipe Trades
Association with area environmentalists in an unprecedented alliance,
one that intervened in the land-use permit application process of nonunion builders. In early 1982, the new allies began to charge builders
with filing inadequate environmental impact statements (EIS). They successfully used this strategy to halt large-scale projects until major reforms
were negotiated to the satisfaction of both environmental and labor union
goals.

Coming to Terms

As word spread, West Coast builders who were members of organizations
such as the Sierra Club and Greenpeace began seeking the approval of
Hunter and his allies before setting major construction projects in motion.
Hunter would recommend the exclusive use of union pipefitters, and the
environmentalists would recommend specific reforms to protect natural
and human resources. The builder was then assured that the new alliance
would not find further cause to challenge an EIS and thereby halt construction. So substantial was the impact of this strategy that the union
share of construction work soared and the negotiated hourly wage set a
new northern California record.

Reinterpreting the Past

Hunter commissioned a sixty-minute color videotape in 1986 to demonstrate that organized labor was the nation's first environmental movement. *In the Community Interest* documents two centuries of efforts by labor to alleviate ecological hazards in the workplace, such as chemicals, gases, coal dust, and cotton lint. Also chronicled in the videotape is the history of the environmental movement, with an emphasis on those efforts related to labor. Widely shown to union locals and environmental groups throughout northern California and the Seattle area, the film illuminates a dimension of American history that has been ignored.

Reclaiming the Present

In 1986, the fledgling JCPP became embroiled in several California community disputes. In Shasta County, for example, members of the building trades sponsored a protest group (Shasta Citizens for Responsible Industry) that fought to deny a developer a permit to build a fifty-megawatt biomass power plant. Air quality controls were criticized as inadequate, and smog and soot, which were likely by-products, would have violated the standards of the Environmental Protection Agency. Such violations, the activists explained, would have disqualified Shasta County from federal programs, including highway construction. Labor's opposition was fueled by the developer's intention to remain nonunion and by the company's threat to move the entire project elsewhere unless it got its way. Although members of the labor-environmental coalition were unable to block the building permit, they won many environmental concessions, such as improvements in effluent controls and the repositioning of tall stacks, and the builder now discusses projects with unions before permits are sought.

In Merced County, the building trades unions focused on United Technologies, a nonunion developer that had submitted a proposal to build a rocket fuel manufacturing plant. An attorney for the unions told county authorities the proposed facility would create a noise hazard and a fuel-burning hazard and seriously undermine the land-use process. Crews of nonunion workers from outside the state would also weaken the Merced economy, the attorney reasoned, since they would send their earnings back to their families rather than spend them locally. Under the pressure of these indictments, the developer agreed to submit an improved proposal.

Finally, in Richmond, California, building trades unions intervened in the EIS process when a new housing tract was proposed on the storage site of old petroleum tanks. Toxicity in the soil threatened both construction workers (nonunion) and prospective residents. Hunter's lawyers urged the authorities to halt the project and think more deeply about the meaning of responsible growth.

Stabilizing the Campaign

As the sequence of local success stories grew and the film reached new audiences, many more locals of the Carpenters Union and of the pipe-fitters association joined the JCPP. The original assessment of $1.25 an hour to launch the project was dropped to 15 cents an hour, and the $400,000 a year the original members had contributed was soon dwarfed by the contributions of new locals eager to participate in both the creation of new jobs and the protection of the environment.

Spreading the Word

When Hunter spoke to Seattle's Local 46 in the spring of 1987, he inspired the five hundred attendees to initiate a program similar to his own. The membership voted a special assessment of 25 cents per hour worked for one year, amounting to a projected $400,000, to initiate the program. Representatives of the United Brotherhood of Carpenters, Local 1144, who attended Hunter's talk offered to contribute a special assessment of 20 cents per hour, assuring $250,000 in a year for the fund's operation, subject to lulls in the construction industry.

Cautionary Note

Jim Freese, the Seattle Fund specialist at Local 46, IBEW, emphasizes the need for unions to move cautiously. His own study of the alliance project reveals how fine the line is between acceptable and unacceptable union action in efforts to block the process of obtaining construction permits. If the line is crossed with rash statements or actions, a union can be cited for "abuse of process."

To avoid legal embarrassments, the Seattle Fund has an environmental lawyer on retainer and employs a full-time environmental specialist, who may be the first in the profession to work for a coalition of building trades unions. Finally, a public relations firm has been contracted to enhance interactions with the media, the various environmental groups, and the public at large.

Listening to "John Q. Public"

Guided by its public relations specialists, the Seattle Fund sponsored a half-day workshop in July 1987. Freese and other union officials listened carefully as Seattle citizens aired their attitudes toward labor in general and toward the building trades unions in particular. A discussion of environmental issues developed into an exploration of labor's responsibility for environmental quality.

On the basis of the workshop discussions, the local decided to commission a poll of five hundred Seattle-area residents. Professionally conducted, the fifteen-minute telephone interview indicated public support for labor's outreach into environmental matters. Specifically, 76 percent of the respondents agreed unions should be involved in community issues such as land-use planning, and 89 percent thought labor should police toxic waste issues, such as water pollution, leeching, and landfill controversies. Moreover, 79 percent felt unions should do more concerning job safety, while 83 percent believed unions should help monitor hazardous substances both on and off the job. Gratified by the public response, Freese and his colleagues feel their new strategies have been vindicated: "We are now doing for ourselves what is good for the public as well, and the public is coming to know and appreciate it."

Battle Plan

According to Freese, a typical Seattle Fund action follows a sequence of careful steps. When a search of public records indicates a developer is seeking permits for a project, the Seattle Fund tries to determine the likelihood that the project will be constructed with nonunion workers by examining past practice and talking directly with the developer. Typically, the nonunion projects pay wages below scale, do not support multiemployer health and pension plans, and show little concern for local employment. Seattle Fund representatives then probe whether the project has the potential for substantial environmental impact. Only if it does and if other individuals or groups are also concerned about the project does the group decide to intervene in the process.

The aim of the Seattle Fund is to force the aggrieved builder to seek a compromise settlement that addresses both the complaints of area environmentalists and labor's economic concerns. If environmentalists challenge a *union* developer, the fund will neither oppose nor support the project, even though many of its members may depend on its implementation, until an informed committee that includes fund members has evaluated the project.

Redefining "Environment"

A special effort to redefine environmental gains and losses is pivotal to the Seattle version of JCPP. Seattle Fund locals know from experience that low-quality developers seeking permits will boast about the number of jobs a project will generate and the amount of money their payroll will add to the community. Freese and his colleagues respond that if the project pays below union scale, it deprives both the workers and the community of needed revenue. They have set a precedent in the Seattle area by arguing that the positive EIS required before authorization of a major building permit must also demonstrate positive economic impact on the host community.

Any such argument by a union, Freese insists, must be reasonable, legitimate, and sincere. Potential impact on the environment must be weighed against a project's impact on the area's economy. Will the project undercut the prevailing wages of area unionists? Will it circumvent the training requirements the state sets for relevant trades? Will it damage a wetlands? Will it destroy a salmon stream? If a concerned local feels the construction threatens the community's best interests, it should intervene in the permit process until reasonable compromises are won.

By carefully explaining the extended definition of environmental impact to community activists, Freese expects to win additional support at EIS hearings. He has documented the contention that builders who seek to undercut wages also cut corners on planning and environmental safeguards. Although labor will not abandon a permit protest once it has begun; the Seattle Fund is prepared for honest differences with its allies. A neighborhood group may persist in opposing a project long after the fund agrees, for example, that new off-street parking has met labor's environmental objection.

Freese is confident the Seattle version of the Hunter Plan, with its bold line of reasoning, will continue to thrive. Many Seattle rank-and-filers welcome cooperation with other environmentally aware citizens and applaud the fund's redefinition of environmental impact to include the economic environment. As Freese says, "If a developer claims the environmental damage caused by their project should be overlooked because it will create jobs, we ask, What kind of jobs? Are they good jobs? We don't like projects that lower our standard of living and wreck the local economy."

Progress of the Seattle Fund

Jim Freese takes justifiable pride in having scrutinized 150 building projects involving more than $3 billion in proposed construction costs. In 1987, three of these projects posed an unacceptable threat to the Seattle-area environment and were targeted for corrective action:

- An office park would have lacked an adequate setback from a blue heron rookery if it was built as originally planned. The nonunion builder involved abandoned his plan when the fund began its campaign.
- A large retail store was planned for construction close to a neighborhood school and a recreational lake. Although the developer some-

times "built union," the fund wanted to see how a revised EIS treated traffic and runoff problems. If these issues were still poorly addressed, the fund would fight for substantial site alterations.

■ A project proposed in a small town with a daily traffic load of six thousand vehicles would have brought in thirty thousand more, an increase the community had no way to handle. The fund requested a copy of the project EIS and scrutinized it with particular concern for the traffic problems.

For its careful and significant work, the Seattle Fund and Freese's IBEW local have been viciously attacked in anti-union newsletters. Freese suggests those attacks are further evidence that the Seattle adaptation of the Hunter Plan is succeeding.

Summary

There have always been isolated instances of cooperation between labor and environmentalists, but the Hunter Plan has solidified the relationship, making a working alliance systematic and cumulative. Both parties have benefited as more and more union members work on construction projects that are environmentally sound.

Building trades unionists have discarded many archaic work-site practices as a result of their cooperation with area environmentalists and are winning more work than ever for rank-and-filers. Many now weigh the economic and environmental impacts of construction with new insight that benefits both the labor movement and the larger community in a very laudable way.

Part VI

Part VI

CREATING A
FINER FUTURE

Many union leaders and rank-and-filers are intent on making the future their own. Chapter 14 documents labor's involvement in futuristics, the exploration of policy options by which labor can determine more of its own destiny. Chapter 15 explores one specific "future-making" strategy, the merger of various unions with one another. Some experts expect, for instance, that the ninety unions in the AFL-CIO will merge into forty or so in the 1990s. The chapter discusses this major tool for modernizing the labor movement.

Chapter 14
Toward the Employ of Futuristics

It is no longer satisfactory in today's dynamic world, where accelerating technological change and lagging social progress are so mismatched, to plan to manage and operate by reaction to unanticipated, unexpected events after they occur.... We must seek to make what happens, in substantial part, a logical result of our having planned that it should happen.

Simon Ramo, *Century of Mismatch* (1976), 204

As insiders begin to gain insight and outlook, they will move toward an articulated philosophy to give long-range direction to their instinctive reactions. In the rise of such a corps of doer-seers will rest the fate and future of American labor and, to some extent, of American civilization.

Gus Tyler, *The Labor Revolution* (1967), 256

AFL founder Samuel Gompers liked to recall how as a young worker in a cigar factory he profited from listening to a co-worker hired by the work force to read aloud. Although the readings varied, requests were generally for political analysts and reformers, including Ferdinand Lasalle and Karl Marx. The cigar makers were not at all averse to heated arguments about broad strategies for changing society, and, through these discussions, Gompers and his co-workers discovered that "they too possessed the ability to contrast current reality with a just and humane potential."[1]

Recognition that the future is created in the present by consequential acts of commission and omission is the essence of futurist thinking. Activities discussed below of the Communications Workers of America and its Committee on the Future, created in 1981, exemplify a robust use of this perspective, as do efforts of the AFL-CIO Committee on the Evolution of Work, with its long-range forecasting, planning, and advocacy.

Background

Despite pro-labor rhetoric that links the movement with change and adaptation, America's unions are not commonly thought of as farsighted and dynamic. For example, James O'Toole wrote in 1986:

Perhaps no institution, save university faculties, is more resistant to change than the trade union movement. Many unions in this country were slow to respond to the needs of women and minority workers, slow to understand the values of post-Vietnam era workers, and slow to respond to the need for cooperation with business to meet the challenge of foreign competition. (To be fair, most employers were no better than unions on these issues.)[2]

Twenty-five years earlier, Clark Kerr characterized labor similarly as a "great social institution remaining virtually unmoving on a plateau, while society all around it keeps on growing and changing."[3]

Unfortunately, this feeling has not been confined to academic experts. In a 1983 poll of national labor leaders and a 1985 poll of local union leaders, some 73 percent of the former respondents and 76 percent of the latter agreed there was "a lack of vitality in the labor movement." Indeed, only 26 percent and 21 percent respectively felt the future of the labor movement was secure.[4]

To understand labor's resistance to change is to understand its deep-rooted suspicion of intellectualism. As long ago as 1923, labor historian Selig Perlman was struck by the "remarkably restricted" role of the intellectual in the movement: "The intellectual with his new and unfamiliar issues has been given the cold shoulder by precisely the trade unionists in whom he had anticipated to find his most eager disciples. The intellectual might go from success to success in conquering the minds of the middle classes; the labor movement largely remains closed to him."[5]

Perlman attributed this "cold shoulder" to a sharp clash of concerns: intellectuals were passionately committed to timeless general theories, while union leaders were primarily focused on specific topical details and grievances. Union leaders wanted to win conventional reforms of working conditions overnight, while intellectuals often wanted far more than "mere amelioration." The two parties naturally remained wary of each other.

Although labor's suspicion of intellectuals persists, the leaders of certain major unions were intrigued by Alvin Toffler's 1970 best-seller, *Future Shock*. As a leading proponent of "applied futuristics," Toffler offered a variety of planning strategies "more humane, more far-sighted, and more democratic than any so far in use." Unlike many such theorists, he made at least occasional reference to unions and advised labor to use advanced telecommunications and other innovations.[6]

The CWA and Futuristics

During the 1970s, corporations, government agencies, and think tanks such as Rand and Brookings made increasing use of new tools such as computer simulations, trend forecasting, a complex technique known as Delphi polling, and cross-impact analysis.[7] Finally, in 1981, a major union dared to try its hand at the game. Acting on the suggestion of a particularly creative unit (locals in District 9), the CWA created the labor movement's first Committee on the Future. According to CWA president Morton Bahr, it was a major component in a thorough effort at modernization. After two years of deliberations, the committee reported its action-oriented recommendations at a special convention at which Alvin Toffler delivered the keynote address. He became thereby the first futurist ever to address a major American labor union.

The CWA's Committee on the Future advised the parent organization to convert itself into a "strategy-driven union," warning that "we cannot afford to deal with external events reactively and in a piecemeal fashion."[8] At the same time, the committee was quick to acknowledge labor's many reasons to resist taking a pro-active stance:

> It is easy... to get so caught up in current emergencies that we lose sight of upcoming problems. [Our] Committee, because of its specific focus on the shape of things to come, has been able to view CWA's present situation within a much broader and longer-term framework. [Our] job has been to jolt us out of the complacency of success and away from the natural tendency to keep doing the same things in the old ways because they have worked for us in the past.[9]

Above all, the committee saw its role as helping the CWA change in "an orderly, organized fashion so that we can help shape the future, rather than be swept along helplessly."[10]

To meet its mandate, the committee had followed a five-part plan:

- Committee members had studied the extensive literature on the future, including the forecasts and prescriptions of labor leaders, economists, and other farsighted and knowledgeable figures.
- Based on its literature review, the committee had drafted a forecast for the upcoming ten to fifteen years, encompassing an artful scenario of extrapolations, speculations, and value preferences.
- The committee had shared its forecast with the executive board of the CWA, with more than thirteen hundred members at the 1982 legislative conference, and with the membership at large through the union's newsletter.
- Guided by carefully considered responses, the committee had developed a profile of a successful information-age union, including the long-term goals, strategic options, and priorities the CWA needed to consider to begin to match the profile.

■ The committee had drafted an interim report which it presented for critical review at the CWA's 1982 national convention.

The committee then refined its recommendations and offered a specific plan "so well designed that the whole would be more powerful and effective than simply the sum of its parts." Several issues were highlighted: "Major technological changes that will profoundly affect job opportunities; structural changes in the telecommunications/data processing industry; changes in the composition, lifestyles, needs, and interests of the workforce; power shifts in business and politics; and economic turbulence and uncertainty."[11]

One issue the committee especially emphasized was employment security, which, more than any other union goal, "touches all of our lives and reaches into the heart of all of our hopes." The key to employment security was making career development and continuous learning "the natural order in the workplace." Some serious introspection was required if the CWA was to take the initiative: "It would be impossible to develop an integrated strategy and change accordingly without self-evaluation, self-criticism, and self-discipline."[12]

The committee was eager to involve rank-and-filers in the process of galvanizing the union: "CWA's strategy for the future must be aired, thrashed out, and subjected to the democratic process so that everyone in the union knows exactly what is being processed and why. Only in this way will CWA develop the broad base of cooperation and support it needs to become the union of the future."[13]

With a frankness uncommon in union matters, the committee made specific forecasts and offered detailed ideas for reform of virtually every aspect of the union, including the grievance and appeals process, funding and budgetary controls, organizing and bargaining, local and district performance, public affairs and image, staff performance and motivation, state councils and legislation, strategic planning, and the commitment to women and minorities.

For strategic planning, or "applied futuristics," to succeed, the committee explained, both members and leaders had to make a significant change in their perspective: "It requires a willingness to plan ahead, to make clear statements of priority, to make tough trade-off decisions after careful analysis, to manage the cross-impacts of union programs, and to maintain a strategic information base. Above all, it means questioning the basis on which CWA's monies are allocated and spent."[14]

In accepting the committee's recommendations, the CWA created a model that has since proved useful to other unions as well:

■ Glenn E. Watts, the CWA's president in 1983, characterized the committee's report as "a guide—a bible—for many years into our Union's future. I see at conventions of the future delegates with their dog-eared copies of this report, leafing through it and challenging CWA leaders as to how they are carrying out the vision of this 1983 Special Convention."[15]

■ In 1983, the Steelworkers' Union became one of the first to emulate the CWA by creating its own Committee on the Future Directions of the Union. Its 1984 report recommended numerous changes in union structure and policy, including that "to insure the process remains a dynamic one, the International Executive Board should continue the Committee on an ongoing basis."[16]

The CWA committe set a valuable precedent with its call for sweeping changes, a call that proved it was "neither an artificial exercise nor a cover for rubber-stamping a set of predrawn conclusions."[17]

AFL-CIO Efforts

Composed of union presidents, the AFL-CIO Committee on the Evolution of Work was created without fanfare in 1982 and caused no special stir a year later when it published its first report, *The Future of Work*. Asked to "review and evaluate changes that are taking place in America in the labor force, occupations, industries, and technology," the committee relied on straightforward government data and made no recommendations for change in union attitudes or practice.[18]

Labor leader Gus Tyler boldly contended, however, that the document's potential impact on unionism was "as profound as that of Vatican II on the Catholic Church."[19] Two and a half years later, the committee vindicated Tyler's position with its second report, entitled *The Changing Situation of Workers and Their Unions*, which was widely hailed for its fresh remedies and bold departure from "business as usual." According to economist Richard B. Freeman, the report represented a "landmark change" in labor's willingness to acknowledge current problems and its eagerness to address them imaginatively. He asked in mock astonishment, "Is this the stodgy old AFL-CIO?"[20]

One particularly controversial suggestion was that a benefits program be created for "associate members," whose ranks could include 27 million former union members and other workers not covered by a labor contract. The committee's report also insisted labor could push harder for pay equity and for workplace management. It recommended revitalization through surveys of members' opinions and new forums for sharing ideas.

Many critics doubted the recommendations would be implemented.[21] Even Freeman, who admired the report, complained about four serious omissions:

- The report sidestepped the question of how labor could engage in new political activity without provoking censure for throwing its weight around.
- The report did not deal with how labor could confront anti-union management without an adequate grasp of business mentality and behavior.
- The report paid inadequate attention to the impact of global markets on traditional union activity, relations with unions overseas, and labor's national economic policy.
- The report did not provide an invigorating vision that would galvanize current members and attract new ones.

Nevertheless, Freeman applauded the committee's document, as did Gus Tyler, for setting the stage for unions "to redefine themselves and to develop a new rationale in troubled times."[22]

Labor journalist A. H. Raskin in his 1987 William Gomberg Memorial Lecture at the University of Pennsylvania welcomed the report as "the finest thing to come out of the labor movement since the merger of the AFL and CIO ended two decades of civil war thirty years ago." He was particularly impressed with its candor and its call for experimentation, features it shared with the 1983 CWA report. Raskin hailed the "encouragement of venturesomeness in a barnacle-encrusted movement" and the "vigor the AFL-CIO high command has shown in breaking out of ancestral straightjackets." He wondered, however, whether any real changes were possible without extensive labor law reform or a wide-scale transformation in the anti-union attitudes of far too many employers.[23]

The committee's 1985 report became the basis for unprecedented self-analysis and planning by grass-roots activists, local union leaders, central labor councils, state federations, international unions, and various departments of the AFL-CIO. Several unions have since established committees to explore the report's relevance to their own concerns. One year after the report was presented, the AFL-CIO proudly noted several related spinoffs:

- the development of TV "performance workshops" for union leaders;
- the creation of a pilot program to increase membership participation;
- the establishment of a membership benefits program consisting of various forms of consumer and insurance programs; and

■ the initiation of a coordinated organizing campaign in the health-care insurance industry.

AFL-CIO president Lane Kirkland was confident American union leaders, "conditioned to see the past as a learning device, will focus on the present and future which confronts them."[24]

Spreading the Word

As a professional futurist, I have taken a small part in encouraging labor's involvement in futuristics. For example, I invited Lynn Williams, president of the Steelworkers, Ed Cleary, president of the New York State AFL-CIO, and others to participate in various meetings of the World Future Society. In 1984, I initiated a course in futuristics in the Antioch College degree program of the George Meany Center, and I have continued to teach it every other year. I base the course on one-day workshops I have conducted for the Steelworkers at their educational center in western Pennsylvania and for two of the annual meetings of the secretary-treasurers of the AFL-CIO unions on the executive council. I have also published several articles on labor's utilization of futuristics.[25]

Summary

An African proverb advises, "You cannot build a house for last year's summer." A small but influential group of labor leaders seems to understand this. As Gus Tyler explained, "The good news is that labor knows what it does not know, and, in this act of wisdom, has undertaken an inquiry into its necessary, proper, and feasible role in the coming decades.... By its generation of new attitudes and acts this process will change the character of American labor and, perhaps, of the total society."[26]

Chapter 15
Making the Most of Mergers

I do not suggest that we deviate in any way from the principle that merger action must be entirely voluntary. I do, however, strongly suggest that the responsible officers of many unions, who by all logic and common sense should merge, might take a broader view of the union as an instrument of progress for working people rather than an institution devoted to its own perpetuation for the sake of sentiment and tradition.

George Meany, *AFL-CIO Constitutional Convention Proceedings* (1965), 21

Union mergers tend to strengthen the entire labor movement. The trend is toward fewer, stronger, and more diverse unions, and the AFL-CIO encourages that trend.

Rudy Oswald, "New Directions for American Unionism,"
***Annals*, May 1984, 147**

Mergers between unions have become both frequent and complex. More have occurred in the past ten years, for example, than in any period since World War II. Not surprisingly, their impact on the number of unions and interactions among unions has been profound. Since the merger of the AFL and the CIO in 1955, the number of AFL-CIO affiliates has declined from 135 to 90, primarily as a result of mergers.[1] In virtually all of these cases, the mergers required careful diplomatic skills, since negotiations are commonly "haunted by Byzantine protocol. Every step in the merger process is like the Paris Peace talks."[2]

Those favoring mergers argue they can end jurisdictional raids that are damaging to all parties involved, such as the 1985 Ohio confrontation in which sixteen unions fought to represent thirty thousand public sector workers who were already unionized. As labor educator Ben Fischer charges, such squabbles are "injurious to unions, damned expensive, and do very little benefit for anyone."[3]

Union mergers can also be an appropriate response to the corporate merger mania now concentrating power in fewer and fewer companies. In 1978, AFL-CIO president Lane Kirkland provided a glowing assessment of mergers between unions with shared interests: "I know of none that has failed to improve the position of workers involved in organizing, administration, collective bargaining, and legislative and political action, and all other areas in which unions must engage today."[4]

Murray Seeger, the AFL-CIO's information director in 1985, expressed similar enthusiasm when he called mergers "one of the most important trends in the labor movement." And various labor scholars have "high expectations... for mergers in the restructuring and revitalization of the labor movement."[5]

At the same time, skeptics warn that mergers can inhibit internal union democracy and weaken local union autonomy. They claim gains achieved by mergers remain on paper, while the dangers of organizational giantism and bureaucratic bloat are very real. The subject received considerable attention in the path-breaking 1985 report of the AFL-CIO, *The Changing Situation of Workers and Their Unions:* "Mergers are difficult to effectuate, and, if poorly conceived, can cause a union to lose that identity which helps bind the members and the organization. Accordingly, both active AFL-CIO encouragement of mergers, and guidelines as to appropriate and inappropriate mergers, deserve a high priority."[6]

Gary N. Chaison, a scholar who has focused on these "exceptionally complex phenomena," believes mergers will "increase in form and frequency, and become a central part of the labor movement's reactions to its present predicament."[7]

Background

Mergers have occurred routinely since the formation of the first unions in this country in the 1700s. They became a leading method for rationalizing union structure toward the end of the nineteenth century when small unions with narrowly defined jurisdictions had limited potential for growth and a high likelihood of jurisdictional conflict.[8]

In the decades since 1900, mergers have provided an honorable end for many organizations (such as the Cigar Makers International Union and the Brotherhood of Sleeping Car Porters) made obsolete by cultural changes. They have also provided a vital launching pad for new hybrid unions, such as the Amalgamated Clothing and Textile Workers Union, the United Food and Commercial Workers, and the United Transportation Union.[9]

Few mergers have occurred quickly and straightforwardly, however. Most have required the resolution of difficult problems in internal politics, local-national union relations, and representational effectiveness. Chaison notes, for example, that before their merger in

1979, the Retail Clerks International Union and the Amalgamated Meat Cutters and Butcher Workmen had been engaged for fourteen years in sporadic discussions about merging and for six years in final negotiations.[10]

Risks

While the historical value of mergers is well established and their potential value remains substantial, skeptics have expressed serious concerns about their actual impact. Some worry that mergers may diminish the role of the individual member by promoting centralized structures at the expense of grass-roots empowerment. In that mergers generally result in additional layers of hierarchy, skeptics warn they create the opportunity for officers to disempower individual members.

Mergers can also weaken the valuable role of union dissidents. By creating additional patronage jobs at headquarters, mergers increase the number of employees who may feel indebted to union leaders. Dissidents may find themselves increasingly out of competition as they try, with diminished resources, to win over a larger and more diverse membership. Of the twenty-five thousand members of the National Maritime Union, for example, only ten thousand are unlicensed deep-sea sailors, once the NMU's main base. Opposition candidates find it hard to reach (merger-acquired) shoreside NMU members who work in factories.

Herman W. Benson, an expert on union democracy and one of its leading guardians, worries especially about this subject: "The more disparate and dispersed the separate pieces, the more uncontrollable becomes the national officialdom and its full-time staff." With union merger mania in fashion, he warns, "the need becomes urgent to strengthen the institutions and practices that make for democratic government in unions."[11]

In addition, mergers can undermine the crucial role of vigorous locals. Rapid expansion in the size of an international union invariably centralizes power, a process that can sap the morale of independent locals. Members of historically feisty and irreverent locals may find it harder to develop meaningful opposition after a merger has boosted the power base of those ensconced at headquarters.

Finally, a merger can enthrone power-hungry leaders. The sudden growth created by mergers can empower officers adroit at exploiting giantism and indifferent to its anti-democratic implications. Often autocratic and self-serving, such unionists know how to use mergers to inflate and insulate their reign.

Forecasts

What does the future hold? Chaison's forecast for the 1990s is provocative in that about fifty of the AFL-CIO's ninety affiliates have fewer than fifty thousand members and another thirty have fewer than one hundred thousand members, leaving them resource-poor and prime candidates for mergers:

- Many smaller unions, especially those with fewer than thirty thousand members, are likely to pursue absorption via mergers as a means of survival.
- Certain large unions will rely heavily for growth on absorption through mergers, rather than face employer opposition to organizing campaigns or the costs and delays of NLRB election procedures.
- Logical merger jurisdictions will become increasingly irrelevant, and many mergers will be plainly opportunistic. As Chaison explains, "Who merges with whom will be determined more by whether mutually attractive merger agreements can be proposed than by whether the merger fits into some broad scheme for uniting unions in related trades or industries."[12]
- The AFL-CIO could find itself resented as it attempts to guide and police the mergers of its affiliates. Affiliates may be angered by AFL-CIO "interference" and may insist that their autonomy be carefully respected.

Chaison expects merger strategies to become far more competitive, complex, and proactive. He recommends two robust innovations. First, the AFL-CIO or the American Arbitration Association or the Labor Department should create a training forum to prepare specialists for mediating the pre- and postmerger process. And second, specialists should prepare detailed guidelines to help the two participants in a merger alleviate difficulties that commonly arise thereafter.

Varied and numerous union mergers are likely to occur in the coming years. Fans are cheered by the bold posture of the nation's largest unions, all of which use merger campaigns as a primary growth strategy. Their pursuit of smaller unions, however, worries skeptics who claim the large unions are merely reshuffling players already on board rather than undertaking the far more difficult task of winning over the unorganized.

One point seems especially important: it will not be enough to use mergers to rationalize union structure, as unionists did at the end of the nineteenth century, if labor loses sight of the greater potential in the merging process. Labor's goal should not be growth for its own sake but on behalf of a more exciting vision of its possibilities. Especially since the amalgamation of the AFL and the CIO, the pro-merger vision has held out eight remarkable possibilities:

- The number of national unions in the United States—currently almost two hundred, ninety of which are in the AFL-CIO—could be reduced to about forty by the year 2000.
- Each of these large unions could have one major industry as its jurisdiction. Each would probably attract weak unions within its industry that were seeking a safe haven from organizing and financial adversity.
- Union bargaining power could be substantially increased as the new conglomerate unions (many with more than 1 million members) more effectively countered the power of expanding conglomerate employers.
- The elimination of deadly competition between unions should stabilize labor relations and free resources for skillful campaigns aimed at organizing the unorganized.
- Extending throughout the country, the new unions should have unprecedented political clout and earn a substantial revision in labor's favor of relevant laws and NLRB regulations.
- The new unions should be able to afford and utilize cable TV, conventional TV, and other vital communications resources currently too expensive for smaller labor organizations.
- The new unions should be able to afford innovative computer technology to support their administrative functions.
- The new unions should be able to afford and retain outstanding talent at every level of their organizations.

Economies of scale, along with an end to interunion wars and the redirection of energy into organizing, could contribute to a labor revival of extraordinary proportions. A robust movement reorganized by sound mergers could have power greater than any known by the unions since World War II. No other blueprint seems to offer dues payers as much, as soon, and in as readily attainable a way as does the merger route to a streamlined and updated labor movement.

EPILOGUE

When it comes to protecting, promoting, and building the movement, we need more experimentation with as wide a variety of techniques as possible.
Joseph B. Uehlein, Labor Notes, August 1987

The most popular contemporary explanation for labor's condition is that times are changing, and the labor movement cannot figure out how to cope with change. This analysis conveniently ignores the fact that the sole reason men and women organize unions is to bring about change.
Lane Kirkland, in Lipset, Unions in Transition (1986)

Certain academicians and conservative columnists insist the American labor movement is caught in a downward spiral from which it cannot recover.[1] To the extent their doom-and-gloom forecasts rest on a perception of contemporary unionism as essentially brain dead, as incapable of adapting to changing circumstance, the forecasts mislead. Those who expect labor's imminent demise mistake the absence of media coverage of union experiments with their actual absence. They confuse manageable setbacks during a trying stage with the terminal stage of a fatal illness.

I have tried in this volume to convey some of the excitement and ingenuity I find in America's largest social movement, one that is very much alive. My examples of robust projects have persuaded me that labor's detractors overlook or undervalue three significant aspects of the current scene:

- Old-fashioned defenders of the status quo are losing power to younger and far more innovative leaders.
- Union innovations are being adapted more and more across the country, thanks in part to the inclusion of a relevant feature story in nearly every issue of the *AFL-CIO News, In These Times, Labor Notes,* and similar publications.
- Consciousness-raising about the urgent need for innovation, along with field-proven "dos and don'ts," occupy more and more space in

union newspapers and more and more time at union conventions and local union meetings.

Although the lure of standard operating procedure remains strong, proponents of a regenerated labor movement have impressive momentum.

It remains possible, of course, that the vital and creative strategies highlighted in this volume may yet prove too little, too late. Labor's robust experiments may be overwhelmed by diehard anti-union opposition. Or by an uneven legal and legislative "playing field." Or by the unwillingness of "me-first!" Americans to continue to support a collective social movement like trade unionism. Or by deep-seated conflict within union ranks over the way to go, as in the case of the UFCW Local P–9 dispute.[2]

This much, however, seems clear: labor has a remarkable will to survive, considerable capacity to innovate, and a militancy long ago turned to bargaining advantage. Close observers note a new set of possibilities, as the following comments by four such observers illustrate:

> The Pittston strike represents the embryonic stirrings of a rebirth of the labor movement... More than a test case, it is a shot in the arm for the labor movement that will help set the course of its resurgence in the 1990's.[3]

> For years the American labor movement has been all but written off as dead.... Now it's beginning to look as if the obituaries may have been a bit premature. In recent months, several unions have exhibited a feistiness that's almost reminiscent of labor's glory days.... Whatever the issue, labor is showing more solidarity these days.... After years of backing down to management, the new militants seem determined at least to show that labor doesn't always have to say 'Uncle' first.[4]

> The strike against Lorenzo sent a message of something more than labor's difficulties. "Lorenzo paid an incredible price and lost over a billion dollars," said Nancy Tauss, vice president of the flight attendants' union.... "We think other employers won't be willing to follow in Lorenzo's footsteps."[5]

> With a sophisticated strategy that even its opponents agree was carried out to near perfection, New York City's major health-care workers' union gained a victory in late September, 1989, that many experts say provides the nation's labor movement with a badly needed ray of hope.[6]

At the heart of the matter, and indispensable if labor is to remain adaptable and keep up its momentum, is the emergence of a new clarity about labor's leadership role in a post–Cold War America: "Unions have to come up with a vision of the future that is broader than the vision the company has for its employees," advises MIT professor Thomas Kochan.[7]

Thanks in large part to its unsung creative projects, the labor movement appears well on its way. If it falters in the 1990s, it will not be because of its own paralysis. Contrary to what its detractors contend, the nation's labor federation, its ninety affiliates, and various non-AFL-CIO unions appear increasingly ready to try new tactics, and the ripple effect of successful experiments appears quite considerable. Examples of robust approaches to organizing, bargaining, and representing working Americans are multiplying rapidly from coast to coast.

As discussed at the beginning of this book, a large and diverse social movement is almost as hard to "steer" as a mammoth oceangoing vessel. All the more strategic, therefore, are trimtabs—those small adjustable flaps that enable deck officers to use only a small amount of pressure to move the main rudder and thereby reset the vessel's course. Organized labor has "trimtabs" in the form of its robust experiments. They may yet enable the movement to set a regenerative course, one guided by a fresh vision that will honor us all.

METHODOLOGY AND APOLOGY

In my search for robust projects, I conducted mail surveys, personal interviews, a computer review of the literature, and phone interviews; attended conferences and workshops; and had many carefully focused informal conversations. The bar at the AFL-CIO George Meany Center for Labor Studies, for example, is widely known as a source of some of the best anecdotes about union life. But even with this diversity of resources, the research confirmed my belief that far too little information is available about union experiments both within labor's ranks and outside them.

In the spring of 1986, I mailed requests for leads to the thirty largest unions in the nation, identified by the U.S. Department of Labor's 1984 *Directory of Labor Organizations* and to more than 250 alumni of the Antioch College degree program for labor unionists conducted at the George Meany Center.[1] To my dismay, I received replies from only ten of the unions (34 percent) and fifteen of the alumni (6 percent). Follow-up phone calls to likely prospects boosted the final tally to 50 percent and 25 percent respectively, but it was clear other resources would be necessary.

I found a relevant report on union attitudes by Brian Heshizer of Cleveland State University, published in the spring 1987 issue of *Labor Studies Journal*. His essay analyzed the responses of 79 national union leaders contacted in 1983 and 139 local union leaders contacted in 1985. Although his return rate was only 37 percent and 26 percent respectively, Heshizer believes the size and industry distribution of respondents indicate his data were drawn from samples "representative of labor organizations."[2] I have made extensive use of his survey results throughout this volume.

I also had the privilege of conducting long and frank interviews with labor innovators from coast to coast. Philadelphia-area unionists with whom I met over the summer of 1986 were especially helpful in that I was able to follow their projects carefully after hearing their stories.

Similarly, during my courses at the Meany Center, I have sought leads from staff and students alike. When invited to speak at Meany Center conferences, I have gone out of my way to explore robust unionism with attendees.

Labor economist Rick Hurd of the University of New Hampshire, a longtime supporter of this research, appealed for leads on my behalf at the 1986 Annual Meeting of the University and College Labor Educators Association (UCLEA). From 1986 on, I asked for leads from sociologists attending sessions of the Labor Studies Division of the annual meetings of the Society for the Study of Social Problems, the Eastern Sociological Society, and the American Sociological Association, as well as the monthly meetings of the Philadelphia chapter of the Industrial Relations Research Association.

Richard Binder of the Drexel University Library helped me undertake several computer scans of relevant books and periodicals. Seven books proved particularly useful:

Future Bread, by Dennis Clark and Merry Guben (Philadelphia: Local 1357, UFCW, 1983), tells the story of the Owned and Operated (O & O) Food Supermarkets in the Philadelphia area and the key role Local 1357 of the UFCW played in their creation.

Concessions, and How to Beat Them, by Jane Slaughter (Detroit: Labor Education and Research Project, 1983), pioneered in detailing alternatives to "submission to capital and management's seductive advances."

Inside the Circle: A Union Guide to QWL, by Mike Parker (Detroit: Labor Education and Research Project, 1985), explores ways unions can either fight or co-opt this new workplace option.

When Unions Merge, by Gary N. Chaison (Lexington, Mass.: D.C. Heath, 1986), proved to be the definitive guide to a complex and controversial process.

Labor's New Voice, by Sara U. Douglas (Norwood, N.J.: Ablex, 1986), explores the media environment in which labor operates and offers sophisticated advice on media "counterstrategies" for use in collective bargaining and public relations.

Mutual Gains, by Edward Cohen-Rosenthal and Cynthia E. Burton (New York: Praeger, 1987), stands out for its candor and constructive hands-on advice on union-management cooperation.

Rusted Dreams, by David Bensman and Roberta Lynch (New York: McGraw-Hill, 1987), offers a powerful account of the human costs of deindustrialization and prescribes programs to restore the steel industry and the Steelworkers' Union.

Thanks to my personal ties with the authors of three of these volumes, I was able, after private conversations with them, to take their leads even further than I expected.

I am aware of only one volume, published in 1984, that is similar to this one, although it depended completely on respondents rather than on direct field research. *Unions Today: New Tactics to Tackle Tough Times* (Washington, D.C.: BNA), covers thirty intriguing projects, although its 140-page length severely limits the attention paid to any one experiment. While the writers shy from constructive criticism, the book remains a valuable starting point.

Far more helpful were such periodicals as the *AFL-CIO News,* the house organ of the labor federation, which reports on an experimental program or innovative project in nearly every issue.[3] Five other publications, often at odds with that organization, also warrant recognition:

Labor Research Review, a biannual journal published by the Midwest Center for Labor Research, is a gold mine of robust material.[4]

Labor Notes, a monthly publication of the Labor Education and Research Project, highlights the creative turbulence that often pits grassroots activists against union officials.[5]

Union Democracy Review, a monthly published by the Association for Union Democracy, explores possibilities for civil liberty gains in unions.[6]

In These Times, a weekly publication of the Institute for Public Affairs, features the biting commentary of labor journalist David Moberg, a man with remarkable reach and valuable inside knowledge.[7]

Workplace Democracy, a quarterly published at the University of Massachusetts, explores robust aspects of worker participation and ownership.[8]

Other publications, such as *Labor Studies Journal* and the *ILR Review,* as well as *Business Week, Fortune,* and the *Wall Street Journal,* occasionally yielded material of value.

One final written source merits attention: the course papers I have required over the past ten years from my Meany Center students were an earnest, engaging, and eye-opening source of leads.

I fully expect to learn that my scholarship has been faulty on this or that sensitive matter. For one, I have probably overlooked early examples of path-breaking ventures. I apologize in advance to any union pioneer who was inadvertently slighted.

Similarly, I would like to apologize to risk-takers whose ongoing ventures were not covered in this volume. I hope to update this book every five years or so and to discuss new projects and assess the state of those covered in this edition. I welcome news of any projects I inadvertently overlooked or of those set in motion by readers who understood and responded to the need for creative risk-taking in the labor movement.

RESOURCE DIRECTORY

The following list includes a few of the many organizations that offer useful labor-related resources. These organizations welcome mail and phone inquiries about their speakers, publications, and other services.

I would be glad to hear from readers who know of additional organizations that should be included in forthcoming editions of *Robust Unionism*.

Asian-American Workers

Asian Week
809–11 Sacramento St.
San Francisco, CA 94108
Asian Week is an English-language journal for the Asian-American community.

U.S. Asian News Service
1053 National Press Bldg.
Washington, D.C. 20045
202–638–1117

Black Workers

A. Philip Randolph Institute
260 Park Ave. S., 6th fl.
New York, NY 10010

Black Resources Information Coordinating Services
614 Howard Ave.
Tallahassee, FL 32304
904–576–7522

Black Workers for Justice
P.O. Box 1863
Rocky Mount, N.C. 27802
919–977–8162
This group publishes a newspaper, *Justice Speaks*.

Coalition of Black Trade Unionists
P.O. Box 13055
Washington, D.C. 20009

National Urban League
1111 14th St. N.W., 6th fl.
Washington, D.C. 20005
202–898–1611

Communications and Media

AFL-CIO Pamphlet Section and Film Division
815 16th St. N.W., Rm. 209
Washington, D.C. 20006
Their catalog, *Films and Video Tapes for Labor,* is available on request (202–637–5153).

California Working
240 Golden Gate Ave., Suite 104
San Francisco, CA 94102
California Working produces a monthly TV show on union topics.

Labor Access
37 S. Ashland
Chicago, IL 60607
312–226–3330
Labor Beat, a guide to relevant videos, is available on request.

Labor Media
c/o Media Network
121 Fulton St., 5th fl.
New York, NY 10038

Labor Video Project
P.O. Box 5584
San Francisco, CA 94101
415–641–4440
A complete list of their half-inch VHS tapes for union use is available on request.

UAW Ammo
8000 E. Jefferson St.
Detroit, MI 48214
Attn.: Dick Olson
The Media Business: A Worker's Guide to the Media is available on request.

"Union, YES!" Campaign
Labor Institute of Public Affairs
815 16th St. N.W.

Washington, D.C. 20006
800–242–UNION

Community Alliances

Center for Community Change
1000 Wisconsin Ave. N.W.
Washington, D.C. 20007
202–342–0519

Human Resources Development Institute
AFL-CIO
815 16th St. N.W.
Washington, D.C. 20006
Specializes in services for displaced workers.

Jobs with Peace
76 Summer St.
Boston, MA 02110
617–338–5783

Lesbian and Gay Labor Network
P.O. Box 1159
Peter Stuyvesant Stn.
New York, NY 10009

Trade Union Housing Corporation
234 Cabot St.
Beverly, MA 01915
508–922–0166
Building Our Communities: Unions and Affordable Housing is available for
$10.*

Urban Institute
2100 M St. N.W.
Washington, D.C. 20037
202–833–7200

Workers and Communities Conference
c/o Labour Studies Programme
Division of Social Science
York University
4700 Keele St.
North York, Ontario, CANADA M3J 1P3

*Prices are effective 1989 and may vary.

Computer Networks

Labor Line Electronic Bulletin Board
c/o Chuck Hodell
George Meany Center for Labor Studies
10,000 New Hampshire Ave.
Silver Spring, MD 20903
301–431–0534

Union PC Users Group News-Letter
c/o Chuck Hodell
George Meany Center for Labor Studies
10,000 New Hampshire Ave.
Silver Spring, MD 20903
301–431–6400

Economic Issues

AFL-CIO Department of Economic Research
815 16th St. N.W.
Washington, D.C. 20006

Big Picture Books
P.O. Box 909
Carlisle, PA 17013
717–245–2768
Sharing the Pie is available on request.

Center for Popular Economics
Box 785-T
Amherst, MA 01004
413–545–0743

Economic Policy Institute
1730 Rhode Island Ave. N.W., Suite 812
Washington, D.C. 20036
202–775–8810

Labor Center
University of Iowa
N251 Oakdale Hall
Iowa City, IA 52242
319–355–4144
Privatization: Confronting the New Leviathan, a pamphlet by Laurie
Clements, is available for $2.

Labor Research Association
80 E. 11th St., Suite 634

New York, NY 10003
212–473–1042

Maquiladora Project
AFSC, Community Relations Division
1501 Cherry St.
Philadelphia, PA 19102
215–241–7134
The Global Factory is available for $7.50.

National Commission for Economic Conversion and Disarmament
Box 15025
Washington, D.C. 20003
202–544–5059

National Jobs with Peace Campaign
76 Summer St.
Boston, MA 02110
617–338–5873
The video *Build Homes, Not Bombs* may be rented for $10.

UAW
8000 E. Jefferson St.
Detroit, MI 48214
Fulfilling the American Dream is available on request.

Family Issues

Child Care Law Center
625 Market St., Suite 915
San Francisco, CA 94105
415–495–5498

U.S. Department of Labor
Office of Information and Public Affairs
200 Constitution Ave. N.W.
Washington, D.C. 20210
202–523–9711
A 182-page report entitled *Child Care: A Workforce Issue* is available for free
on request.

Global Relations

AFL-CIO International Affairs Department
815 16th St. N.W.
Washington, D.C. 20006

African-American Labor Center
AFL-CIO
1400 K St. N.W.
Washington, D.C. 20005

Asia Monitor Resource Center
444 Nathan Rd.
8-B Kowloon, Hong Kong
Partners or Predators: International Trade Unionism and Asia is available on request.

Committee for International Support of Trade Union Rights
P.O. Box 31397
San Francisco, CA 94131

International Labor Reports
P.O. Box 5036
Berkeley, CA 94705

International Labor Rights Education and Research Fund
110 Maryland Ave. N.E.
Washington, D.C. 20002

International Union of Food and Allied Workers' Associations
2000 Florida Ave. N.W., Suite 401
Washington, D.C. 20009
International Conference on Strategies for Global Labor Solidarity: 1989 Conference Proceedings is available on request.

Labor Action on Central America
Box 28014
Oakland, CA 94604
415–272–9951
A bimonthly twelve-page newsletter, *Labor Action: You, Your Union, and Central America*, is available for $10 per year.

Labor Coalition on Central America
P.O. Box 53407
Temple Heights Stn.
Washington, D.C. 20009

Labor Committee against Apartheid
c/o CWA Local 1180
6 Harrison St.
New York, NY 10013

Labor Committee on the Middle East
P.O. Box 421429
San Francisco, CA 94142

Labor Council for Latin American Advancement
c/o AFL-CIO
815 16th St. N.W.
Washington, D.C. 20006

Lawyers Committee for Human Rights
330 Seventh Ave., 10th fl.
New York, NY 10001
212–629–6170

National Labor Committee in Support of Democracy and Human Rights in El
    Salvador
15 Union Sq.
New York, NY 10003
212–242–0700
Critical Choices is available for $1.

North American Congress in Latin America
475 Riverside Dr., Suite 454
New York, NY 10115

Pro-Canada Network
904–251 Laurier West
Ottawa, Ontario, CANADA KIP 5J6

Southern Africa Media Center
149 Ninth St., Rm. 420
San Francisco, CA 94103
415–621–6196

Third World Resources
464 19th St.
Oakland, CA 94612
415–835–4692

Transnational Information Exchange
Paulus Potterstraat 20
1071 DA Amsterdam, NETHERLANDS

Health and Disability Issues

AFSCME Research Department
1625 L St. N.W.
Washington, D.C. 20036
202–429–1215
Fighting for the Rights of Disabled Employees is available on request.

National Health Care Campaign
P.O. Box 27434
Washington, D.C. 20038
202–639–8833

Health and Safety Alliances

AFL-CIO Food and Allied Service Trades Department
815 16th St. N.W., Suite 408
Washington, D.C. 20006
202–737–7200
All Systems Are Go is available on request.

Environmental and Occupational Health Sciences Institute
UMDNJ
Robert Wood Johnson Medical Center
Brookwood II
45 Knightsbridge Rd.
Piscataway, N.J. 08854
201–463–5353
The Occupational Health Resource Guide is available for $15.

The Labor Institute
853 Broadway, Rm. 2014
New York, NY 10003
212–674–3322
The videotape *A Price for Every Progress: The Health Hazards of VDT's* is available on request.

Labor Occupational Health Program
2521 Channing Way
Berkeley, CA 94720
415–642–5507

National Safe Workplace Institute
122 S. Michigan Ave., Suite 1450
Chicago, IL 60603
312–939–0690

National Safety Council
444 N. Michigan Ave.
Chicago, IL 60611

NIOSH
Robert A. Taft Laboratories
4676 Columbia Pkwy.
Cincinnati, OH 45226

Philadelphia Area Project on Occupational Safety and Health (PHILAPOSH)
3001 Walnut St.
Philadelphia, PA 19104
215–386–7000
Injured on the Job is available on request.

Southeastern Michigan Coalition on Occupational Safety and Health
1550 Howard St.
Detroit, MI 48216
313–961–3345
AIDS in the Workplace: Fear or Fact is available on request.

Urban Environment Conference
7620 Morningside Dr. N.W.
Washington, D.C. 20012
202–726–8111
America's Forgotten Environment, a report on solutions for OSHA and workers alike, is available for $4.

Wisconsin Committee on Occupational Safety and Health
1334 S. 11th St.
Milwaukee, WI 53204
414–643–0982
The Deadly Dilemma is available on request.

Workers' Memorial Day Project
AFL-CIO
815 16th St. N.W.
Washington, D.C. 20006
202–637–5210

Workplace Health Fund
815 16th St. N.W.
Washington, D.C. 20006

Hispanic Workers

Consortium of National Hispanic Organizations
2727 Ontario Rd. N.W., Suite 200
Washington, D.C. 20009
202–387–3300

Labor Council for Latin American Advancement
815 16th St. N.W., Suite 707
Washington, D.C. 20006
202–347–4223

National Council of La Raza
20 F St. N.W., 2nd fl.

Washington, D.C. 20001
202–628–9600

U.S. Catholic Conference, Secretariat for Hispanic Affairs
1312 Massachusetts Ave. N.W.
Washington, D.C. 20005
202–659–6876

Labor Culture

Alternative Media Information Center
121 Fulton St., 5th fl.
New York, NY 10038
212–619–3455

Bread and Roses Cultural Project Film Library
415 W. Main St.
Wyckoff, N.J. 07481
201–891–8240

California Newsreel
630 Natoma St.
San Francisco, CA 94103

George Meany Archives
10,000 New Hampshire Ave.
Silver Spring, MD 20903
301–434–6404
Information about the archives' journal, *Labor's Heritage,* is available on request.

John Edwards Memorial Forum
c/o Down Home Music
10341 San Pablo Ave.
El Cerrito, CA 94530
415–525–1494

Labor Heritage Foundation
815 16th St. N.W., #301
Washington, D.C. 20006
202–842–7880

Labor Intensive Quarterly
% Bob Hinkley
1213 Chalkstone Ave.
Providence, RI 20908

Massachusetts History Workshop
P.O. Box 755
Cambridge, MA 02238

New Day Films
22 Riverside Dr.
Wayne, NJ 07470–3191

Northwest Poster Collective
1613 E. Lake St.
Minneapolis, MN 55407

Talkin' Union
c/o Saul Schniderman, editor
P.O. Box 5349
Takoma Park, MD 20912

Wage Slave World News
P.O. Box 3511
Madison, WI 53704
608–255–7031
A sample copy of *Wage Slave* is available on request.

Labor Education

AFL-CIO Education Department
815 16th St. N.W., Rm. 407
Washington, D.C. 20006

American Labor Education Center
1730 Connecticut Ave. N.W.
Washington, D.C. 20009
202–387–6780

Center for Labor-Management Policy Studies
120 W. 44th St.
New York, NY 10036
212–391–0410
Six awards of $3,000 each are available to union officers or staff members to assist them in developing and evaluating new ideas and strategies for their unions.

CWA Education Department
1925 K St. N.W., Suite 823
Washington, D.C. 20006
202–728–2405
Learning about Work: A Kit for Discussion in the Schools is available on request.

Frontlash (Labor and Young Adults)
c/o AFL-CIO
815 16th St. N.W.
Washington, D.C. 20006

Harvard Trade Union Program
17 Dunster St., Suite 205
Cambridge, MA 02138
617–495–9265

Monthly Review Press
122 W. 27th St.
New York, NY 10001
The Power in Our Hands, a curriculum on the history of work and workers in the United States, is available on request.

Pacific Northwest Labor History Association
P.O. Box 75048
Seattle, WA 98125
Publishes a labor history calendar each year.

Southern Appalachian Labor School
Center for Labor Education
P.O. Box 127
Kinkaid, WV 25119
304–442–3157

Trades and Labor Assembly
411 Main St., Rm. 103
St. Paul, MN 55102
Produces a labor studies curriculum for use in kindergarten through high school.

University and College Labor Education Association
c/o Gene Daniels, Treasurer, LERS
Ohio State University
35 E. 7th St., Suite 200
Cincinnati, OH 45202

Workers' Education, Local 189, CWA
c/o Jim Bollen, Executive Secretary
44 Hollingsworth St.
Lynn, MA 01902
Publishes an annual *Directory of Labor Education.*

Older Workers and Retirees

AFL-CIO
815 16th St. N.W.
Washington, D.C. 20006
Publishes *A Guide to Establishing Senior Clubs.*

David Gregory
9436 Cherry Hills Lane
San Ramon, CA 94583
A VHS tape on the Union Club in Sun City, Arizona, can be borrowed.

Labour Council of Metropolitan Toronto
15 Gervais Dr., #407
Don Mills
Ontario, CANADA M3C 1Y8
416–441–3663
Publishes *A Shameful Silence: Older Workers, New Technology, and Retraining.*

National Council of Senior Citizens
1511 K St. N.W.
Washington, D.C. 20005

The Union Club
P.O. Box 1206
Sun City, AZ 85372
602–974–9882

Organizing

AFL-CIO Department of Organization and Field Services
815 16th St. N.W.
Washington, DC 20006
202–637–5280
Published *The Blitz: A Manual for Organizers on How to Run Fast-Paced Pre-petition Campaigns.*

AFL-CIO Food and Allied Service Trades Department
815 16th St. N.W., Suite 408
Washington, D.C. 20006
202–737–7200
Published *Workers' Kaleidoscope.*

AFL-CIO Organizing Institute
1444 Eye St. N.W., Suite 216
Washington, D.C. 20005
202–408–0700
FAX 202–408–0706
Every month the institute accepts qualified applicants into a three-day training program.

Center for Labor Research and Education
Institute of Industrial Relations
University of California
Los Angeles, CA 90024–1478
213–825–9191
Published *Organizing for Empowerment* by Gloria Busman.

The Clerical Research Group
#207–1230 Buraby St.
Vancouver, B.C.
CANADA V6E 1P5
604–689–7822
The group's survey of Vancouver's office workers, *A Heavy Load at Half the Price,* is available on request.

Consumers United Insurance Co.
2100 M St. N.W.
Washington, D.C. 20037
202–872–5390
Offers a low-cost health insurance policy designed to help recruit members during an organizing drive.

Farm Labor Organizing Committee
714 1/2 S. St. Clair
Toledo, OH 43609

Jobs with Justice
P.O. Box 19128
Washington, D.C. 20036
800–424–2872

Political Alliances

AFL-CIO Department of Legislation
815 16th St. N.W., Rm. 309
Washington, D.C. 20006

AFL-CIO Food and Allied Service Trades Department
815 16th St. N.W., Suite 408
Washington, D.C. 20006
202–737–7200
A fourteen-page manual, *City Council to Capitol Hill,* is available on request.

Center for National Policy Review
1025 Vermont Ave. N.W., Suite 360
Washington, D.C. 20005

Center for Popular Economics
Box 785
Amherst, MA 01004
413–545–0743

Center for the Study of Social Policy
236 Massachusetts Ave. N.E.
Washington, D.C. 20002
202–546–5062

Center on Budget and Priorities
236 Massachusetts Ave. N.E., Suite 305
Washington, D.C. 20002
202–544–0591

Joint Center for Politics Studies
1301 Pennsylvania Ave. N.W., Suite 400
Washington, D.C. 20004
202–626–3500

Productivity

Built-Rite
c/o PALM
125 N. 8th St., Suite 500
Philadelphia, PA 19106
215–931–0100

Philadelphia Area Labor-Management Committee (PALM)
125 N. 8th St., Suite 500
Philadelphia, PA 19106
215–351–1176

Strikes and Inside Tactics

AFL-CIO Industrial Union Department
815 16th St. N.W.
Washington, D.C. 20006
The Inside Game: Winning with Workplace Strategies is available on request.

Black Cat Collective (video films)
P.O. Box 511
Cambridge, MA 02238
617–864–4810

United Electrical, Radio and Machine Workers
2400 Oliver Bldg.
535 Smithfield St.

Pittsburgh, PA 15222
412–471–8919
Preparing and Conducting a Strike is available for $4.75.

Union Affairs

AFL-CIO Department of Organization and Field Services
815 16th St. N.W.
Washington, D.C. 20006
The department's booklet *Numbers That Count* contains useful ideas on how to strengthen a local.

AFL-CIO Human Resources Development Institute
815 16th St. N.W., Rm. 408
Washington, D.C. 20006

AFL-CIO News
815 16th St. N.W., Rm. 209
Washington, D.C. 20006
202–637–5032
Subscription: $10/year.

Blade and Whetstone
c/o Paul Rasmussen
2320 S. Dixie Hwy.
Miami, FL 33133

Cornelius Communications Co.
2457 E. Washington St.
P.O. Box 7
Indianapolis, IN 45206
What Is a Union? is a twenty-four-page booklet written especially for elementary school children.

Department of Labor Studies and Industrial Relations
Old Botany Bldg.
Penn State University
University Park, PA 16802
814–865–5425
Among their useful publications are *Changing Labor's Image: A Union Member's Guide* by Paul F. Clark, available for $1.

Labor Notes
7435 Michigan Ave.
Detroit, MI 58210
313–842–6262
Subscription: $10/year.

Labor Research Review
c/o Midwest Center for Labor Research
3411 W. Diversey, No. 14
Chicago, IL 60647

New England Labor News and Commentary
P.O. Box 6419
Nashua, N.H. 03063
603–882–8831
Subscription: $10/year.

Punch Out
401 Broadway, Rm. 911
New York, NY 10013
212–941–7483
Punch Out is an eight-page newsletter intended primarily for rank-and-file activists in the New York area.

Union Communication Services
1633 Connecticut Ave. N.W., Suite 200
Washington, D.C. 20009
800–321–2545
Steward Update is a bimonthly newsletter intended to help stewards represent workers.

Workplace Democracy
111 Draper Hall
Amherst, MA 01003

Union Democracy

Association for Union Democracy
YWCA Bldg., Rm. 619
30 Third Ave.
Brooklyn, NY 11217
718–855–6650
Publishes *Union Democracy Review.*

Teamsters for a Democratic Union
Box 10128
Detroit, MI 48210
313–842–2600

Voice for New Directions
P.O. Box 6876
St. Louis, MO 63144

Women's Issues

ACTWU Research Department
15 Union Sq.
New York, NY 10003
212–242–0700, ext. 208
Particularly useful is a free booklet, *Bargaining on Women's Issues and Family Concerns.*

Equal Rights Advocates
1370 Mission St., 3rd fl.
San Francisco, CA 94103
415–621–0505

National Committee on Pay Equity
1201 16th St. N.W., Suite 420
Washington, D.C. 20036

National Organization for Women
1025 Barry Court
St. Louis, MO 63122

Southeastern Massachusetts University
Labor Education Center
North Dartmouth, MA 02747
Published *Babies and Bargaining,* a manual on bargaining for employer-supported child-care programs.

Women's Economic Justice Center
National Center for Policy Alternatives
2000 Florida Ave. N.W.
Washington, D.C. 20009
202–387–6030

Women's Occupational Health Resource Center
Columbia University
600 W. 168th St.
New York, NY 10032
212–694–3606

Working Women's Health Project
Southeastern Michigan Coalition on Occupational Safety and Health
2727 Second Ave.
Detroit, MI 48201
313–961–3345

Women Workers

Chicago Women in the Trades
37 S. Ashland
Chicago, IL 60607

Coalition of Labor Union Women
15 Union Sq.
New York, NY 10003
212-242-0700

Hard Hatted Women
P.O. Box 93384
Cleveland, OH 44101

The Institute for Women and Work
School of Industrial and Labor Relations
15 E. 26th St., 4th fl.
New York, NY 10010

National Commission on Working Women
1325 G St. N.W.
Washington, D.C. 20005
202-737-5764

9 to 5, National Association of Working Women
614 Superior Ave. N.W.
Cleveland, OH 44113
216-566-9308

Philadelphia Women in Non-Traditional Work
TOP/WIN
P.O. Box 5904
Philadelphia, PA 19137

Tradeswomen
P.O. Box 40664
San Francisco, CA 94140
415-821-7334

Women's Legal Defense Fund
2000 P St. N.W., Rm. 400
Washington, D.C. 20036
202-887-0364

Women in the Building Trades
241 St. Botolph St.
Boston, MA 02115
617-266-2338

ACKNOWLEDGMENTS

U nion specialists who commented in valuable ways on early drafts included Ben Albert, director of public relations, AFL-CIO; Judy Allison, pension coordinator, IUOE; Charles E. Bradford, director of the apprenticeship program, IAM; Phil Comstock, UFCW; the late Frank W. Emig, Department of Community Services, AFL-CIO; James Freese, IBEW, Seattle; Stanley Gordon, Red Cross/labor partnership associate, AFL-CIO; David Gregory, COPE, AFL-CIO; Robert Harbrant, president of the Food and Allied Service Trades Department, AFL-CIO; Jack Lutz, Union Label and Service Trades Department, AFL-CIO; Jack Maher, AFT, Tallahassee, Florida; John J. McManus, Department of Community Services, AFL-CIO; Robert J. McMenemy, legislative director of Local 675, IUOE, Pompano Beach, Florida; Jim Moran, PHILAPOSH, Philadelphia; Hank McGuire, IBEW, Seattle; Kinsey Robinson, Roofers, Damp and Waterproof Workers Association; Bruce Smith, Molders' and Allied Workers' Union; Edward Stubblefield, IAM; and Gerta Williams, American Postal Workers Union. All serve labor with distinction.

Five academic friends read first drafts of various chapters. I am deeply appreciative of help from Patricia Cooper, Department of History, Drexel University; Steven Deutsch, Department of Labor Studies, University of Oregon; Art Hochner, Department of Management, Temple University; Joyce Kornbluh, Labor Studies Center, University of Michigan; and Jack Metzgar, Department of History, Roosevelt University. Joyce, in particular, provided detailed and mind-stretching commentary of the type writers hope to receive and from which they profit.

Thirty-three labor union officers and staff members made time to discuss examples of robust unionism, and I remain, accordingly, deeply indebted to John P. Beck, education director, Paperworkers International Union; Alan Bosch, Department of Community Services, AFL-CIO; Robert Brand, District 1199-C, National Union of Hospital and Health Care Employees; John T. Browning, CWA; Walter Burke, retired secretary-treasurer, USWA; David Camp, District 1199-C, National Union of Hospital and Health Care Employees; Dennis Chamot, Department of Professional Employees, AFL-CIO; Edward Cohen-Rosenthal, education director, International Union of Bricklayers and Allied Craftsmen; B. G. "Pete" Culver, community services/labor liaison, Illinois; Mary T. Dresser, International Union of Bricklayers and Allied Craftsmen; J. E. Eyer, New Mexico Local 1564, UFCW; William Farally, IUOE, Pennsylvania; David Fontaine, Baltimore City Labor Council; Charles Gentile, UFCW, Philadelphia;

Patrick Gillespie, president, Philadelphia Building Trades Council; Captain Roger D. Hall, vice-president, ALPA; Charles Hodell, Meany Center; Kevin Kistler, Organization Department, AFL-CIO; Jeffrey MacDonald, Meany Center; Anne Macko, CWA; Michael McConnell, IBEW, Illinois; Melva Meacham; Victor Munoz, El Paso Central Labor Council; Donald Peters, retired president, IBT Local 743, Chicago; Stan Rosen, UCLEA Local 189; Jim Ryan, District 1199-C, National Union of Hospital and Health Care Employees, Philadelphia; Kathy Schrier, District 37, AFSCME, New York; Dorothy Shields, director of education, AFL-CIO; Mary Ann Snider, El Paso AFT local; Larry Spitz, the Union Club, Phoenix; Elisabeth Szanto, Harvard Union of Clerical and Technical Workers; Ed Toohey, president, Philadelphia AFL-CIO Council; and Dennis J. Walton, business manager, Local 675, IUOE, Pompano Beach.

Similarly, individuals outside the labor movement who made room to talk with me included David Bensman, Department of Labor Studies, Rutgers University; Daniel Cornfeld, Department of Sociology, Vanderbilt University; John Dodds, Philadelphia Unemployment Project; Robert Erikson, Department of Economics, Carlow College; Robert F. Forman, Haverford Community Hospital; Arthur L. Fox II, Esq., Washington, D.C.; Jay Guben, O and O Fund, Philadelphia; Marty Gusoff, O and O Store, Roslyn, Pennsylvania; Howard Harris, Department of History, Pennsylvania State University; Alice Hoffman, Governor's Office, Pennsylvania; Sherman Kreiner, Philadelphia; Andrew Lamas, PACE, Philadelphia; Paul Landsbergis, Rutgers University; Jenny Luray, Harvard Trade Union Program; and Pamela Tate, Council for Adult and Experiential Learning, Chicago.

The following people generously provided articles, reprints, and unpublished material: Jack Barbash, professor emeritus, University of Wisconsin; Erica Bronstein, Labor Education Center, Southeastern Massachusetts University; Elena M. Brown, EAP coordinator, Association of Flight Attendants; Drayton Bryant, housing consultant, Philadelphia; Richard Dwyer, deputy director, George Meany Center; Ann Herson, School of Industrial and Labor Relations, Cornell University; Jack Jeffrey, secretary-treasurer, South Nevada Central Labor Council; Ross Koppel, Social Research, Inc., Philadelphia; John Morawetz, director of health and safety, Molders' and Allied Workers' Union; Amy Morris, office manager, Legal Department, UMWA; Robert Pleasure, executive director, George Meany Center; Dennis Riel, IUE, Massachusetts; Hig Roberts, Department of Labor Education, University of Alabama; Pamela Roby, Department of Sociology, University of California, Santa Cruz; John Scalley, CWA, Philadelphia; Chuck Schwartz, director, Institute for Labor Studies and Research, Providence, Rhode Island; Betty Shostak, my mother and a skilled clipper of union coverage in the press; Gil Whitmer, IUOE, Pennsylvania; and William F. Whyte, professor emeritus, School of Industrial and Labor Relations, Cornell University.

Thirty-eight of my students at the AFL-CIO George Meany Center were especially helpful with this project: Donn Berry, IBEW, Massachusetts; Bill Breslin, Rubber, Cork, Linoleum, and Plastic Workers of America, Ohio; Mary Curley, CWA, Ohio; Dixie Garman, International Brotherhood of Paper Makers, Pennsylvania; Thomas Hummel, ACTWU, Pennsylvania; Carol Kauss, director of labor participation, MEBA-Red Cross, Ohio; Patricia Kuhlkin, regional vice-president, National Association of Broadcast Employees and Technicians, California; Christel Manz, AFSCME, Wisconsin; Harriet Morley, National Association of Letter Carriers, Washington, D.C.; Philip Pope, ACTWU, Virginia; Matthew Rusow, UFCW, Illinois; Roy Silbert, president, Local 54, Hotel and Restaurant Employees Union, Atlantic City, New Jersey; Jerry Sirk, AFL-CIO community service liaison, Michigan; and Anthony Vignola, United Transportation Union, New York. Many others have been mentioned earlier: Allison, Bradford, Browning, Emig, Freese, Gordon, Gregory, Harbrant, Hodell, Macko, McConnell, McGuire, McManus, Meacham, Morris, Riel, Robinson, Scally, Smith, Stubblefield, Whitmer, and Williams.

At a critical point in 1986 at the project's outset, I received assistance in mailing a questionnaire to Meany Center alumni from then-director of the Antioch–Meany Center program, Jacqueline Brophy. Leads secured in this way were invaluable, and I remain in Ms. Brophy's debt.

Thanks are also owed a friend and frequent collaborator, Ross Koppel, founder and president of Social Research, Inc., in Philadelphia. When I was groping for a rubric to make sense of my early insights, he heard me out, reflected on the matter, and produced from his voluminous files an unpublished paper by J. Moses entitled "Reductionism and Holism: Approaches to the Organization of Robust Systems." Honing in on the concept—robust—Ross helped provide a key to the culture of union risk-taking.

Creative and timely support was provided by Drexel University Library staffers Aaron Bernstein, Richard Binder, Ken Garson, Marie Kuhn, Tim LaBorrie, and Debbie Sheesley, without whom it is hard to imagine how this volume could have been completed.

As has often been the case in recent years, indispensable secretarial assistance was graciously provided by Sharon Gehm of the staff of my Drexel University department. Early drafts were ably typed by Jackie Seguin, and finishing touches were contributed by Shirlene Fetlow. Indispensable, creative, and upbeat assistance of a very strategic sort was provided by Denise Weintraut, ably assisted in a closing rush by Nadine Matthews.

Throughout the four years required to travel, explore, correspond, interview, reflect, write, and rewrite, my family—Lynn, Scott, Mark, Matt, and Dan—has seen far less of me and has had far less of my attention than reasonable. I deeply appreciate their forbearance, their frequent inquiries about this project, their patience with my distracted moods, and their acceptance of my preference to stay home and work when I might have otherwise joined in family outings. I hope their reading of this volume leaves them persuaded that our mutual sacrifices have been at least partially requited, and I pledge to try and do it all better the next time around.

Frances Benson, the director of ILR Press, encouraged this project across the several years it took to complete. Her very able associate, Andrea Fleck Clardy, put up gracefully with the stresses inherent in a project as multisided as this one and contributed more to its rewriting than did the editors of any of my other thirteen books. Both Ms. Benson and Ms. Clardy have my respect and gratitude. Erica Fox, the copy editor on the project, helped considerably by increasing clarity, stylistic consistency, and overall flow.

Eight personal friends mentioned earlier—Phil Comstock, Bob Harbrant, Stan Gordon, Joyce Kornbluh, Michael Lucas, Melva Meacham, Jack Metzgar, and Steven Deutsch—made all the difference. And, as with everyone else involved, these friends are owed only credit for the book's merits. Its various remaining shortcomings, despite numerous rewrites, must be regarded, alas, as mine alone.

NOTES

Introduction: The Trimtab Factor

1. Harold William, *The Trimtab Factor: How Business Executives Can Help Solve the Nuclear Weapons Crisis* (New York: William Morrow, 1984), 27. I recommend this cogent volume to anyone interested in an analysis of the possibilities for large-scale change.

2. Bill Berkowitz, *Local Heroes: The Rebirth of Heroism in America* (Lexington, Mass.: D. C. Heath, 1987), 7. I draw heavily on this source in this section.

3. Thomas J. Peters and Robert H. Waterman, Jr., *In Search of Excellence* (New York: Harper & Row, 1982), 12.

Chapter 1: Seeking a Better Way of Work

1. Anonymity was requested by these respondents, all of whom echoed sentiments widely expressed in the literature. See, for example, William Winpisinger, "Rage and Reason," in International Association of Machinists, *Let's Rebuild America: The Original Rebuilding America Act* (Washington, D.C.: Kelly Press, 1984), 1–99.

2. Robert F. Harbrant, "Comprehensive Campaign," in *Union Power in the Future—A Union Activist's Agenda,* ed. Ken Gagala (Ithaca, N.Y.: Cornell University, New York State School of Industrial and Labor Relations, Labor Studies Program, 1987), 137.

3. Ibid., 143.

4. Ibid., 137–38; Charles Craypo, "Union Bargaining Power—Past, Present, and Future," in Gagala, *Union Power,* 119.

5. Eric Mann, *Taking on General Motors: A Case Study of the UAW Campaign to Keep GM Van Nuys Open* (Los Angeles: University of California, Center for Labor Research and Education, 1987), 12.

6. Jerry Tucker, "In-Plant Strategies," in Gagala, *Union Power,* 149.

7. Ibid., 154.

8. Ibid., 155.

9. Tom Balanoff, "The Cement Workers' Experience," *Labor Research Review* (Fall 1985): 18.

10. Thomas J. Peters and Robert H. Waterman, Jr., *In Search of Excellence* (New York: Harper & Row, 1982), 14.

11. Staughton Lynd, "Foreword," in Donald M. Wells, *Empty Promises: Quality of Working Life Programs and the Labor Movement* (New York: Monthly

Review Press, 1987), ix; U.S. National Conference of Catholic Bishops, *Economic Justice for All: Pastoral Letter on Catholic Social Teaching and the U.S. Economy* (Washington, D.C.: U.S. National Conference of Catholic Bishops, 1986), 150. See also Norman Eiger, "Organizing for Quality of Working Life," *Labor Studies Journal* (Fall 1989): 3–22.

12. Michael Massing, "Detroit's Strange Bedfellows," *New York Times Magazine,* February 7, 1988, 20, 24.

13. John B. Judis, "U.S. Automakers Ride on Rough Terrain," *In These Times,* March 28–April 3, 1990, 10.

14. Robert Schrank, "The Future of Unions," *New Management* (Winter 1986): 16.

15. Dennis Chamot, "Unions Need to Confront the Results of New Technology," *Monthly Labor Review* (August 1987): 45.

16. Samuel Gompers, *Seventy Years of Life and Labor: An Autobiography,* ed. Nick Salvatore (Ithaca, N.Y.: ILR Press, 1984), 111; see also Edith Abbott, *Women in Industry: A Study in American Economic History* (New York: D. Appleton, 1910), 257; Daniel Nelson, "Unions' Struggle to Survive Goes Beyond Modern Technology," *Monthly Labor Review* (August 1987): 41.

17. Sumner H. Slichter, *Union Policies and Industrial Management* (Washington, D.C.: Brookings Institution Press, 1941), 201–81.

18. Nelson, "Unions' Struggle to Survive," 42.

19. Ibid., 45.

20. Dennis Chamot, "A Union Perspective on Technological Change," *Looking Ahead* (Summer 1987): 14.

21. Steven Deutsch, "Response to IAM Case Studies," in Donald Kennedy et al., *Labor and Technology: Union Response to Changing Environments* (University Park: Pennsylvania State University, Department of Labor Studies, 1982), 141–43.

22. Russ Allen, "Response to Auto Crisis and Union Response," in Kennedy et al., *Labor and Technology,* 189.

23. Steven Deutsch, "Unions and Technological Change: International Perspectives," in Kennedy et al., *Labor and Technology,* 194. See also Nicholas A. Ashford and Christine Ayers, "Technology Bargaining Keeps Labor and Management Interests Balanced," *Occupational Health and Safety News Digest,* February 1987, 1–3, 20.

24. David T. Lykken, "Polygraphers Are the Last to Know," *USA Today,* December 15, 1987, 10-A.

25. "Making a Difference…in Personal Privacy," *New Republic,* December 14, 1987, 33.

26. Constance Holden, "Days May Be Numbered for Polygraphs in the Private Sector," *Science,* May 9, 1986, 705.

27. Ibid.

28. Robert M. Andres, "Wide Support in Congress for Ban on Lie-Detector Tests for Employees," *Philadelphia Inquirer,* May 18, 1988, 2-A.

29. William Safire, "One Blow for Liberty," *New York Times,* May 26, 1988, A–35.

30. I draw extensively on Mann, *Taking on General Motors.*

31. Ibid., 10.

32. Ibid., 263.

33. Kelly Jenco, quoted in Mann, *Taking on General Motors,* 144.

34. Mann, *Taking on General Motors,* 330.

35. Ibid., 358.

36. See, for example, Jane Slaughter, "Viewpoint: Corporate Campaigns: Do They Work?" *Labor Notes,* September 1988, 11–12.

37. See in this connection Neil Chetnik, "The Intercultural Honeymoon Ends," in Parker and Slaughter, *Choosing Sides,* 119–20.

38. Slaughter, "Viewpoint," 12.

39. See in this connection Harley Shaiken, *Work Transformed: Automation and Labor in the Computer Age* (Lexington, Mass.: Lexington Books, 1986 ed.).

40. Rob Kling and Suzanne Iacono, "The Mobilization of Support for Computerization: The Role of Computerization Movements," *Social Problems* (June 1988): 240–41.

41. Shaiken, *Work Transformed,* 267. "These other possibilities, however, do not mean the technology is neutral. . . . The bias of the designer is built in. The machines and systems themselves embody the relations of power in the workplace" (page 268).

42. Ibid., 274. "Without a more democratic control of the enterprise as a whole, the social control of technology will remain an illusion" (page 277).

43. Kenneth E. Noble, "Paying Workers Extra to Be Their Own Efficiency Experts," *New York Times,* August 28, 1988, E–6.

44. *International Masonry Institute Report* (Washington, D.C.: International Masonry Institute, 1985).

45. See Paula Nesbitt, "Beyond Plant Closure: New Strategies for Corporate Social Responsibility" (Paper presented at the Annual Meeting of the American Sociological Association, Atlanta, August 24–28, 1988).

46. Massing, "Detroit's Strange Bedfellows," 20. See also James B. Treece, "Here Comes GM's Saturn," *Business Week,* April 9, 1990, 59.

47. Gerald W. McEntee, "Introduction," in *Facing the Future: AFSCME's Approach to Technology* (Washington, D.C.: AFSCME, 1986), 1.

48. Edward Cohen-Rosenthal and Cynthia E. Burton, *Mutual Gains: A Guide to Union-Management Cooperation* (New York: Praeger, 1987), 48.

49. Gompers, *Seventy Years of Life and Labor,* 111.

Case Study: Affirming Co-responsibilities

1. "Built-Rite the First Time," *Labor Relations Today,* September–October 1987, 3.

2. Ibid.

3. PALM representative, quoted in "Major Philadelphia Owners Endorse Built-Rite Program," *Construction Labor Report,* October 28, 1987, 961.

4. Based on my notes from the PALM—Built-Rite Forum, April 15, 1988, Ramada Airport Motel, Eddystone, Pennsylvania.

5. The manual *Built-Rite: How It Works* is valuable for understanding the

project's success. It is available from Built-Rite at the address in the resource
directory, page 310.

6. Jim Martin, quoted in "Built-Rite the First Time," 7.

7. Robert Hatch, manager of General Electric's construction and real estate
operations, quoted in "Philadelphia Owners Endorse Built-Rite," 962.

Chapter 2: The Priority of Safety

1. The material in this section is from "Probe Shows Pressure on OSHA,"
AFL-CIO News, April 23, 1988, 1–2.

2. Quoted in "Multinationals Hit Fomenting Global Trade War," *AFL-CIO
News,* February 6, 1988, 6.

3. "Job Safety: A Ceaseless Struggle," *Steelabor,* May–June 1988, 2. So neglected is the topic that only in 1987 did research clarify the number of occupational deaths that had occurred three years earlier (6,553). The Bureau of
Labor Statistics had an earlier figure of 3,750, while the National Safety Council
had estimated 11,500 ("Miners Found to Have Highest Death Rate on Job,"
New York Times, July 27, 1987, A–15).

4. Arlee C. Green, "Willful Safety Violators Evade Criminal Penalties," *AFL-
CIO News,* February 13, 1988, 2.

5. Matt Yancey, "OSHA's Reports Inflated, Panel Told," *Philadelphia Inquirer,* April 20, 1988, 24-A.

6. "Railroad Safety Sidetracked, Unions Charge," *AFL-CIO News,* February
20, 1986, 4.

7. David Corn and Jefferson Morley, "Inflation's Gift to Big Business," *Nation,* March 26, 1988, 404.

8. Cathy Trost, "Occupational Hazard," *Wall Street Journal,* April 22, 1988,
9, 25-R.

9. Congressman Tom Lantos, quoted in ibid.

10. David Moberg, "IBP's Priorities—Pork before People," *In These Times,*
June 8–21, 1988, 8.

11. William Glaberson, "Misery on the Meatpacking Line," *New York Times,*
June 14, 1987, F-8.

12. Andrea Knox, "For Some Workers, the Computer Is a Pain—Literally,"
Philadelphia Inquirer, July 4, 1988, D–1.

13. James L. Corcoran, safety and health director, Civil Service Employees
Association, AFSCME Local 1000, quoted in "Guidelines Set for VDT Use in
New York," *AFL-CIO News,* January 9, 1988, 2.

14. Eric Schmitt, "Judge Thwarts Suffolk's Video-Terminal Law," *New York
Times,* December 28, 1989, B–3.

15. Bill Paul, "IBM to Reduce Radiation from Future VDT Models," *Wall
Street Journal,* November 22, 1989, B–1.

16. Quoted in "Union Corporate Campaign Focuses on Asbestos Hazard,"
AFL-CIO News, January 2, 1988, 5.

17. I draw here on conversations with Kinsey Robinson, a lengthy letter from
John Barnhard, the union's safety specialist, and an extensive packet of union
publications Barnhard sent me.

18. "Table Grape Boycott Pressed by Labor Consumer Coalition," *AFL-CIO News,* January 2, 1988, 6.

19. "At Last, a Worker's Right to Know," *New York Times,* August 25, 1987, A–20.

20. "Chemical Workers Get Safety Training Grant," *AFL-CIO News,* January 9, 1988, 5.

21. *John Herling's Labor Letter,* February 13, 1988, 3.

22. "New York Connects Job Hazard Hotline," *AFL-CIO News,* April 16, 1988, 4.

23. "Food Union Gains Recognition at IBP Beef Plant," *AFL-CIO News,* June 18, 1988, 3.

24. David Weil, "Government and Labor at the Workplace: The Role of Labor Unions in the Implementation of Federal Health and Safety Policy," in *Proceedings of the Fortieth Annual Meeting of the Industrial Relations Research Association,* ed. Barbara D. Dennis (Madison, Wisc.: Industrial Relations Research Association, 1988), 334.

25. Trumka makes a point (as do many other union presidents) of attending the graduation of members of his union who have completed the Antioch College degree program; we talked at the postgraduation reception in both 1986 and 1987, and, at my request, his staff sent me very helpful UMWA publications.

26. "Job Safety," 2.

27. Matt Yancey, "Rules Set for Machine Safety in Workplace," *Philadelphia Inquirer,* April 30, 1988, 3-A.

28. Weil, "Government and Labor at the Workplace," 333; cf. Lance Selfa, "OSHA: When Politics Becomes a Major Occupational Hazard," *In These Times,* February 11–17, 1987, 19.

29. William Serrin, "A Great American Job Machine?" *Nation,* September 18, 1989, 270; Margaret Seminario, "Worker Death and Injury Toll Cries for Remedy," *AFL-CIO News,* March 18, 1989, 11.

Case Study: PHILAPOSH

1. Richard Kazis and Richard L. Grossman, *Fear at Work: Job Blackmail, Labor, and the Environment* (New York: Pilgrim Press, 1982), 271.

2. Ibid., 231.

3. Quoted in Sharon Chess, "In One City, at Least, You Have a Right to Know," *In These Times,* January 28–February 3, 1981, 4–5.

4. This paragraph draws on Moran as quoted in Ellen Cassidey, " 'Corporate Murder,' " *Philadelphia Daily News,* January 21, 1988, 31.

5. Gil Gall, "Book Review," *Pennsylvania Labor* (Winter 1988): 7.

6. PHILAPOSH, *Services for Member Unions from the Philadelphia Area Project on Occupational Safety and Health* (Philadelphia: PHILAPOSH, 1987), 1.

7. Ibid., 2.

8. PHILAPOSH, *Annual Report, 1989* (Philadelphia: PHILAPOSH, 1989).

Chapter 3: Health Promotion at Work

1. William J. Sonnenstuhl and Harrison M. Trice, *Strategies for Employee Assistance Programs: The Crucial Balance* (Ithaca, N.Y.: ILR Press, 1986), 8.

2. William J. Sonnenstuhl. "Contrasting Employee Assistance, Health Promotion, and Quality of Worklife Programs: Disentangling Workplace Health Interventions," *Journal of Applied Behavioral Sciences* 24 (1988): 347–61.

3. Harrison M. Trice and Janice Beyer, "Work-Related Outcomes of Constructive Confrontation Strategies in a Job-Based Alcoholism Program," *Journal of Studies on Alcohol* (September 1984): 117.

4. See Judith Vicary, "The Role of Employee Assistance Programs in Dealing with Employee Substance Abuse," in *Substance Abuse in the Workplace,* ed. Raymond L. Hogler (University Park: Pennsylvania State University, Department of Labor Studies and Industrial Relations, 1987), 37.

5. Richard E. Dwyer, "The Employer's Need to Provide a Safe Working Environment: The Use and Abuse of Drug Screening," *Labor Studies Journal* (Winter 1987–88): 16.

6. "Flight Attendants' Association Honored," *EAP Digest,* July–August 1985, 1.

7. "AFA EAP an Exemplary Program," *Almacan,* August 1986, 1.

8. "Union EAPS: Taking Care of Our Own," *Training,* October 1987, 64.

9. Ibid.

10. Barbara Feuer, "Innovations in Employee Assistance Programs: A Case Study at the Association of Flight Attendants," in *Occupational Stress and Organizational Effectiveness,* ed. Anne Riley (Westport, Conn.: Greenwood Press, 1987).

11. Peter Sutherland, quoted in Howard W. French, "Helping the Addicted Worker," *New York Times,* March 26, 1987, D–7.

12. William J. Sonnenstuhl and Harrison M. Trice, "Social Construction of Alcohol Problems in a Union's Peer Counseling Program," *Journal of Drug Issues* 17 (1987): 227–55.

13. Ibid., 236.

14. We met at the Annual Meeting of the Society for the Study of Social Problems in August 1987 in Chicago and again at the Annual Meeting of the Eastern Sociological Society in March 1989 in Baltimore.

15. Charles E. Bradford, "A National Labor and Industry-Based Program Designed to Train and Place Persons with Disabilities in the Aerospace and Machining Industries," in *Annual Report* (Washington D.C.: IAM, 1987), 2–3.

16. Ibid., 4–5.

17. Ibid., 8.

18. Kirk Spitzer, "Government Program Helps Disabled Workers Find Jobs," *Fort Worth Star-Telegram,* January 10, 1986, 3.

19. Nanette Asimov. "The Road Back to Independence," *San Francisco Chronicle,* June 27, 1986, 1.

20. Ibid., 3.

21. Bradford, "Program to Train and Place Persons with Disabilities," 14–18. See also Dennis Chamot, "The Changing Workplace: The Union View," in *The*

Future of Work for Disabled People: Employment and the New Technology (New York: American Foundation for the Blind, 1988), 63–72.

22. Gregory Spears, "Study: Few Disabled Go Back to Job," *Philadelphia Inquirer,* February 23, 1988, 7-B. See also Harold Russell, *Out of the Job Market: A National Crisis* (Washington, D.C.: President's Committee on Employment of the Handicapped, 1987).

23. Wayne Beissert, "Drug Tests Become Part of Work Place," *USA Today,* June 16, 1987, 3-A.

24. Mark Memmott, "Jobs Hanging on Drug Tests," *USA Today,* June 17, 1987, 7-B.

25. William J. Sonnenstuhl, Harrison M. Trice, William J. Standenmeier, Jr., and Paul Steele, "Employee Assistance Programs and Drug Testing: Fairness and Injustice in the Workplace," *Nova Law Review* (January 1987): 22.

26. James Ellenberger, "AFL-CIO Urges Privacy Protection, Treatment in Drug Abuse Testing," *Business and Health,* October 1987, 58. See also "USWA Confronts Drug-Test Issue," *Steelabor,* April 1989, 14; "Body Invaders," *Nation,* January 8–15, 1990, 39–40.

27. Ibid., 58–59.

28. Quoted in "Court Outlaws Random Testing in AFGE Case," *AFL-CIO News,* March 19, 1988, 10.

29. Thomas F. Hogan in ibid.

30. We talked in 1987 at an AFL-CIO Executive Council session in Bal Harbour, Florida, and in 1988 at an American Federation of Teachers conference in Philadelphia.

31. Richard Kilroy, chairman, Railway Labor Executives' Association, quoted in Laurie McGinley, "Drug-Test Rules for Rail Workers Proposed by U.S.," *Wall Street Journal,* May 6, 1988, 46.

32. Gerald B. Jordan, "U.S. Assails Tampering of Safety Devices That Prevent Rail Warnings from Working," *Philadelphia Inquirer,* February 18, 1987, 3-A.

33. Larry D. McFather, international president, Locomotive Engineers, "Testing Doesn't Make a Drug Program" (letter to the editor), *New York Times,* June 8, 1988, A–38.

34. Ibid.

35. Ellenberger, "AFL-CIO Urges Privacy Protection," 59.

36. Ibid.

37. Elaine F. Gruenfeld, "Smoking, Drugs, and the Healthy Employee," *ILR Report,* Spring 1986, 9.

38. See, for example, Meredith Miller, "Labor Sees Both Merit, Public Policy Concerns in Provider Contracting," *Business and Health,* December 1987, 46.

39. Quoted in Jane Stein, "Labor Speaks Out on Health Concerns," *Business and Health,* November 1986, 53–54.

40. Ibid.

41. Meredith Miller, "Evolution of Flexible Benefits Prompts Second Look by Labor Unions," *Business and Health,* April 1987, 58.

42. Hay Group research, as reported in Albert R. Karr, "Labor Letter," *Wall Street Journal,* July 12, 1988, 1.

43. Milt Freudenheim, "Labor's Effort to Curb Costs," *New York Times,* July

9, 1985, D–2. See also "Union-Made Health Plan Beats All Rivals," *Steelabor,* March–April 1988, 14–15.

44. "Deaf Union Members Sign on at Postal Workers' Session," *AFL-CIO News,* May 7, 1988, 11.

45. Faith L. Ham, "City Textile Workers Union to Direct Medicare Project," *Philadelphia Business Journal,* December 21–27, 1987, 4.

46. Harvey Sigelbaum, quoted in ibid.

47. Rhonda L. Rundle, "Several Employers and Unions Propose to Administer Retirees' Medicare Plans," *Wall Street Journal,* August 18, 1986, 48.

48. John Herling, "AFL-CIO Conference on Safety and Health," *John Herling's Labor Letter,* November 21, 1987, 3. See also Louise D. Walsh, "Labor Studies Center Helps Unions Prepare for Health Benefits Role," *Business and Health,* March 1987, 54–55.

49. See in this connection AFL-CIO Committee on Health Care, *A Battle Labor Can Win* (Washington, D.C.: AFL-CIO, 1985).

50. John Mehring, "Health-Care Workers' Unions Should Take Lead in AIDS Fight," *In These Times,* December 16–22, 1987, 16. See also Jordan Barab, "Lack of AIDS Safeguards Fuels Health Workers' Fears," *In These Times,* November 4–10, 1987, 15.

51. Glenn Kramon, "Bargaining on Fee with a Surgeon," *New York Times,* April 19, 1988, D–2.

52. Angelo Fosco, quoted in "Laborers Extend Health Risk Curbs to Families," *AFL-CIO News,* February 27, 1988, 4.

53. Jim Pinkham, "Automaker and Union Forces in Unique Health and Safety Program," *Occupational Health and Safety News Digest,* August 1988, 4–5. See also Tobi Lippin, "Healthier Workers," *Technology Review,* January 1988, 10–11.

54. "Newswatch," *Labor Notes,* July 1988, 4.

55. Bruce Miller, "A Guide to the Smoke-Free Workplace," *East West,* August 1987, 51. A 1988 survey found that 89 percent of Americans considered tobacco smoke generally harmful to health, up from 58 percent in 1978. See Charles Taylor, "Poll Majority Sees Harm in Smoking," *Philadelphia Inquirer,* April 22, 1988, 8-A.

56. Jeanne M. Stellman, "Environmental Factors Affecting Job Stress," *Business and Health,* October 1987, 19.

57. Miller, "Evolution of Flexible Benefits," 58.

58. Sheldon W. Samuels, health director, AFL-CIO, in "Heart Disease Affects Wage Earners," *Occupational Health and Safety News Digest,* May 1987, 13.

59. *Safer Times,* October–November 1989, 6. The last year for which data are available is 1988.

Chapter 4: Encouraging Membership Growth

1. Duane Beeler and Harry Kurshenbaum, *Roles of the Labor Leader* (Chicago: Union Representative, 1976), 42.

2. William Serrin, "Labor as Usual," *Village Voice,* February 23, 1988, 26; "Labor in the 1990s" (excerpts from the AFL-CIO Executive Council report to the 1989 AFL-CIO convention), *AFL-CIO News,* November 13, 1989, 7.

3. "Union Membership," *LRA's Economic Notes,* January–February 1990, 15.

4. Robert H. Zieger, *American Workers, American Unions, 1920–1985* (Baltimore: Johns Hopkins University Press, 1986), 192.

5. Richard B. Freeman and James L. Medoff, *What Do Unions Do?* (New York: Basic Books, 1984), 221.

6. "Union Membership Down," 5-A; see also *Labor Letter,* March 1989, 2; "Labor in the 1990s," 8.

7. Alan Kistler, "Union Organizing: New Challenges and Prospects," *Annals,* May 1984, 100.

8. Robert Kuttner, "Will Unions Organize Again?" *Dissent,* Winter 1987, 53.

9. Ibid.

10. Freeman and Medoff, *What Do Unions Do?* 222.

11. Kuttner, "Will Unions Organize Again?" 53.

12. Freeman and Medoff, *What Do Unions Do?* 222, 212. "From 1950 to 1980, when unfair labor practices per election increased by sixfold, . . . the rise in management opposition explains from over a quarter to nearly a half of the decline in union success organizing through NLRB elections" (page 238). On labor's premium, see John R. Oravec, "Blue-Collar Workers Lead Strong Union Advantage," *AFL-CIO News,* July 9, 1990, 10.

13. Freeman and Medoff, *What Do Unions Do?* 241–42. "But such a decline is the logical consequence of 1980s patterns of change" (page 242).

14. Quoted in Peter Perl, "The Lifeline for Unions: Recruiting," *Washington Post,* September 13, 1987, H–14.

15. Perl, "The Lifeline for Unions," H–14.

16. Ibid.

17. Ibid.

18. Samuel Gompers, *Seventy Years of Life and Labor,* ed. Nick Salvatore (Ithaca, N.Y.: ILR Press, 1984), 43.

19. Sirabella spoke to a dinner meeting of the Philadelphia chapter of the Industrial Relations Research Association, February 1987. See in this connection Kenneth Gilberg and Nancy Abrams, "Union Organizing: New Tactics for New Times," *Personnel Administrator,* July 1987, 52, 54–56.

20. Roger Starr, "Close Sweatshops, Open Jobs," *New York Times,* January 21, 1988, A–26.

21. Lydia Chavez, "Aliens Balk at Old 'Skeletons,' " *New York Times,* November 17, 1987, B–5.

22. Mizaffar Chishti, quoted in Alfredo Corchado and Dianna Solis, "Immigration Law Creates a Subclass of Illegals Bound to Their Bosses and Vulnerable to Abuses," *Wall Street Journal,* September 2, 1987, 44.

23. Pauline Yoshihashi, "Garment Makers Struggle under the Immigration Laws," *Wall Street Journal,* September 8, 1987, 6.

24. "Labor in the 1990s," 9.

25. Enid Eckstein, "Unions Prepare to Deal with New Immigration Law," *Labor Notes,* March 1987, 11.

26. Peter Applebone, "Amnesty Sale: The Medium Is the Tortilla," *New York Times*, March 1, 1988, B–9.

27. John Herling, *John Herling's Labor Letter*, July 30, 1988, 3.

28. Quoted in Bob Cohn, "Perks for the Rank and File," *Newsweek*, April 6, 1987, 40.

29. Quoted in Jay McCormick, "Union Offers Credit Card as Benefit," *USA Today*, February 14–16, 1986, 1-A.

30. Donahue quoted in "New Union Thrust," *AFL-CIO News* (New Horizons Suppl.), October 24, 1987, 1; Ray Denison, speech to the convention of the AFL-CIO Union Labor Department, Miami Beach, October 22, 1987.

31. Kevin Kelly, "Labor May Have Found a Rx for Growth," *Business Week*, February 22, 1988, 162.

32. Steve Early and Rand Wilson, "Organizing High Tech: Unions and Their Future," *Labor Research Review* (Spring 1986): 47–67.

33. Lisa Ellis, "Labor Aims to Woo Workers in the Booming Health Field," *New York Times*, February 4, 1990, A-1.

34. See, for example, Jack Golodner, "How 'Other Professionals' Bargain: Professional Employees," in *The Unionized Professoriate: A Discriminating Approach*, ed. Joel M. Douglas (New York: National Center for the Study of Collective Bargaining in Higher Education and the Professions, Baruch College, 1986), 49–54.

35. Kelly, "Rx for Growth," 166.

36. Gene Zack, "Organizing Victories Rebound to Eight-Year High," *AFL-CIO News*, May 14, 1990, 6.

37. Michael A. Pollock, "Can Credit Cards and IRAs Rebuild the Labor Movement?" *Business Week*, November 4, 1985, 96.

38. " 'Blitz' Engages Tappan Workers," *Steelabor*, February 1988, 8.

39. Quoted in Pollock, "Credit Cards and IRAs," 96.

40. Arlee C. Green, "Labor Educators Explore Needs of New Decade," *AFL-CIO News*, April 2, 1990, 11.

41. Candice Johnson, "Organizing Institute," *AFL-CIO News*, August 6, 1990, 8.

42. "Labor in the 1990s," 7. The peak figure, achieved in 1975, was 14,070,000 members; in 1989, the AFL-CIO claimed a total of 14,158,000 plus 395,000 associate members, on whom a reduced monthly per capita tax was paid.

Case Study: Reorganizing the Air Traffic Controllers

1. For details on the win and the party, see Susan Kellam, "Air Controllers Vote Overwhelmingly to Unionize," *Federal Times*, June 22, 1987, 3.

2. Irvin Molotsky, "Air Controllers Vote New Union over Issues That Led to '81 Strike," *New York Times*, June 12, 1987, 1.

3. For a full account of the FAA-PATCO relationship, see Arthur Shostak and David Skocik, *The Air Controllers' Controversy: Lessons from the 1981 PATCO Strike* (New York: Human Sciences Press, 1984). Relevant articles include Arthur Shostak, "Let the Air Controllers Return," *New York Times*, September 5, 1986, A-23; Arthur Shostak, "Air Traffic Controllers Offer Labor a

Model," *Philadelphia Inquirer,* September 7, 1987, A-11; and Arthur Shostak, "Second Thoughts on the PATCO Strike," *Social Policy* (Winter 1986): 22–28.

4. Brochure prepared by Aviation Education Systems (10 East 53rd St., New York, NY 10022), 3.

5. I draw here on Alex C. Cullison, "The Forgotten Promise: The Resurgence of Unionism among the Air Traffic Controllers," master's thesis, Empire State College, 1988.

6. "Skyjam," *New Republic,* September 29, 1986, 8.

7. Josef H. Hebert, "Air Traffic Controllers Approve Union," *Philadelphia Inquirer,* June 12, 1987, 9-A.

8. Quoted in Gene Zack, "Air Traffic Controllers Sweep Union to Victory," *AFL-CIO News,* June 13, 1987, 6.

9. John Thornton, quoted in Laura Parker, "Movement for New Union for Controllers Takes Off," *Washington Post,* February 8, 1987, A–10.

10. Quoted in David Lyons, "Kirkland Issues Call to Bolster Union Ranks," *Philadelphia Inquirer,* October 27, 1987, 4-A.

11. Press statement prepared by MEBA and distributed to attendees of NATCA victory celebration, June 11, 1987.

12. See in this connection *FAA Staffing* (Washington, D.C.: General Accounting Office, 1986).

13. On the case for rehiring, see the 1984-to-date issues of *PATCO LIVES* (P.O. Box 15254, Washington, D.C. 20003–9997). See also John F. Leyden, "Time to Rehire Some PATCO Air Controllers," *New York Times,* July 3, 1987, A–26; Moe Biller, "Let's Call Back the Fired Air Controllers," *USA Today,* February 7, 1990, 10-A.

14. On the persistence of workplace discontent, see James R. Carroll, "Air Controllers Say System Needs Help," *Philadelphia Inquirer,* May 26, 1989, 3-A; William Stockton, "Dangerous Traffic," *New York Times Magazine,* June 4, 1989, 40, 56, 61, 68–69.

15. Cullison, "The Forgotten Promise," 100.

Chapter 5: Solidarity with Professional Employees

1. Kevin Kelly, "Labor May Have Found a Rx for Growth," *Business Week,* February 22, 1988, 162; Barry Liebowitz quoted in *The Unionized Professoriate,* ed. Joel M. Douglas (New York: National Center for the Study of Collective Bargaining in Higher Education and the Professions, Baruch College, 1986), 44.

2. Jack Golodner, "Professional Employees," in Douglas, *The Unionized Professoriate,* 49.

3. I draw extensively in this section on Gale Miller, *It's a Living: Work in Modern Society* (New York: St. Martin's Press, 1981), 96–132.

4. Dick Moore, "Actors' Unions," in Douglas, *The Unionized Professoriate,* 46.

5. Ibid., 48.

6. Barry Liebowitz, president of the Doctors Council, "The Physicians," in Douglas, *The Unionized Professoriate,* 41.

7. Ibid., 42.

8. Ibid., 44.

9. Ibid. See also Dirk Johnson, "Doctor's Dilemma: Unionizing," *New York Times,* July 13, 1987, D–1, D–4.

10. Donald M. Fehr, "Labor Relations in Baseball," in Douglas, *The Unionized Professoriate,* 33.

11. "Baseball's Bosses Toss a Curve," *Business Week,* May 4, 1981, 168.

12. Fehr, "Labor Relations in Baseball," 36.

13. Richard Justice, "$10.5 Million Awarded in Collusion Decision," *Philadelphia Inquirer,* September 1, 1989, D–1; see also Murray Chass, "Players Say Trust Is a Big Issue," *New York Times,* December 7, 1989, D–27.

14. Quoted in "NFL's Union Reacts," *Philadelphia Inquirer,* November 9, 1989, F–1. See also Gerald W. Scully, "Tackling the N.F.L. Labor Impasse," *New York Times,* November 26, 1989, S–8.

15. Glen Macnow, "Baseball's Union Drove a Hard Bargain," *Philadelphia Inquirer,* March 20, 1990, 1-A.

16. Mary G. Edwards, "Faculty Unions Must Respond to the Shifts of Power in Higher Education," *Chronicle of Higher Education,* March 23, 1988, B–2.

17. Debra E. Blum, "New Bargaining Units in 1987 Comprised Only Part-Time Professors and Assistants," *Chronicle of Higher Education,* May 11, 1988, A–18.

18. John Herling, "Are Teachers' Unions an Endangered Species?" *John Herling's Labor Letter,* March 26, 1988, 1.

19. Myron Lieberman, "Peer Review and Faculty Self Government: A Dissenting View," in Douglas, *The Unionized Professoriate,* 13.

20. Jack H. Schuster, "The Evolving Faculty Condition: What Is the Relevance to the Collective Bargaining Community?" in Douglas, *The Unionized Professoriate,* 7.

21. Ibid.

22. Ibid.

23. "Almanac," *Chronicle of Higher Education,* September 1, 1988, 3.

24. Gene Zack, "Health Care Workers Turn to Unions," *AFL-CIO News,* April 2, 1990, 6; Milt Freudenheim, "Labor's Hospital Drive Gets a Lift," *New York Times,* May 10, 1990, D–1, D–13.

25. Ibid.; "Nurses Get New Contract at Six New York Hospitals," *AFL-CIO News,* January 22, 1990, 9.

26. Ibid., 10.

27. Teresa Conrow, "Blood and Justice: Red Cross Nurses on Strike," *Labor Research Review* (Spring 1988): 56.

28. Quoted in ibid., 61.

29. See John Fox, "Medical Computing and the User," *International Journal of Man-Machine Studies* 14 (1977): 669–86.

30. Heidi I. Hartmann, ed., *Computer Chips and Paper Clips* (Washington, D.C.: National Academy Press, 1986), 56.

31. Ibid., 56–57.

32. Phone interviews, Membership Department, NEA, and Research Department, AFT, January 2, 1990.

33. *AFT Members Put Ideas into Action* (Washington, D.C.: AFT, 1988), 3. See also Lee A. Daniels, "Florida Teachers' Pact Praised as Education Boon," *New York Times*, July 27, 1988.

34. Interview, Joseph Fernandez, school superintendent, March 3, 1989, Orlando, Fla.

35. Ibid.

36. Harold J. Carroll, quoted in Joseph Berger, "Two Rival Unions Endorse Plans to Help Teachers," *New York Times*, July 6, 1988, B–5.

37. Dale Mezzacappa, "In Rochester, Contract with Teachers Puts the Interests of Students First," *Philadelphia Inquirer*, November 5, 1987, 1-A.

38. Adam Urbanski, quoted in ibid., 14-A. See also Michael Winerip, "$70,000 Salaries and High Hopes for Teachers," *New York Times*, September 18, 1987, B–1.

39. Golodner, "Professional Employees," 51.

40. Ibid., 52.

Chapter 6: Women and Unionism

1. Philip S. Foner, "Women and the American Labor Movement: A Historical Perspective," in *Working Women: Past, Present, Future*, ed. Karen S. Koziara et al. (Washington, D.C.: Bureau of National Affairs, 1987), 154; see also Judith O'Sullivan and Rosemary Gallick, *Workers and Allies: Female Participation in the American Trade Union Movement, 1824–1976* (Ithaca, N.Y.: ILR Press, 1975).

2. Ruth Needleman and Lucretia D. Tanner, "Women in Unions: Current Issues," in Koziara et al., *Working Women*, 188–89; Ruth Needleman, "Turning the Tide: Women, Unions, and Labor Education," *Labor Studies Journal* (Winter 1986): 203. "Women could turn the tide in favor of unions, helping to halt the membership decline and expand the active membership base."

3. Brian Heshizer, "Union Officials Assess the Labor Movement and Labor-Management Relations," *Labor Studies Journal* (Spring 1987): 33.

4. Naomi Baden, "Developing an Agenda: Expanding the Role of Women in Unions," *Labor Studies Journal* (Winter 1986): 244.

5. Nancy Seifer and Barbara Wertheimer, "New Approaches to Collective Power," in *Women Organizing: An Anthology*, ed. Bernice Cummings and Victoria Shuck (New York: Basic Books, 1979), 180.

6. Eileen Ogintz, "9 to 5: An Idea Whose Time Has Come," *Chicago Tribune*, November 20, 1985, 1.

7. Roberta Lynch, "Organizing Clericals: Problems and Prospects," *Labor Research Review* (Spring 1986): 94; see also Gloria Johnson, "Never Underestimate Power of Women in Unions," *New York Times*, April 6, 1989, A–30.

8. Francine D. Blau and Marianne A. Ferber, "Occupations and Earnings of Women Workers," in Koziara et al., *Working Women*, 44–46.

9. Kay Kaboolian, "The Feminization of Unions and Pressure for Pay Equity," in Koziara et al., *Working Women*, 442; Ray Marshall, *Women and Work in the 1980s* (Washington, D.C.: Women's Research and Education Institute, Congressional Caucus for Women's Issues, 1983), 18.

10. Needleman and Tanner, "Women in Unions," 200–1.

11. Michael E. Gordon, "Discussion," in *Proceedings of the Fortieth Annual Meeting of the Industrial Relations Research Association*, ed. Barbara D. Dennis (Madison, Wisc.: Industrial Relations Research Association, 1988), 168.

12. Charles C. Heckscher, *The New Unionism* (New York: Basic Books, 1988), 187.

13. Naomi Baden, "Developing an Agenda: Expanding the Role of Women in Unions," *Labor Studies Journal* (Winter 1986): 245. See also Kaboolian, "The Feminization of Unions," 442; Patricia Thomas, "Pay Equity: Educating for Union Action," *Labor Studies Journal* (Winter 1986): 278–89. "There is no question that this issue will continue to be a central one for unions nationally, given the changing composition of the workforce and of union membership" (page 289).

14. "Panel Votes Bill on Child Care," *New York Times*, July 28, 1988, A–28.

15. Milt Freudenheim, "G.M. and Ford Pacts Provide Custodial Care," *New York Times*, November 2, 1987, D–1.

16. Cathy Trost, "Labor Letter," *Wall Street Journal*, July 19, 1988, 1.

17. Maggie Garb, "Bringing Up Babies," *In These Times*, January 27–February 2, 1988, 12.

18. See in this connection John J. Sweeney and Karen Nussbaum, *Solutions for the Work Force* (Washington, D.C.: Seven Locks Press, 1989), 103–26.

19. Shelly Phillips, "Paternity Leaves Increase, Minus Executive Approval," *Philadelphia Inquirer*, July 10, 1988, 2-J. See also R. A. Zaldwar, "Bush Vetoes Family-Leave Legislation," *Philadelphia Inquirer*, June 30, 1990, 1-A, 4-A.

20. Linda Lloyd, "Firms, Workers Face New Problem: Caring for Elderly," *Philadelphia Inquirer*, April 25, 1988, D–1.

21. Garb, "Bringing Up Babies," 12.

22. Gerald McEntee, "Child Care: A Union Issue," *Child Care Action News*, March–April 1988, 12.

23. Christopher J. Dodd, "Child Care Crises Cries Out for Federal Help," *New York Times*, May 13, 1988.

24. John Naisbitt, *John Naisbitt's Trend Letter*, February 18, 1988, 1.

25. Quoted in Cindy Skrzycki and Frank Swoboda, "A Surge of Support for Child Care," *Philadelphia Inquirer*, February 21, 1988, G–1.

26. Quoted in "American Family Celebration," *Steelabor*, March–April 1988, 7–8.

27. Ibid.

28. Needleman and Tanner, "Women in Unions," 207–11. All of the union statistics are from this source. See also Arthur R. Schwartz and Michele M. Hoyman, "The Changing of the Guard: The New American Labor Leader," in *The Future of American Unionism*, ed. Louis A. Ferman (Beverly Hills, Calif.: Sage, 1984), 64–75.

29. Albert R. Karr, "Labor Letter," *Wall Street Journal*, July 26, 1988, 1. Unfortunately, the government stopped collecting relevant data on women in unions in 1980, and researchers have been unable ever since to convince some unions to share such data. Needleman and Tanner, "Women in Unions," 205.

30. Diane Balser, *Sisterhood and Solidarity: Feminism and Labor in Modern Times* (Boston: South End Press, 1987), 151.

31. Ibid., 208.

32. I draw here on literature sent at my request from CEP.

33. Cosby Totten et al., "Women Miners' Fight for Parental Leave," *Labor Research Review* (Spring 1988): 95.

34. I draw here on Jenny Burman, "Daughters of Mother Jones," *Z*, November 1989, 41–44.

35. Marat Moore, a UMWA organizer who had been meeting for about a year with the women's auxiliary to prepare for the Pittston strike, as quoted in ibid., 44. See also Jonathan Tasini, "Proud to Be a Daughter of Mother Jones," *Z*, January 1990, 36–37.

36. Fred Krebs, director of employment relations policy, Chamber of Commerce, quoted in Garb, "Bringing Up Babies," 12.

37. Donna Lenhoff, associate director for legal policy and programs, Women's Legal Defense Fund, quoted in Garb, "Bringing Up Babies," 12.

38. Mark Hussey, "What Do They Want?" *New York Times Book Review*, July 19, 1987, 3.

39. Quoted in Balser, *Sisterhood and Solidarity*, 164–66. For a helpful British perspective, see Cynthia Cockburn, *Machinery of Dominance: Women, Men and Technical Know-How* (London: Pluto Press, 1985), 244–57.

40. Richard B. Freeman and James L. Medoff, *What Do Unions Do?* (New York: Basic Books, 1984), 28.

41. National Association of Working Women, *The 9 to 5 Profile of Working Women* (Cleveland: National Association of Working Women, 1986), 4.

Case Study: The Campaign at Harvard

1. Quoted in Nina McCain, "Unionizing Harvard's Clerical Workers," *Boston Globe*, January 22, 1988, 1.

2. I draw here on Robert Kuttner, "At Harvard, Two Unions Battle the Administration and Each Other," *Boston Globe*, December 8, 1986, 1.

3. Cited in Bruce D. Butterfield, "Two Unions Compete in Fight to Organize Harvard Workers," *Boston Globe*, February 8, 1987, 1.

4. Ibid.

5. Quoted in Bruce D. Butterfield, "Unions Woo Harvard's Workers," *Boston Globe*, January 30, 1987, 1.

6. Quoted in Butterfield, "Two Unions Compete in Fight," 1.

7. UAW letter to its Harvard organizers, cited in Brian Silver, "Union Gears Up for Vote," *Harvard Independent* (distributed by HUCTW), n.d., 2.

8. Quoted in Silver, "Union Gears Up," 2.

9. Quoted in Susan Povich and Vincent Chang, "HUCTW and AFSCME Merge into the Future," *Harvard Law Record*, March 13, 1987, 1.

10. I draw here on Mark Feinberg, "Long-Timers Join Fray at 'McHarvard,'" *In These Times*, July 22–August 4, 1987, 5.

11. Quoted in Silver, "Union Gears Up," 2.

12. Ibid.

13. Melissa R. Hart, "Union Stages Support Rally," *Harvard Crimson,* February 19, 1988, 1. McEntee said, "We don't pretend to be perfect, but this book is a one-sided and inaccurate portrayal of our union and unions in America."

14. See in this connection Julie McCall, "An Interview with 'The Pipets,' " *Labor Notes,* April 1989, 2. Their two tapes are available for $10 each from HUCTW, 67 Winthrop St., Cambridge, MA 02138.

15. Hart, "Union Stages Support Rally," 1.

16. Kenneth B. Noble, "Union Seeking Affordable Day Care at Harvard," *New York Times,* February 28, 1988, 24.

17. Quoted in Hart, "Union Stages Support Rally," 1.

18. Butterfield, "Two Unions Compete in Fight," 1.

19. Kuttner, "At Harvard Two Unions Battle," 1.

20. Cited in Bruce Butterfield, "Union to Seek Harvard Election," *Boston Globe,* February 23, 1988, 1.

21. Noble, "Union Seeking Affordable Day Care," 24; see also Daniel Golden, "Taking on Harvard," *Boston Globe Magazine,* August 7, 1988, 21, 36–47.

22. Quoted in "First Contract Seals Big Victory at Harvard," *AFL-CIO News,* July 8, 1989, 1.

Chapter 7: "Reorganizing" Members

1. A. H. Raskin, "New Directions for the AFL-CIO," *New Management* (Winter 1986): 12–13.

2. Frank Tannenbaum, *A Philosophy of Labor* (New York: Knopf, 1951), 168.

3. Brian Heshizer, "Union Officials Assess the Labor Movement and Labor-Management Relations," *Labor Studies Journal* (Spring 1987): 32, 40.

4. Ibid., 37.

5. Quoted in Leonard P. Oliver, *Building Union Democracy: The BAC Study Circle Program* (Washington, D.C.: BAC, 1986), 23.

6. Alex Kotlowitz, "Rebuilding Demand for Union Bricklayers," *Wall Street Journal,* August 24, 1987, 31.

7. Oliver, *Building Union Democracy,* 9, 11.

8. Ibid., 22.

9. Interview, George Meany Center, Silver Spring, Md., July 27, 1987.

10. Note in this connection a finding from a study of the experiences of women apprentices in an Ohio local of the Brotherhood of Carpenters: male apprentices were "surprisingly more positive than the women concerning the performance of minorities and women in the program. This difference could be because although men may be less than supportive of affirmative action as a policy, they may be surprised to recognize the contributions of minorities and women once they have an opportunity to work with them" (Susan L. Josephs et al., "The Union as Help or Hindrance: Experiences of Women Apprentices in the Construction Trades," *Labor Studies Journal* [Spring 1988]: 17).

11. AFL-CIO Department of Organization and Field Services, *Numbers That Count* (Washington, D.C.: AFL-CIO, 1988), 2.

12. Jeremy Brecher, *History from Below* (New Haven, Conn.: Commonwork Pamphlets/Advocate Press, 1986).

13. Harold Wilensky, *Intellectuals in Labor Unions* (Glencoe, Ill.: Free Press, 1955), ix–x.

14. Dick Moore, "Actors' Unions," in *The Unionized Professoriate*, ed. Joel M. Douglas (New York: National Center for the Study of Collective Bargaining in Higher Education and the Professions, Baruch College, 1987), 47–48.

15. David L. Perlman, "Veto Override Shows Congress Stands Firm on Protecting Rights," *AFL-CIO News*, March 26, 1988, 1.

16. Quoted in "Shell's Tie to South Africa Protested," *AFL-CIO News*, March 26, 1988, 8.

17. "King's Holiday," *AFL-CIO News*, January 9, 1988, 3.

18. Coalition of Black Trade Unionists, *CBTU* (Washington, D.C.: CBTU, 1987), 1.

19. Lisa Ellis, "Labor Council Excludes Hispanics, Leaders Say," *Philadelphia Inquirer*, November 16, 1989, 5-A.

20. Jack Otero, "Bring Hispanics into Labor's Fold," *Public Employee*, August–September 1988, 18. For data on black unionists, see Gloria Johnson, "Never Underestimate Power of Women in Unions," *New York Times*, April 6, 1989, A–30.

21. Jack Otero, vice-president of the Transportation-Communication Employees Union, cited in "Top Officers Re-elected; 5 Join Executive Council," *AFL-CIO News*, November 27, 1989, 5.

22. Josephs et al., "The Union as Help or Hindrance," 18.

23. Richard T. Ely, *The Labor Movement in America* (New York: Thomas Y. Crowell, 1886), 138, 154.

24. Frank Marquart, "New Problems for the Unions," *Dissent*, Autumn 1959, 388.

Case Study: Utilizing Telecommunications

1. Jack Metzgar and Andrew Banks, "The United Strike," *Nation*, June 29, 1985, 64.

2. I draw liberally on the work of three personal friends: *Electronic Meetings: Technical Alternatives and Social Choices*, by Robert Johansen, Jacques Vallee, and Kathleen Spangler (Reading, Mass.: Addison-Wesley, 1979).

3. Ibid., 137.

4. I draw with appreciation on an interview with Captain Roger D. Hall, first vice-president of ALPA, June 11, 1987. At the time of the 1985 strike, Captain Hall was in charge of the United pilots local.

5. BNA, *Unions Today: New Tactics to Tackle Tough Times* (Washington, D.C.: Bureau of National Affairs, 1985), 83, 86.

6. Sara U. Douglas, *Labor's New Voice: Unions and the Mass Media* (Norwood, N.J.: Ablex, 1986), 105.

7. Metzgar and Banks, "The United Strike," 64.

Case Study: Upgrading Responses to the NLRB

1. "How Do the Contractors View Deklewa?" *SPARKS,* July 1987, 6.
2. 282 NLRB no. 184.
3. Hank McGuire, "Deklewa: Life or Death for Construction Unions?" *SPARKS,* July 1987, 2.
4. Ibid.
5. Ibid.
6. Oscar Neebe, "Organizing," *SPARKS,* June 1986, 5.
7. McGuire, "Deklewa," 2.
8. Ibid.
9. Ibid.
10. Interview, George Meany Center, Silver Spring, Md., July 31, 1987.
11. Michael D. Lucas, "The Deklewa Decision" (Paper for course at George Meany Center, November 1987), 16.
12. Hugh Hafer, quoted in McGuire, "Deklewa," 2.

Chapter 8: Providing More Effective Service

1. This language is attributed to an anonymous community services liaison in Shirley Keller, "Volunteering: Organized Labor's Best Kept Secret," in *A New Competitive Edge: Volunteers from the Workplace,* ed. Shirley Keller (Arlington, Va.: Volunteer—The National Center, 1986), 207.
2. Foster Rhea Dulles, *Labor in America* (New York: Thomas Y. Crowell, 1955); Gus Tyler, *The Labor Revolution* (New York: Viking Press, 1967); Seymour Martin Lipset, ed., *Unions in Transition* (San Francisco: Institute for Comtemporary Studies, 1986).
3. Keller, "Volunteering," 208; Richard B. Freeman and James L. Medoff, *What Do Unions Do?* (New York: Basic Books, 1984).
4. AFL-CIO Executive Council, "Labor in the 1990s," *AFL-CIO News,* November 13, 1989, 8.
5. Leo Perlis, "Pastoral Letter from Bishops Is Both Moral and Practical," *Atlanta Journal,* December 16, 1984, 23.
6. The data that follow are from Frank W. Emig, "Report of the AFL-CIO Department of Community Services" (February 1, 1989, Mimeographed), and from phone interviews with Alan Bosch, AFL-CIO Department of Community Services, July 11, 1990.
7. John Auble, Jr., "Giving the United Way," *St. Louis Globe Democrat,* September 16–17, 1967.
8. Interview, George Meany Center, Silver Spring, Md., February 6, 1988.
9. Interview, Chicago, January 18, 1987. This is reconstructed from notes. I apologize for any inaccuracies attributed mistakenly to Mr. Culver.
10. Interview, AFL-CIO headquarters, Washington, D.C., October 28, 1987; Leo Perlis, "AFL-CIO Community Services: The Human Contract," in *Manual for the AFL-CIO CSA Representative* (Washington, D.C.: AFL-CIO Department of Community Services, 1979), u.p.; see also Perlis, "A Summary Report of the

National CIO Community Services Committee to the Seventeenth Constitutional Convention of the CIO, December 1–2, 1955," in the *Manual*.

11. Richard Lester, *As Unions Mature: An Analysis of the Evolution of American Unionism* (Princeton, N.J.: Princeton University Press, 1958), 45; see also Emig, "Report of the Department of Community Services."

Case Study: Cooperating with the Red Cross

1. Jeanine Derr, *Labor and the American Red Cross* (Washington, D.C.: American National Red Cross, 1987), 2.

2. Ibid., 2.

3. As recalled by Stan Gordon in an interview at the George Meany Center, Silver Spring, Md., July 27, 1989.

Case Study: Cooperating with Retired Unionists

1. Erik Erikson et al., *Vital Involvement in Old Age* (New York: W. W. Norton, 1986).

2. Quoted in Gillian Silver, "Union Club Guards Interests of Seniors," *Sun City Independent*, December 4, 1985, u.p.

3. Ibid.

4. Information for this case study was obtained during research trips to Sun City, Arizona, and confirmed through correspondence with Larry Spitz. For information on how to form a union club, write to the Union Club, P.O. Box 1206, Sun City, AZ 85372.

Chapter 9: Labor Education

1. I draw here extensively on the seminal work of Joyce L. Kornbluh, whose book *A New Deal for Workers' Education: The Workers' Service Program, 1933–1942* (Urbana: University of Illinois Press, 1987) is an indispensable source.

2. Harry Overstreet, in *Workers' Education: A Quarterly Journal* (October 1936): 137, as cited in ibid.

3. Mark Starr, "The Current Panorama," in *Workers' Education in the United States*, ed. Theodore Brameld (New York: Harper, 1941), 90.

4. Quoted in Kornbluh, *Workers' Education*, 129. "The program succeeded in transmitting the legacy of the democratic education ideals and practices of the progressive adult educators of the 1920s to the education of union activists today."

5. Brian Towers, "Labor Education in Depression: A British Perspective," *Labor Studies Journal* (Spring 1987): 8–9.

6. See in this connection Richard E. Dwyer, *Labor Education in the U.S.: An Annotated Bibliography* (Metuchen, N.J.: Scarecrow Press, 1977).

7. See in this connection Helmut Golatz, "Labor Studies: If the Shoe Fits" (Paper presented at the Southwest Labor Studies Conference, Arizona State University, March 4–5, 1977) and Milt Lieberthal, "On the Academization of Labor Education," *Labor Studies Journal* (Winter 1977): 235–45. See also Steven

Deutsch, "University Research and the Labor Movement," *Labor Studies Forum* (Fall 1989): 1–2.

8. Richard E. Dwyer et al., "Labor Studies: In Quest of Industrial Justice," *Labor Studies Journal* (Fall 1977): 95–131.

9. Towers, "Labor Education in Depression," 28; see also Russell Allen, "Labor Education Programs and Universities: Changing Expectations," *Labor Studies Forum* (Fall 1989): 5–6.

10. Charles Derber, "Worker Education for a Changing Economy: New Labor-Academic Partnerships," in *Responding to the Educational Needs of Today's Workplace,* ed. Ivan Charner and Catherine A. Rolzinki (San Francisco: Jossey-Bass, 1987), 50.

11. Ibid.

12. Charles Derber, phone interview, August 12, 1988.

13. Derber, "Worker Education," 54.

14. Ibid., 55.

15. *A College Degree for Union Leaders* (Silver Spring, Md.: Meany Center for Labor Studies, n.d.).

16. Kenneth B. Noble, "Where Labor Goes for College-Style Learning," *New York Times,* August 3, 1988, 21.

17. Ibid.

18. Hig Roberts, director of the Center for Labor Education Research, University of Alabama, Birmingham, and a senior staff member of the Meany Center Antioch Program.

19. Nick Browne, "Education: Today's Bread-and-Butter Issue for America's Unions," *Social Policy* (Winter 1986): 39. I draw heavily on this source for material about CWE and CWL.

20. "Unions: Bread, Butter, and Basic Skills," *BCEL* (Business Council for Effective Literacy) *Newsletter,* October 1987, 5.

21. Quoted in ibid.

22. Browne, "Education," 39.

23. John Ashcraft, "New Jobs Require Both Brains and Bodies," *USA Today,* August 10, 1988, 9-A; Browne, "Education," 39.

24. Noble, "Where Labor Goes for College-Style Learning," 32.

25. U.S. Basics, *The Comprehensive Competencies Program* (Washington, D.C.: U.S. Basics, 1988), 1.

26. Ibid., 13.

27. ILSR pamphlet (Providence, R.I.: Institute for Labor Studies and Research, n.d.), 2.

28. ILSR, *Sixth Annual Report* (July 1, 1985–June 30, 1986); institute newsletter, Winter 1987–88; and letter, May 4, 1990.

29. I talked with Barry Bluestone on June 23, 1988, at the National Press Club in New York; I interviewed Charles Derber by phone on August 13, 1988.

30. "Postal Workers Turn a Page in History," *AFL-CIO News,* June 18, 1988, 3.

31. Arlee C. Green, "Job Corps Proves a Success Story," *AFL-CIO News,* February 6, 1988, 4.

32. Quoted in "Local 1442 Member Gets in the Act," *UFCW Action,* January–February 1987, 6.

33. Shaun Nethercott, quoted in Shaun Nethercott and Buck Buchanan, "Auto Workers Revive Labor Theatre of the '30s," *Labor Review* (May 1988): 7.

34. Judith L. Catlett, "After the Goodbyes: A Long-Term Look at the Southern School for Union Women," *Labor Studies Journal* (Winter 1986): 311.

35. Ronald L. McKeen and Larry D. Terry, "Evaluation of a Minorities Leadership Institute in a Large Labor Union," *Labor Studies Journal* (Spring 1988): 58–67.

36. Susan L. Josephs et al., "The Union as Help or Hindrance: Experiences of Women Apprentices in the Construction Trades," *Labor Studies Journal* (Spring 1988): 10.

37. McKeen and Terry, "Minorities Leadership Institute," 67. "Evaluation plans should be developed and put in place before training programs begin." See also Linda Hartenian and Nancy Brown Johnson, "Criteria for Labor Education Program Evaluation," *Labor Studies Journal* (Fall 1989): 34–47.

38. Stephen Singer, "Making New Inroads: Union Bargaining in 1987," *AFL-CIO News,* March 19, 1988, 8.

39. "Machinists Increase Strike Benefits," *AFL-CIO News,* May 7, 1988, 12.

40. "New Orleans Swings to the Union Label," *AFL-CIO News,* May 28, 1988, 4.

41. Greg Burns, Gene Daniels, and Tony DeAngelis, "Providing Union Leadership Education: For a Change," *Labor Studies Journal* (Winter 1987): 238–57.

42. Robert A. Steffen, "On-the-Job Study of State Government: A Unique Internship for Union Leaders," *Labor Studies Journal* (Fall 1987): 65–76.

43. UAW-GM Human Resources Center, *UAW-GM: United for the Future* (Auburn Hills, Mich.: UAW-GM Human Resources Center, n.d.).

44. P. E. Barton, *Worklife Transitions: The Adult Learning Connection* (New York: McGraw-Hill, 1982); see also Brooke Broadbent, "Identifying the Education Needs of Union Stewards," *Labor Studies Journal* (Summer 1989): 46–60.

45. See in this connection Dorothy Shields, ed., *Labor in the Schools: How to Do It!* (Washington, D.C.: AFL-CIO, 1987).

Case Study: A New Boy Scouts Merit Badge

1. Karin C. Coek, *Encyclopedia of Associations* (Detroit: Dale Research, 1988), 146.

2. Joel J. Gay, "Labor: A Working Partner," *Scouting,* January–February 1971, 3–4.

3. Phone interview, Alan Bosch, staff member, AFL-CIO Department of Community Services, April 23, 1990.

4. "Labor Letter," *Wall Street Journal,* March 19, 1985, 1-A.

5. "A New Boy Scout Badge Merits Attention," *Personnel Journal* (April 1985): 14.

6. Harold Sokolsky, assistant to the chief executive of the Scouts, and J. D.

Owen, merit badge editor, BSA, quoted in Rita McWilliams, "Scouts Badgered on Labor Badge," *Washington Times,* April 5, 1985, 4-A.

7. Bosch, quoted in ibid.

8. "Boy Scout 'Labor' Badge Stirs Controversy," *National R-to-W Advisory Newsletter,* April 30, 1985, 4.

9. Bosch, quoted in McWilliams, "Scouts Badgered," 4-A.

10. Sokolsky, quoted in Rita McWilliams, "Scouts Rethinking Labor Badge," *Washington Times,* July 8, 1985, 6.

11. Quoted in Mark Fritz, "Boy Scout Badge?" *Detroit Free Press,* July 1, 1985.

12. Harry Bernstein, "Labor Column," *Los Angeles Times,* July 10, 1985, 16.

13. Phone interview, Bosch.

Part IV: Introduction

1. Quoted in Frank Swoboda, "Labor's Odyssey: From Bargaining Table to Hill," *Washington Post,* September 4, 1988, H–1.

2. Quoted in ibid., H–3.

3. "Labor Unions Planning Blitz to Aid Dukakis," *Deerfield Beach* (Florida) *Sun/Sentinel,* August 21, 1988, 4-A; see also "Union Families Yield 33 Percent of Dukakis Vote," *AFL-CIO News,* December 10, 1989, 8.

Chapter 10: Improving Public Relations

1. Abe Raskin, "New Directions for the AFL-CIO," *New Management* (Winter 1986): 11.

2. Michael Goldfield, *The Decline of Organized Labor in the United States* (Chicago: University of Chicago Press, 1987), 34.

3. James L. Medoff, "The Public's Image of Labor and Labor's Response," cited in ibid.

4. "Labor's Image on the Upswing, Roper Concludes," *AFL-CIO News,* March 5, 1990, 5.

5. Gary Langer, "Unions Favored, Poll Finds," *Philadelphia Inquirer,* September 4, 1989, 5-A.

6. Murray Seeger, director of LIPA, quoted in David Burnham, "AFL-CIO Trying New Technologies," *New York Times,* October 12, 1983, A–12.

7. AFL-CIO, *The Changing Situation of Workers and Their Unions* (Washington, D.C.: AFL-CIO, 1985).

8. Richard B. Freeman, "Unionization in Troubled Waters," *New Management* (Winter 1986): 10.

9. Lane Kirkland, "Union, YES!" *AFL-CIO News,* May 14, 1988, 3.

10. "American Labor Launches Nationwide Communications Campaign," *AFL-CIO News,* May 7, 1988, 1.

11. Ibid., 2.

12. Ibid., 4.

13. Letters from Chuck Schwartz, July 30, 1987, and May 4, 1990.

14. *Relay,* Spring 1988, 2.

15. Ibid.; see also Laurie Townsend, "How to Put Your Union on Cable

Television," *Labor Notes,* June 1987, 10; Action for Labor Access, "Rank-and-File Cable-TV: A Primer" (available from ALA, P.O. Box 25688, Chicago, IL 60625).

16. Robert Schrank, "The Future of Unions," *New Management* (Winter 1986): 18.

17. Lipset, "Labor Unions in the Public Mind," in Lipset, *Unions in Transition: Entering the Second Century* (San Francisco: Institute for Contemporary Studies, 1986), 321.

18. Interview, Chicago, August 23, 1987.

19. "Tasty Message," *AFL-CIO News,* January 16, 1988, 4.

20. "Union Dedicates Carlough Gallery, Historical Exhibit," *AFL-CIO News,* January 30, 1988, 8.

21. Albert R. Karr, "Labor Letter," *Wall Street Journal,* May 24, 1988, 1.

22. "One Convention Rite Lives On," *New York Times,* July 24, 1988, E-24.

23. Selwyn Feinstein, "Labor Letter," *Wall Street Journal,* May 24, 1988, 1.

24. "Unionists in the News," *AFL-CIO News,* June 4, 1988, 6.

25. Sara V. Douglas, *Labor's New Voice: Unions and the Mass Media* (Norwood, N.J.: Ablex, 1986), 282–83. See also Paul F. Clark, "Union Image-Building at the Local Level," *Labor Studies Journal* (Fall 1989): 48–68.

Chapter 11: Enhancing Union Power

1. David S. Broder, *Changing of the Guard: Power and Leadership in America* (New York: Simon and Schuster, 1980), 190.

2. Quoted in ibid., 215.

3. Broder, *Changing of the Guard,* 218, 219.

4. Brian Heshizer, "Union Officials Assess the Labor Movement and Labor-Management Relations," *Labor Studies Journal* (Spring 1987): 31, 34.

5. Ibid.

6. David Bensman, director of the graduate program in labor studies, Rutgers University, quoted in Edward Power, "Revitalized 'House of Labor' Coming to Write a Workers' Bill of Rights," *Philadelphia Inquirer,* September 14, 1987, 6-B.

7. Quoted in David Moberg, "Unions Are Having Difficulty Fathoming What Went Wrong," *In These Times,* November 21–December 4, 1984, 7.

8. Ibid.

9. Ibid.

10. Moberg warns, however, that "a good percentage of a declining labor movement still means fewer votes and less clout" (page 7).

11. Andrew Rosenthal, "Poll Finds Atlanta Delegates More Liberal than the Public," *New York Times,* July 17, 1988, 17.

12. E. J. Dionne, Jr., "Unions Make Major Gains in '88 Politics," *New York Times,* June 5, 1988, 1. When the members of the National Education Association [NEA], Teamsters, UMWA, and Brotherhood of Railroad Trainmen were included in 1984, the tally reached 25 percent, using the same formula that indicated 27 percent in 1980. The 1988 figure of 23 percent may not be compatible, as NEA and UMWA members may be absent (Harold

Meyerson, "Labor Rebuilds for Grassroots Clout," *In These Times*, August 8–21, 1984, 2).

13. Conversation with David Gregory, George Meany Center, Silver Spring, Md., January 25, 1987.

14. Conversation with Chuck Hodell, George Meany Center, Silver Spring, Md., January 26, 1987.

15. Harold Meyerson, "Winds of Change in Big Labor," *Nation*, January 11, 1986, 9.

16. David E. Rosenbaum, "Jackson Success Brings Scrutiny of Themes That Defy Rival Views," *New York Times*, April 4, 1988, A–12.

17. "Coalition Opens 'Jobs with Justice' Drive," *AFL-CIO News*, June 27, 1987, 5.

18. Quoted in John Herling, "Nation's Largest Unions Launch Campaign for Workers' Rights," *John Herling's Labor Letter*, July 4, 1987, 1.

19. Maria E. Recio et al., "Labor's Long Winter May Be Coming to an End," *Business Week*, February 23, 1987, 145. "For the first time this decade, labor may score a few points."

20. Allan Cors, of Corning Glass Works, quoted in Broder, *Changing of the Guard*, 221.

21. Speech to the National Press Foundation Labor-Management Seminar, November 1987. (Mimeo available from the AFL-CIO.)

22. Robert B. Reich and John D. Donahue, *New Deals: The Chrysler Revival and the American System* (New York: Times Book, 1985), 149.

23. Howard Paster, quoted in ibid.

24. "A Fair and Practical Plant-Closings Bill," *New York Times*, July 12, 1988, A–24.

25. Clyde E. Farnsworth, "72–23 Senate Vote Approves Notice of Plant Closings," *New York Times*, July 7, 1988, 1.

26. "A Fair and Practical Bill," A–24.

27. Quoted in Douglas Harbrecht and Steven J. Dryden, "The Plant-Closing Clause Could Shut Down the Trade Bill," *Business Week*, May 2, 1988, 43.

28. Quoted in Frank Swoboda, "Labor's Question: Did We Win or Did We Lose?" *Washington Post*, April 10, 1988, H–6.

29. See, for example, Roy Godson, *American Labor and European Politics: The AFL as a Transnational Force* (New York: Crane, Russak & Company, 1976); Ronald Radosh, *American Labor and United States Foreign Policy: The Cold War in the Unions from Gompers to Lovestone* (New York: Random House, 1969).

30. Meyerson, "Winds of Change," 9.

31. AFL-CIO Press Release, "The AFL-CIO and International Affairs," October 1987.

32. See in this connection Frank Smyth, "AFL-CIO Is Spanish for Union Busting," *Washington Monthly*, September 1987, 24–27, and "Kirkland Assails Release of El Salvador Killers," *AFL-CIO News*, January 9, 1988, 1–6.

33. See in this connection Daniel Cantor and Juliet Schor, *Tunnel Vision: Labor, the World Economy, and Central America* (Boston: South End Press, 1987); Tom Barry and Deb Preusch, *AIFLD in Central America: Agents as*

Organizers (Albuquerque: Resource Center, 1987); Tim Shorrock and Kathy Selvaggio, "Which Side Are You on, AAFLI?: Workers or Dictators," *Nation,* December 3, 1987, 684.

34. Fred Schmidt, "Workers of the World," *Texas Observer,* June 12, 1987, 13.
35. Meyerson, "Labor Rebuilds for Grassroots Clout," 2.
36. ADA, "Every Reason for Optimism," *ADA Today,* January 1988, 8.
37. Brooks Jackson, "PACs Favoring Incumbents, Especially House Democrats, as Spending Rises 26%," *Wall Street Journal,* May 2, 1988, 52.
38. David Moberg, "From Now on, the Democrats Need to Reach the Blue-Collar Workers," *In These Times,* March 23–29, 1988, 2.
39. I talked with David Moberg in August 1988 during the annual meeting of the American Sociological Association in Chicago.
40. For the poll data, see E. J. Dionne, Jr., "Twin Messages of Protest," *New York Times,* February 10, 1988, A–1, A–23.
41. Arlen J. Lange, "Missing Persons," *Wall Street Journal,* December 4, 1987, 10-D.
42. Joan M. Baggett, committee director, International Union of Bricklayers and Allied Craftsmen, quoted in Recio et al., "Labor's Long Winter," 140.
43. Robert Kuttner, "Getting There: It's Worse than Being There," *New Republic,* February 15, 1988, 22.
44. Ibid. A PAC may give only $5,000 to a candidate in a primary and another $5,000 in the general election, but local unions and other liberal (nonlabor) groups generally follow the lead of the COPE committee.
45. Marick F. Masters and John T. Delancey, "Contemporary Labor Political Investments and Performance," *Labor Studies Journal* (Winter 1987): 223.
46. Selig Perlman, *A History of Trade Unionism in the United States* (New York: Macmillan, 1923), 293.
47. Interview, January 27, 1987, Meany Center.
48. "Union Families Yield 33 Percent of Dukakis Vote," *AFL-CIO News,* December 10, 1988, 8.
49. Aaron Bernstein, "Is Big Labor Playing Global Vigilante?" *Business Week,* November 4, 1985, 92–93; see also "A Classic Debate on Solidarity," *Labor Link,* Fall 1986, and John Russo, "AFL-CIO Foreign Policy Faces Revolt," *In These Times,* October 30–November 5, 1985, 16.

Case Study: Rank-and-File Participation

1. " 'Democracy at Work' Project Draws Praise from News Media," *AFL-CIO News,* June 27, 1987, 2.
2. "See How They Run," *New Republic,* May 4, 1987, 7.
3. Quoted in James R. Dickenson, "Early Labor Endorsement Not Expected for 1988," *Washington Post,* July 31, 1987, A–6.
4. Based on a poll taken in late 1983 by the *New York Times,* cited in private correspondence to me from Ben Albert, director of public relations, COPE, AFL-CIO, August 27, 1987.
5. Quoted in James A. Barnes, "Labor's Mixed Blessing," *National Journal,* March 28, 1987, 84.
6. Transcribed from the videotape, as narrated by actor Ned Beatty.

7. " 'Democracy at Work' Project," 2.

8. Quoted in Dickenson, "Early Labor Endorsement Not Expected," A–6.

9. So firm is this commitment that COPE officer David Gregory, present at a film showing I attended, left when a straw ballot was taken immediately after the screening. In the hallway outside, I asked him why he left. He whispered, "I am barred by my office from being present at any polling on the candidates."

10. COPE, *Presidential Candidate Education Program: Guidelines for State and Local Central Bodies* (Washington, D.C.: AFL-CIO, 1987), 1.

11. Statement by the AFL-CIO Executive Council on "AFL-CIO Presidential Political Process Voluntary Guidelines," May 6, 1987.

12. "Government Unions Augment Videotapes on '88 Contenders," *AFL-CIO News,* June 13, 1987, 2.

13. Maralee Schwartz and David S. Broder, "Labor May Split Support among 1988 Contenders," *Washington Post,* July 23, 1982, A–4.

14. "Voter Education Drive Pays Dividends," *AFL-CIO News,* August 15, 1987, 2.

15. Quoted in Dickenson, "Early Labor Endorsement Not Expected," A–6.

16. Conversation, George Meany Center, Silver Spring, Md., July 30, 1987.

17. "Voter Education Drive Pays Dividends," 2.

Chapter 12: New Forms of Worker Involvement

1. Jennifer Lin, "Firms Are Fighting Unions as Well as Corporate Raiders," *Philadelphia Inquirer,* August 9, 1987, 1-C; see also Steven Hecker and John Hubbird, *Employee Buyouts and Job Retention* (Eugene: Labor Education and Research Center, University of Oregon, 1987). On Pan Am, see Kim Moody, "Union Reformers Clean House at Pan Am," *Labor Notes,* July 1990, 11.

2. Lin, "Firms Are Fighting Unions," 1-C.

3. Irwin Ross, "Labor's Man on Wall Street," *Fortune,* December 22, 1986, 123, 124.

4. Ibid., 126.

5. Pete Engardio, "Frank Lorenzo Starts to Strafe Eastern's Unions," *Business Week,* November 10, 1986, 81–82.

6. Ross, "Labor's Man on Wall Street," 128.

7. Robert Kuttner, "Worker Ownership: A Commitment That's More Often a Con," *Business Week,* July 6, 1987, 16.

8. Interview, Washington, D.C., June 11, 1987.

9. Quoted in John Hoerr, " 'We're Not Going to Sit Around and Allow Management to Louse Things Up,' " *Business Week,* May 18, 1987, 107.

10. Jim Waters, quoted in David Moberg, "Will United Airlines Pilots' Takeover Bid Fly?" *In These Times,* April 29–May 5, 1987, 6.

11. Quoted in ibid.

12. Quoted in ibid.

13. Alex Kotlowitz and Wendy L. Wall, "Pilots Score Victory in Upheaval at Allegis, But Outlook for Union's Bid Still Clouded," *Wall Street Journal,* June 11, 1987, 22.

14. John Zalusky, quoted in ibid; Robert L. Rose, "United's Pilots Leader Stays on Course," *Wall Street Journal,* July 17, 1987, 23; Doug Carroll and

Carolyn Washburn, "Pilots' Union Celebrates Overthrow," *USA Today,* June 11, 1987, 1-B.

15. Frank A. Olson, president and chief executive of United Airlines, and James Waters, ALPA spokesman, quoted in Agis Salpukas, "A Call to Workers by United President," *New York Times,* June 27, 1987, 36.

16. Rose, "United's Pilots Leader," 23.

17. Rick Dubinsky, quoted in ibid; quoted in Robert Moorman, "The $4.5 Billion Buyout," *Airline Pilot,* June 1987, 28.

18. Agis Salpukas, "Owner Backs Sale of United Airlines to Worker Group," *New York Times,* April 7, 1990, 35.

19. Ibid.

20. Quoted in ibid.

21. Kotlowitz and Wall, "Pilots Score Victory," 22.

22. Agis Salpukas, "Pan Am and the Rise of Union Power," *New York Times,* January 25, 1988, D–2.

23. Quoted in Teri Agins, "Pan Am May Get Labor Cost Concessions; Changes in Senior Management Planned," *Wall Street Journal,* January 6, 1988, 2.

24. Agis Salpukas, "New Chief at Pan Am Takes Control Quickly," *New York Times,* January 27, 1988, D–4.

25. Quoted in ibid.

26. Quoted anonymously in Agis Salpukas, "At Pan Am a Calm But Tense Drama Unfolds," *New York Times,* January 18, 1988, D–2.

27. Ibid.

28. Paul Rusen, quoted in Lin, "Firms Are Fighting Unions," 1-C.

Case Study: Turning an ESOP to Advantage

1. Raymond Russell, "Using Ownership to Control: Making Workers Owners in the Contemporary United States," *Politics and Society* 13 (1984): 285.

2. See Louis O. Kelso and Mortimer Adler, *The Capitalists' Manifesto* (New York: Random House, 1958); Louis O. Kelso and Patricia Hetter, *Two-Factor Theory: The Economics of Reality* (New York: Vintage, 1967). For the 75 percent figure, see Anne Zidons, "Avis Puts Workers in Driver's Seat," *USA Today,* December 15, 1988, B–2.

3. Frank Swoboda, "A Labor Buyout Is Rare, But Just as Congress Envisioned," *Philadelphia Inquirer,* April 11, 1990, 10-G.

4. Gary Hansen and Frank Adams, *ESOPs, Unions, and the Rank and File* (Somerville, Mass.: Industrial Cooperative Association, 1989).

5. John Hoerr et al., "ESOPs: Revolution or Ripoff?" *Business Week,* April 15, 1985, 94; J. A. Tannenbaum, "ESOPs Hold Gold for Some Entrepreneurs," *Wall Street Journal,* November 2, 1987, B–2.

6. William Baldwin, "The Myths of Employee Ownership," *Forbes,* April 23, 1984, 108.

7. John Logue, "When Workers Take Stock," *Progressive,* December 1986, 29.

8. Ibid.; cf. Gary S. Becker, "ESOPs Aren't the Magic Key to Anything," *Business Week,* October 23, 1989, 20.

9. Baldwin, "Myths of Employee Ownership," 108.

10. Logue, "When Workers Take Stock," 32.

11. Robert Kuttner, "Worker Ownership: A Commitment That's More Often a Con," *Business Week*, July 6, 1987, 16.

12. Douglas Sease, "ESOPs Weren't Meant to Be Bailouts," *Wall Street Journal* December 2, 1985, 20.

13. James Smith, "The Labor Movement and Worker Ownership," *Social Report*, December 1981, 2–3.

14. Ibid., 3.

15. John Hoerr, "Blue Collars in the Boardroom: Putting Business First," *Business Week*, December 14, 1987, 126. "Unions generally shy away from attempting to seize control, and tend to support professional managers whom they trust."

16. I draw here on Jeremy Brecher, " 'If All the People Are Banded Together,' " *Labor Research Review* (Fall 1986): 1–17.

17. Ibid., 7–8.

18. Michael Kearney, "Neighborly Advice," *Workplace Democracy* (Fall 1987): 11.

19. Michael Kearney, Department of Labor conference, Danbury, Conn., October 20, 1986.

20. Logue, "When Workers Take Stock," 32.

21. Quoted in Brecher, " 'If All the People Are Banded Together,' " 16.

22. Martin Carnoy and Derek Shearer, *Economic Democracy: The Challenge of the 1980s* (White Plains, N.Y.: M. E. Sharpe, 1980).

23. Michael Kearney, quoted in Jeremy Brecher, "Upstairs, Downstairs: Class Conflict in an Employee Owned Factory," *Z*, February 1988, 74.

24. See Edward Cohen-Rosenthal and Cynthia E. Burton, *Mutual Gains: A Guide to Union-Management Cooperation* (New York: Praeger, 1987), 249.

25. Ibid., 253. "The union movement needs to exercise imagination in how to propose cooperative ventures rather than waiting to be called upon" (page 264).

26. Joseph Blasi, "Sociological Practice and Worker Ownership: What Issues Should We Study?" (Paper presented at the 1987 Annual Meeting of the American Sociological Association, Chicago), 42; see also Joseph Blasi, *Employee Ownership: Revolution or Ripoff?* (New York: Ballinger, 1988).

27. See Robert N. Stern and Philip Comstock, *Employee Stock Ownership Plans: Benefits for Whom?* (Ithaca, N.Y.: ILR Press, 1978).

28. See in this connection Henry M. Levin, "ESOPs and the Financing of Worker Cooperatives," in *Worker Cooperatives in America*, ed. Robert Jackall and Henry M. Levin (Berkeley: University of California Press, 1984), 245–56; see also Joyce Rothschild and J. Allen Whitt, *The Cooperative Workplace* (Cambridge, Eng.: Cambridge University Press, 1986), 175–76.

29. Smith, "The Labor Movement and Worker Ownership," 2.

30. Michael Byrne, "Workers Buy Profitable Mill, Take Control of Their Destiny," *AFL-CIO News*, March 19, 1990, 11.

31. "UAW, Colt Ink Pact," *New England Labor News & Commentary*, April 1990, 20.

32. Ibid.

33. Quoted in Anthony Chapin, "700 Colt Strikers May Return," *New England Labor News & Commentary,* February 1990, 3.

34. Peter T. Kilborn, "New Fund to Help Unions Buy Ailing Factories," *New York Times,* February 20, 1990, D–8.

35. Ibid.

36. Quoted in Swoboda, "Labor Buyout Is Rare," G–1.

Case Study: Turning Worker Ownership to Advantage

1. I have made research visits since 1983 and have urged students to provide me with copies of their research papers. My files are available to those who are interested.

2. My answers are based on field research at three Philadelphia-area O & O supermarkets, all unionized by Local 1357, UFCW, on interviews with the officers of Local 1357, and on the research findings of Arthur Hochner and other Temple University academicians.

3. Joyce Rothschild-Whitt, "Who Will Benefit from ESOPs?" *Labor Research Review* (Spring 1985): 72. Responses were secured from forty-nine union presidents or research directors by Robert Stern and Ray Ann O'Brien of Cornell University.

4. William Foote Whyte, "Employee Ownership Yesterday, Today, and Tomorrow," *ILR Report,* Spring 1985, 9.

5. Rothschild-Whitt, "Who Will Benefit from ESOPs?" 72. Responses were secured from forty-two union officers by Joseph Blasi, Doug Kruse, and Eric Asard of Harvard University.

6. Robert Kuttner, "Blue-Collar Boardrooms," *New Republic,* June 17, 1985, 19.

7. Dennis Clark and Merry Guben, *Future Bread: How Retail Workers Ransomed Their Jobs and Lives* (Philadelphia: O & O Investment Fund, 1983), 3.

8. John Merwin, "A Piece of the Action," *Forbes,* September 24, 1984, 147.

9. Ibid., 156.

10. Clark and Guben, *Future Bread,* 4.

11. Quoted in Loren Feldman, "Jay Guben's Back in the Restaurant Business ... Sort Of," *Philadelphia Magazine,* December 1984, 45. Guben had earlier served a student internship as an organizer with Local 1357.

12. Clark and Guben, *Future Bread,* 23, 15, 32.

13. Lucinda Fleeson, "A & P Contract," *Philadelphia Inquirer,* September 28, 1983, 5-B.

14. See Arthur Hochner et al., "Survey of Philadelphia Supermarket Workers in Transition—1982" (Unpublished paper, February 1983 [available from Arthur Hochner, Department of Management, Temple University, Philadelphia]); see also Arthur Hochner et al., *Job-Saving Strategies: Worker Buyouts and QWL* (Kalamazoo, Mich.: W. E. Upjohn Institute, 1988).

15. Clark and Guben, *Future Bread,* 35.

16. Andy Lamas, quoted in Noel Weyrich, "Countering Corporate Pull-Outs," *City Paper,* September 21–October 5, 1984, 4.

17. Ibid.

18. Based on an interview at the Annual Meeting of the Association of Humanist Sociologists, Washington, D.C., November 3, 1989.

19. Leonard Holden, quoted in Noel Weyrich, "Changing the Pace," *New Age Journal*, November 1984, 28.

20. Quoted in John Edgerton, "Workers Take Over the Store," *New York Times Magazine*, September 11, 1983, 176.

21. Quoted in David I. Diamond, "A & P's Worker-Managers," *New York Times*, May 21, 1983, 46.

22. Mike Slott, "The Case against Worker Ownership," *Labor Research Review* (Spring 1985): 93.

23. Ibid.

24. Ibid., 87

25. Ibid.

26. Dan Swinney, "Worker Ownership: A Tactic for Labor," *Labor Research Review* (Spring 1985): 100.

27. Clark and Guben, *Future Bread*, 43.

28. Warner P. Woodworth, "Toward a Labor-Owned Economy in the United States," *Labor and Society* (January–March 1981): 54.

29. Clark and Guben, *Future Bread*, 81.

30. Wendell W. Young III and Robert A. Wolper, "A & P, Super Fresh, and O & O: A Union Success Story," *ILR Report*, Spring 1985, 32.

31. "Introduction," *Labor Research Review* (Spring 1985): 1.

32. Bill Adler, "To Reap What You Sew," *Texas Observer*, June 12, 1987, 9.

33. Kuttner, "Blue-Collar Boardrooms," 23.

34. Clark and Guben, *Future Bread*, 51; see also Frank Lindenfeld, "O & O Markets: The Labor and Cooperative Movements Get Together," *Changing Work* (Fall 1984): 43–46; Lindenfeld, "The O & O Supermarkets" (Unpublished paper, March 16, 1990 [available from Dr. Lindenfeld at the Department of Sociology, Bloomsburg University, Bloomsburg, PA 17815]).

Case Study: Turning Pension Power to Advantage

1. Philip Mattera, "Labor's Lost Lever," *Progressive*, May 1988, 25.

2. "Backing Principles with Principle," *AFL-CIO News*, June 18, 1988, 4–5.

3. Floyd Hyde quoted in ibid., 5.

4. Quoted in ibid.

5. Quoted in Mattera, "Labor's Lost Lever," 25.

6. See in this connection Eugene B. Burroughs, "*Donovan v. Walton* Opinion Provides Guidelines for Fiduciaries," *Pension World*, October 1985, 58–60.

7. Dennis J. Walton, "The Pension Fund Revolution" (Unpublished speech), 3.

8. Ibid.

9. Quoted in Joel Chernoff, "Union Fund's Walton: Visionary or Radical?" *Pensions & Investment Age*, September 2, 1984, 24.

10. *In Our Hands*, videotape made by Local 675, IUOE, 1985.

11. Dennis J. Walton, speech given at a union meeting, September 10, 1982, 1.

12. Quoted in Chernoff, "Union Fund's Walton," 24.

13. Quoted in Joel Chernoff, "Door Ajar for Union Job Tie," *Pensions & Investment Age,* June 10, 1985, 61.

14. Local 675, IUOE, *Trustees' Report* (Pompano Beach, Fla., 1980), 5.

15. Chernoff, "Door Ajar for Union Job Tie," 61.

16. Interview, Dennis J. Walton, Local 675 headquarters, Pompano Beach, July 17, 1987.

17. Dennis J. Walton, "Use of Pension Plan Assets to Promote Social Interests" (Unpublished statement, 1979), 2.

18. Ibid., 7.

19. Quoted in Burroughs, *"Donovan v. Walton,"* 58.

20. Walton, speech at union meeting, September 10, 1982, 2.

21. Dennis J. Walton, "National Council of Unions and Employee Benefit Funds" (Speech in San Juan, Puerto Rico, April 22, 1986), 2; see also Dennis J. Walton, "Participants' Meeting" speech, May 9, 1986, 3.

22. Dennis J. Walton, speech given at the annual Florida AFL-CIO Convention, September 15, 1980, 1.

23. Ibid.

24. Ibid., 5.

25. Ibid., 3–4.

26. Ibid., 8.

27. Ibid., 4–5.

28. Dennis J. Walton, "ERISA: Solely in Whose Interest?" (Speech at Florida International University, March 1983), 26.

29. Quoted in "The Changing Face of Organized Labor," *Florida Builder,* December 1986, 41.

30. Walton, speech at annual Florida AFL-CIO Convention, 1986, 7.

31. Ibid.

32. Quoted in Chernoff, "Door Ajar for Union Job Tie," 61.

33. Walton, speech at Florida AFL-CIO Convention.

34. Gerald Feder, quoted in Dory Owens, "Union Bets Its Pension Fund on Construction," *Miami Herald,* September 15, 1986, 17.

35. Ibid.

36. Quoted in "Trust Investor Dennis Walton," in *Trust Report* (Washington, D.C.: Multi-Employer Property Trust, September 30, 1986), 4.

37. Dennis J. Walton, speech at Union Lawyers Educational Conference, Myrtle Beach, S.C., June 5, 1985, 2.

38. *The Only Way to Discover the True Value of a Seminar Is To ...* (brochure published by Dennis J. Walton, October 1986) 3

39. For information, contact Fund Advisors, Inc., P.O. Box 5243, Fort Lauderdale, FL 33310–5243.

40. Walton, quoted in Joe Brogan, "Labor Unions Generate Jobs with Pensions," *Palm Beach Post,* August 31, 1985, 18-A.

41. Quoted in ibid.

42. Ibid.
43. Ibid.
44. Walton, speech on Indian-labor analog, October 1, 1986.
45. Quoted in "Trust Investor Dennis Walton," 4.
46. Quoted in "Union Fund's Walton."
47. Walton, speech on Indian-labor analog.
48. Cited in a brochure for the February 1986 "Pension Fund Revolution" seminar.
49. Walton, speech on nominations, May 18, 1985, 1.
50. Interview, Local 675 headquarters, Pompano Beach, July 17, 1987.
51. Walton, speech on Indian-labor analog.
52. Interview, Local 675 headquarters, Pompano Beach, July 21, 1987.
53. Ibid.
54. Ibid.
55. Interview, Local 675 headquarters, Pompano Beach, July 17, 1987.
56. Walton, speech on Indian-labor analog.
57. Ibid.
58. Peter S. Canellos, "Bill for Union Housing Trust Wins Support," *Boston Globe,* March 13, 1990, 57.
59. Quoted in Kenneth R. Harney, "Congress Backs Union-Employer Housing Trusts," *Philadelphia Inquirer,* April 15, 1990, 4-K.

Chapter 13: Achieving More Effective Alliances

1. Brian Heshizer, "Union Officials Assess the Labor Movement and Labor-Management Relations," *Labor Studies Journal* (Spring 1987): 32. National leaders were polled in 1983 and local union officials in 1985.
2. Michael Harrington, *The Long-Distance Runner: An Autobiography* (New York: Henry Holt, 1988), 99.
3. Ibid., 100. "The unions... are rooted in the daily necessities of working life. They therefore have a stability, a permanence, that in this society is denied the other opposition movements."
4. Robert L. Rose, "Labor Lending: How a Union Survives in Banking by Pushing Services over Profits," *Wall Street Journal,* December 14, 1987, 1.
5. Ibid.
6. *The Amalgamated Bank of New York* (New York: Amalgamated Bank, 1982), 5, 10.
7. Rose, "Labor Lending," 1.
8. Ibid., 18.
9. Ibid.
10. Ibid.
11. Melissa Chessler, "U.S., OSHA Plans Takeover of California's State System," *Occupational Health and Safety News Digest,* July 1987, 5.
12. Quoted in Kathryn Phillips, "Work-Safety Cut United Labor," *In These Times,* March 9–15, 1988, 6.
13. Andy Schaeffer, consultant for the California Senate Office of Research and the Senate Industrial Relations Committee, quoted in ibid.

14. "Safety Agency Put on Ballot in California," *AFL-CIO News*, June 4, 1988, 2.

15. Ibid.

16. "Union Families Yield 33 Percent of Dukakis Vote," *AFL-CIO News*, December 10, 1988, 8.

17. Quoted in Bruce Schmiechen, "Steelworker Revival: Waking from the American Dream," *Nation*, March 3, 1984, 258. Tri-State is proud to be "one of the few community-based development organizations that has gained the trust of the nation's major labor organizations." "Tri-State Mobilizes Local Support," *New England Labor News & Commentary*, December 1989, 16.

18. Carl Crowe, quoted in Zack Nauth, "Workers Knock Out Chemical Giant," *In These Times*, January 24–30, 1990, 13, 22; Frances Frank Marcus, "Labor Dispute in Louisiana Ends with Ecological Gain," *New York Times*, January 3, 1990, A–16; "OCAW Workers Rewarded after 5 1/2 Year Fight," *AFL-CIO News*, December 26, 1989, 1, 2.

19. Harneen Chernow, Tess Ewing, and Susan Moir, "Gay Activists and Building Trades Unite to Get Clinic Union-Built," *Labor Notes*, February 1990, 4.

20. Kathleen Foster, "Miners Versus Pittston," *Z*, April 1990, 86–89. See also the 1989–90 issues of the *UMW Journal*.

21. Jim Woodward, "McDonald's Boycott Targets City-Suburban Wage Discrimination," *Labor Notes*, April 1990, 5.

22. Quoted in Michael Dawson, "Oregon Activists Build Union-Community Alliance," *Labor Notes*, April 1990, 6. See also Michael Dawson and Dianne Rau, "Community and Inter-Plant Solidarity Highlight Oregon Strike against Morgan Products," *Labor Notes*, March 1990, 11.

23. Steve Wallman, the lawyer who drafted the bill, quoted in Leslie Wayne, "Anti-Takeover Proposal Gains in Pennsylvania," *New York Times*, April 4, 1990, D–2. Cf. Vindu P. Goel, "Many Pennsylvania Firm, Labor Groups Oppose Adoption of Anti-Takeover Bill," *Wall Street Journal*, April 16, 1990, A–14; Leslie Wayne, "Litmus Test in Pennsylvania Anti-Takeover Law," *New York Times*, April 19, 1990, D–1, D–7.

24. "Environmentalists Gain Partial Pesticide Victory," *New York Times*, April 21, 1990, 8.

25. Quoted in Paul Bass, "Connecticut Takes on the Conversion Challenge," *In These Times*, March 28–April 3, 1990, 7.

26. Interview, George Meany Center, Silver Spring, Md., January 27, 1987. The speaker requested anonymity.

27. David Bensman and Roberta Lynch, *Rusted Dreams: Hard Times in a Steel Community* (Berkeley: University of California Press, 1988), 232.

28. Ibid. See also Jeremy Brecher and Tim Costello, "Community Labor Coalitions," *Z*, April 1990, 79–85.

Case Study: Linking Job Creation and Housing Needs

1. Interview, Tom McIntyre, Philadelphia, June 2, 1988.

2. Drayton Bryant, "Spotlight on Labor Initiatives in Housing" (Philadelphia: Task Force for a Labor/Community Alliance, 1988) (Mimeo available from 2106

North Broad St., Philadelphia, PA 19121), 1–2. I am indebted to Drayton Bryant for helping to arrange my conversation with Tom McIntyre and for his own insights into this matter.

3. Interview, Tom McIntyre.

4. Barry Shlachter, "Building the Foundation for Non-Profit Housing," *Philadelphia Daily News,* September 4, 1986, 16.

5. Ibid.

6. Henry B. Schechter, director of the Office of Housing and Monetary Policy, AFL-CIO, "Opportunities for Union-Built, Moderate-Income Housing" (Presented in Washington, D.C., April 12, 1988), 2–3.

7. Interview, Tom McIntyre.

8. Ibid.

9. Linda Corman, "Union Support Spurs Housing," *New York Times,* June 5, 1988, R–29.

10. Interview, Tom McIntyre.

11. Ibid.

12. Ibid.

13. David B. Wilson, "Bargain Houses—No Speculators Need Apply," *Boston Globe,* November 24, 1988, 15. See also Peter Dreier, "Look for the Union Label" (*Progressive,* April 1989, 30), for a discussion of an innovative program to secure mortgage loan guarantees for rank-and-filers, as initiated by Local 26 of the Hotel Employees and Restaurant Employees Union (Boston).

Case Study: Linking Job Creation and Environmental Issues

1. Material is this case study is from several interviews with Jim Freese, the Seattle Fund specialist at Local 46, IBEW, conducted at the George Meany Center, Silver Spring, Md., in January and July 1989. I draw as well on the videotape *In the Community Interest,* prepared by the Northern California Pipe Trades Association.

Chapter 14: Toward the Employ of Futuristics

1. Nick Salvatore, ed., *Seventy Years of Life and Labor: An Autobiography* (Ithaca, N.Y.: ILR Press, 1984).

2. James O'Toole, "Unions: The Good, the Bad, and the Necessary," *New Management* (Winter 1985): 7.

3. Quoted in Leo Perlis, "Labor's Unanswered Questions," *Miami Herald,* March 1, 1985, 5-E.

4. Brian Heshizer, "Union Officials Assess the Labor Movement and Labor-Management Relations," *Labor Studies Journal* (Spring 1987): 31.

5. Selig Perlman, *The History of Trade Unionism in the United States* (New York: Macmillan, 1923), 291.

6. Alvin Toffler, *Future Shock* (New York: Bantam, 1970), 452, 480–83.

7. Helpful here is Joseph F. Coates, "Foresight in Federal Government Policymaking," *Futures Research Quarterly* (Summer 1985): 29–53.

8. CWA, *Committee on the Future Report* (Washington, D.C.: CWA, 1983), 7.

9. CWA, *Q & A: Committee on the Future* (Washington, D.C.: CWA, 1983), 1.

10. Ibid.

11. Ibid., 4.

12. Ibid., 7, 6.

13. Ibid.

14. Ibid., 14.

15. Glenn E. Watts, "Introduction," in CWA, *Committee on the Future Report,* 4.

16. *Forging a Future: Report of the Convention Committee on the Future Directions of the Union* (Pittsburgh: USWA, 1984), 30.

17. CWA, *Q & A,* 7.

18. AFL-CIO Committee on the Evolution of Work, *The Future of Work* (Washington, D.C.: AFL-CIO, 1983), 2.

19. Gus Tyler, "Labor at the Crossroads," in *Unions in Transition,* ed. Seymour Martin Lipset (San Francisco: Institute for Contemporary Studies, 1986), 373.

20. Richard B. Freeman, "Unionization in Troubled Times," *New Management* (Winter 1986): 8.

21. See in this connection David Moberg, "New AFL-CIO Report Outlines Labor Revival," *In These Times,* March 13–19, 1985, 5, 11.

22. Freeman, "Unionization in Troubled Times," 10.

23. I draw here on notes taken at the lecture; see also A. H. Raskin, "New Directions for the AFL-CIO," *New Management* (Winter 1986): 11.

24. Lane Kirkland, "It Has All Been Said Before," in Lipset, ed., *Unions in Transition,* 400.

25. See, for example, Arthur B. Shostak, "High Tech, High Touch, and Labor," *Social Policy* (Winter 1983): 20–23; Shostak, "Organized Labor's Leaders and Followers: On the Urgent Need for a Better Model," in *Leaders and Followers,* ed. Trudy Heller, Jon Van Til, and Louis A. Zurcher (Greenwich, Conn.: JAI Press, 1986), 209–23; Shostak, "Reversing the Decline of Organized Labor" (Paper presented at the 1986 Annual Meeting of the Society for the Study of Social Problems, Chicago); Shostak, "Organized Labor and Research Possibilities" (Paper commissioned by the Graduate School of Social Work, University of Pennsylvania, 1988); Shostak, "The Labor Movement and the Redesign of the Workplace," in *The Future: Opportunity Not Destiny,* ed. Howard F. Didsburg, Jr. (Bethesda, Md.: World Future Society, 1989), 93–104.

26. Tyler, "Labor at the Crossroads," 388.

Chapter 15: Making the Most of Mergers

1. Committee on the Evolution of Work, *The Changing Situation of Workers and Their Unions* (Washington, D.C.: AFL-CIO, 1985), 33.

2. Kim Moody, editor of *Labor Notes,* quoted in Bureau of National Affairs,

Unions Today: New Tactics to Tackle Tough Times (Washington, D.C.: BNA, 1985), 119.

3. Ben Fischer, director of the Center for Labor Studies, Carnegie Mellon University, quoted in ibid., 14.

4. Lane Kirkland, quoted in Gary N. Chaison, *When Unions Merge* (Lexington, Mass.: D. C. Heath, 1986), 40.

5. Murray Seeger, quoted in Bureau of National Affairs, *Unions Today*, 6; Chaison, *When Unions Merge*, 1.

6. Committee on the Evolution of Work, *The Changing Situation of Workers and Their Unions*, 30.

7. Chaison, *When Unions Merge*, 159.

8. See, for example, Theodore W. Glocke, "Amalgamation of Related Trades in American Unions," *American Economic Review* (September 1915): 554–66.

9. Charles Janus, "Union Mergers in the 1970's: A Look at the Reasons and Results," *Monthly Labor Review* (October 1978): 20–24.

10. Chaison, *When Unions Merge*, 7.

11. Herman W. Benson, "New Problems for Union Democracy: The Rise of One-Big Unionism," *Union Democracy Review* (July 1987): 3.

12. Chaison, *When Unions Merge*, 157. See also Howard S. Abramson, "Big Rail Unions Explore Merge to Boost Clout," *Journal of Commerce*, March 2, 1990, 1-B, 2-B.

Epilogue

1. See, for example, Leo Troy, "The Rise and Fall of American Trade Unions: The Labor Movement from FDR to RR," in *Unions in Transition*, ed. Seymour Martin Lipset (San Francisco: Institute for Contemporary Studies, 1986), 75. He declares labor has "entered a new stage in its history, a stage of permanent decline." Economists Stephen Bronars and Donald Deere predict union membership "would fall below 5 percent by the year 2000." They attribute 65 percent of the loss to reduced employment in unionized industries and 30 percent to increased employment in nonunionized fields (Selwyn Feinstein, "Labor Letter," *Wall Street Journal*, April 17, 1990, 1). Cf. Lane Kirkland, "It Has All Been Said Before," in Lipset, ed., *Unions in Transition*, 393–404. "Labor's obituary has been written at least once in every one of the 105 years of our existence, and nearly that many causes of death have been diagnosed. . . . It seems we must be forever perishing so that others may be forever publishing" (page 393). See also Tom Rankin, *New Forms of Work Organization: The Challenge for North American Unions* (Toronto: University of Toronto Press, 1990).

2. See in this connection Kim Moody, "The Legacy of P–9," *Labor Notes*, April 1990, 10. Cf. Dave Hage and Paul Klauda, *No Retreat, No Surrender* (New York: William Morrow, 1989.

3. Greg Tarpinian, "Pittston: Rebirth of the Unions?" *Wall Street Journal*, November 20, 1989, A–18. See also Nicolaus Mills, "Solidarity in Virginia," *Dissent*, Spring 1990, 237–42. Cf. Daniel Seligman, "Liddy's Line," *Fortune*, February 26, 1990, 124.

4. David Pauly, Clara Bingham, and Karen Springen, "The Unions Strike, Again," *Newsweek*, October 16, 1989, 59.

5. Quoted in David Moberg, "Strikers' Creative Tactics Overcome Anti-Union Odds," *In These Times*, December 6–12, 1989, 6. See also Brian Murphy, "Machinists Glad to See Lorenzo Go," *Philadelphia Inquirer*, April 20, 1990, 11-C.

6. Howard W. French, "The Hospital Workers Are the Envy of Labor Now," *New York Times*, October 8, 1989, 22-E.

7. Quoted in Amy Stromberg, "State of Unions," *Deerfield Beach* (Florida) *Sun-Sentinel*, September 4, 1989, 6-A.

Methodology and Apology

1. I could not have completed this phase of the project without the permission and assistance of Meany Center administrator Jacqueline Brophy. I owe her many thanks for this support.

2. Brian Heshizer, "Union Officials Assess the Labor Movement and Labor-Management Relations," *Labor Studies Journal* (Spring 1987): 30.

3. Available for $10 for a one-year subscription from the AFL-CIO, 815 16th St. N.W., Washington, D.C. 20006.

4. Available for $9 for a one-year subscription from the Midwest Center for Labor Research, 3411 W. Diversey, #14, Chicago, IL 60647.

5. Available for $10 for a one-year subscription from *Labor Notes*, P.O. Box 20001, Detroit, MI 48220.

6. Available for $7 for a one-year subscription from the Association for Union Democracy, YMCA Building, 30 Third Ave., Brooklyn, NY 11217.

7. Available for $35 for a one-year subscription from *In These Times*, 1300 W. Belmont, Chicago, IL 60657.

8. Available for $18 for a one-year subscription from *Workplace Democracy*, 111 Draper Hall, University of Massachusetts, Amherst, MA 01003.

INDEX

About the Author

Arthur B. Shostak is a professor of sociology at Drexel University in Philadelphia, where he has taught since 1967. From 1961 to 1967, he was a faculty member of the Wharton School of Finance and Commerce at the University of Pennsylvania. A specialist in labor studies, he earned a B.S. degree from the New York State School of Industrial and Labor Relations, Cornell University (1958), and a Ph.D. from Princeton University in industrial sociology (1961).

Since 1975, he has been an adjunct sociologist in the Antioch College degree program of the AFL-CIO George Meany Center for Labor Studies in Silver Spring, Maryland. He has introduced courses there in industrial sociology, the introduction to sociology, and futuristics.

The author of nearly one hundred published articles, he has also written, co-authored, edited, and co-edited thirteen books, including *The Air Controllers' Controversy, Blue-Collar Stress, Blue-Collar Life,* and *Blue-Collar World.* He is currently working on a book about the functions of unions in a postindustrial society.